Mexico 1910–1982: Reform or Revolution?

Donald Hodges and
Ross Gandy

D1446422

Dedication

We dedicate this book to Raul Sendic of the
Tupamaros and to all the other freedom
fighters in Latin America rotting in dungeons,
dying on torture tables, and surviving in
exile — to the soul of the Latin American
Revolution, a revolution that may be delayed
twenty years but never extinguished. We
recall the words of Karl Marx: "In the scales
of world history twenty years count as but
one day."

Mexico 1910-1982: Reform or Revolution?

Donald Hodges and Ross Gandy

Zed Press, 57 Caledonian Road, London N1 9DN

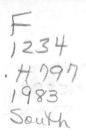
Mexico 1910-1982: Reform or Revolution? was first
published by Zed Press, 57 Caledonian Road, London
N1 9DN in 1983. It is an updated and expanded version
of a previous Zed Press title called *Mexico 1910-1976:
Reform or Revolution?* published in 1979.

Designed by Mayblin/Shaw
Typeset by Donald Typesetting and Jo Marsh
Cover illustration: A Mexican mural

British Library Cataloguing in Publication Data

Hodges, Donald
Mexico 1910-1982—2nd ed.
1. Mexico—Social conditions
I. Title   II. Gandy, Ross
972.08   HN113
ISBN 0-86232-144-1 Pbk

U.S. Distributor
Lawrence Hill & Co., 520 Riverside Avenue, Westport,
Conn. 06880.

Contents

Introduction

In the 19th century Europe bossed the world. Then during the 20th century, world wars brought on civil strife in Russia and China; the colonial revolution broke up Europe's empires in Asia and Africa; and revolutionary struggles shocked into motion the societies of Latin America. Out of this violence arose new social systems, and now 150 nations make the political map a crazy quilt of ideologies and alliances.

The century opened with three great social revolutions, the Russian, Chinese and Mexican. These cataclysms meant civil wars, political change, and mass insurrections: the Russian Revolution ran from 1917 to 1936, the Chinese from 1911 to 1928, the Mexican from 1910 to 1940. Each cast its shadow over the lives of later generations; each sowed the seeds of future revolutions in our century.

Each provided a model for revolution. The Russian model inspired revolutions in Czechoslovakia, Yugoslavia, Albania: the seizure of political power by a communist party with help from the masses, followed by a transformation of the economy and society. The Chinese upheaval showed communists how to mobilize peasants in a combined anti-imperialist and agrarian revolution. The Communist Party under Mao carried forward Sun Yat-Sen's populist goals betrayed by the Kuomintang: nationalism, democracy, and people's welfare. The Mexican Revolution also inspired populist movements for social change. Except for Cuba and (briefly) Chile, Latin America's radical movements turned away from the road opened by the Communist International and chose the Mexican path toward political sovereignty, economic independence, and social justice. The Mexican Revolution continued on an even keel to become a substitute for socialist revolution in the Americas.

The violence of the Mexican Revolution went beyond that of any later revolutionary upheaval in Latin America. Why was there so much fratricidal fury in the country beyond the Rio Grande? In the New World, Mexico holds the record for suffering from foreign invasions and local exploiters. The Spanish conquest was a bloody catastrophe that forever marked Mexican life and customs. To this day Mexicans still slur one another sexually as *hijos de la chingada* or sons of the Great Rape. In 1848 the U.S. robbed the country of half its territory (today's Texas, New Mexico, Arizona, California, Nevada, Utah, and Colorado). In 1863 the French captured Mexico and set up an

1

empire under Maximilian. The struggle against the French occupation, as against the Spanish during the wars of independence, took its toll in blood and tears. By the end of the 19th century, violence was a way of life in Mexico, a land where feudal institutions still survived and slave labour thrived alongside peonage in some parts of the country. The murderous mayhem unleashed by the Revolution was an answer to the violence done to the Mexican people for centuries.

The Revolution brought change to Mexico, but more important were its effects on other nations. Haya de la Torre, the Peruvian revolutionary, internationalized the Mexican Revolution and made it a model for 20 countries. How did he give it this world-historical meaning?

Banished from his native Peru, Haya took refuge in Mexico in 1923. The next year he founded the American Popular Revolutionary Alliance (APRA): it aimed to spread the principles of the Mexican Revolution in Latin America, just as the Communist International celebrated the Russian Revolution throughout Europe. As Haya noted in chapter four of his master work *Anti-Imperialism and the APRA*: 'No historical experience is really closer at hand and more useful for Indo-Americans than what Mexico offers. In my view the Mexican Revolution is *our revolution* . . . her failures and successes, her contradictions and constructive impulses are for our peoples the source of the most favourable lessons.' And again, in chapter eight: 'Historically, geographically, ethnically, and economically, Mexico is a synthesis of all the problems that we see amplified throughout the rest of our great continental nation . . . the Mexican Revolution has been the first contemporary social movement that could offer our peoples an invaluable experience.'

In the revolutionary struggle for economic independence, Haya argued, Mexico went as far as it could at the gates of the imperialist colossus. Mexico had plenty of revolutionary consciousness, but she was alone and isolated. Below her lay a Balkanized continent chopped into twenty artificial republics, which has made revolution difficult in a single country. Nonetheless, in the history of social struggles in our hemisphere, the Mexican Revolution was the first victory of an Indo-American people over feudal and imperialist oppression. As Haya noted in chapter three of *Thirty Years of Aprismo* (1956), the Revolution was also the first example of its kind in the world: 'It antedates the Russian Revolution and, obviously, that of China . . . it is not only an agrarian and anti-feudal revolution, as it referred to itself in its adopted title, but something more. It is an anti-imperialist revolution.' And, he added, it not only parallels, but also rivals, the Russian Revolution on a global scale.

What is needed to make revolution in underdeveloped Latin America? A multi-class party of the Mexican type, Haya believed, a centralized party based on a popular front of workers, peasants, and the old and new middle classes. That was the model provided by APRA, an anti-imperialist party similar to the Chinese Kuomintang (as Haya himself admitted). Though the Mexican model later turned into a parody of its original intent, that is not an argument against the APRA idea. It is a warning against abusing a populist strategy. After all, if there had been no APRA-influenced July 26 Movement, the Cuban Revolution would not have happened.

Between revolutions in Latin America there are family resemblances. If the Mexican Revolution is the father, the children are the Guatemalan Revolution (1944-54), the Bolivian Revolution (1952-64), and the Cuban Revolution (1956-61) — they each show some of the parent's features. Other national revolutions in Latin America had different parents, but with time they came to resemble the Mexican ancestor. The Argentine national revolution under Perón (1943-55) and the Peruvian national revolution under Velasco (1968-75) had starting-points different from the Mexican, but these two national revolutions arrived at results resembling Mexico's achievements. The Mexican Revolution became their adopted parent.

A large number of Third World countries do not take the stride toward socialism, but they do struggle for development free from imperialist pressures. For scores of countries the Mexican Revolution points down a road they want to explore for themselves.

In this perspective the Mexican Revolution opened a series of political revolutions of the same type. This series includes anti-imperialist revolutions in which agrarian reform was not a major issue, as in Turkey (1919-28), as well as the combined anti-imperialist and agrarian revolutions in Egypt (1952-64) and Algeria (1954-66). In Asia the Indonesian Revolution under Sukarno's leadership belongs to the same revolutionary family. These revolutions developed economies that differed in the weights they assigned to their public and private sectors (Egypt went furtherest in favouring the public sector). But these national revolutions charted a common course: they swept away the political rule of propertied interests, mostly coalitions between the big landowners and a financial bourgeoisie.

All these countries came under the rule of military and technocratic sectors of a bureaucracy that differed from both the bourgeoisie and the proletariat. At least a new political order emerged, if not also a new economic one. The result was a bureaucratic political revolution which, as in Mexico, smashed the remaining vestiges of feudalism and paved the way for the economic emergence of an indigenous bourgeoisie.

This new revolutionary family pursues a so-called Third Position between the bourgeois order and the new socialist order arising from the Russian Revolution. The Third Position offers a bureaucratic political revolution without Marxist ideology, a revolution based on a broad populist alliance that includes the middle sectors. Mexico's successive governments were never openly bourgeois. But did the bourgeoisie pull the strings in secret? Or was the Mexican Revolution, like the Russian, moving toward a new socialist order? Both of these views are questionable. At most, the Mexican Revolution prevented the bourgeoisie from wielding both economic *and* political power.

The Third Position goes beyond a mixed economy — a euphemism for a reformed capitalism with a big public sector — to combine with its capitalist economic system a bureaucratic political regime. Whether this regime is a military dictatorship, a one-party state or a populist democracy, it escapes the control of traditional landowning and moneyed interests. So the political right warns that the Third Position is hostile to free enterprise, while the left calls it a swindler afraid to take the road to socialism. The Third Position is pulled in one direction by the capitalist camp and in another by the socialist. In between oscillates the Third Position with its systems of dual authority: one class fastens on political power and another sucks up the economic surplus.

In Mexico the bureaucratic political revolution congealed in an institutional mould designed by Cárdenas through the 1930s, and then there were only two directions in which the Revolution could develop. First, the national bourgeoisie might bring off a political counter-revolution. This bourgeoisie, producing for the home market, was the economic beneficiary of the Revolution. It might use its economic base of privilege to seize political power. Second, the bureaucracy of government administrators, union officials, and peasant leaders might use the levers of political power to overturn the economic system. This political beneficiary of the Revolution could wrest the major part of the economic surplus from the bourgeoisie, and that would complete the bureaucratic revolution by a further economic transformation of society.

But what happened? The Mexican Revolution did not develop but drifted into stagnation. For a state bourgeoisie emerged, people who drew more of their income from private investments than from their salaries as government officials; they weakened the grip of the bureaucratic class on the levers of political power. In 1940–46 the state bourgeoisie backed up by local business began to drive for political power from within the party of the Revolution. They were partly successful (how much we don't know). Yet the overall balance of social forces endured. Mexico became the big argument against an idea popular on the Latin America left, the view that populist regimes are never stable, that they cannot last more than a generation. The Mexican one-party system has lasted half a century and is still going strong.

Mexican historians tend to interpret the main contribution of the Revolution as the agrarian reform which, applied in instalments, finally overcame during Cárdenas' administration the last vestiges of feudalism in the countryside. In contrast, Haya set forth Mexico as a model not only of an anti-feudal revolution, but also of an anti-imperialist one, and hailed it as the first victory by a movement of national liberation against Yankee imperialism in the Americas. Looking back, we can now say that Mexico is also the model of a bureaucratic political revolution. Still the most neglected aspect of the Revolution, it is the one we have chosen to explore.

PART 1
The Mexican Revolution and Its Outcome

1. The Social Volcano

In the 19th century Karl Marx compared European society to a volcano: a cone of privileged orders resting on a base of workers and peasants. The lava of mass resentment flowed underground, but the 'crater of revolution' often erupted to shake Europe to its foundations: 1789, 1820, 1830, 1848. In Eastern Europe the volcano rumbled ever louder. The Nihilists of the 1860s, the Populists of the 1870s, the Terrorists of the 1880s, the Marxists of the 1890s, the Bolsheviks of the 20th century were signs of pressure building toward the explosions of 1905 and 1917.

Through a long series of economic changes and class struggles, social forces press toward a critical point – then comes a great revolution in history. Three examples: Spain, China and Cuba were mountains of social ferment for a hundred years; and they shot off many smaller volleys before their final eruptions in the 20th century – Spain in 1936, China in 1947, and Cuba in 1958.

The Mexican Revolution, one of history's mightiest explosions, also vented subterranean pressures and long-hidden changes. It was the blast of a social volcano formed centuries ago by the impact of Spanish imperialism on an ancient civilization.

The Spanish did not come to Mexico to develop the country, they came to loot it. Cortez's remark, 'I came for gold, not to till the land like a peasant!', warned the world what to expect from his conquest. He did not capture ten or more million Mexican Indians to improve their lot. Mexico was a huge vein of silver; the Spanish opened it to pump its contents to Europe. The Indians, enslaved in the Spanish mines, caught European diseases and almost vanished as a race. By the 17th century only a million remained.

Centuries of Spanish colonialism wiped out Mexico's native crafts and made it a land of plantations and mines sending Europe food and minerals: sugar, tobacco, wheat, and shiploads of silver. The colonial system created a country of Indians and mestizos (or mixed blood) crushed by racist whites. Worked like slaves in fields and mines, the Indians died of hunger and disease; on the haciendas the overseers lashed them without mercy. The law excluded the mestizos from education, and they whined and begged and starved in the cities; usually one of them was hanging from the gibbet in the plaza. As bandits they infested the countryside, and the police nailed them to roadside crosses for a slow death.

Over this colonial barbarism floated *Te Deums* sung by the medieval Church.

The social volcano rumbled and spluttered: there were Indian uprisings on the land and *tumultos* in the cities. On June 8, 1692, the numerous slum elements in Mexico City broke loose, burned down the gibbet and jail along with some buildings, and looted the shops. Ten thousand Indians and half-castes rioted all day, and troops could restore order only by firing on the crowds in the evening. In these *tumultos* the social crust cracked open to reveal lava below.

The Independence War Against Spain and the War of Reform

The first eruption of the volcano was the Independence War of 1810 to 1820. With the cry 'Death to the Spaniards!' Father Hidalgo detonated a social revolution: at the head of a hundred thousand Indians he stormed from city to city to set the Mexican North in flames. Hidalgo demanded land for the Indians and lower taxes. His capture passed the leadership to the half-caste Morelos, once a slaving peon, then a priest discovering a revolutionary mission. Through guerrilla warfare Morelos freed southern Mexico and raided to the outskirts of the capital. But all whites united against his social pro-gramme: republican government, agrarian reform, and the crippling of Church power. They pounded down his revolution with Spanish cannon, and by 1820 they had capped the revolutionary lava.

Suddenly these white landowners declared independence from Spain – they wanted Mexico for themselves. These new Mexican elites formed a rigid social crust over the Indian masses. Independent Mexico had fertile lands, rich mines, many labourers – and a static society. The racist whites did not know how to run a government, for Imperialist Spain had always excluded them from administration. Nor could they operate the mines which the Spanish had abandoned. Nor develop manufacturing: the imperialists had fled with the liquid capital.

English interests rushed in to pump away the wealth of the mines, and the white landowners continued exporting raw materials to Europe. The new administration failed in financing Mexico's government, and the army and bureaucracy bankrupted it. Stable government vanished in exhausting civil wars.

During half a century of anarchy, liberals struggled to smash the medieval Church, ally of the landowners and generals. The Church owned much of the land; the priests controlled education and drained off money to Rome. But the liberal elite feared to mobilize the masses of suffering Indians and mixed bloods. The volcano smoked and rumbled. In Yucatan, Mayan villagers fought the white landowners in the caste wars of the 19th century, sometimes but not always supported by the landlords' Mayan serfs. The white liberals turned away from the people and, with no social force behind them, shot their brilliants ideas into a void.

Spain had so misshaped Mexico that it emerged from the colonial period economically stagnant, without independent businessmen, but with masses of ignorant half-castes, with millions of Indians who spoke no Spanish, vast under-classes who lacked the leadership to free themselves and the nation. As the misery of the massess deepened, a man of the people emerged to lead the liberal reformers — Benito Juárez.

And in 1857 the volcano erupted again.

For ten years, from 1857 to 1867, fratricidal passions split Mexico open and gushed over the land; churches were looted and prisoners shot; guerrillas roamed the country; massacres of civilians followed great battles; liberals and conservatives captured the government from one another; and civil war seemed perpetual. Supported by some mixed-bloods — emergent as a new mestizo race — Juárez and the liberals came out on top. They delivered power-ful blows to the Church. But they failed to carry through agrarian reform, and their constitution brought democracy only on paper. As they died off, Mexico slid toward the shadows of the *Porfiriato*.

The Porfiriato

Porfirio Díaz reigned from 1876 to 1911, Mexico's Age of Iron. Don Porfirio applied the liberals' plan to break up the Indians' communal lands, and new laws about land registration encouraged *hacendados* and speculators to seize the plots of peasants everywhere. Without land most Mexicans became serfs, migrants and beggars, while a few found work in mines and mills — at pitiful wages. The 1910 census reported 840 *hacendados* (big landowners) and approximately 400,000 *rancheros* (landowning farmers, typically owners of family-size farms). Half of Mexico's land was owned by the *hacendados*, while roughly 97% of rural family heads had no land at all.

On the semi-feudal haciendas in central Mexico the peon sweated from dawn to dark, forever in debt to the company store. He slept on a straw mat in a filthy hut with two rooms for his family. When he fathered a child he knew it would probably die: the infant mortality rate was higher than in Asia. The water was bad, and horrible diseases crept about. The peon's diet was the eternal tortilla and the bean, and he was lucky to have it: in Mexico thousands starved to death every year. If he ran away the mounted police hunted him down and dragged him back. If he stole a peso he had to face the lashes of the foreman. Not every peon had access to the *hacendado*. The master might be away in the capital, or even in Paris enjoying the opera. He was like a feudal lord drawing rent. The hacienda produced its work animals and tools, furnished candles for its church, doled out food to peons from the *tienda de raya* or company store. In central Mexico five million peons never handled money. A peon might kill his boss and flee to the mountains: there social bandits like Pancho Villa robbed from the rich and gave to the poor. Sometimes the poor revolted against their masters, but these revolts were quickly crushed.

In the tropical areas farther south there were modern or capitalist forms of production, as in Morelos, where brown men worked under a glaring sun on sugar farms, in distilleries, or loading boxcars. But often enough in the valleys of Oaxaca and Chiapas or on the plantations of Yucatan the coffee and tobacco and hemp were cultivated by slaves. Yes, literally, slaves were bought and sold in Yucatan at $ 40 a head. It is estimated that there were about 750,000 of them. Slavery was abolished in 1835 for the second time — it had been first abolished in 1814 — but the Constitution was honoured more in the breach than in the observance, both on this point and most others. Overseers armed with whips walked up and down the fields, driving the slaves on. At night the foreman locked them in stockades guarded by men with rifles. On a meagre diet the slaves worked to death under the tropical sun. Who were these slaves? Men and women convicted of petty theft, contract labourers tricked into slavery, captured Yaquis and Mayas, and political suspects from every class in society. Conditions were worse than in Tsarist Russia. 'Russia's Siberia is hell frozen over,' people used to say, 'but Mexico's Yucatán is hell aflame.'

Under Porfirio Díaz the nation became modernized, but at a tremendous cost in human suffering.

Foreigners helped Díaz administer the country. The minister of finance was of French origin, and his *científico* friends advised the government. The *científicos* or 'scientists' believed that they could develop the country only with foreign capital. These Mexican businessmen linked Díaz to the foreigners, enriching themselves through financial swindling, land speculation, and the arrangement of concessions for foreign capital. The government had handed over the country to foreign capitalists for plunder: they grabbed a fifth of Mexico's land, including the mineral veins and oil deposits. More gold and silver were lugged out of Mexico's mines than in the previous four hundred years; the oil fields were the richest on the planet. On railways built by Americans this loot rolled north into the United States, along with lead, copper and iron, or it floated away in the imperialists' ships to Germany, France and England. The British planned to run their navy on Tampico's oil.

In the copper mines, textile mills, oil fields, and railways — owned by foreigners — the proletariat slaved thirteen hours a day for centavos. The owners threw injured workers out to starve; unions brought on the wrath of the *patrón*; old age meant the sack and beggary. The foreign capitalists held down wages while profits soared up and out of the country. Could radicals fail to labour in this vineyard? Anarchists went to work; they taught people sabotage and the strike. Between 1906 and 1909 strike waves rolled back and forth over the nation, but Díaz halted them with gunfire. And thus he answered rebelling Yaquis and Mayas — with the bullet and the lash. Standing on a volcano, he thought he could still the shaking earth with a whip.

The dictator had forged his instruments of power: the army, the *rurales*, the police, and the death squad. The regular army garrisoned the towns and could reach most of the country in hours. Who were the *rurales*? Captured bandits formed into mounted state police to terrorize the countryside. Secret police lurked in the capital; uniformed gendarmes infested the cities. For agitators the government death squad came, usually at night, to leave its victims in an alley or gutter. This secret band murdered men who worked against Díaz.

He appointed state governors and political bosses from the top down; congress and the court used rubber stamps. 'L' Etat, c'est moi,' he might have said, but he was the only high leader who didn't know French. While his *científico* ministers bought landed property, he gradually drew more state governors from the *hacendados* than from the generals. And many generals acquired large lands. The landowning oligarchy was the ruling class of Mexico.

Governors gave orders to the army, *rurales*, and death squad; and these kept the sweating masses down, though peasant revolts flashed here and there, strikes steadily increased, and Yaquis fought on in the mountains. Planters and *hacendados, científicos* and foreigners — all worked with Díaz to guarantee their labour force: the Mexican people groaned and cursed, but slaved twelve to sixteen hours a day to escape punishment. There was no way out. The profits squeezed from their toil were among the highest in the world.

Order and Progress! That was the watchword of the Díaz era. And there was certainly progress of a kind, as injections of foreign capital into the economy brought spurts of uneven development.

In 1880 there were only 1,000 kilometres of railroad in the vast extent of Mexico, but by 1910 the nation had 25,000 kilometres of track. Huge locomotives chugged across one of the largest railway grids on earth At the same time the telegraph network stretched out to remote areas — a sevenfold increase in size. The number of post offices tripled. The earth vomited up coal; there was a flood of oil at Tampico. Díaz was building the framework of an industrial economy: transportation, communication, energy.

Mexico was still 'El Dorado', and the silver miners at Guanajuato continued their 400-year-old quest for the mother lode. But at last Mexico diversified her exports. Copper, lead and iron ore came out of the sierras; the tropics yielded up rubber, hemp, tobacco, vanilla, coffee, sugar; the northern lands threw cattle and goat leather onto the world market.

Alongside luxury imports for the aristocrats' use, shiploads of steel and machinery docked at Veracruz. This usually went to mining camps, railroads, and oil fields; but foreigners and Mexicans were also building textile factories in the centre of the country.

During the *Porfiriato* Mexico awoke from her age-old slumber: the cities

began to grow; most of the state capitals doubled in size. Migrant labourers
followed the harvests across the country, and tens of thousands streamed into
urban centres. Though foreigners owned much of the industry and sucked
profits abroad, the railroads and oil derricks stayed put. Díaz and his *científicos*
said they were building a nation.

As the dictator turned eighty, the *hacendados* celebrated his birthday at
fashionable parties; in Chapultepec Castle twenty carloads of champagne
were downed toasting the 'Hero of modern Mexico' as well as Hidalgo's
mestizo and indian army! The year was 1910.

The Struggle Against Díaz, 1910-11

In that year the crater erupted against the old order in Mexico and continued
to explode for a decade of great battles, the bloodiest in Mexican history.
French advisors, Church power, regular army, secret police, *rurales*, serfdom
and slavery disappeared in the fiery lava of the Revolution. This time the lava
changed the political landscape forever. How did this breakout happen?

Every serious revolution in European history since 1700, Karl Marx once
observed, was preceded by an economic and financial crisis. The Mexican
Revolution also fits this pattern. In the centre of Mexico the traditional
haciendas could not grow the grain to feed the country, and as food grew
scarce prices rose. Expensive food caused people to starve. Agricultural
Mexico exported minerals and imported food! From 1900 on, the world
market prices of Mexico's exports curved downwards. The government,
borrowing more and more abroad, slipped toward financial crisis in 1910.

In the same decade the Díaz regime drifted toward a political crisis. In
1904, at the age of seventy-four, the dictator prepared to run for President
again. But what would happen to the government when he died in office?
Díaz *was* the State. Would his disappearance bring chaos, take the lid off the
volcano? The ruling class urged him to pick a Vice-President — the brilliant
científico Limantour or the competent mestizo General Reyes. Reyes' faction
saw him as a new and enlightened edition of Díaz, while the white *científicos*
hoped to advance Mexico with Limantour. Instead Díaz chose Ramon Corral,
the race murderer of the Yaqui Indians, a man feared by both factions. Could
he rule after Díaz's death? The dictator grew older and the nation drifted.

As the 1910 'election' approached, the local bourgeoisie clamoured for
a share in the government. Business families like the Maderos — active in
banking, mining, manufacture, and agriculture — resented a government
favouring American capitalists over Mexicans. Francisco Madero, the leader
of the local bourgeoisie, asked the eighty-year-old Díaz to give up the presidency. Díaz stuck to his original choice. Madero writhed on the horns of a
dilemma: he foresaw chaos if Porfirio Díaz was not removed in time, yet
feared that removal by force would unplug the crater. 'Porfirio is not an
imposing leader,' said Madero. 'Nevertheless, to topple him will require a
revolution. But who will it topple after that?'

The upper classes could not go on in the old way, and Madero called for revolution. His call came from Texas, for the United States offered him a sanctuary. This was a change in American policy: for years the U.S. government had deported Mexican revolutionaries across the Rio Grande; with their prey the *rurales* galloped away into the desert; shots rang out and the prisoner died while 'attempting to escape'. Madero avoided this fate, for Washington encouraged him against Díaz. Porfirio Díaz had angered American businessmen. As U.S. capital embraced his nation with increasing force, like a boa constrictor, he shook off the coils of Standard Oil. The black gold now gushed from his wells into *British* tanks. American oilmen said that the old dictator had turned senile. They plotted to retire him.

From Texas Madero's *Plan de San Luis Potosí* promised democracy and agrarian reform: the programme called upon Mexico to rise in revolution against the dictator. Democracy fired the imagination of the native bourgeoisie; Latin businessmen dreamed of *Mexican* capitalists in Chapultepec palace. And land reform? That promise burned through the rural masses to strike powder: explosions happened in Chihuahua and Morelos. Guerrilla warfare flamed up in Mexico's North and South. The Villista guerrillas were a motley crew of frontiersmen, bandits, cowboys, and peons; the Zapatistas were 'free' villagers who had been stripped of their lands as the big growers in Morelos doubled sugar production between 1905 and 1910. The huge, lumbering mass that does the fighting in most revolutions began to move.

In the opening months of 1911 horsemen thundered across the wilderness of Chihuahua, raiding mining camps in the sierra, haciendas on the plain, and isolated federal garrisons. These mounted guerrillas flashed out of nowhere and disappeared like shooting stars. One of the brighter lights was the former peon, Pancho Villa, the Robin Hood of the North. In the South, riding through the mountains below Mexico City, Emiliano Zapata's peons attacked the haciendas and towns of Morelos. Out of thousand-year-old villages crept these little men, communing in Nahuatl, to mount horses and grasp rifles. They wanted their village lands back.

'It is an evident fact,' Engels once remarked to his friend Karl Marx, 'that collapse of discipline in the Army has been a condition of every victorious revolution.' This collapse usually occurs (says modern sociology) through defeat of the regular army in war. But not always: for decades the Mexican dictator was victorious in the only war he fought — the one against his people. In that war Díaz crushed uprisings in the towns, where he threw in thirty men for every rebel; his regulars machine-gunned Yaqui warriors armed with bow and arrow; his soldiers hunted Mayas for the slave farms. And troops fired on striking workers with deadly aim. But now guerrillas began to spread across Mexico: raging in and out of the forested sierras, concentrating to slay a column of regulars, then vanishing like demons — these fighters were new. Díaz ordered his army to attack, but some generals were as old as he, and their lieutenants had white hair. They responded too slowly or too late.

The handwriting was on the wall. Flashes of dynamite lit up the letters as Pancho Villa blasted his way into Ciudad Juárez. Foreseeing defeat, Limantour persuaded Díaz to resign in May, 1911. Spring passed into summer, and the dictator passed out of history. 'Madero has released a tiger in Mexico,' said Díaz sailing for France. 'Let's see if he can handle it.'

Madero in Office: His Assassination

In the fall of 1911 an election made Madero President. Uncles, brothers, and cousins got high posts; local businessmen had captured executive power. But did they control the State? The old Díaz army lay coiled in the new President's rear, waiting for a false move. Would the army strike?

The native bourgeoisie flexed weak muscles as its President threatened foreign capital. For years this tiny group had longed to grow, while Díaz's policies kept it a dwarf. How could it build heavy industry without raw materials? The imperialists carted these off with Díaz's blessing. How could it build light industry without a market? In foreigners' factories worked wage slaves, on the haciendas debt slaves, in the Tropics chattel slaves — they lacked money to buy any goods produced. How could the bourgoisie compete with American know-how? Díaz had laughed at its plea for protection. American capitalists owned more of Mexico's industry than Mexicans did, and the *gringos* had twice as many investments as the other imperialists together. A third of United States overseas investment had taken root in Mexico. Even conservative historians admit that by 1900 Mexico was an economic colony of the United States.

Now Díaz was gone, and native businessmen had a champion in Madero. Who was this little man and the clan he brought to govern? The Maderos, one of the richest families in Mexico, were *hacendados* turning into manufacturers. They grew cotton and set up textile mills; they drew sap from rubber trees and processed it; they raised mountains of grapes and squeezed out the wine in presses; they founded the first *Mexican* bank in the North. On their lands they discovered copper. They mined it and set up their own smelters, which became an important *Mexican* industry. The American Smelting and Refining Company, owned by the super-rich Guggenheims, sullenly stared at this rival. The Guggenheim interests hated the Maderos. And the Maderos, like the class they led, despised foreign capital.

This bourgeois class, a drop in the sea of *hacendados* and foreigners, thrived in the North. On the national scale a pigmy, but in the states along the Rio Grande a young giant, this new bourgeoisie blew life into northern politics. The states of the North were growing strong. They gave the bourgeoisie political clout in the nation.

Madero became the political leader of the democrats. A revolutionary democratic wave swept him toward the presidency, and he turned to his first task: taming the tiger loose in Mexico. He ordered Zapata to disarm revolutionaries in the South. Zapata asked Madero if the old Díaz officers, still commanding the Federal Army, would tolerate the revolution after it surrendered its weapons. Also, Zapata demanded agrarian reform in exchange for the rifles. 'Look, Señor Madero,' said Zapata (rifle in hand), 'suppose I relieve you of your gold watch. Suppose that next time we meet you're armed: wouldn't you demand your watch back?' The *hacendados,* Zapata went on, had robbed his villagers of their land; now his men had rifles — and demanded their lands back. Why should they lay down their weapons?

Armed revolutionaries urged President Madero to go forward with reforms; *hacendados* and foreigners insisted he stand fast. Madero and his class sweated coldly. Janus-faced, the bourgeoisie stared at the masses behind and the reaction before. Madero again ordered Zapata to disarm, and slapped a tax on foreign oil companies. He looked for a compromise. But the agrarian revolt flared up in the Zapatista South; and the American ambassador, an agent of Madero's rivals the Guggenheims, began to dream of a coup from the right. In 1912 several revolts occurred; Madero snuffed them out. He allowed the urban workers to organize anarchist trade unions into a labour central, The House of the World's Worker; he sent troops against Zapata's agrarian radicals; he made speeches against foreign capital. He wobbled back and forth, riding a tiger.

The Zapatistas fought on in the South. They wanted land. Madero's commander took a leaf from the Americans' book: in the Commanche and Philippine wars they had shown how to wipe out guerrillas, and so General Robles now went to his work with gusto. He burned villages, herded peons into concentration camps, and hunted down peasants at large. They fled to lengthen Zapata's columns. Madero tried another general, Felipe Angeles. This new general burned Zapatista villages, massacred prisoners, but wrung his hands over it. The guerrilla war deepened and spread, while the *hacendados* fretted in Mexico City. Madero rejoiced that the 'dark vandalism' of the peasants did not overflow to the North, and his generals continued their bloody work.

In Mexico City the foreigners fumed and plotted. The Americans wondered if Dollar Diplomacy couldn't help Mexico find a better president. Early in 1913 a coup developed. Madero, the idealistic tribune of the local bourgeoisie, waved the national flag from the balcony, while the reaction lured his hard nosed brother into a trap and tortured him to death. The American ambassador, Henry Lane Wilson, sat on the junta that planned the President's removal. General Huerta assassinated Madero and seized the presidency, while the *hacendados* cheered him as 'the saviour of Mexico'.

All the imperialists but one rushed to recognize him. In the United States a new president, Woodrow Wilson, was taking office, and he wanted to know more about Huerta. He sent John Lind to find out. Lind suggested that the United States withhold recognition. Alarming reports reached Wilson from other sources: as more and more oil thundered to Mexico's surface General Huerta favoured the British companies — against Americans! The Protestant Wilson and his Bible-quoting aides began to speak of righteousness and justice, of Huerta's 'wickedness', of constitutionalism and democracy, of the usurper's dictatorship, of the need for a legal Mexican President. Weighed in the balances, Huerta was found wanting.

What kind of man was Huerta? Amid the applause of *hacendados* and foreigners he calmly murdered the liberals. The anarchist workers resisted, and he drove them underground. He moved from one saloon to another, holding cabinet meetings in bar-rooms, greeting ambassadors glass in hand. He strengthened the army. In 1913 he planned to take up where Díaz left off. He would plug the sputtering volcano with balls of iron.

The Struggle Against Huerta, 1913-14

For a hundred years the volcano had built up its cone: periodic eruptions released pressure from below but did not blow off the archaic social structure. In 1913 this structure trembled and cracked. Huerta would hold it together, and he went savagely to work. The Church sang praises to him. His officers followed orders. The *hacendados* voiced support through their press. And the English, French, German, Spanish, and Japanese ambassadors shored up his government.

Throughout 1913 the magma of revolution was working toward an explosion that would change Mexico. The Zapatista South erupted in a People's War against the dictator; loud noises came from the North as Coahuila, Chihuahua and Sonora smoked with revolt. Huerta felt the crater shaking beneath him.

In the northern states three men symbolized the social movements emerging there: Obregón of Sonora, Pancho Villa of Chihuahua and Carranza of Coahuila. United at first, these men (and their movements) would end fighting one another. 'This is the fate of all revolutions', Friedrich Engels once remarked: 'No sooner is the victory gained against the common enemy than the victors become divided among themselves into different camps, and turn their weapons against one another.' But in 1913 Zapata, Obregón, Villa and Carranza had a common enemy – the new dictator, General Huerta.

Carranza, the middle-aged governor of Coahuila, rose against Huerta first. An educated *hacendado* with a law degree, Carranza had served Porfirio Díaz three terms in the senate ('the herd of tame horses'). In 1909 he frowned on Madero and swore loyalty to Díaz, then asked for the governorship of Coahuila. Díaz refused him, and Carranza decided that the eighty-year-old dictator was too feeble to rule. So this forward-looking landowner backed Madero's thrust for power, joined his cabinet, and got the governorship of Coahuila. Carranza was content until Huerta shot Madero and seized the presidency. Then he called his fellow Mexicans to arms and proclaimed himself 'First Chief' of all the rebels.

The liberal Carranza concentrated in his proclamation on political reforms and the struggle for free elections. Once in power, he would not support even these. The historical evidence is overwhelming: he opposed the growing social revolution and did everything he could in order to prevent it from happening.

This was not clear to Pancho Villa in Chihuahua, where guerrillas buzzed about the state, stinging Huerta's federal army. Villa accepted the leadership

Map of Mexico

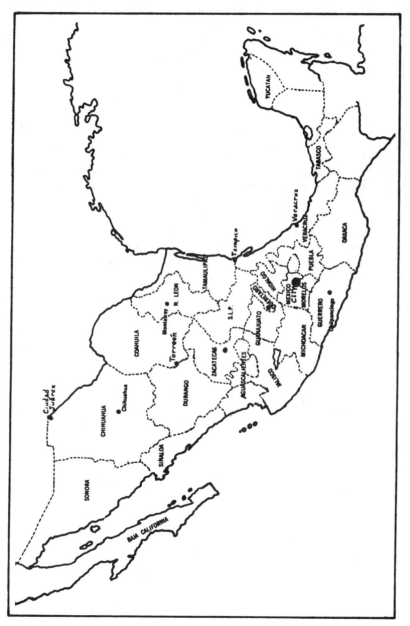

of the First Chief. But Villa intended a social revolution: first a peon, then a roving Robin Hood, and now a revolutionary chieftain, he knew how Mexico's masses suffered, he shared their longing for the land. Slowly he built a guerrilla army. In the fall of 1913 he captured a federal train, hid troops on board, and chugged into Ciudad Juárez. The Villistas poured out of their Trojan Horse to capture this border town. Across the American border flowed modern weapons, paid for with rustled cattle. Villa turned south and took Chihuahua City on the long railway to the capital. There in the spring of 1914 he formed his *Division del Norte*. From every fissure in the old order people streamed into his army: railwaymen, miners, drifters, cowboys, smugglers, rustlers, bandits, peons, workers, servants, prostitutes, beggars, deserting soldiers, mule drivers, migrant labourers, Yaqui Indians – the wretched of the earth. Villa barely trained his army. Some of his recruits he put to work on construction projects. He lowered the price of meat and distributed clothes to the poor. He promised sixty-two acres to every male in Chihuahua. His army's morale rose steadily; the Villistas were marching into a new age. A wave of hope swept over the ragged foot soldiers as they tasted the first fruits of social revolution. They would fight to the death.

Obregón had seized control of Sonora early in 1913, and he too recognized Carranza as First Chief. A former employee on a chickpea hacienda who had become a small *ranchero*, Obregón mirrored his class: he supported Madero, he wanted to limit monopolies and foreign capital, he favoured agrarian and labour reforms. Most observers agree that he was no radical. Yet this able organizer calculated that social change must occur in Mexico, and recruited into his army foot soldiers from the rural proletariat: miners, peons, migrant labourers, railway workers, and hundreds of Yaquis armed with bow and arrow. He made them salute and drill. Carranza came to Sonora, and for many years Obregón took orders from the First Chief.

In Sonora, Carranza made windy speeches while Obregón organized his Army of the Northwest; in Chihuahua the *División del Norte* sharpened its teeth under Pancho Villa. Throughout 1913 these revolutionary storm centres sucked youth toward the North. Many others fled the southern cities toward the storm gathering over Mexico. Many could find no place in the old society. There were trained engineers without work: in the factories and railways run by foreigners jobs went to French and American personnel. Men with diplomas could not get jobs in the government bureaucracy, for there weren't enough to go around. Some rejected a society that had rejected them. New ideas danced in their heads; some joined the revolution to find a place in the sun. Teenagers brought the hope of youth with them. This gust out of the South accelerated the tornados whirling over Sonora and Chihuahua.

In the North 1913 was a year of guerrillas congealing into armies: weapons crossed the border into Chihuahua, Obregón put uniforms on his ragged men in Sonora. Carranza, the former Porfirista landowner now wearing a liberal mask, firmly took command; his programme was simple – to remove Huerta and hold 'elections'. Obregón was a genuine liberal, and he knew that only social reforms could bring peace. Villa, the agrarian radical, dreamed of transforming Mexico into a society of peasants, ranchers, artisans, and small producers. Everyone followed the First Chief.

General Huerta, now President, ordered the federal army to fall back on Torreón. This desert city, on the railroad leading south, blocked the way to the capital. There the Federals built fortifications and assured Huerta that Torreón was impregnable. They had Villa trapped in the North. Could they crush him? They were too busy in the South, where the war was spreading over six states. In the mountains of Morelos the Zapatista guerrillas galloped near Mexico City.

In March 1914 Villa hurled his *División del Norte* upon Torreón. The fortifications held, and desperate fighting began. From the Villista trenches John Reed reports of the battle:

> Now the trench was boiling with men scrambling to their feet, like worms when you turn over a log. The rifle fire rattled shrilly. From behind us came running feet, and men in sandals, with blankets over their shoulders, came falling and slipping down the ditch, and scrambling up the other side — hundreds of them. They almost hid us from the front, but through the dust and spaces between running legs we could see the soldiers in the trench leap their barricade like a breaking wave. And then the impenetrable dust shut down and the fierce stabbing needle of the machine gun sewed the mighty jumble of sound together. A glimpse through a rift in the cloud torn by a sudden hot gust of wind — we could see the first brown line of men reeling altogether like drunkards, and the machine guns over the wall spitting sharp, dull red in the sunshine.

The battle raged for twelve days, as the Villistas fought from trench to trench, from house to house, from grave to grave. Torreón fell, and the federal trains retreated. The Federals fortified Zacatecas in the South, still blocking the rails to Mexico City.

Obregón's army crept down the Pacific coast, urged on by the landowner Carranza — he must beat Villa to the capital. In June 1914 Villa's ragged troops stormed the mountain citadels of Zacatecas, breaking open the road to Mexico City. Carranza cut off Villa's coal supply to halt his trains. Villa cursed while Carranza's faithful Obregón marched toward the capital.

The United States had slowly pressed Huerta to the wall. From the beginning Huerta had favoured the British imperialists. Britain grew stronger in Mexico. As the Revolution frightened out American investment, Huerta stretched out his hand to British oil companies. Oil was feeding the 'second industrial revolution' in the developed nations, and Mexico's fields were the richest on earth. Over the diplomats' meetings hung the ugly smell of petroleum. The fumes fuelled ideological engines in the White House, and phrases about 'democracy' floated south toward the Mexican dictator — a menacing cloud. President Woodrow Wilson and his Secretary of State, William Jennings Bryan, beat their breasts over Huerta's dictatorship. Bryan, a frequent visitor to Mexico for many years, had publicly said in 1907: 'We should all thank

17

Porfirio Díaz for his great work.' But Huerta's work with the British enraged Bryan, and he remembered democracy. The democratic phrases were followed by American actions. The United States refused the dictator recognition, watched arms flow to Villa, and warned off the British. In April 1914, U.S. marines killed hundreds of Mexicans to seize Veracruz, cutting off Huerta from the customs' revenues. His government's financial artery was severed; it rapidly bled to death.

In the South, Huerta's government rested on a foundation that was honey-combed, ready to collapse. From Guerrero to Veracruz, Zapata's guerrilla bands had tunnelled through it like termites. The guerrilla war had spread to meet Huerta's attacks. In the spring of 1913 he sent General Robles to deport 20,000 peasants for slave labour in Quintana Roo. If the guerrillas swam through a peasant sea Robles would empty it of people. 'How wonderful it will be when we are rid of the people of Morelos', he said. 'If they resist me I'll hang them from the trees like earrings.' In May he deported 1,000 peasants in boxcars. Soon the hoofbeats of approaching troops sent villagers into the ravines, only to return after the soldiers left. In July Robles herded families into concentration camps and deported 2,000 people. His ruthless Colonel Cartón murdered peasants, burned fields and looted villages. The villages emptied, as even the women and children fled to Zapatista camps in the mountains. Starving, wrapped in blankets under the night rains, some died of pneumonia. Children wandered homeless, while women seized weapons to form roving bands. The men swelled Zapata's guerrilla army.

A People's War exploded in Mexico. The cry *Tierra y Libertad* grew louder, and the war overflowed to the neighbouring states: Guerrero, Mexico, Oaxaca, Puebla, Tlaxcala, Hidalgo, Veracruz. In Morelos the people seized the *hacendados*' lands. By September Huerta gave up and sent troops north to fight Villa; in the South his generals retreated into the cities while rebels held the countryside. Zapatistas raided to the limits of Mexico City. To guard the capital Huerta used troops needed in the North.

Zapata could not take the cities to end the war, for he lacked cannon and bullets. But Chilpancingo fell to him in March 1914. There he captured General Cartón and his mass murderers. These officers faced a People's Court, then a firing squad. (In Morelos 20% of the people had died). In April Zapata encircled Cuernavaca. In the summer his army campaigned on the outskirts of Mexico City and ran out of bullets. He strengthened his *Plan de Ayala*: the *hacendados* would lose their lands to the people without compensation.

Pressured by the victories of the Constitutionalist armies in the North and harassed by Zapata's forces in the South, the dictator Huerta resigned in July, 1914. Huerta then fled into exile to drink himself to death in peace.

The Split in the Revolutionary Forces: Carranza Triumphs

Obregón liberated the capital in August. In Mexico City he reopened the House of the World's Worker, headquarters for the anarchist labourers, and urged them to join Carranza's movement. The workers turned a deaf ear. Carranza, they said, was no friend of the working man. Obregón, promising labour reforms, continued to woo them. He felt more and more uneasy: the urban workers rebuffed Carranza; Villa roared 'Treachery!' and threatened to march on the capital from Zacatecas; in vain Zapata urged Carranza to accept the South's *Plan de Ayala* legalizing land seizures across the nation.

Carranza's speeches made these radicals suspicious. The Revolution, he had shouted pompously, is not just a matter of distributing land, of honest elections, of opening new schools, of sharing the nation's wealth equally; the Revolution is a matter of something greater and holier; it is a matter of establishing justice, of searching for equality, of achieving national economic equilibrium. Carranza's deeds — before and after 1914 — spoke even louder. When his liberal generals carried through reforms he quashed them. Lucio Blanco divided a *hacendado's* lands among peons; Salvador Alvarado swept out Yucatan's slavery by labour reforms; Francisco Mújica ordered empty churches turned into schools. Carranza tried to annul these acts. Surrounded by fawning lawyers, the old landowner argued that reforms should wait until he became president.

With Huerta gone, the radicals, Villa and Zapata, slowly turned against Carranza. Their suspicion fractured the Revolution. As the split widened, Obregón suggested calling a Convention to smooth things over. Villa and Zapata sent intellectuals and revolutionary generals, while Carranza sent generals and lawyers. In the fall of 1914 they gathered in Aguascalientes to decide the fate of the Revolution. 'In periods of revolutionary crisis,' Karl Marx once observed, 'people conjure up the spirits of the past and borrow from them battle cries and costumes in order to present the new scene of world history in a time-honoured disguise.' And so the radicals in this Revolutionary Convention claimed the French Jacobins of 1793 for a model. They declared the Convention sovereign in the land, and *talked* of revolutionary decrees, laws, and programmes that would remake the nation. From afar, Carranza washed his hands of them.

In the Convention Obregón came forward, hiding his ambition. He urged mulish Carranza and radical Villa to step from the stage to permit a compromise. They refused, and Obregón's centre group had to choose between them. They chose Carranza and left the Convention to the radicals and their flaming oratory. In November 1914 Obregón again asked the Mexico City workers to join Carranza, but they had eyes only for the radical Convention. Obregón and Carranza, weaker than Villa, withdrew their army to the port of Veracruz, and the Convention marched on the capital. The Revolution had split open.

In Mexico City the Convention ruled for two months; many anarchist leaders worked closely with it. But the powers behind the Convention — Villa and Zapata — could not answer the question 'What is to be done?' Zapata had only his *Plan de Ayala*, granting land to ancient village communities in the South; and Villa had no plan at all. 'This town is too big for us,' Villa told Zapata. 'Things are better out there [in the countryside].' Villa felt at home in Chihuahua, Zapata in Morelos. Zapata left some intellectual lieutenants in the capital and rode away to the South. Both leaders preferred the saddle to the chair of *el Presidente*. Neither was educated enough to run the government: during the Revolution they read books for the first time. Both were men of the people, and yet the people they knew were in a rural *region*. How well did the two chieftains know the *nation*?

The Mexican nation was a kaleidoscope of classes and regions: Mayan slaves in Yucatán, mestizos in the mine pits of Sonora, enserfed peons on Durango haciendas, Yaquis in the sierra, textile workers in Puebla, cowboys on the Chihuahua plains, waiters in Mexico City restaurants. roughnecks in Tampico, labourers in the shoe factories of the capital, metal workers in northern smelters, peasants in Zapatista villages, hordes of servants in the cities, bandits in the countryside, migrant labourers in the North, and Zapotec Indians in the South. Train engineers, illiterate peons, anarchist migrants, tiny farmers, cattle rustlers, rural schoolteachers, poor blacksmiths, streetcar drivers, telegraph operators, electrical workers, roving unemployed — such were the little people of Mexico. As this kaleidoscope of races, classes, and regions whirled in revolution, Villa and Zapata went colour-blind. Each could see only one region — Chihuahua or Morelos, the *patria chica*. They strained to glimpse the whole through the lens of Zapata's agrarian programme. Zapata focused his *Plan de Ayala* on the nation, announced that the *Plan* could work, and Villa promised support. With this *Plan* Zapata thought to transform Mexico from the Texas border to Yucatán. The vision of the two men was national but the content utopian: a republic of small peasants.

In December 1914 in Mexico City, Villa's soldiers looted the rich to celebrate victory. The soldiers obeyed only Villa; the Convention (and its President Gutiérrez) became a shadow government. For trivial reasons the leader of the Zapastistas in the Convention, Paulino Martínez, was murdered by Villista soldiers. This and other differences between the two groups created a breach in the agrarian revolution.

In the capital the Convention talked and debated, but no dramatic laws gripped the nation. Across the land workers and peasants sweated from sun-up to sun-down. Where was the decree promising land to the tiller? The President was busy calling rioting troops to order. Where was the law guaranteeing every worker a minimum wage? The Convention was occupying itself with colourful speeches. Disorder spread, and the food flow into the capital slowed to a trickle. The Mexico City workers began to starve.

From December 1914 to January 1915 the armies of Villa and Zapata patrolled the nation; they had Carranza trapped on the coastal strip running from Tampico to Yucatán. Would they drive him into the sea? They let the weeks fly past them. While the Villistas enjoyed the fleshpots of the capital, the Zapatistas tilled the fields of Morelos. In Veracruz the Carrancistas built up their army. In December 1914 Obregón finally had his way: Carranza announced to the nation he would carry out political, legal, labour, and land reforms *during his struggle against Villa*.

Carranza's promises of December 1914 were a shout of despair. With his back to the sea he faced a nation dominated by radicals. To survive he had to steal their thunder. So he appealed to the miners, peons, clerks, Indians, workers, storekeepers, peasants, migrants, slaves, teachers and unemployed, to all the little people of Mexico, to the *populus*. He forgot no class or region in his new populism. He talked to the whole nation.

In January 1915 his populist politics gathered momentum with a new Agrarian Law. From Veracruz he promised land to the Indians, peasants, villagers, and peons of Mexico. How many noticed that Article 10 provided compensation to big landowners whom the courts had decided had been damaged by redistribution? Or that the Law placed land reform in the hands of authorized generals and the governors of each state? (In Zapatista country the haciendas were seized *by the people themselves*.) These details escaped most Mexicans.

Obregón led Carranza's strengthened army out of Veracruz towards Mexico City; Villa withdrew toward Querétaro to prepare for the last battle. Obregón, master of the new populist strategy, marched into the capital.

In February 1915 he found the capital paralyzed: worthless paper money littered the streets; shops were boarded up; factories stood idle; water was in short supply; food no longer rolled into the city; and the workers were starving. Obregón set up aid posts, executed food speculators, and struggled to organize the capital. He began to woo the anarchist workers again. To the House of the World's Worker, the organization of unions, he gave buildings and printing presses. His agents handed the union leaders money for desperate workers. He invited the anarchist House to join Carranza's movement, but the retreating Convention drew the workers like a magnet — they did not trust Obregón. When the electricians' union struck against the telephone company Obregón settled the dispute quickly: he turned over the company to the workers. He pressed his suit of the anarchist House harder. An open assembly attended by rank-and-file workers refused him. But a secret meeting of leaders finally accepted an alliance with Obregón. He sent them to Carranza.

In a pact with Carranza the leaders promised to organize union members into battalions for the army. The leaders agreed to spread Carrancista propaganda among the workers throughout Mexico. With bad grace Carranza consented to labour reforms. In February 1915 these labour leaders tried to recruit soldiers for Carranza. The rank-and-file workers, more radical than their leaders, had no love for the 'First Chief'. But thousands faced starvation in the hapless capital. To get food and money they joined Obregón's army: carpenters, masons, tailors, mechanics, printers, metallurgists, bakers, cobblers, waiters, conductors, and textile workers. They formed six Red Battalions to fight against Villa. The radical workers and peasants had split.

The critical importance of the industrial proletariat during the Revolution, the influence it wielded, went far beyond its actual numbers. According to Obregón's memoirs, 9,000 recruits joined his army in Mexico City, the greater part consisting of industrial workers from the House of Labour. Considering that the size of his army at the decisive battle of Celaya was barely 20,000, it is fair to say that roughly one-fourth consisted of industrial workers. Unlike the peasant masses who outnumbered them many times, industrial workers were organized in unions and constituted a disciplined political force. The important task of recruiting a new army to fight Villa was assigned to the trade unions. On the morning of February 11 the headquarters of the House of Labour were voluntarily closed and all trade-union work was suspended, according to the resolution of the workers' general assembly, 'until the victory of the revolutionary cause which we support'.

It is true that the House of Labour was divided. The Electricians' Union, which had the backing of the rank and file and, the following year, would lead the workers in Mexico's first general strike, refused to aid Carranza and Obregón's Constitutionalist army. At the workers' assembly on February 8, which first discussed the question of organizing Red Battalions, more than 1,000 trade unionists participated without being able to reach an agreement. Against the anarcho-syndicalist opposition the leaders of the House of Labour had to convoke a second assembly on February 10, this time with picked delegates meeting in secret, in order to impose their will.

Although historians point to Obregón's ability to manoeuvre the industrial workers into forming battalions, the pact between the Constitutionalist government and the House of Labour was also an indication of the government's weakness. If it wanted to defeat Villa's peasant army, it was virtually compelled to rely on the industrial workers to tilt the balance. The government's concessions went so far as to admit Red Battalions into the regular army. The designation 'Red' was not Obregón's idea; it was imposed on him by petty bureaucrats from the House of Labour in their effort to win over the rank and file.

Obregón's army with its Red Battalions marched north. During his advance he carried on revolutionary propaganda about Carranza's programme of land and labour reforms. Students and generals called meetings to discuss the revolutionary ideology. They explained the Agrarian Law to the people. As Obregón sped towards Villa he left the House's labour agitators in his wake; they organized unions and spread Carrancista promises.

In the spring of 1915 Obregón and Villa clashed in a series of great battles first at Celaya and then at Leon and Aguascalientes. Obregón's advisors had learned trench warfare in Europe: they laid rolls of barbed wire between machine-gun nests. In battle after battle the Villistas, against professional advice, charged Obregón's trenches only to hang up on the wire under roaring machine guns.

They repeated mistakes and failed to learn. Had their will to win weakened? In war, Napoleon once said, moral factors are to material factors as three to one. The Villistas' morale was slowly fading: in the capital they muffed their chance to govern; next they lost contact with Zapata's guerrilla armies; then they watched the urban workers desert to Obregón; and finally they let him steal the agrarian revolution by populist promises.

Obregón's populism flared up brighter than ever. In the midst of the great battles he decreed a minimum wage for all areas under Carranza's control. Debt peons, house-maids, factory hands, migrant labourers, copper miners, plantation slaves, textile workers, restaurant waiters, foot soldiers, northern

cowboys, southern serfs, urban proletarians, rural day labourers — to all these
he appealed for support. Under his machine guns Villa's armies broke up,
and Obregón pursued the remnants toward Chihuahua. To secure the cities
in his rear the House's labour agitators organized unions.

In October 1915 the American government finally grasped the class
lines separating the agrarian radicals from Carranza: the old *hacendado*,
in spite of his demagogic populism, was more conservative than either Zapata
or Villa. Carranza, now winning, promised law and order, and the Americans
wanted an end to chaos. Only then would the profits again flow north to the
United States. Washington recognized Carranza, sent him aid, and laid down
an arms embargo against Villa. This was the death blow: without modern
weapons Villa slid back into guerrilla warfare. For years a thousand Villistas
held out in the mountains of Chihuahua.

With the armies of the northern agrarians crushed, Carranza dropped
his populist mask to reveal the Porfirista senator. He betrayed his promises to
the people. This turn to the right worried his populist commanders: Villarreal,
Mújica, Alvarado, Obregón.

The Red Battalions were dissolved. In the opening months of 1916 Carranza
ordered his generals to arrest militants of the House of the World's Worker.
He closed their Mexico City Headquarters. In July the House paralysed
the capital with a general strike; Carranza jailed the leaders and broke the
strike with death threats. Obregón met leaders in hiding to suggest they dissolve
the House until things calmed down. Posing as a friend of labour, Obregón
had his way: the anarchist confederation of unions quietly vanished.

In 1916 Carranza sent his most reactionary general, Pablo Gonzales, to
attack the Zapatistas in Morelos. There in the South the agrarian revolution
was complete: the villagers had divided up the *hacendados'* lands: some sugar
fields and distilleries were owned in common; and a people in arms defended
the new order. Generals in Zapata's popular army wore sandals, and the
soldiers seemed a militia, ready to exchange ploughs for rifles.

Carranza's general began a scorched earth campaign in Morelos. Pablo
Gonzales robbed, burned, sacked, raped, and massacred the people. He
deported prisoners to slave labour in Yucatán. And the old pattern
recurred: a People's War surged up against him. Driven back into the cities,
his shattered army caught the virus of revolution. It grumbled against the
policy of murdering peasants.

The social volcano rumbled under the nation. Villa's guerrillas fought on
in the North; a People's War raged in the South; the general strike paralysed
Mexico City. Carranza's turn to the right alarmed his populist ideologists and
generals. They were the vanguard of the revolution, and they wanted to stay
in power. They saw that power required at least the passive consent of the
people.

They made Carranza call a convention to write a constitution for the
nation. In December 1916 these leaders met in Querétaro to cast their populism in legal form, and by January they had forged the law of the land. The
Constitution of 1917 was — in that year — the most radical in the world.

The 1917 Constitution

By 1917 the nucleus of a new political and military bureaucracy had formed in Mexico. Emerging from the Carrancista army, it had spread over the nation to penetrate the people's life, like mould on bread. In its core lurked the army's generals (there were many generals, one for every two hundred soldiers). Government careerists near Carranza formed part of the core. Civil servants and army officers made up the expanding layers of this new and influential group.

The writers of the Constitution of 1917 were not brokers, bankers, merchants, rentiers, investors, or factory owners living off profits – they were not capitalists. Rather they were men drawing a salary: schoolteachers, journalists, engineers, government officials, and numerous generals. They belonged not to the bourgeoisie, but to an emerging bureaucracy or 'new middle class'. This bureaucracy, clutching an unsteady throne, saw that social reforms might close the jaws of the revolution yawning below. As 1917 opened, the nation wavered over the abyss: almost two million people had died; paper money choked the economy; the mine pits were empty; haciendas lay in ruins; in outlying states generals ruled by whim. People went about their labours armed. Columns of guerrillas snaked through Chihuahua and Morelos, while American regulars hunted Villa in the Mexican sierra and threatened to roll across the nation 'to restore order'. A Mexican nationalist might urge reforms to keep the nation from going under; an idealist might demand reforms from love of the people. Such motives drove a few of the constitution-writers, but most of the Carrancista generals and political bureaucrats backed reforms out of an instinct for survival. To retain power they needed peace.

In 1917 Mexico cried out for reform: the Church, though weakened, still spread ignorance; a few big owners held most of the land; and the army pushed civilians around at gunpoint. Workers and peasants, slaving long hours for poor fare, could not read and write. At Tampico foreigners still sucked up the nation's oil and shipped it home. But the old regime was gone, and this opened the door for social change.

The Constitution of 1917 outlawed the old Mexico and declared a new society. Yet the old society lingered on. Did the Constitution's authors think to abolish militarism, clericalism, and landlordism with their clattering typewriters? Not at all: the Constitution was a programme for social change, a programme made into the law of the land. The Constitution gave this promise: the Mexican people, in their struggle for a new order, could count on the government for help. This promise aimed to quieten the masses.

The Constitution fired a volley of promises at three important classes: peasants, workers and businessmen. To the peasants it promised land reform: village communities would get back the fields and waters stolen from them by great owners, and in addition the rest of the rural population would receive land. The big owners would have compensation – someday. (This convenient *mañana* frightened rich Mexicans.) And the haciendas must dissolve into smaller plots, each state fixing the maximum size for farms. Thus the Constitution appealed to all the little people who wanted land: peasants, peons, villagers, Indians, migrants, and *rancheros*.

To the workers the Constitution guaranteed a better life. Accident compensation, a share of the employers' profits, the right to unions and strikes — these appealed to men working in railways, factories, and mines. There were also measures aimed at women: no more child labour, an end to night work for women, and equal pay for equal work regardless of sex. The Constitution, turning toward the peon, ordered a day of rest once a week, the end of debt peonage, and the closing of company stores. For all workers there would be social security, the eight-hour day, and a minimum wage.

To businessmen the Constitution seemed reassuring, for private property was guaranteed. Through the Constitution ran the themes of 19th century liberalism — everyone has a right to property. Private property, individual enterprise, and free competition are the basis of the economic system.

But the movement of the Mexican Revolution from 1910 to 1917 contained anti-capitalist features. Though the masses usually did not know what to put in place of the old Díaz system, some Zapatistas had collectivist tendencies, and anarchist workers wanted communism. To placate these people, the constitution-writers added several paragraphs with a socialist tendency. The nation has the eternal right, declared Article 27, to give private property the forms dictated by public interest. The State can limit the size of farms, says the Constitution, and by implication the size of many things (corporations, incomes). The State must break up monopolies; and for the public good it curbs the individual pursuit of wealth. All lakes and rivers belong to the State, and also the diamonds, copper, gold and iron in the mountains, along with the oil in the earth. Individuals can own only the land's surface. They can freely develop their property only if they further the interests of all. The State guards the interests of the nation against the greed of individuals.

Thus the Constitution contradicts itself. It springs from 19th century liberalism, yet contains a sharp attack on this tradition. That did not disturb its authors, for populist ideologists are rarely consistent. They become, like St. Paul, all things to all men. They try to bring men together, to make the social system work. Far from preventing capitalism in Mexico, their constitution may have strengthened it. In the 20th century, ruling classes in many countries copied the Constitution's famous Article 27.

This article gave great power to the State. The government bureaucracy, growing ever larger, would use it to build up its power over other classes — through the presidency. The republican constitution, providing for a congress and a court, would become a fig leaf covering the nakedness of the President's power (and he is the bureaucracy's man). Today he makes all law for the nation; Congress and the Court use rubber stamps.

In Article 123 the Constitution allowed the State to step into conflicts between the three principal classes: workers, peasants, and employers. Strikes are legal *only if* they aim to restore social equilibrium, to harmonize the relationship between labour and capital. In such conflicts arbitration committees have the final decision, committees with equal numbers of employers, unionists, and state bureaucrats. This gives the State the decisive voice, for it can side with either business or labour. The State is the great dictator, the brain that makes the body's members work in harmony.

The Constitution set the stage for the State to co-opt and control workers, peasants, and businessmen. And the Constitution gave the bureaucratic State weapons against those ancient enemies of the Mexican people – the Army, the Church, and the Oligarchy.

The Army was boxed in with rules: in peacetime no requisitioning, no quartering of troops in private homes; all town garrisons under federal control – to avoid future coups. The Church faced a battery of regulations: foreign priests were to leave Mexico, religious schools to close, and the State was to take all Church lands – and buildings! As for the landed oligarchy, big haciendas were to break up into small plots, and every state government was to limit the land a person could own.

The Constitution of 1917 contained the promise of social revolution, a programme for levelling the social volcano. It was the work of populist ideologists and commanders backed by Obregón. The President decided to ignore the Constitution; Carranza would sign but not enforce it.

In 1917 he launched his second scorched earth campaign against the Zapatistas, in 1918 a third. By 1919 Morelos suffered famine; one half the original population was dead. There was talk of American intervention. Zapata was betrayed and killed in an ambush. His movement broke up, but villagers kept lands seized during the Revolution. In 1920 Pancho Villa laid down his arms in the North.

The Armed Struggle for the Presidency: Obregón Replaces Carranza

The military phase of the Revolution drew to a close. The last act in this drama, an armed struggle over the presidency, took place in 1920. As Carranza's term ended, the nation looked for the old 'liberal' to allow the election of Obregón. But Carranza betrayed his promise of democracy; he prepared the 'election' of a stooge he could control. Obregón revolted, the Army rallied to him, and the nation backed his march to the capital. Carranza fled with government gold but was betrayed and killed in the mountains. The road to the presidency opened before Obregón. He brought his populist style of politics to the government, and Mexico was surprised by – peace!

Obregón had survived them all – Villa, Zapata, Carranza – and now he controlled Mexico. How did this come about?

Students of revolution will see that, in the twisting torrent sweeping Mexico toward a new order, Obregón had the advantage of the centrist position. In the French Revolution the centrist Robespierre joined with Danton's right to destroy the left; then Robespierre sent the right to the guillotine, and the centre emerged triumphant. The process recurred in the Russian Revolution. Stalin played Robespierre to Bukharin's Danton and crushed the left; then Stalin purged the right opposition and the Stalinist centre came out on top. In Mexico the Revolutionary Convention was the first act in the same drama, unfolding scene after scene, from Obregón's split with Villa in 1914 to Carranza's death in the mountains in 1920. Obregón's centrists worked under the rightist Carranza to destroy Villa and Zapata, then Obregón eliminated Carranza, and the populist centre became the government of Mexico.

How did Obregón lead his pack of generals and bureaucrats to their triumph over the revolutionary masses? He had strengthened his hand in 1915 by dividing the workers from the peasants: his urban Red Battalions followed him against Villa's rural armies. Thus he prevented the worker-peasant alliance that Marx advocated in the 19th Century and that Lenin was to lead in Russia in the 20th. On 14 February 1918 in a letter to General Jenaro Amezcua, Zapata recognized that the worker-peasant split had weakened the agrarian radicals. Obregón aimed to divide radical workers from peasants, then co-opt each into his movement. During his presidency from 1920 to 1924 he applied this policy with great success.

But the key to Obregón's victory, from beginning to end, was his populism. He promised something to everyone: land reform to the peasants, labour reform to the workers, guarantees to businessmen, and defence against imperialism to all classes. To the Army he offered plunder and promotions, to the bureaucrats the spoils of power. He gave intellectuals government posts.

His enemies helped by limiting their appeals. Villa never got beyond a mild agrarian law, and this came late in the struggle. Zapata's *Plan de Ayala,* promising the return of stolen lands to villages, captured the hearts of southern peasants — there were free villages in the South. But what could Zapata's programme mean to workers in Puebla textile mills, to enserfed peons on haciendas in Guanajuato, to labourers on Yucatán's hemp plantations, to miners in Sonora? The Zapatistas finally published a programme of reforms aimed at these groups. But the programme forgot to mention the minimum wage and came too late to do any good — the radicals were broken.

The labour unions preached a class-oriented anarchism to their workers and ignored everyone else. This anarchist ideology was beyond many proletarians; they could not read, they came from rural areas, they lacked a nation-wide union to lead them.

By contrast, Obregón wooed the Mexican masses with simple appeals and popular slogans. He talked the language of many classes and races — he could speak some Yaqui and Maya. To everyone he made promises. His vision was national, for he craved power, and he knew it lay in Mexico City. He would use it to manage the masses. He gave the land distribution agency to Díaz Soto's peasant leaders, money to Luis Morones' unions, and government posts to intellectuals like José Vasconcelos.

Were the Mexican revolutionaries thus betrayed? No. They were co-opted.

2. Soldier, Priest and Landlord

From 1910 to 1920 the social volcano blew away huge pieces of its cone, but the crater remained. In 1920 the medieval Church towered over the people, cast shadows of superstition across the country, and preached disobedience toward Obregón's new government. Foreigners and *hacendados* clung to Mexico's land, though there were fresh faces among the landowners — the brown faces of mestizo half-castes. These were revolutionaries turned rich. And the Army's generals began to behave like officers of the 19th century: they enriched themselves and shot protesting civilians. In this the new military followed an old tradition. Since the War of Independence against Spain a thousand military attacks on the Mexican government had taken place. The new 'revolutionary' army mouthed the old threats and demanded high salaries; a starving nation dug into its pockets to pay.

The old crater remained — the Army, Church, and Oligarchy. In 1920 the volcano stopped erupting, but had it gone dead? There were rumblings down below. Everyone knew its power: for ten years the nation had suffered chaos; more than two million Mexicans had died; and a ruling class had lost the government. Mexico's new rulers wanted to avoid a similar fate. From 1920 to 1940 they slowly levelled the crater, as successive Presidents — first Obregón, then Calles, and finally Cárdenas — provided populist leadership for popular struggles against the old order.

This social change did not turn Mexico into a democracy, nor did it raise the popular classes out of their misery, nor shake off the chains of economic imperialism. But it brought a political stability unknown in Latin America. The political movement that emerged in 1915 has held continuous power for half a century — longer than any ruling party on the planet. It allows opposition parties to run but not to reign. The Mexican party, father of firm government, has not freed the masses; it has managed them. With their help it has broken the traditional blocks on Mexico's development (Army, Church, Oligarchy) and released powerful economic forces. These forces have driven the nation ever deeper into the maelstrom of world capitalism. While Mexico's capitalist development has brought wealth to a few, the lot of the little people hardly improves. Yet the State continues to manage them. For sixty years it has applied its tested formula — violence plus co-option — with increasing success. This formula works in the corporate state built by the revolution of 1920-40. How did this society come into being?

The Struggle to Control the Army

Mexico tamed the beast that devours governments in Latin America — the Army. In Latin countries politicians often wake up in jail or exile; each country is occupied by its own army. This makes for unstable regimes: in 150 years Bolivia has had 180 governments. In 1920 Mexico wallowed in this violent tradition, for the previous hundred years had seen a thousand *pronunciamientos* in this unhappy country, a record in Latin America.

To Mexico the Army meant crime and corruption, and by 1920 the monster had swelled to twice its normal size. It staggered under the weight of its huge head — thousands of officers, a general for every two hundred soldiers. There were generals nineteen years old. The Revolution had thrown up these officers overnight, along with roving bands of armed men, and the nation was at their mercy. They lacked discipline and uniforms, and though some were idealists, many were little better than bandits. Their salaries gobbled up the federal budget while the nation shivered in poverty. How could Mexico get rid of them?

Obregón Tames the Revolutionary Generals

When Obregon became president in 1920 he attacked the problem in a roundabout way. While he prepared to suppress the generals in the long run, he moved to co-opt them at once. Into the federal army he brought the irregular generals. They squirmed and cursed, but Obregón demanded submission. He gave them generals' pay, and soon the Army was eating two-thirds of the government's budget! In buying them off he bought time. He encouraged the restless to enrich themselves and announced the bitter truth: 'No general can resist a blast of 100,000 pesos'.

Meanwhile he trained new officers to replace the wild men of the revolution. He set up a national military academy, and sent the best students to Spain, France, Germany and the United States for further study. He prepared professional officers loyal to the nation.

Rebellious generals lurked in the regular army and remained a threat to the President's power. As he looked for allies against them, his eye fell upon the Colossus of the North. He decided to win the support of the hated *gringos* for his struggle against the military chieftains, for he remembered that Mexico's history was a graveyard of parties and factions that had antagonized the United States, and he knew that his government had infuriated American capital. The iron, oil, gold, and copper in the earth, said the Constitution of 1917, no longer belonged to private companies, but to the Mexican government. Obregón promised Washington he would not enforce the Constitution against oil and mines already worked by foreigners. The U.S.A. then threw its colossal weight behind him.

He made workers and peasants his allies. He favoured the peasant league of Díaz Soto y Gama, the Zapatista ideologist, and protected Luis Morones' labour confederation. During any showdown with the Army he could count on mass support.

The showdown came. By 1924 most of the soldiers were up in arms: fires of rebellion had flared up in Jalisco, Oaxaca, and Veracruz. In Veracruz, General Sánchez returned the peasants' lands to the *hacendados* and marched on the capital. While peasants attacked Sánchez's army in the rear, Obregón rallied loyal troops to fight. The United States rushed him rifles, bullets, and airplanes! The common people of the North supported him, Mexico City workers applauded him, and peasants took up arms for him. He snuffed out the military rebellions one by one.

Then began the bloody business of reprisals. Rebel generals faced firing squads, and the President sent politicians into exile. But as he cut off heads with one hand, he rewarded with the other — scores of loyal officers became generals. Disloyal officers fled the country, and graduates of the new military academy took their place. The loyalty of the new men reached beyond local commanders to the nation itself.

Thus Obregón, the Revolution's leading general, crushed his colleagues with the hammer of the State. Some historians believe that this was his greatest deed as president. In four years he cut into military corruption, shaved the Army's size, and trimmed its slice of the federal budget to 40%. But he only dented the Army's power. Though the 1924 bloodletting weakened the military dragon, it continued to breathe fire and smoke over the nation. The local generals were often robber barons: corrupt, drunken, violent men, who ran haciendas and gambling houses for themselves and protected land-owners against the peasants. Someday these violent men could devour the State. Would the next president slay the dragon?

Calles Builds a Professional Army

In 1924 the new President, Calles, took up the challenge. In three years he slashed off a further third of the Army's body; the men he let go were of doubtful loyalty. As the Army shrank, the government threw it smaller chunks of the federal budget. More federal money was left for schools and public works.

Calles wooed workers and peasants partly from fear of the Army; he wanted a counterweight to military power. He distributed land to the free villages and took union leaders into his government. People's militias could help him against the rebellious generals.

He modernized the military academy and sent graduates to regiments he didn't trust. Between the cowboy generals and their private armies he spread layers of careerist officers loyal to the government. The government gave some generals posts far from their units.

The Mexican foot soldiers, peons saluting *their* general, lived in ignorance and squalor. If their commander ordered an attack on the government, they followed him blindly. They knew little of the world beyond the barracks. Calles tried to turn the barracks into schools, to occupy the troops with base-

ball, or put them to work building roads. He improved their living conditions
and so increased their resistance to the promises of disloyal generals.

All this was progress. Yet in 1927 the Army still gobbled up one-fourth
of the government's pitiful funds while the nation went barefooted. In the
giant U.S.A. there were 64 generals, in little Mexico 456! With an 'election'
approaching they grew restless.

Elections were fraudulent, for the men that counted the votes always
won — they were the governing party. In the 1920s both government and
opposition campaigned at election time, then began armed struggle to decide
the outcome. In an election they were cocks strutting their colours before
the death fight.

There was opposition to Calles' government: part of the Army disliked
him; Catholics hated him for enforcing the Constitution against the Church;
and landowners resented his programme of agrarian reform. In 1927 the election campaign against him began. Then the generals, fed up with his moves
against their power, persuaded many officers to join them — the death struggle
was on. Within a month Calles crushed them. He stood the leaders against
the wall, and the dragon bled again.

As Calles stepped down from the presidency, the Army had weakened —
but not fatally. Many of its generals were murderers, ready to kill anyone in
their way, and they would never be satisfied with provincial commands.

From 1928 to 1934 Calles was the nation's *eminence grise*, moving puppet
presidents across the political stage in Mexico City. He continued his policies
of shifting and retiring the old 'revolutionary' generals. In 1929, during the
'election' of a presidential puppet, the generals struck again; according to the
historian, Tannenbaum, they carried away most of the Army. Calles took
charge of the fight against them.

He could count on the professional officer corps drawn from the academy;
worker groups supported him; and thousands of peasants hurried to help
the government. The United States again sent large shipments of arms: chaos
in Mexico was bad for American business, and Washington wanted the rebellion
crushed. With aid from the popular masses Calles smashed the revolt in two
months. Shootings and exiles followed.

The Workers' Militia and General Cedillo

Was the military monster mortally wounded? President Cárdenas (1934-40)
was not sure; he continued to undermine the power of the remaining chieftains. He retired generals, shifted commands, and made the troops build
roads and schools. He passed a law against political activity by officers and
required competitive examinations for promotion. In 1936 he sent some
generals into exile. The Army's share of the federal budget slipped to one-
sixth. The government saved money for its modernization programme: roads,
dams, schools, railways, industry.

In the 1930s the world economic crisis was shaking up societies everywhere, and social unrest spread to Mexico. Cárdenas answered strike waves
and agrarian revolts with labour and land reforms. A few generals, by now

31

Mexico 1910-1982: Reform or Revolution?

hacendados or businessmen themselves, turned against a president calling for union power and land to peasants. As a check on these generals, Cárdenas distributed rifles and organized a militia among the peasants. The handful of reactionary generals muttered threats. Would the Army follow them? For a generation officers loyal to the President had trickled out of the academy into the Army. President Cárdenas took no chances: he formed a workers' militia, equipped it with rifles and uniforms, and pointed their weapons at the generals. His militiamen soon outnumbered the soldiers two to one. For the Army it was checkmate.

General Cedillo, the boss of San Luis Potosí, could not believe it. Cedillo had entered history as a peasant revolutionary, gained control of a state, and turned it into his private kingdom. He became rich, Catholic, and conservative. With thousands of personal troops this barely literate strongman rose against Cárdenas and called for Army support. But the Army was a new creature, staffed by officers loyal to the President, whoever he might be. Cárdenas sent the Army against Cedillo, forced his surrender, and shot him. No general ever tried a coup again.

An End to Military Coups?
In the 1940s Mexican presidents suspiciously watched their generals, but the army was a paper dragon. By 1940 Obregón, Calles, and Cárdenas, relying on mass support, had turned the Army into a tool of government. Since then the Army finds enough to do putting up schoolhouses, repairing roads, planting forests, building hospitals, and digging canals. Civilians control the ruling party, the big motor that drives the small motor of the military. Today the Army bites out only one-tenth of the budget; it absorbs a smaller percentage of national production than almost any military in Latin America.

In the 1950s the U.S.A. built a war economy and expanded its economy and military power over scores of nations; by 1960 Latin American armies had received millions in U.S. guns, bullets, tanks, and planes. The Latin armies took this aid like alcoholics sipping a bottle of rum. Latin politicians who angered Washington first saw the bottle stoppered, then heard tanks smash the gates of the presidential palace, and finally found themselves in exile. But the Mexican army never became an addict of U.S. aid. Though the Mexican generals wanted to accept Washington's offer, the politicians pushed the bottle away: they thought it contained a genie beyond their control. Through years of struggle they had tamed the Army, and they wanted it weak and obedient. Today the Mexican Army's links with the Pentagon exist but are fragile.

Today the Army's task is to enforce the will of the ruling party inside Mexico. Every town has its garrison on the hill, and the troops put down any rebellion. In a nation of suffering millions, where violence is common, the Army guards banks in the cities, shoots Indian tribes in revolt, hunts guerrillas in the sierra, or scatters demonstrations of striking workers. It has even fired on university students. Though the Army cannot legally take part in political struggles it is hardly neutral — it supports the ruling party. In the underdeveloped world Mexico's little army stands out for its servility; most of the non-communist countries in Asia, Africa, and Latin America are run by generals. Mexico has curbed its officers. In doing this the nation broke its century-old tradition of militarism and became the exception among countries south of the Rio Grande.

The War Against Organized Religion: The Church Retaliates

Beside this struggle with the Army ran Mexico's war against the Church, several terrible battles growing out of the contest between priest and president, a rivalry with roots in the 19th century. Mexico was born in 1821. The new nation suffered from a tumour it carried within — the Catholic clergy. In Europe, before the tumour could become cancerous, it had been slashed by radical surgeons: Diderot, Voltaire, Robespierre. In Mexico it grew ever larger. As the Industrial Revolution hurled Europe forward into the 19th century, the Catholic Church dragged Mexico back into the feudal past. For the Church was an economic power; it owned half of Mexico's land down to Juárez's reform in the 1860s, then got some of it back under Díaz. As the nation's banker, the Church sat on the liquid capital or sent it to Rome. It controlled education: while Frenchmen studied Copernicus, Laplace, and Lamarck, Mexicans learned how the sun goes round an earth created by God in six days. The Church was a political force; priests propped up governments to their liking and sabotaged the rest. No matter what crime a priest committed he faced a Church court — the State could not touch him. The Church was a state within the State.

In the 1860s Juárez and the liberals weakened the Church, but it got back some of its influence under Díaz' regime. In 1910 it was still a major landowner and controlled many schools. It encouraged mass ignorance, supported dictatorial governments, and ran medieval convents in the 20th century.

The Revolution of 1910-20 met an implacable enemy in the Church. The religious hierarchy and the Catholic press backed dictators Díaz and Huerta, sided with the *hacendados* against the people, and turned a stone face toward Carranza's government. So in the Constitution of 1917 the federal government urged the states to limit the number of priests within their borders, declared all religious buildings government property, outlawed the ownership of land by the Church, and banned foreign priests from giving the sacraments. Since many of backward Mexico's priests came from the surplus in Spain and Italy, the Constitution was a death sentence for the Church. But Carranza refused to enforce it.

Obregón (1920-24) took parts of the Constitution seriously. The Church preached disobedience to his government and sneered at the Constitution, the highest law in the land. Priests behaved as if the year were 1820 instead of 1920. Ten years of revolutionary violence had smashed the old political system, robbed the Church of its lands, and raised the hopes of poor peons and hungry miners, of peasants in remote villages and the under-classes in the cities. The voltage of the Revolution had shocked Mexico's static society into motion; the popular masses longed for social justice. But justice in this world did not interest the Church. 'Blessed are you poor,' Jesus had said, 'for yours is the kingdom of God.' A kingdom in the *next* world, the priests added, for in this life the poor must suffer the wickedness of the rich. For centuries Mexicans had listened to the Church's message: 'Obey!'

By 1920 the mood of the people had changed. They welcomed the new programmes of land reform and mass education. Obregón began his administration with a literacy campaign based on a simple idea that those who can read should teach those who can't. Soon reading classes were meeting in plazas, in homes, on street corners. Mexico, where eight out of ten people could neither read nor write, had begun to drag itself out of the Middle Ages. The Church frowned on this new progress.

The economic base of the Church had disintegrated in the Revolution, but its ideological superstructure was as rigid as ever: the priests preached ancient dogma and ritual in a foreign language, fostered superstition and ignorance among the peasants, and *fought against education for the people*. Like Pope Pius IX (1864) the priests remained irreconcilably opposed to progress, liberalism, and modern civilization. The Catholic leadership feared that education would turn millions from the Church, as the schools had done in Europe. But the government needed mass education to build a modern nation. On the horizon loomed a war between Church and State.

In its schools the Church dished out medieval instruction to a few and worked against the government's efforts to enlighten the many. Obregón's government printed a million textbooks for those learning to read. His state presses published the classics in cheap editions; for the first time the literate poor could sample Plato, Shakespeare, and Calderón. Obregón's programmes sent teachers into the countryside with a revolutionary mission.

These teachers went to live in the villages, and by the end of 1924 the peasants had built themselves a thousand schools. President Calles (1924-28) deepened and spread this missionary programme. The teachers were young idealists who disliked religion – to them it seemed superstition. Soon the village became an arena for the struggle between teacher and priest. For centuries the priest had argued against Indian beliefs that man had descended from a jaguar; now the teacher said he had come from an ape. The priest counter-attacked. By pointing to a drought as an act of God against these devilish ideas, the priest sometimes persuaded peasants to stone their teacher. But usually the peasant thirst for education was too strong, and the priests lost ground all along the line. The Mexican peasants enjoyed their taste of progress.

In the 1920s agrarian agitators organized peasants to demand the land reform promised in the Constitution. The religious hierarchy sided with the landowners against these reformers, and priests undermined the work of peasant leagues in the countryside. The agrarian reformers redoubled their efforts. A few governors helped them regain lands stolen by *hacendados*.

By 1926 the Church, thoroughly fed up, began to move against the government. The archbishop announced that Mexican priests would never observe the Constitution's regulation of religious activities; the bishops called for Catholics to demand constitutional changes. President Calles urged Catholic leaders to compromise, but the bishops and their conservative supporters wanted a showdown. So Calles accepted the challenge: he ordered foreign priests out of the country and closed the religious schools; he began to enforce the Constitution. The Church went on strike and refused to give the sacraments in Mexico — priests walked off the job. Did they expect Catholic Mexico to rise in revolt and destroy the government? Many historians believe they did.

There were Catholic rebellions. From 1926 to 1929 violence raged across Mexico in the Cristero War against the government. In this civil war several social tendencies surfaced: in Morelos peasant radicals fought for land; in Jalisco greedy generals massacred Catholics to seize their goods. But the essence of the Cristero rebellion was conservative. *Hacendados* rallied to it, as the faithful in Jalisco, Nayarit, and Durango rose in arms. The government crushed them, and they took to guerrilla warfare. The guerrillas killed the new teachers or cut off their noses; federal troops hung peaceful Catholics from telegraph poles; the religious rebels murdered agrarian reformers in the countryside. Three years of senseless violence shook Mexico. Jesuit priests with machine guns, teachers without noses, dynamited passenger trains, demolished schoolhouses, burning cornfields, government massacres — scene after scene of the tragedy rushed past. By 1929 the Church saw that the government was stronger than ever, for most of the people did not support the Cristeros. The Church ended its strike and the war stopped. Church and State struck a compromise.

The priests had learned their lesson; they wanted the truce to become a permanent peace. But Calles had tasted blood and like it. As the nation's *eminence grise* he goaded subsequent presidents to revive the anti-religious campaign in several states; during 1931 it flared up brightly in the work of the Revolutionary Anti-clerical League of Mexico. In Veracruz bombs exploded in churches, and the state government limited the number of priests to one per 100,000 people. In Tabasco the Red Shirts killed Christians and marched with banners that showed fat priests collecting money from the starving poor. In 1932 every state passed laws limiting the number of priests. The Church, worried by the threat of another war it could not win, ordered Christians to avoid violence and condemned sporadic outbreaks of guerrilla warfare against the government.

Ex-President Calles, now becoming rich and politically moderate, wanted to disguise himself as a continuing revolutionary. In 1934 he issued his famous Call from Guadalajara: 'The Revolution has not ended; its eternal enemies ambush it, try to nullify its triumphs; we must enter the new period of the Revolution, that I would call the psychological revolutionary period.' He planned to secularize the *minds* of the next generation through 'socialist' education — children must grow up atheists. President Cárdenas (1934-40) accepted this plan and tried to carry it through.

Cárdenas had dubbed Tabasco, where Red Shirts terrorized priests, 'the laboratory of the Revolution'. He made six years of 'socialist education' for every child in Mexico a constitutional principle. This simply meant that education must be rationalist.

The President set the pace for all those who hated religion. In 1935 waves of government persecution swept over the Church: hundreds of buildings were confiscated; only 300 priests remained in the country. Caught up in the momentum of this de-Christianization campaign, Cárdenas was out-rivalled only by President Calles' own campaign against the Church.

Thousands of guerrillas rose again in a second religious insurrection. For three years they murdered agrarian reformers, wrecked schools, killed teachers, and cut off two hundred pairs of ears. The priests condemned these religious warriors and ordered the faithful to turn them in: the Church had learned that it could not beat the government. With radios and airplanes the federal armies hunted down the guerrillas to give them a martyr's death.

At last the Church had become a loyal supporter of the government, while 'socialist' education aroused resistance to Mexico's greatest President. Cárdenas called off the campaign against religion and ended rationalist propaganda in the schools. Socialist symbols vanished. The strains of the *Internationale* no longer floated from classroom windows.

By the end of Cárdenas' term Church and State were at peace. The Church accepted the Mexican Revolution as irreversible; the government stopped enforcing the Constitution against religion. Since 1940 the Church has drawn closer to the poor of Mexico, and today a part of the clergy is to the left of the ruling party. The clerical engine has jumped its 500-year old track to break new paths among the people.

The Campaign for Agrarian Reform

Between 1920 and 1940 the Mexican Revolution resulted in a dramatic change in the social relations, says Hans-Rudolf Horn in his *Mexico: Revolution und Verfassung* (p.58). The old native and foreign landowners had possessed 60-70% of the nation's wealth; this class almost completely disappeared. The thousands of millionaires in today's Mexico acquired their wealth after 1930. The transfer of the bulk of the economic.surplus from the landowning oligarchy to a rising class of capitalist farmers and industrialists took place in the 1930s and 1940s. Wasn't this a transformation of the economic basis of society?

Opposition to Land Redistribution under Obregón and Calles
The change in social relations on the land began under Obregón. In 1920 he confronted the land barons, a bloc that had come through the military phase of the Revolution unbroken. Individual landowners had not always survived the fighting; some had been killed or fled abroad. But their haciendas rarely went to the peons who worked them. Sometimes a rising mestizo warlord

seized the *hacendado's* land for himself; sometimes peons abandoned a great estate to join Villa's armies. Then after 1917 the exiled landowner returned to his fallow fields, rebuilt the ruined hacienda, and put the jobless to work. The age-old methods of production, clumsy and primitive, continued as before. Abuses like debt-peonage were against the new Constitution, but the law was rarely enforced. How much had really changed in Mexico?

The faces of some landowners had changed. During the decade of revolutionary battles, foreigners had fled the country in tens of thousands; a few of them were landowners, leaving forever. The Church, the greatest landowner of all, was a target for men on the make, who helped themselves to its goods. In 1921, in Puebla alone, the government confiscated 59 mortgages and 9 haciendas belonging to the Church; the men of God lost their lands to the nation's new masters. And finally there were 'revolutionary' generals turning into landlords.

But, though some of the personnel had changed by 1920, the landowning oligarchy was intact. In the populous areas most of the land still belonged to the huge estates called haciendas, covering thousands of acres. At the centre of the hacienda stood the great house, surrounded by a high stone wall, with a church, a workshop, and a store inside. There were filthy huts for the workers. The landowner carried a gun and lorded it over the peons as he had for centuries. These owners held sway in the central and northern states: Michoacán, Jalisco, Nayarit, Sinaloa, Guanajuato, Querétaro, San Luis Potosí, Zacatecas, Durango, Coahuila, and Nuevo Leon. Against these powerful people Obregón could do nothing. His shaky government dared not begin land reform in their states, for it would mean class war: this might split the country and topple the president.

In Mexico one-fifth of privately owned land still belonged to foreigners (usually Americans). In some north-western states, for example, they owned 40% of the land, some of it fertile, some of it rich in minerals. The new Constitution threatened the lands of foreigners, who held a big chunk of the nation's wealth in metals and ores, in crops and oil. The U.S. State Department ordered Obregón to announce formally that he would not enforce the Constitution against property already owned by foreigners. He delayed; and the U.S.A. refused to recognize his government. With the sword of intervention hanging over him, Obregón could not think of land reform in the areas run by Americans. Near the end of his term, facing internal revolts, he formalized the hated promise to Washington: Mexico would never touch Americans' land if the U.S. government would shore up *el presidente*.

Thus, in the field of agrarian change, history tied the hands of Mexico's President. People threw him proposals for land reform, which he kicked away as smouldering dynamite. He was consolidating his young government. And he did not really believe in dividing the great estates into small plots producing for a family's need, for who then would feed the cities?

Yet he needed land reform as a safety valve for mass anger, for the restless men throughout the South where Zapatistas had led the agrarian revolution for *'Tierra y Libertad'*. In the South peasants were not helpless peons. There free villagers occupied the plains and valleys; they wanted back their ancestral fields and woods. The great owners were weaker in the southern states: Guerrero, Morelos, Puebla, Veracruz, Oaxaca. Here Obregón could distribute token bits of land to the people.

His government was walking a tightrope, balancing the demands of workers and peasants against those of foreigners and landowners. The landowners were clever and powerful. Could the peasants drive the government to move against the *hacendados*? These land barons hired armed bands to terrorize the peasants. In a nation charged with violence, the armed bands (called White Guards) kept the poor cringing in fear. To this threat of bullets priests added the fear of hell: they warned the peasants that poverty was blessed, that land seizures were robbery, and that the government was run by rebels and atheists. Would the peasants act?

Throughout Mexico during the 1920s, people moved about the countryside organizing demands for the land promised in the Constitution, people who sympathized with the masses: urban intellectuals, school teachers, agrarian reformers, labour agitators, peasant leaders — the *agraristas*. To rouse the masses into action these agrarians risked their lives for a generation, and thousands died under the bullets of Cristero guerrillas and the landowners' gunmen. No agrarian was safe; sometimes White Guards hung even government officials. But these agitators kept the peasantry in ferment.

Rural Mexico divided into two regions. In the central states the hacienda peons were born on the plantation and died on it; the master ruled over their work, fiestas, and prayers; theirs was the psychology of dependence. In the South, where Zapata rode his white horse over the mountains in popular legends, men lived in free villages — theirs was the courage to revolt. Here Díaz Soto y Gama, the Zapatista intellectual, founded the National Agrarian Party in 1920. These agrarians supported President Obregón, who promised a land distribution programme: free villagers were to get their stolen lands back. But Obregón was in no hurry to keep his promise to the South.

His government handed the land reform to judges who entangled it in red tape. Every village must count a certain number of family heads, must become a legal persona, must put its claim through the courts. The villages, spurred on by agrarians, fed their claims into the bureaucratic machine; the gears clanked in endless court cases. The Mexican peasantry was tormented by the fires of land hunger, and Obregón sprinkled drops of water on the flames.

In the southern states the peasants went so far as occupying land in Morelos, Veracruz, Yucatán. In Yucatán the state government had curbed the power of the *hacendados* and begun to regulate the hemp industry. Hemp brought high prices on the world market, and these profits gave Yucatán room for manoeuvre: its government toyed with radical policies; the popular masses pressed for action. The Socialist Party of the Southeast and Carrillo Puerto's Resistance Leagues were struggling to shorten work hours and raise wages for the Mayan serfs who cultivated hemp. In 1922 Carrillo Puerto became governor. The organized workers and peasants helped push through reforms, including distribution of land to villages. He translated the Constitution of 1917 into Maya and taught peasants their rights. For two years the peasants struggled forward. In 1924 the landowners carried through a counter-revolution and shot Carrillo Puerto and his associates.

In Veracruz, Governor Tejada supported peasant movements, while the state's army commander sided with the landowners. As these *hacendados* tried to drive villagers from newly won lands, the peasants counter-attacked. They seized great estates; they welcomed socialists pouring out of the cities to organize the countryside. In 1923 a congress of peasant leagues sent agrarians throughout the state, and soldiers killed many organizers. The landowners' hired thugs burned peasant villages, while army cavalry destroyed their crops. Obregón ignored the defenceless peasants, yet they supported him when General Sánchez and the landowners rose in revolt against Mexico City. Obregón distributed rifles to the peasants, who harassed rebel columns from the rear as they marched toward the capital. In 1924 the rebel officers faced a firing squad.

Not only in the southern states was there an agrarian struggle. Here and there across Mexico agrarians organized peasant leagues. In Michoacán the peasant, Primo Tapia, tried to organize Tarascan Indians to demand the return of ancestral lands to their villages. Governor Mújica supported his efforts, but the state army commander helped the landowners. So did the priests. When the governor wanted to return lands to the villages of Patzcuaro, the priests persuaded the Indians that God would curse them as robbers — and they turned from state aid. Agrarians travelled around teaching the rural masses about land reform, and White Guards and soldiers hunted them down. But the landowners could not catch Primo Tapia. He slipped in and out of the peasant villages, explaining their constitutional right to former lands. To the villages Governor Mújica distributed 50,000 acres — a drop in the sea. Yet he had made a beginning. In 1922 generals and landowners carried out a counter-revolution and drove Mújica from the government. They searched for Tapia in vain; by 1923 he was leading a secret peasant association. The rich murdered its leaders, castrated peons, and cut off ears — but the league grew. In 1924 Tapia's native village got its land back. And some generals faced a firing squad.

Peasant leagues across Mexico sent delegates to a National Agrarian Congress; Obregón's government paid their fares to Mexico City. At the Congress the Zapatista intellectual, Díaz Soto, called for arms to the peasant and warned that many generals and priests were holding back agrarian reform. The peasants were moving toward a nation-wide organization.

In 1924 Calles became president. 'Land for the peasants,' he said, 'prevents revolutions.' He developed programmes that echoed his old slogan: 'Land and books for all.' He deepened the literacy campaign and distributed land to the free villages three times as fast as Obregón. But he too was attacking the flames with a sprinkler.

In the countryside the class struggle raged on. In 1925 in Aguascalientes, General Talamantes, working with the big owners, killed peasants or drove them from their lands. The labour organizer, Miguel Ricardo, arrived to investigate, and Colonel Estrada shot him. Next year the Colonel tried the same approach in Nayarit and died in a peasant ambush. Violence crackled across rural Mexico.

The peasant leagues spread. From 16 of the 27 states, leaders poured into Mexico City to found the National Peasant League. This organization decided for co-operatives and socialism. It endorsed Article 27 of the Constitution, and declared for any government working to free peasants from priests and landowners. The League called for solidarity with proletarians around the world in their fight against capitalism. The leaders of the League, Montes and Rodríguez, were later assassinated.

In 1926 the Cristero War broke out, and landowners supported the rebellion of the priests. But in Morelos, the country of Zapata, landless peasants raised the flag of agrarian revolt and also joined the uprising against a government they hated. Their leaders carried the guerrilla war into Guerrero and raided near Mexico City. Old Zapatista generals rode again: Benjamin Mendoza, Maximiliano Vigueras, Victorino Bárcenas. The roads of Morelos were unsafe; guerrillas attacked buses and trains in broad daylight. Morrow, the American ambassador, narrowly escaped capture on the road to Cuernavaca. The Zapatistas wanted their lands back.

Calles neared the end of his term. While Zapatista peasants fought on in Morelos, clouds of reaction gathered over the nation: foreign interests screamed that Calles was a Bolshevik; American businessmen demanded intervention against him; the Church encouraged Cristeros to shoot at his government; and landowners plotted to do him in. So, in 1928, he cut back on land distribution. He was also worried by the rising agrarian debt, for the government was compensating the expropriated landowners with twenty-year bonds. Where would backward Mexico find the money to pay?

The governor of Tamaulipas, an agrarian named Portes Gil, became interim President in December. He stepped up land distribution in the South, and the powerful Calles tried to restrain him. The new President answered that the government must win peasant loyalty. In Morelos the Zapatista commander, Vigueras, seemed everywhere at one: his secret network of peasant supporters used telegraphs in the cities to track regular army movements, and weapons streamed to him through the underground from the capital itself! On December 27 fate caught up with Vigueras — capture, torture, death. But his Zapatista guerrillas continued the war for 'Land and Freedom'.

The power behind the throne was Calles. During 1929 this *eminence grise* protested the land distributions of Portes Gil, the interim President. Portes Gil warned him that another 'election' was approaching, with its inevitable coup from the army: the government must arm peasants to help fight off the military, and only land grants could gain supporters from the tillers of the soil. The coup came. Peasants fought the Army, and the government survived stronger than ever.

In the early 1930s weak presidents danced from the strings of Calles, who pulled them as best he could from Cuernavaca. He and his cronies, acquiring estates for themselves, had grown rich and conservative; they slowed the machinery of land reform to a crawl. The result was growing unrest among the peasants. Popular pressure increased on those reformers remaining in the ruling party; workers and peasants pressed for a turn to the left. Calles saw the handwriting on the wall, and in 1934 allowed a young reformer to run for president.

Cardenas Unleashes a Social Revolution in the Coutryside

Lázaro Cárdenas took the election seriously (though the ruling party could not lose) and campaigned thousands of miles across Mexico. He visited villages in the valleys, hamlets in the mountains, and peons on the haciendas. He heard the peons and peasants of Mexico threatening, he listened to their demands for land. Was a revolutionary storm like that of 1910-17 brewing, a hurricane that would sweep away landowners and president in a new civil war?

In 1935 Cárdenas surveyed the enemies of the ordinary people of Mexico. He saw foreign interests crippled: the national income of the United States down from 87 billion dollars to 39 billion; one of every three American workers out of a job; breadlines spreading. The Colossus of the North showed feet of clay. The Mexican Church, that old friend of landowners, lay defeated in the Cristero War and begged the government to call off the de-Christianization campaign. Obregón and Calles had so reduced the Army that generals-turned-landowners had not tried a coup in six years – a sign of weakness.

On his left Cárdenas sensed the impatience of the popular classes. Strike waves rolled over the nation. In 1933 there were 13 strikes; in 1934 at least 200; in 1935 650. (Unofficial sources report more than 1,000 strikes during Cárdenas' first year in office.) Violent strikes of agricultural workers exploded around the country: on the commercial haciendas in Michoacán, on the hemp plantations of Yucatán, and in the cotton-growing regions of north-central Mexico, the people working from dawn to dark had reached the end of their tether – they demanded better wages and shorter hours. Groups of the landless seized soil for their use; the peasants were on the move. From the nimbus of peasant anger, lightning flickered over the countryside, as agrarians and big owners clashed throught the land.

For 15 years the time-bomb of peasant frustration had ticked under the nation. Cárdenas and his government wanted to detonate it, but under controlled conditions. The regime prepared to unleash the rural masses against the landowning class.

The landowners affected by reforms had received compensation in twenty-year bonds, but the rising agrarian debt made it ever harder for the government to carry on land distribution in good conscience. Cárdenas' government sent the agrarian debt to the devil; land must go to the peasants whether owners got paid or not. Up to now, land had gone only to free villages. But almost half the rural families did not live in these villages – they were hacienda peons. The government turned to these peons in the Centre and North of Mexico with the slogan: 'Land to the tiller!' The hour of the *hacendados* had struck.

The President was embarking on an unknown and risky course, a revolution in the countryside. What if it ran away from him? In July 1935 he ordered the creation of peasant leagues in every state, then the merging of all existing leagues in a confederation run by the government. The peasants, working up from local committees, could petition the government for land; the state would grant land and organize these committees into peasant leagues. Cárdenas wanted top-down control of the land distribution.

Landlords destroyed peasant villages to keep them from asking for land. The White Guards burned peasant crops and killed men, women, and children. Peasants organized for self-defence. 'I will give to the peasants the Mausers with which they made the Revolution,' said Cárdenas, 'so they can defend it and the village and the school.' On January 1, 1936, he ordered governors and army commanders to distribute weapons and organize a peasant militia. The landlords tried to win over army officers commanding parts of the militia; in Chihuahua, Guanajuato, and San Luis Potosí such tactics worked. Sometimes rifles meant for the militia went to the White Guards. There were battles between the landowners' mercenaries and armed peasants throughout Mexico — thousands died in the struggle. The peasant militia grew, and by 1940 contained 60,000 men, all with arms, half with horses.

Without waiting for the government to grant land, some groups of peasants began to occupy it. Cárdenas struggled to retain control of the movement: in March 1936 he ordered army commanders to repress all spontaneous land seizures. He rushed to grant land to the peasants.

The distributed land took three forms: small plots, *ejidos*, and collective farms. *Ejidos* were village communities that owned land in common; each family, assigned its plot, could neither rent nor sell it — an Indian tradition. The formation of collective farms was the President's most imaginative move. He remembered the recent general strike in north-central Mexico, with its million acres of cotton and wheat. In October 1936 he broke up the scores of plantations there, mostly belonging to foreigners. He gave the land to the workers and organized them into commercial collective farms. Then came the turn of other areas boiling with discontent: Yucatán's hemp plantations, the haciendas of Sonora's Yaqui valley, and the big sugar-growing area of Los Mochis in Sinaloa. Foreign owners gnashed their teeth.

As plotting against the government increased, Cárdenas armed a workers' militia in the capital. In 1938 General Cedillo, allied to landowners and foreigners, rose against the government. He was defeated and shot. In the United States a reformist president, Franklin Roosevelt, was busy fighting economic paralysis at home, and voices for intervention against Cárdenas cried in vain. The Mexican leader moved to take over American oil in Tampico. His country united behind him.

From 1935 to 1938 half the landowning class lost its holdings to the peasants. On tiny plots most peasants raised food for their families; not much was left over to feed the towns. To feed the rising cities in the 1940s, the government irrigated vast tracts in the North and turned them over to businessmen. Huge capitalist farms, using new seeds, fertilizers and tractors spread through the northern states. Today agribusiness flourishes in Baja California, Sonora, Sinaloa, Chihuahua, and Tamaulipas. The giant factories and farms of Mexico are run by modern businessmen. The wealth of the nation is in their hands; the old aristocracy of landowners has either disappeared or gone modern. The little people barely get by: mass unemployment, subsistence farming, migrant labour, pitiful wages, poor food, illiteracy — misery is their lot. This misery is surprising in the tenth largest country in the world. One-third of its 70 million people are functionally illiterate; almost half live in dwellings with no running water, a dirt floor, and five people to a room. Half the nation is without proper medicine. At least one-third of the labour force is unemployed, and that means frightening poverty; three-fourths of the people must divide among themselves one-third of Mexico's personal income left to them — after the elites have taken their huge slice.

In the 1920s Mexico was an agricultural country. In the countryside power and riches depended on possession of large tracts of land, on owning haciendas. From father to son the haciendas passed down through inheritance. But after the agrarian reform of the 1930s, riches no longer came from owning large lands. During the reform, half of the big owners vanished. The rest soon found that owning haciendas was no longer enough, that traditional large-scale farming was doomed. The ancient methods of production were slowly disappearing in the face of agribusiness. The new business farmers of the North drew wealth from capital and technology: control of credit, knowledge of the market, management ability, soil engineering, tractors, fertilizers. To learn to compete, the remaining *hacendados* sent their sons to Texas A. & M. College. Today the old barons of the soil are gone; in both agriculture and industry Mexico's wealth belongs to the transnational corporations and to native millionaires; capital and technology rule.

In 1920 life on the hacienda went on in the centuries-old way. The peon was born into debt: the *hacendado* loaned tokens for his baptism, his first white clothes, his marriage feast. The peon built his hut on the hacienda and drew corn, candles, and pulque from the company store. From there came the white *manta* to make his clothes; he rarely saw money. If the hacienda was sold, his debt was transferred to the new owner — the peon could never get away. Should it surprise us that many historians have called him a serf?

Article 123 of the new Constitution had ordered an end to debt peonage an the closing of company stores. 'But enforcement of Article 123 depended on the state governments,' says Henry Parkes' standard history of Mexico (p. 374), 'and throughout most of the country peonage remained the reality, if not the law.' The revolution of 1910-17 had weakened the debt system; there were less hacienda peons than under the old dictatorship. But the system continued to survive.

The agrarian struggles of the 1920s brought a gradual enforcement of the law. By 1933 the historian Tannenbaum could write, in *Peace by Revolution* (p. 213), that 'the system of both token coin and payment in kind, as well as the *tienda de raya*, is still to be found, but it is confined to isolated places instead of being in general use.' The agrarian reform of 1935-37 hit the debt system a mortal blow, and the rise of agribusiness finished it off: a rural proletariat has grown up in the Mexican countryside, with migrant labour and mass unemployment.

In the 1930s and '40s Mexico underwent rapid industrialization. Mexican business had no competition from foreign producers, as depression and war in the developed countries halted their export of capital. Since 1940 Mexico's businessmen have made fortunes in steel, chemicals, banking, bottling, brewing, hotels, real estate, consumer goods, and sports arenas. 'The majority of the truly big enterpreneurs date the beginning of their fortunes to the 1920s and 1930s,' says the sociologist, Frank Brandenburg, in his *The Making of Modern Mexico* (p. 220). During those years the bulk of the nation's wealth passed from landowners to the rising businessmen. The nation entered a new epoch, an age of entrepreneurs and large corporations.

Summary

Between 1920 and 1940 Mexico shook itself free from Army, Church, and Oligarchy, built itself schools and factories, and stepped toward the modern world. Though one foot dragged behind and the other sank into the slough of dependence on the power to the North, who can deny that the nation lurched forward?

This advance came through both leadership and mass struggles. Obregón, Calles, and Cárdenas worked to rid the Army of disloyal officers while peasant and worker militias fought down praetorian uprisings. Most Mexicans withheld support from the Church during its showdown with the government; Calles could therefore isolate the Cristero rebels and crush them. By the 1930s Church and Army had bled into weakness, and the government dared to unleash peasant leagues against that great enemy of the people, the landowning oligarchy. Without allies the landowners were finally defeated.

Soldier, priest, and landlord: thundering down an historical track of misery, that huge troika had pounded Mexico for centuries, until its collapse brought forth a new economic order. That was the social revolution.

3. Managing the Masses

Three-fourths of the world's non-Marxist sociologists study and write in the U.S.A. They tell us there are no classes in modern society, that people live in harmony, and that governments worry about the public good. Society, they think, is like a farmyard where everyone knows his work: the foreman orders men about, the children do chores, the oxen drag a plough from dawn to dark, and pigs eat happily toward the day of slaughter. This picture of social peace would astonish Mexicans from peon to president. For them society is a jungle red in tooth and claw, and there is a struggle for the bones left over from survival eating. Can the government contain the struggle between the classes? That question has worried every Mexican leader to our day.

The Mexicans' mental image of a social jungle arises from their experience in the 20th century. Again and again internal war has wrecked their country: guerrilla war, peasant war, religious war, civil war. Under Don Porfirio's dictatorship the class struggle had already exploded the illusions of people preaching social peace. In the last years of the *Porfiriato* strike waves lashed Mexico. In 1906 the railway yards rebelled against starvation wages. The strikes leaped from city to city: Chihuahua, Torreón, San Luis Potosí, Monterrey, Aguascalientes. At the station of Cárdenas in San Luis Potosí a violent clash left eighteen dead in 1907; a huge strike exploded in protest. In 1908 strikes sizzled over the nation's railway grid, and the workers won sympathy from people in many walks of life.

From 1903 to 1910 federal troops rained bullets on strikes sputtering in the mine pits of Mexico. The largest of these strikes flared up in Sonora. At Cananea, in the copper mines owned by foreigners, the workers laid down their picks in 1906 and American foremen fired on unarmed demonstrators. The workers searched for weapons and fought back, as the Americans shot them down with dum-dum bullets. Both American volunteers and the Mexican *rurales* rushed to Cananea to slaughter workers.

In 1906 and 1907 workers struck in the textile factories of Veracruz, Tlaxcala, and Puebla, where working conditions made every mill an inferno. This general strike caused a nationwide lockout of textile workers. The strike movement led to the government massacre of men, women, and children in Rio Blanco.

In mines, railways, and factories Mexico's workers showed fighting spirit against the dictatorship. Their economic strikes took on a political tone, an anti-State bias encouraged by anarchists. These agitators preached direct action to bring down the government.

Peasant guerrillas knocked down the *Porfiriato*. Under the liberal Madero, workers organized the House of the World's Worker in Mexico City; the House spread anarchist propaganda and worked toward a labour central. General Huerta killed Madero and restored the dictatorship. The House became the urban centre of historic resistance to Huerta, the new dictator. Against him the Mexico City workers carried out a monster demonstration; he brutally drove their leaders underground. With Huerta's fall the House surfaced again.

Obregón urged the workers to join Carranza's movement against Villa and turned over the telephone company to the striking labourers led by the electrician, Luis Morones. Finally, many labour leaders accepted Obregón and formed the Red Battalions. To get food, workers joined up and left the starving capital. They fought battles, and in the wake of Obregón's advancing armies they organized unions. Unionism swept the nation; soon there was hardly a branch of industrial activity without a labour union.

Carranza, frightened by this growing power, dissolved the Red Battalions, jailed labour organizers, and shut down their newspapers. In 1916 strike waves foamed across the nation, washing into Mexico City in the summer. A general strike paralysed the capital; President Carranza broke it with troops and violence. He swung the death penalty over the heads of strike agitators. The House of the World's Worker vanished, and the movement of the workers ebbed away. With the storm past, Carranza gave in to their demands for salaries, not in worthless paper, but in gold.

As the military phase of the revolution drew to a close, Mexico's workers had proven themselves a social force. Red Battalions, militant unions, anarchist ideology, general strikes, sabotage — the workers waved the red flag of revolution. Mexico had stepped into the 20th century with a fighting proletariat.

This class was too small to impose its revolutionary will on Mexico and reshape society. Yet that society was falling apart. After a decade of civil war the haciendas lay in ruins, mine pits were empty, railways were destroyed, guerrillas stalked the land, administration had broken down, and men went about their labours armed. The new government, trying to put Mexico together again, faced an explosive proletariat that threatened to burst the bubble of consensus blown by Carranza's populist commanders. How could the government fit this class into the social order?

The Co-option of Mass Organizations by Obregón

In 1918 the fighting died down, and Obregón set in motion the machinery of co-option. First, he persuaded President Carranza to sponsor the Congress of Workers' Organizations, and out of it came the Regional Confederation of

Mexican Labour — the CROM. Second, when leaders of the Zapatista movement organized a rival peasant party in 1920, Obregón gave it his blessing. Behind the scenes Obregón reached agreement with both the CROM and the new National Agrarian Party. He got the government to subsidize the CROM; he rewarded its leaders with government posts in return for keeping the lid on labour discontent. And he promised a radical programme of land reform if the peasant party would support the government. Thus Obregon with great skill divided workers from peasants and prepared to deal with their leaders separately.

Morones and the CROM

Díaz, Huerta, and Carranza had failed to tame the workers with bayonets and police clubs. Then Obregón suggested to President Carranza a new tactic: the pretence of friendship. Grudgingly Carranza offered to pay the workers' fares to the Congress of Workers' Organizations in Saltillo. In 1918 over a hundred organizations sent their people to the government-sponsored Congress. A key figure in its executive committee was Luis Morones, once an anarchist revolutionary, then a man in contact with the AFL craft unions in the United States, and finally an organizer working to help labour through government action. Obregón was soon plotting with Morones; both labour boss and revolutionary general rode the workers' movement toward power. Obregón had switched the proletarian locomotive onto tracks leading toward a government station.

'The emancipation of the working classes,' Karl Marx used to say, 'must be the work of the workers themselves.' Socialists, anarchists, and syndicalists had shared this idea; Luis Morones was abandoning it for Obregón's view that to achieve their aims the workers must look to the bureaucratic state.

In the birth of Mexico's large labour central (the CROM), the government acted as midwife; and this enraged many radical workers. Though at first the CROM seemed independent of the government, some radicals looked upon it with suspicion. They refused to join; they worked to organize rival labour centrals. In 1919 workers and intellectuals founded the Mexican Communist Party, which cried out for revolution.

Obregón's star was rising. The nation expected him to become president when Carranza's term ran out in 1920. Luis Morones and his Action Group inside the CROM secretly proposed a pact to Obregón. In the struggle over the presidency, the CROM would support Obregón in return for these guarantees: creation of a Ministry of Labour headed by Morones; material and moral support for the CROM from the government; presidential consideration of the CROM's views on all proposed reforms affecting the nation; and government money to build links between the Mexican proletariat and the international working class. Obregón signed this pact with the Action Group. Neither rank-and-file labour nor the Mexican public knew what had happened in a smoke-filled room.

Obregón needed the CROM's support, for Morones had returned from an instructive visit to England's trade unions and their parliamentary group to found a party of Mexican workers. His Mexican Labour Party, political instrument of the CROM, was in 1919 the first great party of the Revolution. It backed Obregón in his life-and-death struggle with Carranza. Morones accompanied Obregón on his journeys across the nation, while in different states party leaders whipped up support for the famous general. The weight of the working class tipped the scales in favour of Obregón. The election degenerated into an armed struggle ending with Carranza's death in the mountains.

In 1920 Adolfo de la Huerta became interim president while Obregón staged a nationwide election of himself to the highest office. The workers, feeling their power, pounded the nation with strikes. Ninety thousand walked off the job: the oilworkers of Tampico, the railwaymen of the Veracruz-Mexico line, the miners of Zacatecas and Coahuila, the farm labourers of the haciendas in north-central Mexico. These workers toiled for foreign companies, and de la Huerta's government adopted a hands-off policy toward labour disputes. The United States machine-gunned de la Huerta with threatening diplomatic notes (fourteen in six months). The cannon of foreign intervention pointed into Mexico.

Into this turmoil walked the new president, Alvaro Obregón. Caught between a militant proletariat on his left and the formidable United States on his right, he stepped onto the tightrope of his presidency and began a clever balancing act. Impressed by the power on his right, Obregón moved to divert the seething energy of the proletariat into government channels. He began to carry through his secret promises to the Action Group inside the CROM.

Huge sums of government money flowed to the CROM for organizing workers. According to official figures, membership in the CROM rose in a spectacular way: from 7,000 in 1918 to 2,000,000 in 1928. Whatever the true figures, no one denies that the giant CROM became Mexico's dominant labour central in the 1920s.

Communists and anarchists organized a rival labour central, the General Confederation of Workers (CGT), which soon claimed 100,000 members. Anarchists became its guiding influence and preached direct action and revolution. Many radical unions formed regional confederations, like the Societies of Railwaymen, that stayed clear of the labour centrals. The government-sponsored CROM mushroomed over the nation and tried to smother its rivals. In the shade of this giant they struggled to grow, but they were cut off from the nourishing rays of Obregón's sun: massive financial aid, protection in disputes with employers, and for CROM leaders posts in government.

What kind of posts? Obregón made Morones chief of the Manufacturing Establishments. The CROM's Richard Treviño (an anarchist) was elected to the Chamber of Deputies, along with the brilliant lawyer Lombardo Toledano (who would later become a leading Marxist). The CROM also put the famous socialist, Juan Sarabia, in the Senate and carried off 50% of the municipal offices in Mexico City. Two years later Morones and a host of CROM leaders were in the Chamber of Deputies — they dominated the Congress on vital questions. They could pass laws favourable to labour.

Obregón made CROM men governors of states: thus Toledano came to power in Puebla. Observers began to speak of a Workers' Government in Mexico.

Was it a Workers' State? Obregón urged the workers to support him 'to keep capital from gaining control of the government.' But if businessmen were not in power, it was hardly clear that labour ruled. Obregón talked of the Constitution's promise of social security and wrote a law guaranteeing aid to workers injured on the job or retired by old age. He sent the law to Congress, but did not push it through, nor did the CROM congressmen struggle to pass it. The anarchist CGT carried out or supported the major strikes of the period, but Obregón excluded its newspaper from the mails, persecuted its leaders, and expelled its foreign-born agitators from Mexico. He often sent troops against these strikes.

He favoured the CROM. In 1921 the number of strikes reached a large figure: 310. That was too many for *el Presidente*, and both he and Morones worked to strengthen their control over the unions and to organize more workers. Next year the strikes were less and usually not for higher wages or shorter hours – the workers struck to gain recognition of unions by management. The government intervened in these strikes to favour employers twelve times and the workers ninety! For Obregón the proletariat was a stallion, untamed and dangerous, but the unions might ride it. By 1924 the number of strikes had dropped to 125 a year.

Through the government purse the President influenced the labour central; he fed money into the Action Group inside the CROM. Luis Morones ran this shadowy group of 20 men. It steered the CROM's central committee and bent the national conventions to its will. It was a springboard to high government posts. The Action Group placed directors in workers' organizations around the nation, meddled in the elections of union committees, manipulated debates in the assemblies, organized demonstrations against people it hated, fought strikes outside its control, screened out rebels against itself, sent orders to agents in state government, dangled thousands of workers on its salaries, paid professionals to do its bidding, swung the Labour Party by the tail, and pushed and shaped working-class opinion across Mexico. No wonder its opponents became suspicious of leadership and drifted into anarchism.

Obregón developed a carrot-and-stick policy toward the working class. In one hand he held a whip: jail for communists and anarchists, troops against strikes by 'red' unions. In the other he held rewards: money and posts for friendly labour leaders, pay hikes for 'yellow' unions. Between repression and co-option oscillated *el Presidente* – the master politician.

Díaz Soto y Gama's National Agrarian Party
This political strategist laboured to keep the urban workers divided from the peasants. The division had roots deep in the Mexican Revolution. When revolutionary bands of dark-skinned Zapatistas thundered into Mexico City late in 1914, the white working-class leaders in the capital looked upon them with suspicion. The workers' leaders had recently arrived from Spain, and their heads were filled with anarchism and atheism. They watched the peasant

guerrillas gallop past with religious flags, virgins stamped on their huge sombreros, capes flying in the wind. The Zapatistas celebrated victory amid the pealing of church bells, the churches anarchists had just sacked. Then the peasants went from door to door in the rich suburbs, hat in hand, politely begging their tortillas from the 'bourgeoisie'. The workers' leaders, proud of their mastery of Bakunin's writings, turned away from these dark, illiterate masses. The workers poured into Obregón's 'Red Battalions' and marched off to fight against Villa's peasant armies. Obregón had deepened the split between workers and peasants.

But in 1919 the peasant war in the South raged on. With 10,000 guerrillas Zapata harassed government troops; Carranza could not extinguish the last flames of the People's War. The peasants who had torn Mexico in half were proving harder to handle than the workers. The peasants wanted land.

Zapata died in an ambush, and the government allowed many peasants in Morelos to keep lands already seized. The guerrilla war stopped. The CROM labour central, based in the cities, decided to organize peasants as well. Morones probably thought to build his Mexican Labour Party on a worker-peasant alliance. This would make him a great power in the new Republic.

Antonio Díaz Soto y Gama, the Zapatista intellectual, accused Morones of dishonesty and worked to bring peasant leaders and agrarian thinkers into a rival party. In 1920 Díaz Soto founded his National Agrarian Party. President Obregón quickly threw his weight behind Díaz Soto. The President made a pact with the National Agrarian Party.

In running for president, Obregón had come out in favour of land to the people, but warned against breaking up the productive estates into tiny plots for a family's needs. What could the great general mean? For land to the tiller often meant smashing haciendas into subsistence fragments. Obregón did not really believe in 'dividing up', though he consented to the formation of a country of farmers that were small but efficient.

Once in the presidency he saw that some land would have to go to the people to prevent revolution. So he promised Díaz Soto's agrarians that free villages in the South would get their stolen lands back — a radical programme. Then he produced a tangled legislation about the way this would happen, and turned the process over to the courts. The bureaucrats fulfilled his hopes; the reform soon struggled in a swamp of treacherous and annoying legal traps. The peasant villagers marched into this wilderness to attain the promise on the other side.

While the agrarian knights worked off their energies jousting with the bureaucratic dragon, Obregón thought up another way to keep them busy. He handed the land distribution agency to the National Agrarian Party. The party used the regional agencies to organize peasants, and soon Leagues of Agrarian Communities were flourishing in many states. In these leagues Obregón spotted a means of controlling the turbulent countryside; so he invited leagues and agrarians to a national congress in 1923, with the government paying the bill. Over 1,000 people gathered in Mexico City to respresent hundreds of thousands of peasants in stormy debate. The fiery Díaz Soto thundered to the Congress about forces blocking agrarian reform: medieval priests preaching loyalty to landlords; *hacendados* with private armies of White Guards; federal generals united with big owners to hunt down agrarians; state governors refusing to enforce the law and courts reading it in favour of the rich. He forgot to mention the foreigners who owned 20% of Mexico's arable land, people backed by the United States, with its dozens of interventions in Latin America between 1910 and 1920. Díaz Soto called for arms to the peasants. The Congress hammered out resolutions agreeing with his general conclusions.

The high point of the Congress was the ending; *el Presidente* himself came with a speech. He pointed out that his appearance was something new in Mexican history: 'immediate contact between the popular masses and the representative of the Public Power.' He cautiously played upon Díaz Soto's theme of wicked forces fighting agrarianism, identified himself with the peasant struggle, and repeatedly called for popular support. He ended with this appeal: 'I only need for the popular will to support me as it has supported me to this day, in order to counteract all the influences that try to oppose our humanitarian programme, whether they be influences that come from outside our country or influences from inside. Return then to your homes and tell your comrades and co-workers that the entire people of the Republic is in perfect communion with the man wielding the Executive Power, and take to each of your companions a warm greeting from the revolutionary who the Mexican people have entrusted with the highest post of the present administration.' The agrarians applauded happily.

Díaz Soto stepped to the podium and called Obregón the real executor of the thought of Emiliano Zapata.

In 1924 Calles, Obregón's understudy, ran for president; he began his political campaign with a pilgrimage to the tomb of Zapata, where he swore to carry on the dead fighter's programme. Calles was a man of the people. Though the Revolution raised him to high office, where he improved his mind with reading, he remained crude and unpolished to the end. This helped him to carry out that essential task of Mexican presidents: management of the masses. The National Agrarian Party lined up behind him. 'We have faith in General Calles, in this man of the people,' said the peasants' maximum leader, Díaz Soto, 'for Calles is a man of deeds, not words.'

Voices of Dissent and Corruption under Calles

Obregón's measured pace had finally exhausted the peasant's patience, and under Calles there was increasing violence in the countryside: more clashes between agrarians and White Guards, and in 1926 the resurgence of Zapatista revolt in Morelos. Calles tripled the pace of land distribution from a walk to a trot, enough to keep the peasant nag from breaking the bit. But he dared not allow the agrarian left to gallop ahead, for the power on his right was rising steadily. The Church idealized feudal land tenure and encouraged armed rebellion against Calles' government. Generals turning into landowners threatened him with their guns. And the agrarian debt was soaring, for the government paid landowners with bonds for confiscated acreage. These bonds drifted into the hands of bankers in the United States. Where would the Mexican treasury find the money to pay? Yet, some day, pay it must: in the dozens of armed interventions by the United States in Latin America, Mexico had suffered the whip more than any other nation.

Ursulo Galván and the National Peasant League

Calles teetered on the tightrope of his presidency, for the agrarians were growing more radical. In 1925 the agrarian leader, Ursulo Galván, went to the International Peasant Conference held in Moscow and returned with new ideas. In 1926 he called together the first national congress of peasant leagues in Mexico City. The government lent a hand: Adalberto Tejada, a minister in Calles' cabinet, helped Galván bring together the leagues. In the capital they founded the National Peasant League, made up of peasants from 16 states. The League surprised Calles with its communism.

The League became a centre of gravity for the agrarian forces. They shifted away from Díaz Soto toward this radical magnet: the programme of the National Peasant League sparkled with communist ideas. The programme called for an alliance with the urban proletariat. It urged solidarity with rural struggles around the world in working toward a Peasant International. It took the colour red for a symbol. It blessed Mexico's distribution of land to semi-communal villages (*ejidos*), but saw these as a station on the way to social-ization of the land and all the means of production.

Calles' view of the *ejidos* was different: they were a detour on the road to capitalism in the countryside. His ideal was France, a nation of prosperous farmers; but Mexico's southern peasants lived in semi-communal villages as old as the Aztecs, and the President knew he must do something for these rebellious people. They craved land. He gave some land to the *ejidos*, but it was rocky soil watered by the whim of the rain god. The new dams built by Calles irrigated rich lands, and these he turned over to small famers with funds and education; he set up a National Bank of Agriculture to supply them with credit. The miserable peasants scratching the *ejido* soil also demanded credit; and the sympathetic ear of the President, always turned toward these recent revolutionaries, heard their groans and threats. He launched four *ejido* banks. But he forgot to give the banks money, and they soon foun-dered and sank.

Corruption in the CROM

Under Calles' administration, there continued the contest between the agra-rian party and Morones' CROM, a struggle for allegiance from people in the fields. An example: in Morelos the CROM had formed a peasant union in Tepoztlán; in 1925 two government agents from the rival movement came to Tepoztlán to distribute hacienda land; these two died suddenly, probably by the hand of the CROM. In 1926 the CROM claimed 1,500 peasant workers' unions as it own.

Though Calles did not encourage the CROM's work among peasants, he had raised labour leaders to the pinnacle of power in the cities. During his campaign for president he called in Morones to make a deal for CROM support. The labour boss was licking his wounds after a shoot-out in the Chamber of Deputies. Calles and Morones reached a secret understanding, then later signed a pact: the CROM promised to warn the state of all strike plans and to support government decisions and decrees; the presidential candidate agreed to finance the labour central, to back its actions, and to make Morones the Minister of Labour. In power Calles quickly took Morones into his cabinet. The CROM got one-fifth of the Congess, two governorships, and control of Mexico City's administration.

There were more secret agreements between President and labour chief. To stabilize Mexico the CROM agreed to suspend strike actions. But the government made sure that CROM labourers got wage hikes, better times at the work.place, inspection of factory conditions, and other favours from the State. The number of legal strikes slowly fell away to zero.

What is a legal strike? Here the Constitution of 1917 talks of strikes that 'aim to harmonize the relations between capital and labour'. The government spots such a strike and declares it legal. 'Harmony' is for the government to define, and Calles decided it meant no strikes at all. Morones had the CROM announce that no member union could strike without approval from the central committee in Mexico City. He was striving for control over the rank and file.

Unions broke away from the CROM and joined the anarchist CGT. The anarchist labour central led or supported the major strikes of the Calles period. The government attacked the CGT's newspaper and hurt its circulation; its director, Valadés, was dragged into court for insulting the king of Italy! The CROM sent hit men against the CGT's agitators, and a latent civil war between the labour centrals built up tension in the cities.

The radical CGT opened up against Calles' regime with a strike in Tampico protesting against the firing of oilworkers. The President answered as he would throughout his term: he declared the strike illegal and sent federal troops against the workers. Railway workers struck many times and met similar treatment. In 1926 the railwaymen on the Isthmus walked off the job; the government rushed in scabs from other areas.

But the government nourished the CROM with huge sums and improved the condition of its rank and file enough to keep their support. During the first two years of Calles' reign, people spoke again of a Workers' State. B. Traven's proletarian novels named the government a Workers' Regime; international monopolies screamed against Calles' 'Bolshevism'. There was widespread belief that Mexico aimed at socialism. A few honest socialists provided moral cement to hold the CROM together. They gave Mexico City one of the best municipal administrations it had seen. Toledano worked as governor of Peubla to serve the people. Ezequiel Salcedo was a model senator.

But the CROM finally dropped class-struggle philosophy to call for patriotism and nationalism. The nation was approaching a new time of troubles. Foreigners threatened Calles with intervention; the Church preached rebellion; generals waited for their chance. Calles told the labour leaders that the government needed the support of the working class. Since the workers were too weak to seize power, reasoned the leaders, they should back a government that favoured the proletariat within capitalism. The President persuaded them to come out for 'class peace' during the industrialization of Mexico. Employers applauded the new policy.

Corruption had been growing in the CROM leadership since its collaboration with Obregón; how could labour bureaucrats resist diverting some government aid, big and secret, into their pockets? They invested in real estate and stocks for themselves; they became rich and powerful. Under Calles the corruption came into the open and spread. Morones set the pace. Surrounded by bodyguards, he drove about in a large automobile, flashing diamonds on his fingers. The diamonds, he explained, were the workers' funds being kept safely away from shaky banks. His sparkling fingers were a revenge upon capitalists who wanted to see workers in rags. Or, even less credible, his riches were an inheritance from his father! As Minister of Labour he allowed the acid of corruption to filter from the unions into collective bargaining. The CROM regularly blackmailed employers: they must pay off or suffer strikes. Anarchist agitators called Morones the 'Mexican Mussolini', but others decided that the *Duce* was the President himself. To the national body he fastened the legs of the young proletariat and made them march to a government drum.

Corruption ate into the foundation of the CROM and cracks appeared throughout — it began to sink. The rank and file tired of Morones. In 1928 Obregón campaigned for president: he fired volleys of criticism at the CROM, and unions jumped from this sinking ship to join the next captain of state. An assassin struck him down. But interim President Portes Gil, an enemy of Morones, pounded the disintegrating CROM with government power. Police and troops went after its unions; in the CROM's disputes with employers the state ruled against it. Without Calles' protection both CROM and its Labour Party slowly went under.

President Cárdenas Cements Unity out of Chaos

In 1929 the CROM lost its hold over the labour movement, and by 1930 the National Peasant League was losing control over people on the land. The movements of the popular classes split up. Rival factions competed for the allegiance of the workers, and peasant groups squabbled among themselves. The early 1930s saw a babble of tongues among the Mexican masses. The nuclei of new labour centrals failed to grow; peasant organisations sputtered along out of gear. A firm hand at the helm of state was missing: a series of weak presidents sat out two-year terms while strongman Calles manoeuvred from Cuernavaca. When Lázaro Cárdenas, Mexico's greatest President, took over in 1935, the situation quickly changed; he organized workers and peasants into huge, new confederations of leagues and unions.

Obregón had emerged from the chaos of the first revolutionary decade to become a strong president. Under him popular organizations flourished: CROM for the workers, and the Agrarian Party for the peasants. Calles was stronger, and he raised the CROM to new heights, while peasant currents flowed into the National League and built up its power. Next came the presidential candidate's assassination in 1928, triggering a political crisis that stretched into six years of division and weakness at the top. At the base the big organs of popular will fell apart — confusion was king. A deepening economic crisis drove the masses toward another explosion like that of 1910. Then President Cárdenas, a populist leader of great ability, repaired the state engine, hitched people's organizations behind it, and steered them against landlords and foreigners.

After the lid blew off in 1910, the desperate and illiterate Mexican masses were a steaming sea of social energy, churning up revolutionary storms that threatened to sweep away all elites, along with the nation itself. Slowly the new state learned to channel that energy in different directions, collect it into organizations, and turn these against special military, religious, and propertied interests. Thus the bureaucrats sought to divide and rule. In government, strong leadership led the nation through the agony of budding industrialization, but weak presidents drifted into crisis.

The death of the presidential candidate in 1928 opened a period of weakness. For a year an interim president, the civilian Portes Gil, attempted to rule with Calles looking over his shoulder. Ortiz Rubio, an engineer, then tried to govern with Calles' approval, but people were not sure where the decisions came from — until Ortiz suddenly resigned. Calles appointed a general to take his place. The general lasted until 1934, but checked his actions with the shadowy power in Cuernavaca. Thus the government remained divided.

In 1929 Calles had tried to seal the cracks opening in the state structure by founding a national party to hold together the groups thrown into power by the revolution: political bosses and their local followers; state governors with administrative hierarchies; restless generals commanding divisions; labour chiefs with union bureaucracies; congressional leaders and their clients; the president himself surrounded by top officials. At first the ruling party was a weak alliance of many groups, but it gained in strength every year, and by 1934 developed a bureaucratic machine for directing the new men of power. Yet the machine lacked a skilful conductor.

In 1929 General Cárdenas, the governor of Michoacán, was one of the main personalities among the men of power; he would quickly become the leader of the ruling party's left wing. The right wing of the party rallied behind Calles, who grew more conservative every year. He openly said that Mexico must be capitalist; he slowed agrarian reform to a crawl and announced to the peasants that land distribution would stop. Mexico was still a nation of huge estates: of the privately owned land a few thousand landlords held four-fifths, while 700,000 men in the semi-communal *ejidos* held only a tenth as much, and 2.3 million peasants *had no land at all*. So after 1930 peasant support for the government melted away, as the rising cry for land got a deaf ear from Calles and the party's right wing. There was growing trouble in the countryside, and by 1933 land seizures and strikes of farm workers were spreading. Peasant uprisings exploded in Zacatecas, Guanajuato, and Michoacán; in the state of Veracruz 15,000 people revolted. In rural Mexico gusts of discontent were blowing up a tornado of mass anger, while the government drifted before the wind.

In 1929 the crisis of world capitalism gripped the Mexican economy. On the world market the price of silver tumbled, and a vital sector of Mexico's big mining industry sickened. The disease got worse, as gold, copper, lead, and zinc went down. Oil production, already dropping in the 1920s, fell ever faster; plantations in the cotton-growing regions of north-central Mexico slid into bankruptcy. Around the nation, layoffs and wage cuts dragged the proletariat toward starvation. Food prices were rising; floods, droughts, and frosts ruined a third of the corn crop and cut the bean harvest in half. Mexico's economy, based on export, had always swung with the ups and downs of the world market. In the 1930s it collapsed.

In the disorganized working class there were spontaneous struggles and strikes; the government answered with swift repression. Layoffs led to workers' claims against companies, jacking up the number of labour conflicts year by year. Starting in 1929 with 13,000 the number of conflicts rose annually: 21,000; 29,000; 37,000. Workers' demonstrations for a government return to policies favouring labour met rebuffs from Calles. 'I am convinced,' he said about the workers' demands, 'that in every man greed and selfishness are basic.'

By 1933 a practised eye could spot the elements of a revolutionary situation: repressive government, political crisis, economic disaster, increasing misery for masses of people with a fighting tradition, and a sharp rise in their actions against existing conditions. In the cities there were labour disputes, suppressed strikes, marches, speeches, demonstrations; in the countryside, roaming migrants, squatters' movements, land seizures, clashes between peasants and big owners, and armed uprisings setting in motion thousands of people.

While Calles and the right wing of the ruling party remained blind to the abyss opening beneath their feet, the left wing gazed into the depths with fear. By 1933 the left had converted the bulk of the party to its vision. A Six Year Plan vaguely calling for socialism was drawn up, and the left's leader became the next candidate for president. Lázaro Cárdenas was to be the greatest agitator in Mexican history.

Cárdenas had rocketed out of a poor family to make a general of division at age thirty-two. Riding the wings of the revolution to glory, he showed all the strengths of the populist commander amid the usual weaknesses. A man of the people, he lived simply and worked long hours to serve the peasants he loved. He knew how to listen to their problems and hopes; he was patient with their slowness. He often spent the night talking with people in a remote village, only to continue sleepless on his journey the next day. As governor of Michoacán he mobilized the people to fight for their rights; together they distributed land and built schools.

He was a self-educated man, not an intellectual, and he took his political views from the grab bag of leftist ideas available in Mexico. Like all populist ideologies, *Cardenismo* was full of contradictions: the state must mix capitalism and communism into a brew called Mexican socialism; the President should protect private enterprise while educating the people to hate it; a handful of producers' co-operatives would grow through decades into a just society. Cárdenas was a passionate democrat. He trusted the elemental power of the masses to right wrongs and rebuild the social order. At the same time he believed in a strong state supported by the popular classes, *but also obeyed by them*, as the only way to avoid chaos. (The memory of the civil war and its horrors ate at his mind.) He wanted to organize the masses in defence of their class interests and to make the State work for them.

In 1934 Cárdenas launched his campaign for president. In this campaign his ruling party could hardly lose the 'election', but something more than votes was at stake: the nation was a primed mine, and an explosion might come any minute; the presidential candidate was struggling to defuse the bomb of the popular wrath threatening the government. Cárdenas moved over the length and breadth of his vast country, travelling thousands of miles to talk with peons and Indians, with miners and ranchers in remote areas. He made speeches off the top of his head, using simple ideas, and he listened to peasant committees stammering out their griefs and hopes. He saw that many no longer believed in the promises he was making for the government, and he knew that when president he must do something quickly. Everywhere he preached that a new deal was coming to Mexico, called for land to the people who tilled it, and shouted against the foreigners exploiting the nation's ores. factories, oil, and agriculture. In the fields and factories he never tired of telling the labourers to organize themselves, to press their demands on their enemies, and to throw the weight of the people behind their government. He urged the atomized workers and peasants to unify their fragmented organizations into leagues and centrals; he took a hand in healing their quarrels. He met peons, migrants, unemployed, workers, women, and youth with the same slogan: Get organized! A man of the people, he felt their suffering and dreamed with them of a new order; he convinced many that he was leading the nation toward a just society.

The hour had produced the man.

The Role of the Mexican Confederation of Labour
At the end of 1934 he became President and looked around for allies. His eye fell upon the fragmented working class, and he encouraged the unification of the labour movement. For two years union leaders had called for unifying the pieces of the old labour centrals, and here and there they had congealed into larger blocs. In 1933 there had been more than a dozen confederations,

scores of federations, and hundreds of loners. Then Lombardo Toledano formed a new central out of dissidents from the ghost of the CROM. Toledano's central called for the overthrow of capitalism, preached syndicalism, and returned to the idea of direct action: meetings, demonstrations, boycotts, sit-downs. To fight low wages the central organized walk-outs and in 1934 a general strike. Toledano and his workers became a centre of attraction for the drifting unions.

In 1935, with President Cárdenas in office, waves of strikes encouraged by the government shook up the industrial system. In the summer Calles publicly warned the President away from leftist policies and threatened him with a coup; this won huge applause from the business class. But Cárdenas dismissed conservatives in his cabinet and retired generals of doubtful loyalty. As the crisis deepened, he put out congressmen suspected of plotting, fired a number of state governors, and purged the ruling party of its right wing. Among the workers there sprang up a Committee for Proletarian Defence aiming at a single labour central to back the President. The Committee directed more and more strikes, demonstrations, and unity meetings. It threatened to drive Calles out of the country with a general strike. Around it rallied workers of all tendencies: socialists, communists, syndicalists, reformists, and former anarchists. In December it filled the streets of the capital with 100,000 workers, peasants, and students in a giant demonstration led by Toledano to the central plaza where Cárdenas swayed the masses with words. To support him they could unleash a general strike. The agitation swept out of the capital across the country; there were marches and meetings for Cárdenas in cities throughout Mexico. Labour was getting together.

At the beginning of 1936 several thousand delegates met to form the Confederation of Mexican Workers (CTM) with Toledano at its head. He dissolved his own central in this big one, and many others merged with it. Although some unions stayed out, like the corrupt CROM and anarchist CGT, a single central was uniting the Mexican proletariat. The CTM built itself out of industrial unions and ordered craft organizations to regroup in the new way.

At the CTM's founding congress Toledano declared independence from the government: 'We have not received money from anybody nor have we asked anyone for anything; we are free, positively independent, autonomous.' The CTM was supposed to grow on its own. The new central began with 200,000 members and carried on organizing around the country. Fidel Velázquez, the secretary for organization, sent propaganda and agitators into every corner of Mexico. The CTM umbrella opened out over the working class: by the next year it counted half a million members, and this growth went on year by year. By 1940 it contained more than a million. The CTM sucked into itself the unattached unions in the country.

The labour central's leaders publicly denied government aid during this spectacular growth, but somebody was paying huge sums for organizers and buildings, and it was hardly the Mexican workers on subsistence wages. Government and party officials spoke of aiding the CTM. Thus in 1936 the party's official newspaper declared: 'The public power has distributed fairly the material elements it has been possible to give, in order to stimulate the realization of alliances, conventions, and arrangements that aim to unify the industrial proletariat.' Historians have guessed that Cárdenas was financing the astonishing growth of the labour central. Anyone familiar with Mexican history must suspect that.

At least the CTM leaders were honest. Fidel Velázquez was a tireless organizer who made the young central grow into a giant. From the organizing secretariat he built a bureaucratic machine inside the central and gathered power into his hands. Above Fidel's bureaucratic camarilla was suspended the central's brilliant General Secretary, Lombardo Toledano. He matched Cárdenas as the other mass leader of the period, but with a difference: behind Lombardo's word-magic lay a mastery of Marxist theory.

He reasoned that some day the tiny Mexican proletariat would grow big enough to seize power and march toward a classless society. Meanwhile, semi-colonial Mexico orbited the imperial sun of the U.S.A., and only a revolutionary explosion at the centre of this system could free the periphery for socialism. So Mexican socialism might be a long way off. For the time being, concluded the union leader, the tasks facing Mexico's labour movement were twofold: (1) a struggle to free the nation from the United States' grip on its oil, ores, and land; and (2) a defence of the workers' wages against capitalists during the course of the democratic revolution against feudalism. This second point was the essence of Toledano's tactical programme — successful strike action.

By contrast, President Cárdenas did not expect that the proletariat would some day seize power to push the nation violently toward a classless society. Mexico would evolve toward state-regulated socialism over several decades, as producers' co-operatives and capitalist factories existed happily side by side. For the time being, thought the populist President, the State must undertake not only to free the nation from economic dependence on the United States, but also to stimulate Mexican entrepreneurs to expand industry and modernize the country. This last point was the essence of Cárdenas' tactical programme: the creation of a consumers' market by jacking up wages through pressure from organized labour.

With different ideologies the President and the labour leader had come to the same conclusion: the workers' starvation wages must rise to a reasonable level; the unions must force businessmen to come around. That, and not revolution, was the task at hand. Cárdenas made a pact with Toledano. The CTM would back the President in his struggle against landlords and foreigners while the State would support labour's strikes. The working class would not try to seize state power, for the President would share power with the organized proletariat or at least with its leaders.

The misery of the industrial workers worried Cárdenas. Their wages were so low that they lacked food, their desperation was turning into rage. In the explosive atmosphere of the 1930s the urban proletariat was inflammable material, and the reformist President wanted to soak that dry tinder in food and drink. He gave a green light to the engines of social integration – the militant unions. They pushed ahead with strikes.

Under the Mexican Constitution, in labour disputes the State holds the whip hand: the government can declare a strike illegal and smash it with troops, or recognize it as legal and arbitrate in favour of labour. The figures in the table tell a dramatic story.

Number of Lawful Strikes in Mexico, 1927-1938

Year	Number of Lawful Strikes
1927	16
1929	14
1931	11
1933	13
1935	642
1936	674
1937	576
1938	319

From 1935 on, there were actually more labour conflicts than these figures show. Unions threatening a strike informed the government; state arbitrators then rushed in to settle the dispute before a walk-out. Between boss and worker slipped the government official, ready to oil the machinery of collective bargaining. He was determined to have the workers eating enough to keep them from fainting on the job. Wages were often so low that workers barely had enough to buy poor food, and the slightest emergency might send them to work with empty stomachs.

Cárdenas pushed through social reforms. He struggled to enforce the minimum wage law and passed legislation requiring pay for workers on Sundays. Sunday pay knocked up the power of mass consumption by 16%. The President said he was only trying to restore social equilibrium. In fact, the economy picked up rapidly, as the new buyers demanded goods from industry. 'The acts of my government,' Cárdenas said in 1940, 'have always been inspired by a desire to raise the great working masses' capacity to consume, to raise national demand and thus national production.' As output soared, even the bankers stopped calling him a communist.

At the foundation of the CTM in 1936, Toledano had insisted on his independence from the government, and though the state may have aided his organizing efforts with money, he was determined to be his own man. His pact with Cárdenas made the CTM the main social prop of the President's reformist policy, but Toledano might withdraw support some day. He was, after all, calling himself a revolutionary Marxist, and the CTM had inscribed on its banner the slogan *Towards a Classless Society*! Its final goal was the seizure of state power. Cárdenas, by contrast, believed in a strong state suspended above society; he thought no Mexican President could surrender power to the workers, though he might share it with them. Cárdenas watched his Marxist ally with suspicion, for the labour leader was gaining strength with every month of the CTM's growth.

Toledano longed to build a worker-peasant bloc by using the CTM to organize the countryside. Success in this project would bring the Mexican masses into one big union and make the labour leader (with his golden tongue) the most powerful man in the Republic. So the CTM organized unions of agricultural labourers on the great plantations. Thousands of sugar, cotton, and hemp workers swelled its ranks. The labour central planned to swallow up millions of Mexican peasants, and openly said so.

The National Peasant Confederation

Cárdenas threw the weight of his government against the CTM's project. He said that the Mexican State reserved for itself the right to organize the peasants, and he urged agrarians to boycott the CTM's efforts. He played on the old suspicions of peasant leaders (like Díaz Soto) who feared the labour movement. The biggest peasant league ordered its members to stay out of the CTM, and the government raced ahead with the construction of its own nationwide organization on the land.

The CTM protested to the President and demanded the right to organize peasants, but Cárdenas was like stone. CTM calls to peasants for unity with the working class usually fell on deaf ears. The labour central complained bitterly, but finally allowed the State to have its way: once the official peasant confederation had won the organizational race, the CTM's unions of sugar, hemp, and cotton workers transferred to the government association.

How did Cárdenas build his National Peasant Confederation? He and organizers from the ruling party travelled up and down the country calling for peasant unity. The President spent half his time on the road; he visited villages in mountains and jungles where no top leader had ever gone. For an hour daily he opened the telegraphs to Mexico City so that peasants could talk to their President. His populist style invaded Mexican politics, and state governors went out to meet the people.

For several years Cárdenas' agrarian revolution and the construction of his Peasant Confederation marched hand in hand. To get land, peasants must form an agrarian committee to petition the government; then the state granted land. But once the agrarian committees appeared, the ruling party brought them together into regional committees. Next the regional committees in each state were united in a peasant league. And finally the ruling party merged the leagues into a National Confederation.

In the summer of 1935 Cárdenas began the process, and by 1936 there were 14 peasant leagues. This first period saw violent struggles. Many peasants, suspicious of official promises, forgot about agrarian committees petitioning the government for land – they marched out to seize it. The President wanted control of the agrarian revolution, and he ordered governors and generals to stop spontaneous invasions of land 'by whatever means you think suitable' – an invitation to bloodshed. To keep the revolution from sweeping beyond the government, Cárdenas revved up the machinery of land distribution to meet peasant demands. Before some peasants could ask for land for their *ejido* village, big owners sent White Guards to kill, burn, and destroy. Villages vanished. To villages the State handed out rifles for a militia to defend the land reform. Over the Cárdenas years the militia grew into a people's army with 70 battalions and 75 regiments of cavalry — firearms protected the new lands. While the men worked in the fields their women stood guard with Mausers and fought off the *hacendados'* gunmen. Gunfire lit up the map of Mexico, as battles between agrarians and White Guards exploded around the nation.

By the end of 1937 the ruling party had organized 28 peasant leagues. Across Mexico the rural teachers, often peasants themselves, brought the tillers of the soil into agrarian committees. The teachers' work at the base helped the ruling party catch over a million people in its organizing net. These agrarian cadres often died in the struggle. During the first years of the reform, the White Guards murdered 2,000 agrarians in Veracruz State alone. The teachers never tired of explaining to peasants what the government was doing, and their ideas undermined the work of hostile priests and political bosses. When the fat Catholic Indian, General Saturnino Cedillo, rose in arms to stop Cárdenas' reforms, the rebel called for support from the confused peasants of San Luis Potosí. As peasants rallied to his cause, the rural teachers marched with them to explain what was happening. They went over to Cárdenas.

By the summer of 1938 there were 37 peasant leagues and unions; and the government called them into the capital to found the National Peasant Confederation (CNC). The CNC was to remain a creature of the state. To this day its members, grateful for the land, back the ruling party.

The base unit of the CNC was the *ejido*, the semi-communal village rooted in the mythical past. The village owned the land and assigned to each family a plot; the peasant could till the land but not rent or sell it; forest and pasture land were held in common. An *ejido* assembly was supposed to run the common affairs of the village and send delegates to the peasant league. Thus in theory the CNC was democratic.

Obregón and Calles had thought the *ejido* transitional to private property, but Cárdenas treasured it as the germ of a socialist society. He not only gave the *ejido* villages land. He aided them with credit, schools, dams, and roads, for they were his ideal of a new order. 'To solve the agrarian problem,' the President had said in his electoral campaign, 'I don't think giving land to the peasants will be enough. The Public Power must give the *ejido* men all material and moral aid, so they can prosper economically and free their minds from ignorance and prejudice.' The government must build up the *ejido* sector until it produced food for the growing cities; the State must integrate the peasants into modern life.

In December 1935 the state founded the Ejido Bank to give the villages credit for fertilizer, seed, and tools. From the beginning Cárdenas planned to use the Bank to organize production and distribution in the countryside. His revolution would go beyond a change in land tenure to rebuild the economic and social life of rural Mexico. The State would lead the peasants into a new world.

The Ejido Bank became more than a moneylender. It stored and sold harvests, bought machinery and taught peasants to use it, fought crop plagues and developed new seeds, built power plants and repaired irrigation canals. The Bank set up consumers' co-operatives. It grew into a giant brain for administration and planning, with bureaucratic nerves linking it to a thousand villages. Through this monster the governemnt got more and more of the seething countryside under control.

The Bank's money came from the State's limited funds, and there was not enough to go around — only a minority of *ejido* men got credit. Cárdenas funnelled the money into explosive areas where strikes and rebellions had threatened authority. The Laguna region of north-central Mexico, the rice fields of Nueva Italia in the state of Michoacán, and the Yucatán hemp fields commanded attention. In such areas the agrarian transformation may have prevented another *jacquerie* like that of 1914.

The Laguna cotton-growing area, a million acres cultivated by over a hundred haciendas, saw bloody strikes throughout 1935. The foreign owners refused to meet their peons' demands.. In 1936 a general strike brought the crisis to a head, and the government decided to turn the haciendas into collective farms run by the workers. So the foreign owners wrecked irrigation canals and carried off machinery. Workers' detachments guarded the canals while the State reorganized two-thirds of the area into 300 collective farms. These collectives used land, water, machinery, and credit in common. Everyone in the collective had a card noting the number of days they laboured, and profits were distributed to each according to their work. The collectives got massive aid from the Ejido Bank.

A strike movement shook up the rice plantations of Lombardía and Nueva Italia in Michoacán; the President handed the farms to workers' collectives. In Yucatán the big hemp growers had created chaos to sabotage Cárdenas' struggle for agrarian change, and by 1937 reformist efforts there were paralysed. The frustrated peons threatened to break loose against the old order. The President rushed to Yucatán to give the land to the workers, along with the hemp growers' machinery; to the emerging collectives he promised big credits from the Ejido Bank. The wheat fields of the Yaqui valley in Sonora, the sugar-growing region of Los Mochis (Sinaloa), the coffee plantations in Chiapas — all these areas sprouted collective farms. The foreign landowners were going down under the blows of Mexico's greatest nationalist.

From 1935 to 1938 the ruling party hit native *hacendados* and foreign owners with the power of mass movements, and pieces of Mexico returned to the little people on the land. The party entangled the people in the meshes of the CNC, and the Ejido Bank captured their villages in its tentacles. Cárdenas hoped that he was mobilizing the people to build a democracy: he intended that peasant organizations should express the popular will.

The Organization of Professional Workers and Public Employees

The President believed in the magic of organization, and early offered its blessing to the state bureaucrats. He abolished the spoils system and gave public employees job tenure, then urged them to form unions. At the base these white collar workers wanted to join Toledano's CTM, and in 1936 the labour central declared it would organize the civil service. This would give the CTM great power, for a strike by the bureaucrats' unions could paralyse the government.

As the organizing moved forward in 1937, the government worked to bring the bureaucrats into unions outside the CTM. The labour central repeatedly attacked the official policy, and between the State and the CTM there developed a struggle for the public employees. 'The employees form part of the state organization,' said Cárdenas, 'so that it is their duty to identify completely with its ends . . . .' He threw the weight of his office against Toledano, and in 1938 the CTM's bureaucrat unions transferred to a new labour central, the Federation of Unions of Workers at the Service of the State (FSTSE).

The organisation of the teachers also took place outside the CTM; they finally joined the bureaucratic central. This was encouraged by Cárdenas' policy, and the CTM complained that it was a violation of the right to associate freely. The President was determined to check the CTM's power, for he feared that his pact with its Marxist leader would some day break down. But once the chief of state had lined up the peasant CNC and the FSTSE behind the government, the CTM was likely to maintain its alliance with him, for Toledano would go where the power lay.

Mobilizing for the Corporate State

Toledano's CTM did back up Cárdenas. In fact, the most dramatic example of its power to rally Mexicans behind the President occurred in 1938. In Tampico the foreign oil companies refused to obey a government ruling, and Cárdenas plotted to seize the petroleum industry. He wondered if the United States would send its fleet to Tampico to stop him. He had already taken the lands of North American owners to build collective farms, and Roosevelt had done nothing, for the engines of the United States' economy barely idled, the American President was busy with repairs, and peace was needed on the border. But the oil might bring U.S. warships snarling down the Gulf, and Cárdenas wanted Mexico to back him up. He asked the CTM to mobilize the nation.

The CTM prepared its unions for demonstrations around the country; the labour central urged other organizations into action: the CROM, the CGT, the socialist youth, the communists, the ruling party. They shifted into gear, and drove more and more Mexicans into the demonstrations of March 1938. Cárdenas fired off his decree nationalizing the oil. Like a rocketburst it signalled for a national fiesta: Mexico City schools vomited students into the streets; shopkeepers closed up to join the crowds; 200,000 workers surged down thoroughfares to paralyse the capital. Demonstrations broke out in cities around Mexico. The press applauded, while peasants, women, youth, professionals, bureaucrats, and labour unions declared for the President.

The Ruling Party Reorganized

Riding this wave of popular enthusiasm, the mass leader stepped up his efforts to turn the ruling party into a working democracy. For two years he had struggled to strip the party of its old image. To Mexicans it had always seemed a bureaucratic machine, the instrument of an elite, a tool for settling disputes among the groups in power. Then President Cárdenas said he preferred a political organization controlled by the masses. So in 1937 the ruling party arranged for assemblies of workers and peasants to ratify the people put forward as candidates for office. At the party's national assembly after the oil expropriation in 1938, Cárdenas herded flocks of celebrating workers into the fold. Millions swelled the party's ranks. The President marched them into what he called a 'popular' sector, a 'labour' sector, and a 'peasant' sector. (There was also a military sector, but the party soon dropped it.) At the centre of each sector he placed a large organization orbited by smaller groups. In the popular sector stood the bureaucrats' FSTSE, surrounded by associations of professionals, intellectuals, shopkeepers, women, and youth. In the labour sector around the giant CTM hovered the smaller centrals and independent unions: the CROM, the CGT, the Miners Union, the Electricians Union. The peasant sector was roughly the CNC.

Each peasant in an *ejido* and every worker in a union became a member of the ruling party. Cárdenas thought he was turning the elitist party into a mass party, but in fact it became a party of corporations: workers belonged to the party because they were members of the FSTSE, or the CTM, or the CNC. A migrant labourer on the land, a penny vendor in the city, a foot soldier in the army, a prostitute in the street, an Indian in the high sierra, a peon on a big estate, a maid slaving in the kitchen, an errand boy in the market, all the drifters, the unemployed, the illiterate, the wretched of the earth — these were not members of the party. On the other hand, anyone in the bureaucrat, labour, or peasant unions could not escape it. To get a teaching job an eighteen-year-old woman must join a union and thus *become a card-carrying, dues-paying member of the party.*

The three sectors were supposed to control the workers' party from the bottom up. On the national level they would elect a candidate for president, on the state level candidates for governors, and on the local level people to run for municipal offices. The popular, labour, and peasant sectors should act as pressure groups on the President, pushing him to make state policies in favour of working people.

The reconstructed party, says its declaration of principles, 'considers as one of its fundamental objectives the preparation of the people for building a workers' democracy, for arriving at a socialist regime.' The 'class enemy' is big business. The great industrialists, merchants, and bankers cannot join the workers' party, but the law requires them to organize in associations:

the Chamber of Industry, the Chamber of Commerce, and the Bankers' Association. Through such associations they can express their interests in an orderly way before the people's state. The workers' party was supposed to lead the nation toward socialism, and such a project meant a struggle to transfrom the economic institutions of society.

By 1938 the Mexican government dominated the banking system, operated the railways, ran the oil industry, and encouraged the *ejido* sector in agriculture. The State controlled the commanding heights of the economy. A Leninist strategy would mean state planning to broaden gradually this socialized sector into a new society.

The Struggle Against Marxist Socialism
Cardenas disliked the doctrines known as Marxism-Leninism, for he thought they were leading to bureaucracy and statism in the Soviet Union. He turned away from 'scientific socialism' to something he supposed more original. Mexican socialism, for him, would emerge through building producers' co-operatives in the cities and collective farms in the countryside; the workers themselves would run these in a pluralistic economic order. During his term the state created some collective farms and factories. He hoped that these would grow and multiply, that future presidents would sow more such seeds. Cárdenas expected the workers' party to keep up this labour for decades, until Mexico reaped a socialist society in the remote future. His programme of socialist education in the schools, his slogans against capitalism and the Church, would prepare the country for the change; his efforts toward technical training for working people would enable them to take control of production some day. He believed a revolution was under way.

During the 1930s the economic crisis of world capitalism and the belief that the Soviet Union was building socialism brought Marxist ideas into fashion everywhere. In Mexico, Marxists appeared inside the governing party. The pictures of Marx and Lenin in school textbooks, the socialist rhetoric of the party and Cárdenas, his founding of a few collective farms and producers' co-operatives, his nationalization of the railways and oil — all this convinced some Marxists that a transition to socialism had begun. They forgot that the party was not Marxist, that economic planning was hardly present, and that Cárdenas must soon step down from the presidency.

From Cárdenas to certain Marxists, from reformist socialists to populist reformers, there was hope that in some way a revolution against private property was developing. But if a transformation of Mexico's economic order was going on, it was not destruction of private property; whatever revolution there was led Mexico straight toward industrial capitalism. What went wrong?

Undermining Workers' Democracy
Cárdenas' attempt to transform the ruling party into a working democracy backfired. In the big unions at its base the party suffered all those tendencies that organization gives rise to: the emergence of bureaucracies and chains of

command, with the shifting of control into the hands of a few internal oligarchs. 'Who says organization says oligarchy,' wrote Robert Michels 60 years ago, and Mexico's political experience confirms this famous sociologist's idea. This highly organized nation has failed in democracy. The barely literate masses have not made the party unions work for them, nor have the politicians encouraged participation at the base. 'There are few people in Mexico who really want democracy; everyone tries to impose his will on the others,' said Cárdenas. 'It's a selfish and sad picture, but we are going to do our best to put the brakes on that tendency.' His efforts failed.

The 1930s drew to a close; the economic crisis ebbed away. As the excitement of the popular classes cooled, party men manipulated their organizations from the top down. In an economy with little to offer the average man, the workers' leaders discovered the road to well paid jobs in the ruling party. Already in the elections of 1937 large numbers of worker and peasant leaders were taken up into the government to become members of Congress. Their high salaries made them eager to do what the party wanted in hopes of being chosen for other posts later.

In the elections at local, state, and federal levels, democracy never developed beyond assemblies of workers and peasants ratifying candidates proposed by the ruling party from above. The President picked the candidates for governorships, and the party sectors approved his choices. This process also worked at lower levels. Cárdenas thought it a transitional phase that must pass into full democracy, but his expectation was not fulfilled. To this day nomination of candidates for office occurs from the top.

Cárdenas stepped from the presidency in 1940, and a more conservative man moved in. The fiercely independent Lombardo Toledano lost the General Secretariat of the CTM, and the servile organization man, Fidel Velázquez, took over. He was more interested in posts in Congress than in pressuring the new President to meet labour's needs. From that time on, the party has raised the labour leaders into fat jobs in government, and the CTM has become a creature of the state.

The peasant CNC had been that from its birth. Authority flowed down to its *ejido* base where the Agrarian Department manipulated village assemblies. The poor and ignorant peasants slipped under bureaucratic control.

The FSTSE and professional associations showed more energy than the other sectors; so the party took their interests to heart. It showered the state bureaucrats with excellent medical care, retirement pensions, and low-priced goods in special commissaries. But the bureaucrat unions did not democratize the party.

The popular, worker, and peasant sectors failed to become pressure groups moving the President on a leftward course. They turned into interest groups: the ruling party took into account their needs, made concessions to the rank-and-file, and co-opted the organizational leaders. Today the real pressure groups lie outside the party. On the left are independent trade unions and peasant associations, the student movement, and local committees of popular defence. On the right are the associations of big business which carefully advise the government about their economic plans. The government often submits draft laws to the business associations for criticism and advice. This does not mean that businessmen indirectly run the government or determine its policy outcomes. The interest groups within the party come before the pressure groups on the outside. Nonetheless, business does have considerable influence in determining economic policy. Could it be otherwise in a capitalist system?

From 1940 on, President Ávila Camacho steered Mexico down the capitalist road of development. The government's Ejido Bank no longer worked with socialist forms of agriculture to strengthen them; instead the Bank struggled to turn a profit. It gave credit to the few *ejidos* and collectives that promised the Bank returns. Those who got money for machinery and fertilizer found themselves working for the Bank, which sold their harvests on the market, sent bureaucrats to regulate production, and forced the peasants into a new kind of bondage. The number of *ejidos* receiving credit dropped, for the government was spending more money on dams and roads to service agribusiness.

In the cities businessmen applauded the new direction of the Bank. Through it they invested in the collective farms, and profits flowed into their pockets. The Bank forgot its old mission. In its huge body spread the cancer of corruption; it floundered in a slough of fraud and red tape. Its officials got rich off peasant sweat.

The government returned some collective farms to the old landowners. President Camacho slowed the distribution of land to *ejidos* and talked of encouraging small owners. But in fact the state aided the rise of great capitalist farms in the North. This continued under President Álemán (1946-52). New roads and irrigation canals opened up arid areas for cultivation. These lands went to friends of the politicians in Mexico City. Tractors ploughed the new lands to grow food for the cities, while the *ejido* sector withered into plots feeding peasants.

Over the last generation, the State has not struggled to expand the public sector of industry across the economy. The government has been content to invest in energy, transportation, and communication, leaving the profitable areas to private enterprise — production in mines, factories, and farms. The state has provided fuel oil and power dams, railways and roads, while businessmen went after the profits in industry. The Mexican government set the table, says one scholar, and private enterprise came to the feast.

The table is rich indeed, and for the past three decades foreign capital has followed the smell of profits into Mexico. The transnational corporations now control the bulk of consumer goods production, over half the mining, and a slice of agricultural output including four-fifths of the tobacco and rubber industries.

Mexico's capitalist industrialization has not brought economic independence. Two-thirds of the nation's imports come from the United States, and half of these are tools, machines, and spare parts. Mexico cannot make capital goods. Its dependent industry produces consumer goods for that fourth of its population able to afford them. So there has been progress for a few: the Gross National Product now ranks high among the 150 nations in the world.

A thousand years ago John of Salisbury offered a theory of stable society by comparing the state to a body. The prince was its head, the senate its heart, soldiers its hands, tax agents its stomach, and workers its feet. All co-operated, said John, for the good of the total inter-related society; each organ, in doing its job, helped toward the happiness of the whole body. For more than a century Catholic political thinkers have referred to any society run on this model as a 'corporate state' (from the Latin word *corporatus*, 'formed into a body').

Obregón, Calles, and Cárdenas were not theorists; they had never read John of Salisbury. But in Mexico between 1920 and 1940 they slowly built a corporate state. They started with a turbulent society full of class struggles, religious rebellions, internal colonies, army coups, racial strife, peasant uprisings, and widespread violence. How could they fuse the hostile groups into a single nation? They worked from the Mexican tradition that sees the President as dictator and struggled for top-down control of society. Each President followed the age-old tactic of divide and rule with increasing success. He herded the people into organizations run by the government, or scooped up unions and leagues with the net of the catch-all party.

Cárdenas was the architect of the corporate state; on the foundation laid by Obregón and Calles he built the most stable political structure in Latin America. He thought he was steering the Mexican economy toward socialism. Mexico was indeed pregnant with a new order, and Cárdenas acted as midwife, but the system he delivered we now recognize as capitalist. The Cardenistas have long since grasped the truth about their revolution. People who make a revolution, Friedrich Engels once remarked, 'recognize the day after that they had no idea what they were doing, that the revolution made does not in the least resemble the one they would have liked to make.'

Latin American socialists are haunted by the Mexican Revolution's irony.

4. Diagnosing the Revolution

Revolution has bounced into the centre of political discussion more than once in the 20th century, but our generation has batted around the concept until it's almost meaningless: people talk about everything from the urban revolution to the sexual revolution. So we need to define this concept that appears in the title of this book.

Political Revolution and Social Revolution

In the United States, an influential student of revolutions is Samuel P. Huntington, who studies them with the same end in view as his sometime associate, Henry Kissinger. 'A revolution,' he tells us in his *Political Order in Changing Societies* (p. 264), 'is a rapid, fundamental and violent domestic change in the dominant values and myths of society, in its political institutions, social structure, leadership, government activity, and policies.' The respected professor wants to use 'revolution' only for sweeping historical changes in the modern world, like the upheavals in France and Russia. The social cataclysm that modernized Mexico (1910-40) is a good example of a revolution.

But this definition jerks most of history's revolutions from under the label. When the poor citizens of ancient Samos violently seized the government from aristocrats to cancel debts and divide up land — leaving values, myths, political forms, and social structure intact — that too was a revolution (412 B.C.). When the Brazilian military captured the government, smashed left-wing parties, and gathered half of the economy into a state sector run by generals, the army rightly referred to its doings as a revolution (1964-72).

Marxism has often shown its strengths in the historical treatment of revolution; even conservative scholars have sometimes accepted its definitions. We, too, have found these definitions useful. For a look at them we must go back to the turn of the century when Karl Kautsky — 'the Pope of Marxism' — was lecturing to Dutch socialists in Amsterdam. His lectures were later published as *Die Soziale Revolution* (Berlin, 1902). There he laid down a distinction that has passed into the intellectual heritage of Marxist social thought: he separated a political revolution from a social revolution.

A political revolution is the transfer of political power from one social class to another. Political power usually includes the government executive; it may be control of a lawmaking body; but it surely means command of a loyal army and police force. As a political revolution moves from one phase to another, the struggle for the army usually decides its outcome. In Chapter One we mentioned Engels' generalization that every victorious revolution in European history was preceded by a collapse of discipline in the army. A class that commands the loyalty of a reorganized army has captured political power. World history is filled with political revolutions: civil wars, popular insurrections, and colonial revolts have often shifted control of the government from one class to another.

Occasionally such an overturn in government opens the door to *a social revolution, the transfer of economic power from one social class to another.* What is economic power? Karl Marx wrote in section two, chapter ten, of the first volume of *Capital* that economic power means ownership of the means of production — the land, tools, and machines. The class with economic power sucks up the bulk of the surplus product.

The surplus product of a society, Marx said, is what remains after paying for the food, clothes, and housing of the productive workers and replacing used-up tools and materials. The large amount left over is taken by an exploiting class, whether Egyptian priests, Carthaginian landowners, Indian zamindars, Etruscan theocrats, Roman patricians, Norman barons, Inca administrators, Mexican *hacendados*, Mississippi slave-owners, 19th century capitalists, or Soviet and Chinese bureaucrats.

This concept of surplus product defines economic power in history. 'The whole development of human society beyond the stage of savagery begins on the day when the labour of the family created more products than were necessary for its maintenance,' wrote Friedrich Engels in chapter five of part two of *Anti-Dühring*. 'A surplus of the product of labour above the costs of maintenance of the labour . . . was the basis of all social and intellectual progress. Throughout history this surplus has been the property of a privileged class.' A social revolution transfers the lion's share of the surplus product from one class to another.

In modern times such a revolution usually means that the economic power passes from an ageing social class to a dynamic rising one. The great bourgeois revolutions brought land reform and industrial growth: the aristocracy slowly ceased to suck up the bulk of the surplus product; the rising business and commercial class became the economic beneficiary.

In the middle of the 19th century, Marx and Engels imagined themselves on the threshold of a final social revolution. 'The impending social revolution,' wrote Engels in the passage quoted above, 'will for the first time make the surplus . . . a really social fund by taking it away from the privileged class and transferring it to the whole of society as its common property.' Or, as Marx summed up this transfer in the celebrated chapter thirty-two of *Capital*: 'We have the expropriation of a few usurpers by the mass of the people.' The surplus product would be transferred from the privileged class to

71

the propertyless class.

When a political revolution happens, a social revolution may or may not follow — a thunderstorm only occasionally produces a tornado. Once in a while, a political storm may send a great social tornado smashing through the economic structure of a nation. Then the political and social revolutions together bring on a cultural revolution — Huntington's 'change in the dominant values and myths of a society'.

You can see that we have broken his broad concept of revolution into sub-concepts: political revolution, social revolution, cultural revolution. Can't the label 'revolution' fit all of these? It's all right to put a common label on bottles with different contents, so long as you add a qualifying adjective to each.

Political revolutions were common in the ancient world, but social revolutions were rare, if they took place at all. In the modern world too, political revolutions happen more often. But social revolutions also occur: in France and Russia they flared up at the watersheds of modern history; in Vietnam, Algeria, and Angola they were the consequence of successful wars of independence from foreign domination.

To compare and classify social revolutions as bourgeois, proletarian, or bureaucratic, we have to carry out class analysis. But how do we diagnose a gigantic revolutionary process like that of 1789-1814 or that of 1917-1936? The problem is not only to discover which class begins the process, nor even which class becomes its driving force (by doing the fighting). One must also ask which class reaps the economic benefits of the revolution by finally capturing the lion's share of the surplus product. We agree with the method of the sociologist, Barrington Moore, in his *Social Origins of Dictatorship and Democracy* (Boston, 1966). Moore throws revolutions into this bag or that because of their broad institutional results.

For three chapters the historical facts have piled up before us, the crucial events of the Mexican Revolution in its insurrectionary and post-insurrectionary phases. What is the meaning of these events? We must now interpret the revolutionary period.

There are many characterizations of the Revolution, and some of them fit the data better than others. In Mexico, indeed in all of Latin America, Marxist interpretations of the Revolution are widespread. But the conceptual rigidity of the traditional Marxist framework has led to an artificial bending of the data, a forcing of the facts into a pre-existing interpretative schema. By contrast, non-Marxist interpretations are so vague, so lacking in sharp distinctions that history remains in its primitive state — a blooming, buzzing confusion of events.

Marxist Interpretations

Under the Marxist umbrella huddle a score of interpretations of the Mexican Revolution. They run the gamut from the standard interpretations by the Old

Left to the neo-Marxist interpretations by the New Left (under the influence of the Cuban Revolution).

The North American political sociologist, James Cockcroft, broke with the standard interpretations in his thesis of an abortive proletarian revolution. His Mexican counterpart in the New Left, Arnaldo Córdova, interprets the Revolution as a populist political upsurge, the first historical instance of its kind and a model for later revolutions in Brazil, Argentina, and Peru. The Argentine Trotskyist, Adolfo Gilly, while imprisoned in Lecumberri Penitentiary in Mexico City, wrote an incisive work on the Mexican Revolution: he saw it as (1) an abortive peasant revolution, (2) combined with a petty bourgeois political revolution, (3) the political revolution taking the form of a bonapartist transitional regime. In common with other interpretations by the New Left, Gilly dates the bourgeois political and social revolutions in Mexico from the period *before* the Mexican Revolution of 1910. Departing from these New Left interpretations, the independent Marxist and former dean of the National University of Mexico (UNAM), Pablo González Casanova, offers the best summary of interpretations by the Old Left: he sees the Mexican Revolution as an unfinished bourgeois political and social revolution. His thesis coincides with an important Soviet interpretation of the Mexican Revolution by M.S. Alperovich and B.T. Rudenko. Let us examine these Marxist interpretations in order.

An Aborted Proletarian Revolution

Cockcroft, in his *Intellectual Precursors of the Mexican Revolution 1900-13* (Austin, 1968) and continuing through his contributions to *Dependence and Underdevelopment* (Garden City, 1972) and *Latin America: the Struggle with Dependency and Beyond* (New York, 1974), denies that the Mexican Revolution was a classical bourgeois (anti-feudal) revolution. He conceives of the *Porfiriato* (1876-1910) as a bourgeois political regime sitting on a capitalist economic structure dominated by foreign investors. He argues that, insofar as there was a revolution at all, it took the form of an explosive confrontation between proletarians and capitalists. Proletarians made up the driving force of the Revolution, but with this qualification: most of them were rural peons, men loosely described as peasants tied to the haciendas through a form of debt peonage, *yet increasingly migratory and wage-oriented*. This migratory labour force of 'landless peasants' moved from harvest to harvest; the migrants even wandered from farm to factory over vast expanses of territory.

There are two premises behind Cockcroft's thesis. First, from the Spanish Conquest to the *Porfiriato*, the Mexican economy was dominated by mercantile, mining, and agrarian capitalists. Feudal, neo-feudal, or semi-feudal landlords were not the main element. Not feudalism, but capitalism was the driving force of the colonization of Mexico. Second, toward the end of the 16th century, the system of forced labour was replaced by a 'free' labour system. This meant that early in Mexico's development the class structure was polarized into a small commercial bourgeoisie at the top (white creole) and an exploited proletariat at the bottom (Indian, then mestizo).

On these premises Cockcroft argues that the hacienda system was not a feudal import from Spain. The hacienda was a commercial form of agriculture aimed at increasing production for the market; it was a system designed to exploit labour power better than the earlier methods relying on naked force. As a corollary of this thesis, he argues that the so-called peasantry attached to the haciendas was not made up of peasants in the Marxist sense of independent rural owners. At best they were share-croppers or tenant farmers, and he includes them with the bulk of indebted peons in his category of proletarians. In this perspective the Mexican Revolution of 1910-17 could not have been a bourgeois struggle against feudalism in the countryside.

Before the Revolution, argues Cockcroft, the most influential economic group was neither a rural oligarchy nor a local bourgeoisie. It was a foreign bourgeoisie. Zapata's revolutionary movement was a direct threat to the system from which that foreign bourgeoisie directly benefited. But Zapata's revolution was not successful. (In a Marxist framework, revolutions occur only through the transfer of political or economic power from one social class to another.) Cockcroft concludes that the Mexican Revolution was a frustrated, 'misdeveloped', and aborted proletarian revolution. In other words, at most it transferred political (and maybe economic) power from one sector of the bourgeoisie to another, from the foreign sector to the indigenous sector of the same class. The mis-styled 'Revolution' meant a temporary setback for the foreign bourgeoisie, but after 1940 this group (we are told) recovered its stranglehold on the economy.

To judge Cockcroft's interpretation of the data we must look at more than his basic premises. We must examine his definitions of feudalism, capitalism, bourgeoisie, and proletariat. Cockcroft is a late arrival to Marxist theory, and he follows on the heels of Andre Gunder Frank, whose conceptual framework is a misinterpretation of Marx's.* Cockcroft wants to push the genesis of modern capitalism back into the Renaissance during the 13th and 14th centuries in Western Europe. (This is also the fashion among Roman Catholic and liberal historians.) Thus Cockcroft defines feudalism as a 'socio-economic system characterized by a closed economy unconcerned with the accumulation of capital and its progressive reinvestment for profit' — an economy typical of the Middle Ages in Europe. By contrast, he defines capitalism as a 'socio-economic system in which all or most of the means of production and distribution . . . are privately owned and operated for profit,

---

*Andre Gunder Frank's *Capitalism and Underdevelopment in Latin America* (1967) has influenced an entire generation of Marxist and non-Marxist thinking on the left. Unlike Marx, he equates production for profit with capitalist production. But history shows that profit is compatible with the most diverse modes of extracting surplus labour including slavery and peonage. For Marx, the mode of extracting surplus labour through the wage contract was fundamental to his definition of capitalism, not the exploitation of pre-capitalist conditions through production of commodities for a profit.

the accumulation of capital, and the progressive reinvestment of capital, with a corresponding development of wage-labour, salaried classes, and regularly paid functionaries, all of whom interrelate within a relatively open, competitive market economy.' His definitions come from the academic traditions in the developed capitalist countries, but they are passed off as Marxist coinage. Can this be why some historians south of the Rio Grande have accepted them?

Basic to these definitions of feudalism and capitalism are two notions: (1) a market economy, and (2) production and exchange for profit. Such economic *relations* can indeed be traced back to the Renaissance in Europe and to the beginnings of the 17th century in Mexico. But are they sufficient conditions of a capitalist *system* of production? A market economy, contrary to Cockcroft, may or may not constitute a capitalist system in Marx's sense. (Marx distinguished a simple market economy, for example, from capitalist commodity production.) In Marx's framework a market economy and production for profit may coexist within a feudal society, within an economic system in which the bulk of production is agricultural, a system in which most of the producers are serfs coughing up revenue to feudal landlords.

In Europe the mercantilist 17th and 18th centuries were given to the accumulation of liquid capital. But is capital accumulation a sufficient condition of capitalism? In Western Europe capitalism did not emerge as the dominant mode of production, in Marx's sense, until after the Industrial Revolution was underway (the beginning of the 19th century). In short, for Marx, feudalism is a mode of production defined by two characteristics: serfs or semi-serfs do most of the work; and the lion's share of the economic surplus takes the form of revenue from the ownership of land. By contrast, capitalism is a mode of production with different characteristics: most of the labour is free rather than forced; the bulk of the economic surplus takes the form of revenue from the ownership of capital. [As we saw earlier in this chapter, economic surplus means the revenue remaining after the payment of the wages of the so-called productive workers who directly or indirectly produce the goods and services of society. Examples include landowners' rents; businessmen's profits, interest, dividends.]

What is the weakness of Cockcroft's conceptual apparatus? Its weakness is the missing of crucial distinctions, causing it to wallow in confusion. For Cockcroft there is no difference in kind between a landlord producing for the market and a capitalist farmer, between debt-peonage and wage labour, between share-croppers and proletarians.

For the sake of argument let us assume as correct Cockcroft's view that the only revolution in Mexico was an aborted proletarian one, a revolution that merely transferred political and economic power from one sector of the Mexican bourgeoisie to another. Does this thesis contradict, as he claims it does, the classical Marxist interpretation of the Mexican Revolution as bourgeois and anti-feudal? Not really. Because of his confusion of the categories of liberal and Marxist historians, his thesis provides support for the very interpretation he is arguing against. For consider: the transfer of political and economic power from one sector of Cockcroft's 'bourgeoisie' (pre-1910 *hacendados*) to a modern capitalist sector (post-1930 industrialists) is the same in Marxist terms as a bourgeois revolution, as the smashing of the semi-feudal *hacendado* system. In Cockcroft's acceptance of Frank's conceptual model, we have a vulgarization of Marx's terminological distinctions.

Let us apply strictly Marxist terminology and ask two questions. First, did the Villista and Zapatista movements, as Cockcroft claims, wind up in an aborted proletarian revolution? Second, what about his claim that there was no bourgeois revolution in Mexico, neither during the 1910-17 period nor during the post-insurrectionary stage?

Cockcroft argues well that in Morelos, where the haciendas were organized along capitalist lines, most of the peasants had already been reduced to a landless state. Since (in Marx's usage) a landless peasant is a contradiction in terms, the peons in debt to the haciendas were not (strictly speaking) peasants. Actually, the so-called peasant war in Morelos was mainly a proletarian struggle supported by armed villagers. But what was true of Morelos was hardly true of the rest of Mexico (except maybe Veracruz and the farming plantations of Yucatán). More, Cockcroft underestimates the peasant ideology of the Zapatistas: there was a discrepancy between the supposedly rural proletarian make-up of the movement and its peasant programme of recovering lands to convert the peons back into small owners.

There is the evidence we cited at the end of Chapter Two that before the Revolution native and foreign *hacendados* were taking the bulk of the economic surplus, but that by the 1940s there had arisen a class of millionaires getting its revenue from the modern capitalist sectors of commerce, banking, and industry. Research is lacking to show when the semi-feudal sector ceased to take over the bulk of this surplus. The shift must have occurred sometime after the traditional *hacendados* lost their positions of political power, i.e. after the defeat of Huerta's dictatorship in 1914. In Morelos the peasant lution helped shift most of the economic surplus from the *hacendados* to the urban bourgeoisie. Why did this shift occur? Not because the bourgeoisie became richer but because the haciendas were taken over by the local peasants. The same thing happened nationally. The agrarian reform began under Obregón, continued under Calles, and triumphed under Cárdenas, smashing the backbone of the traditional landowning class. The emerging entrepreneurs, both in agribusiness and industry, were soon getting the bulk of the surplus. This was a bourgeois revolution by default. And so, during the post-insurrectionary period the bourgeoisie, though not directly sharing political power, became the main beneficiary of the economic system.

Let us assume with Cockcroft, however, that the most influential sector under the *Porfiriato* was the foreign bourgeoisie. Suppose further that this influential sector was also the main beneficiary of the economic surplus. If the bulk of the economic surplus was sucked up by foreigners, the principal investors during the *Porfiriato*, doesn't that prove Mexico to have been a capitalist country in 1910? In Marxist terms it implies only this: the foreign sector of the economy was capitalist. In legal terms, the enclaves making up this sector were foreign property rather than local; so we have to label the local economy independently of these foreign enclaves. (National liberation movements find their basis in this distinction, in the struggle to recover foreign-owned properties for the nation.) In 1910 Mexico as a geopolitical entity might bear the label 'capitalist'; but this name is misleading, for it suggests that the Mexican ruling class was itself capitalist.

Cockcroft's arguments (modelled on Frank's) are an attack on the dual economy thesis, the idea that Latin American countries have a semi-feudal economy in the countryside but a modern capitalist sector in the cities. This idea about Latin American society was the basis for the politics and strategy of the established communist parties. The idea discouraged support for Cuban-inspired movements of national liberation aimed at a socialist political revolution. For the communists, the problem was to make an anti-imperialist agrarian revolution with the help of the national bourgeoisie. This objective meant completing the bourgeois democratic revolution through overcoming feudal survivals in agriculture and taking over foreign enclaves.

Of course, social thought has a practical function that includes the development of a theory for political and social revolutions. But, in showing that a socialist revolution is not premature in Latin America, Frank and Cockcroft transformed scientific theory from the basis of political practice into its vassal. They needed to study the data to provide a reasonable basis for revolution; instead they ignored data that undercut their political objective of socialism. Since a Marxist conceptual apparatus had served to discourage a socialist revolution in the Americas, then (oh, irony!) they abandoned Marx's approach for a liberal one. Did socialist revolution lack a scientific foundation? Then they must sacrifice science for their political objective. Such theoretical voluntarism is ill suited to the risks people run in making a revolution.

Cockcroft's critique of the dual economy thesis, in application to the Mexican Revolution, missed its mark. He did establish the existence of a market economy in the Mexican countryside, but his concept of an integrated economy geared to profit contains confusions. It confuses profits from urban enterprises with profits from the large haciendas. Who were the men owning these haciendas? Following the method of discovering the relations of production from which a person draws his or her living, we can ask whether in 1910 the Mexican *hacendados* got their gross revenue mainly from their ownership of capital or of land. Most historians say that during the *Porfiriato* the profits of Mexican *hacendados* came mainly from their ownership of land rather than from capital invested in improving it. The *hacendados* were like feudal lords drawing rent. And so a semi-feudal sector did indeed coexist with a capitalist one — a dual economy in Marx's sense.

A Populist Revolution under the Leadership of a New Middle Class
For a better intepretation of the Mexican Revolution there is Arnaldo Córdova's trilogy *La formación del poder político en Mexico* (1972), *La ideología de la revolución mexicana* (1973) and *La política de masas del cardenismo* (1974). (Córdova, like Cockcroft, represents the New Left.)

Underlying his basic thesis is a modified Cockcroftian interpretation of the pre-Revolutionary epoch: that period saw, in his view, the beginning and consolidation of a bourgeois social and political revolution during the *Porfiriato* (1876-1910). Córdova does not trace the capitalist origins of Mexico to the dependent mercantile economy of the 16th and 17th centuries; he finds those origins in the political unification of the country during the last two decades of the dictator, Porfirio Díaz. Mexico lacked a feudal past, thinks Córdova, but the absence of feudalism did not spell capitalism. Nor did the Mexican Revolution much alter the social and economic structure — that had already changed during the *Porfiriato*. The Mexican Revolution issued neither in a bourgeois revolution nor in a new post-bourgeois social order.

But Córdova believes that there was a significant change in the political regime. The rebellion of 1910-17 was, if not a social revolution, at least a political one. The insurrection hurled from power an unpopular and privileged bourgeois oligarchy, replacing it with a popular front government led by the old and new 'middle classes'. These classes of independent small owners and salaried intellectual workers became the new rulers; some of the proletariat and peasantry shared this rule in an active but dependent way. The bourgeoisie went on influencing the government, but did not dominate it. The system was still bourgeois, because the bourgeoisie was its main beneficiary in an economic sense; the government continued to serve primarily bourgeois interests. But under the *Porfiriato* the bouregoisie had had political as well as economic power, and this was no longer true. Cockcroft, as we saw, stopped short of these crucial distinctions.

What were the new elements in the political regime that emerged from the Mexican Revolution of 1910-17? Córdova traces everything new in that regime to Articles 27 and 123 of the Constitution of 1917. The political revolution did not begin with Madero (1911-13), for he only planned a reform of the old political order — effective suffrage and no re-election. Nor was the political revolution the work of popular forces under Villa and Zapata, men concerned with agrarian reform (1910-16). Not once, notes Córdova, did any popular leader try to rule Mexico directly: neither Villa, nor Zapata, nor Morones. Yet how could the Mexican Revolution become a revolution of the oppressed classes? Only by the workers' and peasants' movements seizing direct political power. And the peasant movement suffered defeat on the field of battle, while the workers' movement slid under the political leadership of the middle classes.

The Constitutionalist forces, led by Carranza and generaled by Obregón, carried through the Mexican Revolution (1913-17); these forces aspired to an independent capitalist development for Mexico. During the fighting after Madero's defeat, says Córdova, the middle classes realized that a revolutionary change in the political order could only come through the struggle of the masses for social reforms. To prevent such a popular explosion from getting out of hand, the middle classes decided to lead it. The social reforms proclaimed by the 1917 Constitution aimed to prevent popular explosions against the new equilibrium established by the middle classes, who were the political beneficiaries of the new regime. Under Madero these classes had tried to revive the 19th century political order, Córdova argues, but under Carranza they discovered a new form of political revolution urged upon them by the discontented masses.

The Constitutionalist army represented a third force between a bourgeois political dictatorship (Madero-Carranza) and a political dictatorship by the proletariat and peasantry (Villa-Zapata). (In the 1930s President Cárdenas would argue that revolutionary nationalism was an alternative to both capitalism and communism, that it was a synthesis of both.) The indigenous bourgeoisie was only budding, Córdova goes on, and so the main threat to the new political order seemed to come from the proletariat and the peasantry (1920-40).

The workers, peasants, and middle classes made up the three divisions of the ruling party: unionized labour, *ejido* peasants, and the popular sector. Because of their dependent participation they had less influence on the government than the native bourgeoisie, politically marginalized but *independent*. The bourgeoisie, says Córdova, bypassed the ruling party to put secret pressures on the government at the highest level. The ruling party fostered these fictions: the government is of, by, and for the workers; the political state belongs to the masses; workers and peasants directly control the party. Yet Córdova notes that after Cárdenas (1934-40) there occurred an inversion of the earlier relationship between government and bourgeoisie: the government no longer pushed around the bourgeoisie; the bourgeoisie ended by controlling the government.

Córdova is not sure how to use the usual Marxist categories to define this regime, so he tries his hand at others. He considers and rejects the term 'reformism' because the Mexican regime is too authoritarian. For him the term 'bismarckian' does not fit the masses' controlled but active participation in political power. Marx described a syndrome called 'bonapartism', but to Córdova the Mexican political system showed only some of its features: though a strong executive ruled above the proletariat and the bourgeoisie, the new regime lacked a charismatic leader supported by shock troops from the lumpenproletariat.

Yet each of these terms has a limited relevance for Córdova. First, the victorious Constitutionalist forces wanted to exorcise the social revolution by meeting some of the basic demands of the workers and peasants. Though the measures of the revolutionary government aimed to co-opt and control the masses, there were basic reforms. Second, the new regime was paternalistic and authoritarian. The chief executive got extraordinary powers: he had total control over private property (Article 27) and he could arbitrate in conflicts between labour and capital (Article 123) — powers found in bismarckian and neo-bismarckian regimes. Third, the new regime proposed to rule above class interests and to work for the national welfare. This included the industrialization of the country, the gaining of economic independence, and capitalist development directed by the state. The new regime also proposed to reconcile the social classes, to force each to make concessions, to create the conditions for their coexistence. That is typical of bonapartist regimes.

To label the new political regime, Córdova chooses the term 'populism', a name broad enough to cover the above features. The Mexican government was reformist, had bismarckian traits, and combined characteristics of a bonapartist state — the new regime was all that rolled into one. Of course the term 'populism' had disadvantages. The word recalls the programmes of Vargas in Brazil and Perón in Argentina, programmes for capturing political power with mass support. But their regimes were transitional, never fully institutionalized. By contrast, the political regime thrown up by the Mexican Revolution got an institutionalized and corporatist form under Cárdenas. And so Córdova extends the use of the term 'populist' beyond mass-based movements led by the middle classes to cover mass-based government enduring a long time. The Mexican political regime, he concludes, is no longer transitional: it is a model showing the capitalist class how to dominate a dependent, underdeveloped country by co-opting organized labour and the peasant masses.

What are we to make of Córdova's many claims? His interpretation rests on presuppositions not supported by the evidence. Was there a bourgeois political and social revolution during the *Porfiriato*? As early as Juárez's first reform government (1856) a bourgeois revolution made a successful take-off, but it soon faltered and crashed. Nor did it recover its wings during the *Porfiriato*. In the first decade of the 20th century, the federal government slipped under the financial control of the business-minded *científicos*, who made fortunes mediating between the state and foreign interests. In his classic work *Porfirio Díaz* (1932), Carleton Beals claims that 75% of all federal government appointments in 1910 (including Congress) came from the *científicos*. But this comprador bourgeoisie in the federal government had little power in the interior of the country. 'Land barons' ruled the interior; they had most of the governorships. In 1909, says Beals, more governors were land barons (feudal-type *hacendados*) than business-orientated *científicos*. A year later, as the Revolution broke out, the land barons still prevailed over their business rivals. Beals concedes that the barons were losing ground, as the *científicos* nominated governors for rural areas. But Díaz was not a *científico*, nor was all Mexico ever run by elements of the bourgeoisie.

In fact, there were two sectors of the Mexican State: a *comprador* sector busy with financial matters, with serving foreign interests, with self-enrichment; and a *hacendado* sector controlling most of the state governments through a union of political and economic power in feudal style — this power reached down from the governor to the haciendas with their courts and prisons. On balance, the rulers of Mexico in 1909-10 were not the *científicos*, but the *caciques* (political bosses who were also *hacendados*). More, the Army under Díaz's command openly hated the *científicos*. If political power grows out of the barrel of a gun, (and surely Mao Tse Tung was right that in modern society the men who command the guns have the power) then the federal government was run by *hacendado* and *cacique* interests.

With Madero (1911) the local bourgeoisie captured the presidency at last, but in most states semi-feudal *hacendados* went on ruling as governors and generals. While *hacendado* and bourgeois interests agreed, the Army obeyed Madero. But when peasant risings threatened the *hacendado* system, the Army overthrew him and bourgeoisie (1913). Thus there was a bourgeois political revolution neither under the *Porfiriato* nor under Madero. If we grant Córdova's thesis about a populist revolution in 1917 led by the bureaucratic new middle class and petty bourgeoisie, then Mexico has yet to have a successful revolution led by the bourgeoisie.

There was a symbiosis of political and economic power under the *hacendado* system. How should we define the indigenous sector of the Mexican economy while that system was still working? Within a Marxist framework, contrary to Córdova, we cannot label it capitalist. (Of course the imperialist sector was strongest, but it was not really Mexican.) Mexico's system under Díaz was still feudal or semi-feudal. Thus Córdova's thesis of a bourgeois social revolution during the *Porfiriato* collapses like his idea that Mexico also underwent a bourgeois political revolution.

The Mexican Revolution did not change the social and economic structure, says Córdova, but this hypothesis is questionable. Remember: the *hacendado* system disappeared only *after* the upheaval of 1910-17 (Beals, Tannenbaum, and most historians agree on this). When did capitalism become the dominant mode of production in Mexico? The Mexican transition to capitalism occurred sometime after the insurrectionary period. So the Mexican Revolution (1910-40), sweeping away remnants of the semi-feudal mode of production, did change the social and economic structure. This is the paradox: the Revolution resulted in a bourgeois social revolution without a bourgeois political revolution, without political leadership by the bourgeoisie. Obviously the Mexican economic system has been capitalist for decades. Where did Córdova go wrong about this system? He dated its origin in the last quarter of the 19th century. Did his error stem from disagreement with Beals' interpretation? No, the error arose from Córdova's failure to distinguish the Mexican economy from its foreign enclaves.

The struggle against the *Porfiriato* (and Huerta in 1913-14) resulted in a populist revolution under the leadership of the 'middle classes' with dependent participation by workers and peasants — this hypothesis is Córdova's big contribution. Who were these 'middle classes'? The old middle class of small urban owners did not play a leading role in the Revolution. Not the petty bourgeoisie, but the new middle class of military and political bureaucrats led the Consitutionalist forces to victory. Recruited chiefly from small freeholders, peons turned revolutionary soldiers, and professionals themselves, this new middle class was also the main political beneficiary of the Revolution.

A new middle class can lead a political revolution with or without the active collaboration of the masses. In Mexico it is evident that the masses actively participated in making the Revolution. That is why Cordova is right in preferring the term 'populist' to the traditional Marxist term 'bonapartist'.

(Bonapartist regimes soar above the reach of the masses.) Córdova's distinction between bonapartist and populist political revolutions is thus crucial for diagnosing the Mexican Revolution.

The Constitutionalist forces, Córdova correctly notes, steered a middle course between the interests of the privileged and the demands of the people. But with more precision he becomes misleading: he locates the Constitutionalist Third Force between a political dictatorship by the bourgeoisie and a social revolution by workers and peasants. President Cárdenas was also confusing, for he put the Third Force halfway between capitalism and communism. Where do these judgments go wrong?

Once firmly in power, the new middle class saw itself threatened on two fronts: (1) there was a spectre of a political counter-revolution that would hand over the state to the bourgeoisie, the class about to become the economically dominant one; (2) there was the menace of a social revolution that would turn over the economy to the workers by expropriating the bourgeoisie. Why did the regime fear this social revolution? A social struggle could undermine the political power of the new middle class. The struggle might capsize the ship of state.

The 'socialist' project was bound to attract mass support; that happened during Cárdenas' term (1934-40). Yet a successful social revolution would not have transferred the bulk of the economic surplus to the proletariat. The lion's share, as in the Soviet Union, Eastern Europe and even China, would most likely have fallen to the class of salaried and professional workers. And there is the irony: fear of failing in such an anti-capitalist enterprise has so far kept the new middle class from using political power to carry through a bureaucratic social revolution, a revolution making the new class the main economic beneficiary by default.

A Socialist Revolution Interrupted by a 'Petty-bourgeois' Transitional Regime
The Cuban Revolution has inspired New Left interpretations, but we can trace them back to Trotsky's reflections on the Mexican Revolution during his exile in Coyoacán (1937-40). In an essay on 'Nationalized Industry and Workers' Management' (1938), he gave the first Marxist-Leninist interpretation to break with Old Left views of the Mexican upheaval as an unfinished bourgeois democratic revolution. Here is a passage worth quoting:

In the industrially backward countries foreign capital plays a decisive role. Hence the relative weakness of the national *bourgeoisie* in relation to the *national* proletariat. This creates special conditions of state power. The government veers between foreign and domestic capital, between the weak national bourgeoisie and the relatively powerful proletariat. This gives the government a bonapartist character *sui generis*. It raises itself, so to speak, above classes. Actually, it can govern either by making itself the instrument of foreign capitalism and holding the proletariat in the chains of a police dictatorship, or by manoeuvring with the proletariat and even going so far as to make concessions to it, thus gaining a degree of independence

from foreign capitalists . . . . The present policy [of the Mexican govern-
ment] is an example of the second [type of alliance]; its greatest conquests
are the expropriation of the railroads and the oil industry.

The best Trotskyist interpretation of the Mexican Revolution is Adolfo
Gilly's *La revolucion interrumpida* (Mexico, 1971). Gilly wrote his book
while a prisoner in Lecumberri penitentiary in Mexico City; Fidel Castro
made the work required reading for the Central Committee of the Cuban
Communist Party. There are two premises underlying his complicated interpretation of the Revolution. First, under the *Porfiriato* (1876-1910) there
was a bourgeois political regime, and the bourgeois regimes of Madero, Huerta,
and Carranza (1911-20) were continuous with it. In 1855 the 'Revolution
of Ayutla' carried Benito Juárez and his Liberal Party to power, and according to Gilly this was the beginning of the bourgeois revolution. There was
a setback during the counter-revolution of the Conservatives, backed by the
French occupation and Maximilian. But the Civil War (1857-67) ended with
the Liberals back in power, with the triumph of the Reform. That was the
bourgeois political revolution. And so the political revolution of 1910-20
was neither bourgeois democratic nor bourgeois despotic.

Second, a bourgeois economic system emerged under the *Porfiriato*. This
capitalism followed on the heels of Juárez's liberal reforms. The landed oligarchy or 'old bourgeoisie' lacked capital for improvements, but it had to
begin modern methods of farming. In the countryside its new capitalist
system rested on wage labour and production for profit. (The ancient system
used bonded serfs to produce for the landlords' consumption.) So the Mexican
Revolution of 1910-20 did not result in a bourgeois social revolution, either
− that had already happened under the *Porfiriato*.

In common with other New Left interpretations, Gilly's two premises date
the bourgeois political and social revolutions before the Mexican Revolution.
They are the heralds of the Revolution, not its children.

From these premises Gilly advances two hypotheses about the character
of the Revolution. It was a *combined revolution*: an abortive peasant revolution combined with a petty-bourgeois political revolution in the form of a
bonapartist transitional regime. The bulk of the 'peasants' were rural proletarians, says Gilly, but their leaders were small freeholders, like Zapata, or
peons turned revolutionary generals. Gilly uses the term 'petty bourgeoisie'
not only for small, independent owners, but also for professional people
working for themselves, for students and the middle strata of salaried people
including soldiers, technicians, school teachers, office workers, and so-called
intellectuals. This class, he argued, seized political power from both the old
bourgeoisie and the rural proletariat. The petty bourgeoisie established an
intermediate regime that maintained itself by playing off the interests of
those two great classes against each other.

What is Gilly's second hypothesis? The Mexican Revolution is a *continuing
revolution*: though the old bourgeoisie was forever thrown out of political
power, the new bourgeoisie (enriched revolutionary generals) seeks to recoup

it. This new bourgeoisie writhes under the fetters of the peasant agrarian reform and the limits imposed by the nationalized sectors of the economy. At the same time, the masses tend to push forward radical demands of their own. The new political regime, argues Gilly, is intrinsically shaky. Repeated efforts to replace it with a despotic form of bourgeois rule have failed to undermine it, so it can only end in the triumph of a proletarian revolution. Hence the transitional nature of the bonapartist regime and the continuing (but interrupted) character of the Mexican Revolution.

In this perspective the Mexican Revolution has had two ascending phases. During the first phase (1910-20) the Revolution deprived the landed oligarchy or old bourgeoisie of political power, and it attacked that class's economic base with Articles 27 (agrarian reform) and 123 (workers' rights). During the second phase (1934-40) the Cárdenas regime enforced those articles and in addition undermined the economic power of the *new* bourgeoisie by nationalizing the dynamic sectors of the economy. Neither the old bourgeoisie nor the new bourgeoisie can replace the bonapartist state with a classical bourgeois regime of political parties. Such a classical regime would hurl the petty bourgeoisie from its perch above the great classes and reduce that upstart to its place, to its original role as a mere agent of the bourgeoisie.

Gilly's first hypothesis of a combined revolution develops out of the following claims. From the beginning, from Madero's *Plan de San Luis Potosí* in October 1910, the driving force of the Revolution was the peasantry. In the winter came the first armed actions under Pancho Villa; they echoed the trumpet call of the *Plan's* third article promising land to peasants robbed during the *Porfiriato*. To stop the peasant revolt from growing into a big revolution, says Gilly, Madero tried to negotiate a legal transfer of power from Díaz. In May 1911 negotiations resulted in the City of Juárez Accords: the dictator would step down for free elections, the peasants would lay down their arms, and the third article about agrarian reform would be forgotten. Villa co-operated in the North, but in the South Zapata was wary. In November 1911 he answered Madero's presidential election with the *Plan de Ayala*. It called for giving back stolen lands to peasants, named Madero a traitor to his own *Plan*, demanded his removal as President, and promised to continue the Revolution.

On a national scale the height of the peasant revolution came in December 1914: the victorious armies of Villa and Zapata occupied the capital. On a local scale, the height curved through 1915 while Carranza's forces sent Villa reeling North: *in Morelos Zapata was free to develop the first soviet-type government in the hemisphere*. In Zapata's own state, notes Gilly, the political power of the *hacendados* (or old bourgeoisie) temporarily disappeared before the people in arms. The old bourgeois state and police collapsed; people's militias replaced them. The Morelos Commune went beyond this political revolution, says Gilly, to launch an anti-capitalist social revolution: the sugar mills, the lands of the *hacendados*, and private enterprises were expropriated.

All this was in sharp contrast to the events in Mexico City. There Villa and Zapata installed a new national government, but the liberal and radical wings of the petty bourgeoisie staffed its posts. In the last analysis, Gilly argues, this was a government of the bourgeoisie, for it failed to carry out an anti-capitalist revolution, nor did it destroy the political apparatus of the bourgeois state. In brief, on a national scale an aborted peasant revolution issued in a successful petty-bourgeois political revolution: this cut down the economic power of the old bourgeoisie and helped create a new bourgeoisie out of the revolutionary generals in power.

Gilly's second hypothesis of a continuing revolution is developed in connection with the following theses. The peasant revolution (1911-19) occurred at the meeting point of the two world epochs: capitalism and socialism. It came too early to take a proletarian direction; it came too late for the bourgeoisie to stamp it out completely. During the Zapatista period the peasant revolution could have triumphed only under the leadership of the proletariat. The proletariat was unable to provide that leadership, so the peasants were defeated and succumbed to the bourgeoisie's co-optive efforts. The bourgeoisie made its concessions in Articles 27 and 123. At the same time, the bourgeoisie had to play second fiddle to the petty bourgeoisie, which ruled through a bonapartist transitional regime. After 1920, says Gilly, the Mexican political system combined the features of 19th century bonapartism with the bonapartism typical of today's underdeveloped capitalist countries. The earlier bonapartism balanced a timid indigenous bourgeoisie against a young proletariat exhausted by an abortive attempt to seize political power with peasant help. In contrast, today's bonapartism balances an aggressive imperialist bourgeoisie against an organized indigenous proletariat.

In 1920 the old bourgeois political regime, continuous with the *Porfiriato*, came to an end at last — the bourgeois *hacendados* had lost political power forever and were soon to be displaced economically as well. What took the place of the old regime? A presidential despotism, a bonapartist government of the petty bourgeoisie. From its own ranks the petty bourgeoisie generated a new bourgeoisie (enriched revolutionary generals and *nouveaux riches*), says Gilly, but the sons have yet to take the place of their fathers; the new sector of the bourgeoisie has yet to take state power. The bonapartist regime kept this new bourgeoisie from gaining control of the state, for the regime supported organized labour and peasant leagues fighting the return of the bourgeoisie to political power. That is why the regime still has a bonapartist character. The regime staggers onward and will some day receive a death blow not from the bourgeoisie, but from the proletariat.

What are we to say of Gilly's interpretation of the data? He underestimates the differences between the forms of compulsory labour during the *Porfiriato* and the forms of wage labour in modern capitalist production. He sees some differences between the traditional haciendas and modern agricultural enterprises, yet he wrongly identifies the *hacendados* of the *Porfiriato* with a sector of the old bourgeoisie. Gilly veers away from Marx. For the great economist distinguished the epoch of primitive capitalist accumulation from a later stage in which capitalism becomes the dominant mode of production, while Gilly telescopes these two stages into a single stage — the *Porfiriato*.

To support this claim he brings in two sets of evidence. First, he cites the colonization laws dictated during the *Porfiriato* These laws encouraged certain companies to survey a quarter of the national territory, supposedly untilled lands, occupied by free villages and Indian communities. The laws aimed to attract foreign settlers. The villagers and Indians would become peons on the settlers' new haciendas. The land companies, for their part in this programme, got a third of the soil surveyed; they took over one-twelfth of the national territory. The result? An operation of plunder, aimed at seizing communal lands and exploiting them with dependent labourers. The haciendas conjured up by the colonization laws, concludes Gilly, represented a backward form of capitalist penetration of the Mexican countryside.

What can we say of this evidence of Gilly's? He is partly right: this internal colonialism was Mexico's version of the enclosure laws in 16th century England that paved the way for the capitalist mode of production. But who can believe that in three decades Mexico finished what England took more than two hundred years to accomplish?

His other set of evidence is a statistical table at the end of chapter one, a table showing that imperialism is the factor explaining Mexico's dash through primitive accumulation into backward capitalism in the countryside. In 1910, of total capital only 4% was invested in agriculture, but of that fraction 96% was foreign owned. Of total capital, 17% was in mining, but 98% of that came from abroad. The *Porfiriato's* railway grid helped capitalist penetration of the interior. Of total capital, 40% was in railroads, and of that 28% belonged to foreign companies and another 34% to foreign capital invested in the state-owned railways, bringing foreign participation to 62%.

Gilly's data derive from a study by the Méxican economist, José Luis Ceceña. This study shows that (excluding agriculture, a tiny fraction of the total) 9% of investment was in the indigenous private sector, 14% in the public sector, and 77% in the foreign sector. Of the total capital invested in Mexico at the end of the *Porfiriato*, 44% was U.S. owned; most private Mexican capital was owned by local *hacendados*. The ratio of U.S. to private Mexican capital was about five to one. What does this mean? It shows that the Mexican contribution to an indigenous capitalism was practically nothing — a conclusion that wrecks Gilly's interpretation. It suggests that in the indigenous private sector, pre-capitalist and semi-feudal modes of sucking out the economic surplus held sway.

From Gilly's unproved and dubious premises we go on to the hypotheses based on them. First, was the Mexican Revolution a combined one? If we grant that it was, we must still ask: did the abortive peasant revolution result in a petty-bourgeois political revolution? Gilly's use of the term 'petty bourgeoisie' is a curious revision of Marx's. In it Gilly includes more than the old middle class of independent owners and people working for themselves; he sweeps under the term the new middle classes of salaried employees. In

Mexican history what happened in fact? With Obregón's coup in 1920 the revolutionary generals and political bureaucrats tightened their grip on the Mexican state; political power passed to a bureaucratic stratum (hardly a petty bourgeoisie in Marx's sense). So there was no petty-bourgeois revolution. Was there a bureaucratic revolution? Only if a bureaucratic stratum is a separate social class.

In Marx's model the political-military bureaucracy is not a social class: (1) it plays no role in the production of commodities, and (2) it owns no factor of production (like capital or land). But what about the bureaucracy of administrative and professional workers in industry drawing salaries? Marx includes such workers in the privileged, upper stratum of the proletariat.

There are inconsistencies in Marx. In his model, absentee landlords, though they produce nothing, belong to the landowning class; absentee capitalists, who are not entrepreneurs, are members of the bourgeoisie. Do they have any role in production? They are mere owners of a factor of production — land or capital. Unlike them the state bureaucrats do get into the act: they enforce the laws governing workers on the job. The machinery of the state performs a number of economic services, enforcing industrial discipline and making workers stick to labour contracts. Yet Marx does not think of the bureaucrats as a class.

Marx even makes mistakes. The state imposes industrial discipline and organization, but this hardly reduces to Marx's three factors of production (land, capital, labour). Economists as far apart as Alfred Marshall and Mikhail Bakunin see *organization* as a fourth factor of production. With land, capital, and manpower must go *organization*. It is the visible expression of administrative and professional expertise; it is more than a higher form of labour power measurable in either calories or standard man-or-woman-hours. What marks it off are professional skills valued for their uniqueness, not their common denominator.

There are other grounds for thinking of the bureaucracy as more than a stratum, reasons for seeing it as a separate class. The proletariat is an exploited class, but what about the bureaucracy? Administrative and professional workers share in power and enjoy a monopoly of highly specialized skills. They get nice salaries; they take goods and services equivalent, in terms of number of hours worked, to far more than what they give. Are professional and administrative workers in industry just a skilled stratum of the proletariat? We see that they are more than that. Here we must correct Marx, *for the bureaucracy is a class.*

This correction preserves the usefulness of Marx's model, and we can use it to rework Gilly's thesis. What came out of the abortive peasant revolution of 1910-20 was not a petty-bourgeois political revolution; it was a bureaucratic revolution. The abortive peasant revolution was combined with a bureaucratic political revolution.

But wasn't there also a bourgeois social revolution? Evidence cited by Gilly himself shows that the enforcement of Article 27 (agrarian reform), beginning with Obregón (1920) and stepped up by Cárdenas (1935), crippled the Mexican *hacendado* forever. About 45% of the land went to the *ejidos*. If we believe Gilly's own data, under Cárdenas the new bourgeoisie must have become the main indigenous beneficiary of the Mexican economy. As the *hacendados* collapsed, the bourgeoisie became the beneficiary of the surplus by default. What does this mean? The bourgeois social revolution did not occur under Díaz (in Gilly's view): the social revolution was a byproduct of Obregón's bureaucratic political coup (1920), which in turn followed Zapata's abortive peasant revolution. In sum: an abortive peasant revolution in combination with a bureaucratic political revolution paved the way for a bourgeois social revolution.

Gilly's second hypothesis implies that the Revolution did not come to an end in 1940, but was merely 'interrupted'. The longest continuous period in Mexican politics since the insurrectionary phase of 1910-20 covers the post-revolutionary years since 1940. Yet Gilly calls it an 'interruption'! His interpretation of the Revolution as proletarian and socialist from the start, and as being the work of Villa and Zapata rather than Obregón and Calles, is patently unrealistic. Gilly thinks that Cárdenas revived the socialist impetus of Zapata, but we agree with Córdova that the Cárdenas period was mainly a continuation of the policies of Obregón. Cárdenas' commitment to 'social-ist education' has to be seen within the broader perspective of his overall commitment to a third position between capitalism and socialism. During the bonapartist transitional regimes of Obregón and Calles (1920-34), the bureaucratic class generated from its ranks a new bourgeoisie that threatened to become the politically dominant class. But, contrary to Gilly, the bona-partist system came to an end under Cárdenas (1934-40), who nailed the political power of the bureaucracy to an institutional framework and made it permanent.

The resulting political system, says the Mexican sociologist Rodolfo Stavenhagen, is the present bureaucratic-corporatist state. Gilly is warranted (for the wrong reasons) in claiming that the Obregón-Calles period slowly dammed up the revolutionary current while the Cárdenas regime issued in a new revolutionary flow. But what was Cárdenas' main contribution? Not the strengthening of mass organizations, nor his nationalizing of the oil and railways. We think his great work was to firm up the political power of the bureaucratic class: under him it gained control over the mass organizations and used them to offset the rising power of the bourgeoisie.

Gilly's thesis of a continuing (if interrupted) revolution is mistaken, including the main actors. By 1940 the new bureaucratic class had succeeded on two fronts. Contrary to Gilly, it had fastened down its own political power and it had finally made a bourgeois social revolution. Under Alemán's sub-sequent presidency these two revolutions became institutionalized; after that they weren't going anywhere. What makes the Revolution a continuing one, Gilly thinks, is a bonapartist transitional regime; he thinks it can only end with the proletariat as the politically dominant class. But we have shown that Cárdenas ended the transitional regime in 1938, not by establishing workers' power, but by hardening the power of the bureaucracy.

True, the bureaucratic revolution remains incomplete: the politically dominant bureaucracy has yet to transfer to itself economic power through a bureaucratic social revolution. Such a revolution may be lurking off stage, waiting for the bourgeoisie to mismanage the private sector until it proves itself incompetent to serve national interests. So the bourgeoisie's day of ' judgment is yet to come. But does a bureaucratic social revolution have to be fed by the bureaucratic political revolution that preceded it? And does a socialist revolution in Mexico have to take the form of a proletarian state?

Our interpretation of the Mexican Revolution does not rule out a future workers' state. But we see the coming socialist order in the emergence of the bureaucracy as the economically privileged class. Although the proletariat with peasant support may force a social transformation, the bureaucracy is in a position to steal most of the benefits. However begun, the end product would be a bureaucratic social revolution, a new departure, not a continuation of the old Revolution of 1910-40.

By socialism we mean a society in which the State and self-managed collective enterprises are the main owners of the means of production, displacing the capitalists and landowners, who draw profit, interest, and rent from private ownership. In socialist society, the managerial, bureaucratic and party elite is a new ruling class like the class of capitalists under capitalism. Under socialism the basic division of classes is into bureaucrats and workers. Socialism is a mode of taking the bulk of the surplus through salaries — a comparatively innocent form — instead of through profit and rent. Under socialism the proportion of the new ruling class to the mass of ruled tends to be larger; the rate of economic advance is greater; and there are more scientists and engineers in the higher levels of party and government. These are the progressive features of socialism.

An Unfinished Bourgeois Political and Social Revolution
In a chapter of *La democracia en México* (Mexico City, 1965) Pablo González Casanova develops the main Old Left interpretation. He summarizes the traditional Marxist analysis. His summary agrees with the thesis of an unfinished bourgeois democratic revolution that is defended by Soviet historians M.S. Alperovich and B.T. Rudenko in *La revolución Mexicana de 1910-17 y la política de los Estados Unidos* (Mexico City, 1960). There is one important reason for considering González Casanova's interpretation: it coincides with the view of the established communist parties in Latin America, but their politics and strategy have not influenced the development of the thesis by the famous professor. In his hands it becomes an independent and scholarly argument.

Before the Revolution, Mexico was a semi-feudal and semi-colonial state — those ideas are basic to González Casanova's interpretation. During the 19th century and the first decade of the 20th, he claims, the dominant *hacendado* mode of production had little in common with capitalist farming in the United States. The Mexican system was more like the old feudal mode of production in Europe. The *hacendados* were more like feudal landowners than agrarian capitalists, while the hacienda peons resembled medieval serfs more than the modern wage labourers replacing them. Many features of the *Porfiriato* are still present in Mexico today: the foreign enclaves' sway over the private and public sectors has hardly changed since the Revolution; and there survives the system of internal colonialism (metropolitan centres exploiting backward sectors of the country).

From these premises González Casanova moves to the following hypotheses. First, the Mexican Revolution, under conditions of dependence on the foreign bourgeoisie, was *un unfinished bourgeois political and social revolution*. Second, the task of the Mexican working class is not the struggle for socialism but *the completion of the bourgeois national democratic revolution*. The working class must fight the anti-national role of foreign enclaves and the undemocratic survivals of internal colonialism. Pre-capitalist blocks on the internal market, the iron chains of imperialism, the dwarflike nature of indigenous business – all this means that the bourgeoisie needs more leverage. Since the bourgeois national democratic revolution is incomplete, the socialist revolution cannot begin. A revolution cannot skip stages when carrying an old society to the grave.

Professor Casanova's first hypothesis rests on several claims. He argues that the Constitution of 1917 was an instrument for the development of capitalism, the instrument of a budding bourgeoisie co-operating with organized workers and armed peasants against *hacendados* allied to foreign interests. González Casanova identifies this budding bourgeoisie with a petty bourgeoisie of small owners and government officials. Later, it developed into a bourgeoisie proper that replaced the *hacendados* as the main indigenous claimants to political and economic power. But this bourgeoisie did not break the stranglehold of foreign capitalists on the economy. Dependence on foreign capital and technology has held up the bourgeoisie's march toward wealth and power. Each step forward for the bourgeoisie, maintains the professor, was a step backward for native capitalism.

He sees many symptoms of this unfinished bourgeois revolution: the violation of the Constitution by bourgeois governments; the dictatorship of the ruling party; the despotic power of the President; federal intervention in state government; and the absence of internal democracy in the labour unions, in the peasant leagues, in the official party, and in the Mexican government. The Mexican political system is not democratic – it is despotic. A weak indigenous bourgeoisie, fearing division in its ranks, does not want a number of political parties; it prefers the single party. Political despotism results, but this is the bourgeoisie's best defence against the foreign monopolies. While imperialism grinds down the Mexican economy, claims González Casanova, bourgeois democracy will not flower: several political parties succeeding one another peacefully in power – that is a dream for the future.

Democracy, he thinks, is the logical form of government by the bourgeoisie, the form suited to its interests. What follows from that? Since the Mexican political system is not democratic, the country has not developed an independent bourgeoisie, has not developed a mature capitalism. Mexico is a pre-democratic country, he argues, so it must be pre-capitalist. What are the roots of its pre-capitalist structure? The country's economic dependence on imperialist nations, the internal colonialism woven into its relations of production — there lies the difficulty. No capitalist system has ever built democracy in its internal colonies, nor has Mexico done so.

The Mexican working class must struggle for the bourgeois national democratic revolution — that is González Casanova's second hypothesis. It rests on several claims. Mexico faces unfinished national tasks, like the fight against imperialism and the struggle against internal colonialism. As long as the country faces such tasks, he argues, class interests must fade before national interests. These national interests are in keeping with the development of Mexican capitalism. So the struggle for socialism must wait. Under Cárdenas, Mexico took its big step in fighting for national interests with a popular front including the national bourgeoisie; it wiped out the *hacendado* system, it took over the oil. But since 1940 the national bourgeoisie no longer desires a popular front: its economic fortunes are linked to foreign interests. A revival of the politics and strategy of an anti-imperialist front with the national bourgeoisie is a utopian project, our author concludes, because the class interest of the bourgeoisie no longer agrees with the national interest.

Then what is the answer? There is no reason to expect the national bourgeoisie to join the struggle for economic independence and internal democracy. But can some other fraction of the bourgeoisie take its place?

There is no longer a conflict of interest between the bourgeoisie serving the domestic and foreign markets, González Casanova concedes, but the bourgeoisie displays antagonisms between its public and private sectors. This finds political expression in the squabble between the ruling party (PRI) and the National Action Party (PAN). The public sector of the bourgeoisie, unlike the private sector, upholds national interests. The public sector sees that capitalist development and political democracy must come; this sector wants to sweep away the blocks on the nation's progress. The brakes on capitalism and democracy make the bourgeoisie as a whole seem incompetent. These fetters must vanish, or the bourgeoisie may lose its political and economic dominance. So the public sector struggles to curb the foreign monopolies, to limit the greed of private enterprise, and to democratize the political system.

What is the composition of this public bourgeoisie? Our author finds several components. Certain government bureaucrats, using their office to get rich, have become entrepreneurs on the side. Other bureaucrats are not exactly capitalists, but they have power and wealth: top men in government, managers of public enterprises, technocrats working for the state. Finally there is the so-called petty bourgeoisie or new middle class of government employees reaching down to school teachers in the countryside.

So González Casanova favours a popular front of the proletariat, peasantry, and public bourgeoisie aiming to complete Mexico's bourgeois political and social revolution. While bourgeois power is undeveloped, he says, the workers and peasants cannot have independent organizations able to fight the privileges of the bourgeoisie. In the struggle to complete national tasks, the bourgeoisie co-opts into its ranks the best among the oppressed; labour and peasant leaders rise in the official party to become part of the government. The completion of these tasks is the condition of a showdown between labour and capital. The unification of the proletariat as a class-for-itself depends on first finishing the build-up of bourgeois power, says our author, even though national unity tends to split the proletariat.

In the proletariat this split develops between opportunist and sectarian tendencies. Opportunism is the loss of organizational independence through an alliance with the more powerful bourgeoisie. And sectarianism? In preparing the conditions for a socialist revolution, this tendency gets into a premature fight with the bourgeoisie. Against both tendencies González Casanova favours a strategy of critical support for the public bourgeoisie. The proletariat and peasantry must build an alliance with this bourgeoisie, while maintaining their organizational independence and struggling for their own goals. Short of carrying out national tasks, short of finishing the bourgeois social and political revolutions, the opportunist/sectarian split cannot be healed. Fulfilling national tasks and completing the Mexican Revolution are conditions for the internal unity of the proletariat as well as the peasantry. And such unity is in turn a condition of a future socialist revolution.

Now we turn to criticism of González Casanova. The premises of his interpretation are sound, but his first hypothesis is false: the Mexican Revolution (politically considered) was neither bourgeois nor unfinished.

In his thesis of a bourgeois political revolution, he fails to see that the so-called public sector of the bourgeoisie is really a bureaucratic class. His concept of the public bourgeoisie reduces (for the most part) to a political-military bureaucracy. And so he provides support for our counter-thesis of a bureaucratic political revolution.

Second, his thesis of the unfinished character of the political revolution hinges on the claim that it was a bourgeois revolution. But the logical form of bourgeois rule, he correctly says, is democracy. The Mexican political system is not democratic, he concedes, but despotic. Thus he provides support for our view that the political revolution was not bourgeois at all. (It was bureaucratic.)

Third, his thesis of the unfinished character of the bourgeois social revolution assumes that in underdeveloped countries imperialism corresponds to a pre-capitalist stage. (Here González Casanova departs from Old Left interpretations. For Haya de la Torre, imperialism is the first stage of capitalism in Latin America; for Lenin, imperialism is the last stage.) For González Casanova what is unfinished in Mexico's bourgeois social revolution is the transfer of the bulk of the economic surplus from foreign monopolies to local businessmen. But that is a struggle inside the bourgeois class. In Marxist terms, a struggle internal to the bourgeoisie is not a revolutionary struggle, for a revolution means the transfer of political or economic power from one class to another. In fact, the social revolution in Mexico had already taken place: under Cárdenas (1934-40) the bulk of the economic surplus sucked out of Mexicans passed from the land-owning class to the local capitalists.

What is González Casanova's second hypothesis? The struggle for socialism is premature; the task of the Mexican left is to complete the bourgeois revolution. Ths idea, so irritating to revolutionary socialists, is based on the fallacy just mentioned. The imperialist bourgeoisie is not a class distinct from the native bourgeoisie. This means that a Mexican take-over of foreign enclaves does not transfer economic power from one class to another. Such a take-over is not the completion of a social revolution. What's more, in Mexico, beginning with Cárdenas, the struggle for democracy was not part of a pro-gramme to complete a bourgeois political revolution. Once Cárdenas had established the political power of the bureaucracy, the struggle for demo-cracy favoured an anti-capitalist revolution, a bureaucratic social revolution. What does such a revolution mean? Not state capitalism run by the 'public bourgeoisie', but a new socialist order – i.e. one similar to the post-capitalist social systems in the U.S.S.R., Eastern Europe, China, Vietnam, North Korea, and Cuba. (For doctrinaire Marxists this usage is evidently contro-versial.)

The struggle for democracy, we believe, is not premature; and Mexico is aching for a drive toward socialism. Just as the bureaucracy had to make the bourgeois social revolution for the bourgeoisie, so the Mexican working class will have to make the bureaucratic social revolution for the bureaucracy. Between 1920 and 1940 bourgeois and landowning interests interlocked – that discouraged the bourgeoisie from making its own social revolution. Today the interdependence of bourgeoisie and bureaucracy gives the bureau-crats a short-run interest in defending Mexican capitalism. But in Mexico the struggle for socialism is not premature. That struggle goes along with the real interests of the bureaucracy as the politically dominant class.

Elitist Interpretations

Now we turn to the non- Marxist interpretations of the Mexican Revolution. Their most significant contributions also rest on a model of social conflict, but their analysis involves a distinction between political and economic elites – not socio-economic classes. Next to the Marxists, the successors to the Italian school of theoretical *realpolitik* have contributed most to under-standing the political forces of the Mexican Revolution and the development of post-revolutionary society. This school works from the tradition founded by Vilfredo Pareto, Gaetano Mosca, and Robert Michels. A Paretan or elitist model need not rival, but may actually supplement, a Marxist interpretation. The élitists have a different conceptual framework. But we translate their conclusions into Marxist categories and find they support our own judgment of the Revolution. A new bureaucratic élite, they argue, was the political beneficiary of the social order arising from the Revolution. Their analysis converges on ours.

Frank Brandenburg's *The Making of Modern Mexico* (1964) was the first elitist interpretation to make a splash in the sea of works about the Revolution. After his seminal work came Roger Hansen's *The Politics of Mexican Development* (1971) and Albert Meister's *Le Systeme Mexicain* (1971) – both rely on Brandenburg's concept of the 'Revolutionary Family'. From now on we refer to these three interpretations as the Brandenburg model, for they have an intellectual common denominator.

The elitist presuppositions of this model show the indirect influence of Harold Lasswell's *Politics: Who Gets What, When, How?* (1936) and C. Wright Mills' *The Power Elite* (1956). Brandenburg focuses on the question 'Who rules Mexico?' Hansen looks into the question 'Who gets what, when and how?' – an obvious reference to Lasswell's work. Meister's identification of the political elite with a 'power elite' is a bow to C. Wright Mills. Of our three writers, only Brandenburg worried about the whole Revolution from beginning to end. Hansen and Meister worked on special problems and focused on the period after 1940. But in their studies they also threw out interpretations of the Mexican Revolution and its background in the earlier *Porfiriato* period.

It is more than curious that Mexican and Latin American interpretations of the Revolution are mainly Marxist in character, while elitist analyses are chiefly the work of North Americans and West Europeans. But one influential Mexican writer, Manuel Moreno Sánchez, implicitly follows an elitist interpretation. The main political contest in post-revolutionary Mexico, he argues in *Crisis política de Mexico* (1970), is a conflict between a political-economic oligarchy and the so-called middle classes. Today three groups make up this oligarchy: the top political bureaucrats in the ruling party and government; the managers of state industries; and the principal capitalists in industry, agriculture, commerce, and finance – they are the most influential group. Under the *Porfiriato* landowning interests held sway, says Moreno, and land (not capital) was the mark of wealth. But with the Revolution the new political-economic oligarchy replaced these old interests.

Moreno is implicitly committed, in Marxist terms, to the thesis of a bourgeois social revolution coming after the armed struggle of 1910-17. The bourgeoisie, he argues, became the main economic beneficiary of the Revolution, but it did this through the patronage of a military-bureaucratic political elite. (In other words, the bourgeoisie's economic triumph was the result of a bureaucratic political revolution.) Only after World War II (1939-1945), he holds, did the bourgeoisie get control of the ruling party and government. How did this happen? The spoils of office formed many bureaucrats into a new state bourgeoisie.

Moreno's theses share common ground with the Brandenburg model, and his interpretation of the Mexican oligarchy suggests the elitist thesis of a symbiotic relationship between the political and economic elites. But his concept of the new oligarchy comes from a Latin American tradition of political analysis, not from the North American and West European sociological tradition based on the idea of a political elite. So we don't include Moreno as a representative of the Paretan model.

What are the basic features of the Brandenburg model? First, its supporters share assumptions about the old order overthrown by the Revolution. They agree among themselves that the economic order of the *Porfiriato* was a semi-feudal system, with debt peonage or virtual serfdom, dominated by the interests of the *hacendados*. Except for Hansen, our elitists agree that under the *Porfiriato* the traditional *hacendados*, not the bourgeois *científicos*, held political power. Second, our authors agree that from the armed struggle (1910-17) and Cárdenas' reforms (1934-40) came a capitalist agro-industrial order. (In Marxist terms that means a bourgeois social revolution.) Third, they agree that during the first stage of the Revolution, during its praetorian phase (1920-46), a new political order replaced the old one, a new order run by a military-political elite. (This is our thesis of a bureaucratic political revolution.) Fourth, they agree with one another that, as this bureaucratic political revolution matured under Cárdenas, there was an abortive effort to follow the 'socialist' path of development. Such a development would have made the new bureaucratic elite the main economic beneficiary of the system.

Finally, our authors agree that during the second stage of the Revolution, during its institutionalized phase beginning with President Alemán (1946) and the rebuilding of the ruling party (1947), the bureaucratic elite had to share more and more political power with the new capitalist economic elite. All three writers point to a symbiosis of the political and economic elites. Except for Meister, they agree that after 1947 business interests prevailed, that the party's top bureaucrats used the spoils of office to become capitalists in their own right. If the worker, peasant, and popular sectors of the ruling party had really run the government, argue Brandenburg and Hansen, then Mexico would have become a workers' state. It did not become a workers' state. Why not? Because the worker, peasant, and popular sectors did not control the political elite — businessmen got control of it. This is like saying in classical Marxist terms that a bourgeois political revolution knocked off a bonapartist transitional regime. We would say, in our new terms, that a bureaucratic political revolution succumbed to a bourgeois political counterrevolution.

What are we to think of the Brandenburg model? The *Porfiriato* was feudal; the Revolution against it resulted in a bureaucratic political revolution; there was a capitalist transformation of the economy between 1920 and 1940 — these three theses match our judgments of the Marxist interpretations of the Mexican Revolution. But doubt arises concerning the fourth and fifth theses.

Cárdenas, claims the fourth thesis, unsuccessfully tried to drive Mexico down the socialist path of development. That the great populist chose the socialist road seems exaggerated to a Marxist. But our authors may be using the term 'socialist' in a non-Marxist sense. They probably follow Durkheim's usage: for him socialism meant ending hands-off-the-economy policies in government; it meant state controls on production and distribution. Translated into Marxist language, such a 'socialist' period in Mexico's development is the founding of a state-directed capitalism. In Marxist terms, Cárdenas did not try to launch a socialist economy; he aimed at a mixed economy balancing the public and private sectors. But the mixed economy he created gave way to a capitalist (basically private) economic order. How could he have kept the balance? Only through a strategy of progressive nationalization, for the private sector grew fast after 1940. But, by then, moderate presidents had replaced Cárdenas, nor would he have known what to do in their place.

The fifth thesis claims that big business has secretly captured the Mexican government. Here our sociologists move into marshy terrain: speculation about what goes on behind locked doors in smoke-filled rooms. On this shaky ground Meister is more careful than the others; he argues for a symbiotic relationship between the political and economic elites that keeps each from enjoying an advantage. But his I'm-betting-on-both-horses approach dodges the question of who rules the country. It is more likely that one elite or the other actually rules. Without more evidence (examined in the next chapter) we cannot say who commanded the ruling party and government after Cárdenas, the bourgeoisie or the bureaucracy.

Bureaucratic rule prevailed during the praetorian period ending in the early 1940s. What about the period beginning with President Alemán in 1946? At most, Brandenburg's evidence suggests that businessmen increased their voice in the inner councils of the ruling party and government. But the elitists go beyond the facts into speculation: after Cárdenas, they claim, the Mexican political system became (in Marxist terms) mainly bourgeois.

The limitations of the elitist model spring from its conceptual apparatus. The concept of a political elite lacks an economic dimension. A Marxist framework, with its concept of a politically dominant or *ruling class,* contains the economic dimension. This concept gives more information and correlates more variables than Brandenburg's *elite.* That is why the class concept brings less confusion.

Brandenburg and Hansen confused two concepts: the 'political elite' and the 'Revolutionary Family'. There are three tiers in the pyramidal 'Family'. Brandenburg's research is supposed to show the following. Since 1952 the 'Family's' top inner-council contains 20 favourite sons, with the family head having the final say. In this group are the President, past presidents, the presidential candidate, prominent cabinet members, and the top national and regional leaders of the ruling party. Below this top level is an intermediate council containing two hundred 'relatives', on the fringes of power because of intimacy with the family head. In this group are the big shots from private industry, agriculture, commerce, and finance; spokespersons from the opposition parties, the press, and educational, religious, professional, and social organizations; leaders from labour unions, farming co-operatives, and civil service federations; and people from the ruling party, government ministries, public industries, federal agencies, state governments, and the armed forces.

Finally, there is a bottom layer of the 'Family' containing the huge political machine: this includes the ruling party and government bureaucracy at national, state, and local levels. This third tier has no say in choosing the President and governors. While the inner circle of the 'Family' commands the decision-making process, this third tier is made up of hangers-on who sniff power but never taste it. Why does Brandenburg include them in the political elite? This bottom layer does not rule Mexico. Brandenburg's and Hansen's own arguments show that the third tier has no active share in political authority. They have confused the 'Revolutionary Family' with the 'governing elite'.

Their model also fails to distinguish the main components of the political elite, though our authors see differences between narrow group and professional interests. Brandenburg draws for us a body with many fleeting faces that look alike, except for two ideological colours: there is a difference between the revolutionary left (*Cardenismo*) and the revolutionary right (*Alemanismo*), between the partisans of 'socialist' (a misnomer) and capitalist solutions for Mexico's economic problems. Behind these ideological differences, we believe, lurk class differences within the political elite. Originally this elite contained only political, labour, and military representatives of a bureaucratic class. But some top bureaucrats have used their office to get rich, they have become a new state bourgeoisie; the bulk of their income comes from investment they have made in the private sector. So here is a reasonable hypothesis: capitalist millionaires have surfaced inside the 'Family's' inner circle, and that explains the nation's drift to the right after 1940.

The elitist model fails to distinguish the principal components of the economic elite (beyond its breakdown into captains of industry, agriculture, commerce, and banking). Our authors leave us to guess what antagonisms may exist inside this elite, and of course, never explain them. But we find conflicts of interest between three sectors of the economic elite: (1) the managers of public industries who make up the economic part of the state bureaucracy; (2) the state bourgeoisie of new capitalists risen from the political or economic bureaucracy; and (3) the traditional bourgeoisie in the private sector. The interest of the traditional bourgeoisie is to build up the private sector and force the public sector into a corner. The state bureaucracy, in contrast, gains more by strengthening the public sector through progressive nationalization. This is also what the bureaucracy itself believes, according to the research by Raymond Vernon in his *The Dilemma of Mexico's Development* (pp. 127,137,149). And the state bourgeoisie? It has a foot in both camps: though its main income comes from the private sector, it wants balanced economic growth that keeps autonomy for each sector. So any big shift in the balance between the sectors finds its explanation in shifting class interests inside the economic elite.

The Outcome of the Revolution?

How are we to explain the outcome of the Mexican Revolution of 1910-40? We are left with two hypotheses, both seemingly plausible. First hypothesis: it was a bureaucratic political revolution betrayed; political and economic power finally passed to the bourgeoisie. Second hypothesis: it was a successful bureaucratic political revolution that brought on a bourgeois social revolution; after that the bureaucracy shifted from its alliances with the proletariat and peasantry to an alliance with the bourgeoisie. Both hypotheses see the first phase of the post-insurrectionary period (1920-34) as a bureaucratic political revolution, with the military-political bureaucracy ruling through an alliance with workers and peasants. Both hypotheses agree that under Cárdenas (1934-40) the bureaucratic political revolution hardened into a neo-corporatist party and state that smashed the economic power of the landlords while the bourgeoisie picked up the pieces — a bourgeois social revolution by default. But our two hypotheses disagree about what happened after Cárdenas stepped down in 1940.

After 1940, claim both hypotheses, the ruling party's inner circle slipped more and more under the influence of ex-bureaucrats, who had turned into capitalist millionaires. But the two hypotheses disagree about the extent of that influence. Have the capitalists taken over or not? (The first hypothesis says, Yes; the second, No.) There is no direct way we can discover the membership of the inner circle. Nor can we figure out the precise ratio of new capitalists to political, military, and labour bureaucrats. In the top and intermediate echelons of the party, the bureaucrats far outnumber members of the state bourgeoisie. But these bourgeois may have great power. The past presidents, powerful figures within the 'Revolutionary Family', were more often bourgeois (businessmen) at the end of their terms of office. Within the party the sheer weight of the bureaucratic elements is offset by the privileged role of these past presidents.

It is a complex task to choose between the two hypotheses and there may be others we have to consider. More evidence is needed. We look for that evidence in an examination of the post-revolutionary period.

5. The Post-revolutionary Regimes

Today the Mexican President is the most powerful elected official in the world. No system of checks and balances curbed his increasing power over the years, and he grew into a despot.

In the nations of North America and Western Europe, both a lawmaking body and a high court rise beside the executive to check his power. But in Mexico the President appoints the cabinet as he pleases; he names state governors, members of Congress, and justices of the Supreme Court. Behind the fiction of Mexican democracy hides the fact of presidential despotism. How does *el presidente* do it?

Presidential Despotism

He is the real head of the government's Institutional Revolutionary Party (PRI). As first chief he picks his candidates for government posts throughout Mexico, then has the PRI's mass organizations whip up support among workers, peasants, and the middle classes. If this doesn't elect all the President's men, the ruling party can resort to fraud. To keep up appearances the party encourages token opposition.

Since the organization of the first government party in 1929 Mexico has chafed under one-party rule. The party is controlled by the government, and the government is under the President's thumb.

The Mexican President is an elective dictator with power that must turn kings an envious green. All the powers of government together cannot match his strength. He appoints his own successor; he can get rid of elected officials at any level; he interprets the Constitution by enforcing it as he wills. He can direct the Army and police to arrest, torture or kill political enemies.

The law is no barrier to his personal ambition. His office is a racketeer's dream, but the golden opportunity only lasts six years, and he must line his pockets while he can. He often does so. At least half of the six presidents since 1940 took office as bureaucrats living off their salary, but retired as multi-millionaires. Those who used their office to rise into the ranks of the big bourgeoisie were Miguel Alemán (1946-52), Díaz Ordáz (1964-70), and Luis Echeverría (1970-76).

Mexican politics at the top shows everyone down the ladder the way to work — the President leads, the rest follow. Corruption is rife. Corrupt bureaucrats translate presidential despotism into a version all their own, no less hateful for its pettiness. Citizens must bribe them to do their jobs. Police use the law to exact their 'bite', and enforce the law to their personal advantage.

Mexico has one of the most socially advanced systems of law in the world. The Constitution, a document written in six weeks by revolutionaries, could lead directly to socialism. But the Mexican political system interferes with its enforcement.

Mexico has never been a democracy. The State leans over citizens' organizations like a powerful father watching every move: it keeps independent groups from defending their economic and political interests. The State claims to defend those interests and sometimes does so. But the people don't decide about the matters that concern them. And when large numbers of people swing into motion, some government purpose is usually prodding them along.

The Mexican political system is authoritarian, and this encourages the highhanded use of power. Over the forest of governmental bureaucracy towers the presidency like a giant sequoia. The presidency with all its branches is the one institution that the Revolution strengthened. The rest were changed or swept away.

Several critics have likened government after the Revolution to the despotic regime of the 19th century. There is the old *Porfiriato*, we are told, and there is the *neo-Porfiriato* based on a new historic bloc of classes. The old and the new differ in substance, but are similar in form.

The new substance underlies the despotic presidentialism of the revolutionary and post-revolutionary regimes. The hammer of the President's power pounded into shape a new political system. Early in the revolutionary period running from 1910 to 1940, the old bloc in power fell apart and a new one emerged. The bourgeois *científicos* allied to foreign capital and to the semi-feudal *hacendados* disappeared from the scene. The question still not settled is: Who took their place?

During the revolutionary regimes from Obregón through Calles to Cárdenas (1920-40), presidential despotism briefly served the Mexican people. But today we live in the post-revolutionary period (1940-80), and growing numbers of Mexicans are disturbed by the direction of their government. Patriots and nationalists, intellectuals and students, reformers and communists — all want Mexico back on a revolutionary path.

Can the Mexican Revolution revive? Or has the post-revolutionary interruption broken its momentum forever? In Mexico City the political cafes ring with debate.

Can progressives transform society a second time by using the President's despotic powers and the PRI government? Or must the revolutionary struggle overthrow both? These are the questions dividing the Mexican left today.

To answer them we examine the political anatomy of the post-revolutionary situation. We dissect the muscles of the Mexican political system to reveal the heart of presidential despotism.

Social scientists have turned powerful lamps of analysis upon the period after 1940, but they don't agree among themselves. Glaring differences of interpretation light up the successive presidential regimes in harsh colours.

Manuel Ávila Camacho's presidency ran from 1940 to 1946 with Cárdenas as defence minister after 1941. Some historians paint his administration as an extension of Cárdenas' work. Ávila Camacho continued in Cárdenas' wake, we are told, flying the ship of state with support from the left wing of the Revolutionary Family. Others find his regime evenly balanced on both wings, gliding along the 'revolutionary centre'.

Most writers see Miguel Alemán (1946-52) making the party's right wing the force of the government. But while some interpret this shift as a political counter-revolution by the Mexican bourgeoisie, others see it as a change in the bloc of classes in power. This change, we are told, broadened the revolutionary alliance to include the bourgeoisie.

Some say that Adolfo Ruiz Cortines (1952-58) followed the path of Alemán, but a broad current of opinion identifies his administration with the revolutionary 'centrism' kept up by the next three presidents.

Adolfo López Mateos (1958-64) is interpreted as a president in the revolutionary tradition, sometimes as slightly left of centre, at other times as a centrist. The centrist school nicknamed him Belly Button, because he was neither to the left nor to the right — and good for nothing! A few interpreters even place López Mateos on the right, a link in the counter-revolution begun by Alemán.

His successor, Gustavo Díaz Ordáz (1964-70), has also called forth contradictory descriptions as a representative of the counter-revolution and as a centrist president.

Finally, many-faced Luís Echeverría (1970-76) is seen variously as a revolutionary nationalist, a centrist in the tradition of Ruiz Cortines, and a counter-revolutionary demagogue throwing sops to the left.

A shortcoming of these interpretations of the post-revolutionary presidencies is their failure to analyse the character of the Mexican ruling class. Because these interpretations fail to penetrate the surface of Mexican political life, they tell us little about the social classes competing for economic and political power. So we pass over these interpretations and focus instead on structural theses about post-revolutionary Mexico (1940-76).

Interpretations of the Post-revolutionary State

Four major theses deserve attention. Each is based on a prior analysis of the revolutionary period. But we have already weighed in the balance the principal interpretations of the Revolution of 1910-40, so there are strong reasons for rejecting those theses that are built on weak foundations. Nevertheless, we must consider them for the light they shed on the post-revolutionary situation.

The first thesis is that the bourgeoisie *consolidated* its political power after 1940. (This presupposes that the Revolution of 1910-40 was basically bourgeois, a hypothesis we have come to reject.) The second thesis is that the bourgeoisie acquired political power after 1940, which agrees with our assessment that this class did not become politically dominant prior to World War II. The third thesis is that the political power of the state bureaucracy has steadily *eroded* since 1940. (In agreement with our own account of the earlier period, this presupposes that the bureaucrats already had political hegemony.) The fourth thesis is that the state bureaucracy *consolidated* its authority after 1940, so that it is now more firmly entrenched in power than before.

The first and second theses agree that the ruling party is forever ruined as a force for revolution by three decades of wrongdoing since 1940: killing peasants, smashing strikes, massacring students, stealing funds, taking bribes, and faking elections. Bourgeois interests have infiltrated and captured the ruling party, and this robs the bureaucracy of its independence — if it ever had any. The Mexican Revolution of 1920 to 1940 has run into a dead end. There is no way out or around or through, and the Revolutionary Family must give way to a new democratic and socialist revolution.

The third and fourth theses have not given up on the ruling PRI, provided that the workers organize independently and follow their own economic and political interests. Bourgeois interests have infiltrated the PRI but have yet to capture it. They may never take it over. Meanwhile, it is open to pressure from below. The Mexican Revolution has not come to a dead end; it is only sidetracked. The Revolution may still return to its course: a bureaucratic transition to socialism through a policy of progressive nationalization and gradual restrictions on private and foreign capital.

Now we must look underneath each thesis for its foundation in argument.

The Consolidation of Bourgeois Power
The first thesis is supported by the Mexican Communist Party (PCM) and sectors of the Mexican New Left grouped around Alonso Aguilar and his publishing house Nuestro Tiempo. They differ concerning the dating of the bourgeoisie's emergence as the dominant political force, so there is also disagreement about the beginning of bourgeois consolidation. For the PCM the consolidation of bourgeois political power begins only after World War II, while the Aguilar group traces it back to the start of the post-insurrectionary period in 1920. For both groups it was completed during the post-revolutionary epoch.

The Communist Party's Analysis: The PCM's analysis of the post-revolutionary era occurs in the second, third, and fourth parts of the New Party Programme adopted at its 16th Congress in October 1973. Beginning in the early 1940s, we are told, the monopolies emerge gradually and take over the national economy. During the Revolution of 1910-17 the triumph of the independent bourgeoisie and bourgeoisified landlords over the revolutionary forces paved the way for this later triumph of the monopoly bourgeoisie. In the 1930s the state sector became the decisive lever of the bourgeoisie for pushing its economic interests, until by World War II capitalism was already the dominant mode of production in Mexico. The spread of capitalism throughout the economy helped the bourgeoisie to consolidate its political power during the post-revolutionary era.

Big monopolies emerged. Did they win out in a competitive struggle with independent capitalists, pushing aside entrepreneurs who dawdled over three-hour business lunches in Mexico City? Not at all, argues the PCM, for the chic cafes along the Paseo de la Reforma were filled with businessmen every afternoon, big ones as well as little ones. No, big monopolies emerged because they were subsidized through the accumulated capital of the Mexican state.

Something unusual happened in Mexico. The stronger the public sector became, the less it served the public interest. The public power, the PCM maintains, strengthened the private sector in many ways: tariff walls, tax concessions, guaranteed markets, assured credits, cheap energy, low railway tariffs, and government-controlled unions.

What did this government favouritism toward the bourgeoisie bring about? A growing financial oligarchy tied to U.S. imperialism. This oligarchy gradually began to influence the group in political power. In the beginning the oligarchy did not govern directly. But since World War II the political bureaucracy has been responsive to it instead of as formerly, to independent local businessmen.

What was the relationship of this powerful fraction of the bourgeoisie, the Big Money, to the state bureaucracy? The PCM thinks that the relationship was instrumental. This means, we are told, that the Big Money dominated the economy but did not run the government. The bureaucracy governed under the domination of the big bourgeoisie until by 1970 the Big Money began to share directly in the government.

The communist programme describes the Revolution of 1910-17 as bourgeois-democratic, but maintains that bourgeois democracy has never arisen in Mexico. In the Revolution the under-classes surged up toward democratic goals, and these aims were written down in the Constitution of 1917. But they never hardened into institutional forms, for the Constitution has yet to be applied.

The outcome of the Mexican Revolution was not bourgeois democracy, but a system that made the state an all-powerful 'Father'. The control board of this paternalistic system stands in front of the presidential chair. The victory of presidential despotism! That was the meaning of the bourgeois-landlord triumph over the revolutionary-democratic forces in 1917. The presidency became an instrument of the bourgeoisie for fattening itself as a class and building its own dictatorship.

The post-revolutionary period of ascendancy by monopoly capital, we are told, has now come to an end. It has ended in the monopolies' triumph. For 30 years there was an uneasy balance between the monopoly sector on the one hand and the competitive sector on the other. But by the 1970s this equilibrium had vanished. What wrecked it? The steady penetration and growth of foreign capital, its fusion with Mexican finance capital, its spread throughout the national economy.

This spreading cancer strangles the competitive sector of small and medium private business. The bureaucracy could not defend this sector and so lost its support; now the bureaucracy is defenceless against rising pressures from the financial oligarchy allied to multinational corporations. The monopolies, warns the communist programme, are pushing for direct control of the state machine. The birth of a new socio-economic system is taking place in Mexico: monopoly capitalism brings forth *state monopoly capitalism*.

With the crisis in the economy comes a political crisis. The political ideology of the Revolution is breaking down; every year fewer people believe in it. The system of presidential despotism is spluttering along on three cylinders. Its authoritarianism and paternalism are not working, for the Mexican people no longer see the President as a god among men. The shadow of his authority no longer awes the masses, so he holds down their organizations with violence. Since the terrible massacre of October 1968, when the government unleashed the Army against peaceful demonstrators in the capital, the long confrontation between the PRI government and the Mexican people grinds on and on — a sharpening political crisis.

For the combined political and economic crisis, we are told, two solutions are at hand. One is the move to a higher stage of imperialist dependency, to state monopoly capitalism. The other is the solution offered by the Communist Party — a new democratic and socialist revolution.

The evidence cited by the Party for the structural crisis in the economy falls under five headings: first, the penetration of foreign capital brings denationalization of the economy; second, monopolies smother small businesses to centralize capital in ever fewer hands; third, hurricanes of inflation and devaluation hit some parts of the country harder than others; fourth, while investment drops and growth slows, one recession follows on the heels of another; fifth, as the maldistribution of income worsens, the rich grow richer and the poor poorer: the swelling numbers of unemployed have nothing to lose but their chains.

Hand in hand with these events march the facts of the political crisis. The ruling classes cannot control growing popular resistance. New forms of opposition from independent groupings in the worker, peasant and middle sectors escape the vertical controls of government organizations. The government's answer? Increasing violence to hold down the masses.

The communist programme does not tell us when this disintegration set in, but other Party documents do. The Political Resolution approved by the 16th Congress traces the political crisis back to the rise of popular resistance in 1968. What is the basis of the sharpening political crisis? A structural crisis that infected the economy about the same time.

A New Left Analysis: Alonso Aguilar and Nuestro Tiempo: Part of the New Left grouped around Alonso Aguilar, his journal *Estrategia*, and the publishing house Nuestro Tiempo accepts the basic ideas in the analysis given above. *Only the dating is different*. The Aguilar group traces the beginning of state monopoly capitalism back to the end of the 1940s and the beginning of the 1950s — to the presidency of Miguel Alemán. And the Aguilar group pushes the transitional phase to monopoly capitalism back to the opening of the century.

Aguilar's best statement of this thesis appears in a book he wrote with Jorge Carrión, *La burguesía, la oligarquía, y el estado*. In the first part Carrión says that in the Revolution of 1910-17 the forces of Madero, Carranza, and Obregón got the upper hand. Who were they? A revolutionary sector of the bourgeoisie kept out of the bloc in power under Porfirio Díaz. This power bloc under Díaz was led by the financial bourgeoisie or *científicos* linked to foreign interests. Capitalism had already filled out most of the Mexican economy: the Revolution against Díaz was nationalist and anti-imperialist, but not anti-feudal. This idea clashes with the PCM's analysis of the Mexican Revolution and of the period before it.

After the 1910-17 Revolution the new middle and small bourgeoisie directly ruled the country, says Carrión, but it soon lost its nationalism as the world capitalist market loomed up around it like a giant stockade. In a chapter on 'The Dominant Class Dominated' Carrión argues that many of the reforms pushed through by the revolutionary government between 1920 and 1940 paved the road to power for the oligarchic sector of the bourgeoisie. In Mexico's system of dependent capitalism the dominant bourgeoisie must suffer domination. Domination by the political bureaucracy? No, by the imperialist bourgeoisie.

Carrión traces the main influence on the federal government and the ruling party after 1940 to the organizations of the bourgeoisie: the National Confederation of Popular Organizations (CNOP), the National Confederation of Industrial Chambers (CONCAMIN), and the National Confederation of Chambers of Commerce (CONCANACO). But the bourgeoisie itself must listen to the harsh voices of the International Monetary Fund and the multinational corporations. Although nationalism survives as the ideology of bureaucratic sectors in the government, Carrión concludes, they never had much clout in the Mexican political system.

Aguilar takes up the argument for the period after World War II when state capitalism supposedly gave way to state monopoly capitalism. In the chapter 'The State and the Oligarchy' he develops his thesis. In Mexico the capitalist mode of production expanded over the economy under the *Porfiriato* and the *científicos*; the decisive role in this drama was played by foreign capital. In the Mexican Revolution of 1910-17 the national bourgeoisie hurled from power the pro-imperialist bourgeoisie, then beginning with Obregón in 1920 capitalism took on the new form of *state capitalism*. Was this a mixed economy, a public sector thriving beside a private sector? No, the public sector had to serve the private, and Mexico became a capitalist society from top to bottom.

What reasons does Aguilar give for dating the switch to state monopoly capitalism at the end of the 1940s rather than at the close of the 1960s? The world depression of the 1930s sent the Mexican State into the private sector to nationalize several of its main branches. World War II created conditions for a rapid concentration of capital and the long range economic development of Mexico. The State took advantage of the War and became a motor of economic growth. After the War the State was permanently cast in this role, while the monopolies demanded that regulation continue. More and more contacts between the monopoly sector and the State machine taught them to live and work together — structural cohesion emerged. The onset of the Cold War and the penetration of U.S. capital set the stage for the structural integration of the State with monopoly capitalism: the structure stretched to take in the foreign-based multinationals.

With the explosive growth of capitalism under the *Porfiriato*, Aguilar sums up, the Mexican bourgeoisie came to command the economy. It also captured the government. But later, during the period of state capitalism the bourgeoisie's manner of governing was indirect. Then with the triumph of state monopoly capitalism the bourgeoisie moved from influential manoeuvres outside the government to manipulation from within.

The public sector embraces about 2,000,00 employees, but at the top of the bureaucratic pyramid are 9 or 10,000 who are part of the bourgeoisie. They are almost bourgeois. This controlling nucleus, Aguilar maintains, is made up of owners of securities, real estate, and means of production. Whether their ownership of these means of production is direct or indirect, it lets them bite into the surplus thrown up by the working class. Aguilar does not argue that these bureaucrats are bourgeois because they get the bulk of their income in the form of profit, interest, dividends, and rent. For him it is enough that they receive part of their income in that manner.

There is more evidence to back up his thesis. It is reasonable to suppose that of the 10,000 top bureaucrats only 500 are really influential; these would be the best paid, able to change themselves from professional bureaucrats into capitalists. Aguilar cites a long list of names to show the increasing role in recent years of well-known capitalists in public office.

Unfortunately for his thesis, these state bourgeois do not have the upper hand in the cabinet. It is mainly after stepping down from the highest offices to become governors, senators, or ambassadors that big bureaucrats pile up enough to draw *the bulk of their incomes from business instead of government.*

The Bourgeois Conquest of the State
We now turn to the second thesis listed at the beginning of the chapter. We may call it the thesis of bourgeois ascendancy. Whatever may be said of the period from Obregón through Calles to Cárdenas, it was not the bourgeoisie that wielded political power; governmental power rested in the hands of an independent state bureaucracy.

For this thesis it doesn't matter whether we call these administrations bonapartist, populist, or bureaucratic. What does matter are the developments after 1940: the bourgeoisie seized control of the state and turned it away from a socialist direction.

This was a giant step backward. It was a counter-revolution, for a bourgeois government is a less advanced political form than the bureaucratic regimes of the 1920-40 period. Bourgeois rule can never break out of the boundaries of capitalism while bureaucratic rule, whether of the bonapartist-military or civilian-populist type, is widely recognized by Marxists as a transitional form with the potential of moving in a socialist direction.

On the Mexican left two groups champion the thesis of emerging bourgeois ascendancy. The first is the Mexican Workers' Party (PMT). The second includes the editorial board of *Punto Crítico*, a widely read magazine of political commentary.

The Analysis of the Mexican Workers' Party: The President of the Mexican Workers' Party, Heberto Castillo, has set out his views of the post-revolutionary epoch in two books. Castillo, who took part in the popular demonstrations ending in the Tlatelolco massacre of 2 October 1968, was tried and sent to Lecumberri penitentiary. *Libertad Bajo Protesta* (1973) covers the trial leading to his imprisonment. Then he wrote *Por qué un Nuevo Partido*? (1975) with Francisco Paoli, the Party's secretary for cultural relations. This book gives the Party's position on the political situation in Mexico: it despairs of change and renewal coming from within the ruling party.

In the Introduction to the first work Castillo argues that the Popular Student Movement (MEP) of 1968 was the national answer to 28 years of growing repression against the people of Mexico. Beginning with Ávila Camacho in 1940, each of the presidential regimes smashed the successive struggles of miners, petroleum workers, telephonists, electricians, railwaymen, teachers, medical personnel, and students. The future organizational secretary of the PMT, Demetrio Vallejo, suffered a cruel imprisonment of eleven and a half years for leading the Great Railroad Strike of 1958-59. In response to this government repression, the students demanded 'Freedom for Political Prisoners!' This slogan pointed up the popular orientation of the student movement.

Castillo seems to reject the pendulum theory of presidential regimes since 1940. According to this theory current among North American analysts and others sympathetic to the ruling PRI, the post-revolutionary presidencies have swung back and forth between two poles: the Cardenist left wing and the Alemanist right wing of the ruling party. Ruiz Cortines supposedly stood for the party's centrist forces; these gave way to a centre-left coalition under López Mateos; and this in turn to a centre-right grouping headed by Díaz Ordáz; and that to another centre-left formation under Echeverría. Castíllo, in contrast, focuses on the common denominator of police repression and knuckling under to bourgeois interest during all these regimes — that is his merit. From this standpoint the ruling party's right wing has been in the saddle ever since 1946.

The evidence piled up behind this thesis is too long to cite. Giving more leeway to foreign capital, the organization of agricultural monopolies, stopping credit for the co-operative sector, government slowdown in land reform, growing political corruption, the Army breaking strikes and demonstrations, the murder of peasant leaders like Rubén Jaramillo, the jailing of labour leaders, open control of trade unions and peasant leagues — all that and more make up the list.

In the second chapter of *Por qué un Nuevo Partido?*, Castillo argues that the Cárdenas period, compared to the other presidential regimes, belongs in a class by itself. Cárdenas' Party of the Mexican Revolution (PRM) encouraged the labouring and peasant classes to take part in politics. And so it parted company with both the PRI that came after it as the ruling party, and the PNR that went before. Cárdenas limited the powers of the local bosses and tried to democratize the ruling party. While Obregón and Calles based their power on taming the Army and co-opting the local bosses, Cárdenas looked for support from the people's mass organizations.

Castillo lists the reasons why the transformation of the ruling party by boring from within is a hopeless task. In chapter eight he says that the government camarillas have an overriding purpose: to help the leader up the ladder of power so that the members of his team can also win promotion.

The Mexican political system defends interests both inside and outside the ruling party. In first place outside are the interests of the bourgeoisie, tied ever tighter to the multinationals. And efforts to change the system from within rarely get beyond official statements: these declarations, not backed by actions, in fact confuse the masses.

Does this revolutionary demagogy help to change the system? No, it keeps the system going. Efforts to change the government from inside mean an unspoken alliance with the people's oppressors, an agreement to work within the rules of the game. What is this but a surrender of popular power to control from above? It means giving up freedom to criticize the government.

Those who want to change the government from within, pleads Castillo, should ask themselves, 'Who can enter the government and by what means?' The answer is clear: only a few professional people and workers' and peasants' leaders can enter. To do so they must join a camarilla and serve someone whose powers do not come from the people. Usually entering the government ends in the co-option of reformers with the promise of money and privilege. If not, it forces them to soften their criticism and suspend the class struggle to stay in office.

In brief, the Mexican political system is not an instrument of the poor but of the rich. There is no way to swing it to the service of the Mexican people.

The Analysis of Punto Crítico: This analysis of the PMT is shared by *Punto Crítico,* whose principal founders quit the PCM in 1967. In the summer of 1973 its editorial committee organized a seminar for studying the present correlation of social forces in Mexico. The committee invited comrades from other revolutionary publications to take part and presented the thesis of a bourgeois counter-revolution in Mexico as a topic for debate. This thesis later saw print in 'Notas para el estudio de la coyuntura mexicana' in a section entitled 'Perspectivas Políticas' (August 1973).

Since 1940, the editors argue, the developing capitalist system has allowed sectors of the bourgeoisie to participate in political decision-making. Before 1940 the State soared high above the main social classes, but now the financial oligarchy has pulled it down and tied it to the apron-strings of the big bourgeoisie. This bourgeoisie has seized the political initiative and bends national decisions to its interest. The state bureaucracy has surrendered its political independence to the bourgeoisie, but without breaking up the ruling party. Unlike most Latin American countries, in Mexico the fusion of big capital with the state bureaucracy took place without a military coup.

Was the agent of this transformation the bourgeoisie's own instrument, the National Action Party (PAN)? No, the great change was carried through by the political apparatus of the majoritarian populist party itself.

The result: the ruling party has watched its popular support slowly crumble away. It turns to government violence and buying off union leaders — to gangster methods. So part of the proof for a bourgeoisie counter-revolution is the rising anger of the masses against the ruling party and government.

The Erosion of Bureaucratic Power

We turn next to the third interpretation of the post-revolutionary period, and baptize it the thesis of bureaucratic erosion. Support for it comes from a diversity of interests. Vicente Lombardo Toledano's Popular Party (PP) was the first to articulate it, and his thesis has since been reaffirmed by the recently established Socialist Workers' Party (PST). Rafael Galván, the leader of Mexico's independent trade union movement, has also given it his support. And it has been further reaffirmed by a number of prominent journalists and professional people independently committed to a revo-lutionary nationalist perspective.

The Popular Party's Analysis Reaffirmed by the Socialist Workers' Party: In 1948 Toledano organized the PP to block the inroads of the local bourgeoisie and U.S. imperialism on the government and public sector. In 1955 he argued Miguel Alemán's presidency marked the end of military bureaucracy and the start of rule by the 'burcaucratic bourgeoisie'.

We agree the power of the military and civil bureaucracies and the state eroded. The 'bureaucratic bourgeoisie' (i.e. public functionaries and union bureaucrats) had used official posts to enrich itself and join the bourgeoisie. Though performing bureaucrat functions, they were not in the bureaucratic class once business provided their main income. But the term 'bureaucratic bourgeoisie' is misleading: it suggests bureaucrats have become bourgeois both by becoming capitalists, and by drawing high salaries. That is not our usage. Our term 'state bourgeoisie' is for those who live mainly off their investments though they go on holding public office. They are bourgeois in Marx's sense, not in the sense of being simply rich.

By 1958 the PP had reached an understanding with the ruling PRI since in its view the world correllation of forces had shifted to the left and this meant in Mexico that the bureaucracy and government could be recaptured from the state bourgeoisie by the popular forces. In 1960 the PP renamed itself the Socialist Popular Party (PPS) and abandoned its original thesis of an erosion of bureaucratic powers. Its new analysis was: the PRI government has returned to the revolutionary path of national liberation from U.S. imperialism and the local bourgeoisie. The role of the PPS was to push the government further to the left, to encourage it to follow a socialist course.

Ironically, this meant a sharp turn to the right for the PPS, winding up in its currying favour with the government party. Suddenly Mexico was without an independent Marxist party in the revolutionary nationalist current. (The Mexican Communist Party still followed the Soviet line.) The PRI had turned to the right after World War II, and now the PPS was following it. In 1968 the PPS ruined itself with the Mexican left by publicly defending the government's massacre of at least 300 demonstrators on October 2. In answer to this government violence, urban and rural guerrillas appeared, and the PPS denounced them for 'objectively' serving imperialism and its internal allies, for unknowingly working with agents of the United States' Central Intelligence Agency. The need for a Marxist party to fill the vacuum left by the retreating PPS was obvious to many on the Mexican left.

Out of the political crisis of 1968 emerged an organ aimed at filling this political vacuum, the National Committee of Investigation and Organization (CNAO). This Committee finally brought forth new mass parties: the Mexican Workers' Party (PMT) and the Socialist Workers' Party (PST). The PMT, we have seen, took up a position between the Communist Party of Mexico and the old Popular Party. And so it was the PST, a little further to the right of all these, that finally filled the void. A national assembly in July 1973 set up the machinery for building the new party; it officially launched the Party on May Day 1975.

The PST's judgment of the Mexican political system is even tougher on the PRI government than was the old PP's own analysis. The fundamental enemy is still imperialism and its internal ally, the big bourgeoisie. But instead of dating the PRI's return to revolutionary nationalism with the presidency of López Mateos (1958), the PST dates it from the inauguration of President Echeverría twelve years laters in 1970.

In the resolution on the national situation adopted at the 7th plenum of its Central Committee in September 1976, the PST attacks the government's 'national unity' strategy since World War II for representing bourgeois interests; it also criticizes the new sector of the PRI in power. What does the PST want? It calls for a Revolutionary Popular Alliance favouring the interests of the working class through development of the public sector.

The Democratic Tendency in the Labour Movement: Rafael Galván's Analysis: Sectors of organized labour also defend this thesis of an erosion but partial recovery of bureaucratic power. The most important of these groups is the independent trade union movement led by Rafael Galván, general secretary from 1960 to 1972 of the Federation of Electrical Workers of the Mexican Republic (STERM). The STERM's journal *Solidaridad* became the focus of the resistance movement within the trade unions until it stopped publishing at the end of 1972. STERM was the big mouthpiece of revolutionary nationalism in the labour movement until it merged in 1972 with the National Federation of Electrical Workers belonging to the government controlled CTM. Then it organized a new movement, the Democratic Tendency within the new union. This movement has two basic aims: to expand nationalized industry as a step toward freeing the workers from imperialism and its local allies; and to democratize the trade unions in an effort to replace the union bureaucracy which has sold out to the government.

In a historic document, 'The Declaration of Guadalajara' (5 April 1975), Galván's Democratic Tendency within the new United Federation of Electrical Workers of the Mexican Republic (SUTERM) presented its analysis of the Mexican political situation. Since 1940 the Mexican Revolution has been sidetracked from its course of progressive nationalization of big local and foreign businesses. For three decades the 'developmentalist deviation' of the governing circles has handed over the national patrimony to imperialism and the big bourgeoisie. During this period special interests inside and outside the government plundered and looted the revolutionary national State. The result? 'Thirty years of counter-revolution.'

But this counter-revolution has yet to undermine the State, for the nationalized sector belonging to the State shapes the basic structure of the economy. Inside the government and ruling party are people who see the need to swing Mexico back to revolutionary nationalism. Echeverría, we are told, is a champion of this change.

This means that it is still possible to work within the Mexican political system. It is not the system that is rotten, but the government's unholy alliance with imperialism and the big bourgeoisie. The corrupt politicians, the labour bureaucracy, and the managers of state owned enterprises make up a new privileged elite. Together they plunder the working class, the peasant co-operatives, and the state sector.

Here we have the thesis of an erosion of the independent power of the State and the state bureaucracy: only a mobilization of the workers can stop it. For this kind of thinking a new revolution is hardly necessary; it is enough to revive the old one.

Supporting Arguments: Another version of this thesis claims that the erosion of bureaucratic powers has not been interrupted but is continuing. For this view, President Echeverría's administration marks a return to the revolutionary nationalism of the Cárdenas period *in words only*. Echeverría, we are warned, has carried on the policies of the presidents before him. Here there are three works to look at: Gastón García Cantú's *Politica Mexicana* (1974), a collection of articles published in the Mexican daily *Excelsior*; Mario Huacuja's and José Woldenberg's *Estado y lucha política en el México actual* (1976); and Juan Felipe Leal's *México: Estado, Burocracia y Sindicatos* (1976).

The term 'counter-revolution' for the post-revolutionary regimes beginning in 1940 is used by García Cantú in his article 'Constitucion ó Capitalismo' (3 September 1971). In a section on 'The Counter-Revolution' he lists the reactionary measures of the administrations of Ávila Camacho and Miguel Alemán.

He holds Ávila Camacho responsible for the following acts against the Mexican people. The massacre of the workers in the war materials co-operative went unpunished. His government shed the blood of students at the Politécnico. He allowed the pell-mell accumulation of capital in the private sector to whittle down the role of the public sector and the co-operatives. Agricultural production was turned away from the home market and aimed at export. Ávila Camacho ignored the laws for strengthening popular education. He gave in to the bourgeoisie, and this encouraged it to co-operate with U.S. interests and to spread anti-nationalism and anti-communism.

During the administration of Miguel Alemán the counter-revolution gathered force and has gripped the nation ever since. Alemán, seeing the McCarthy Era inquisition in the U.S. under President Truman — the investigation of 'security risks', the Hiss and Rosenberg cases, the purging of Communists from union leadership — launched his own petty version of the Cold War. He ruined trade union democracy. He hunted down peasant leaders. He put the government into debt to subsidize the projects of private capital. He organized a network of political spies. He made Mexican diplomacy kowtow to U.S. interests. He developed exports instead of the home market. He started a counter-reform that favoured capitalism in agriculture against the semi-communal *ejidos*. His programme led to the inevitable strengthening of the local bourgeoisie and of foreign participation in the economy.

The replacement of Cárdenas' Party of the Mexican Revolution (PRM) by Alemán's Institutional Revolutionary Party (PRI) meant more than a re-organization of the government party. It was also a change of programme, a point underlined in García Cantú's article 'El Programa del PRI' (27 October 1972). Still, the 'counter-revolution' did not triumph over the Mexican Revolution; it only surged up as a tendency undermining Cárdenas' reforms. Although the bourgeosie captured economic power after 1940, the PRI has yet to surrender political power.

In the opening chapter of *Estado y lucha política en el México actual*, Huacuja and Woldenberg assign tremendous importance to Articles 27 and 123 of the Constitution. These authors argue that the articles gave great authority to the political bureaucracy. The bureaucracy, not the bourgeoisie, holds the political power in Mexico.

What is the state bureaucracy? It is not a class, we are told, but a stratum with no economic interests of its own. The Constitution gives this stratum nearly unlimited authority over private property. The legislative and judicial powers of government are sucked up by the executive branch, and this branch is the final arbiter in the class struggle between labour and capital. This 'State of exception' — as the Mexicans call it — allows the bureaucracy to play off the interests of one class against another. That is how the bureaucracy keeps for itself the lion's share of political power.

Beginning in 1940 and moving ever more boldly, the respresentatives of finance capital have pressured the government to meet their demands. The authors note how the fusion of industrial and banking capital turned the financial oligarchy into the most powerful group in the bourgeoisie. This fraction of the bourgeoisie grew strong enough to challenge the independence of the governing bureaucracy. Meanwhile the popular basis of bureaucratic power was crumbling away. The popular forces, faced with government sell-outs to the monopolies and official violence against workers and peasants, turned from the State with aversion. This resulted in an erosion of the political power of the bureaucracy. Though the ruling party hangs onto the decision-making power, the financial sector of the bourgeoisie is taking it over bit by bit.

In *México: Estado, Burocracia y Sindicatos*, Leal backs up this thesis with more arguments. Since 1940 popular support for the governments of Mexico has slowly withered, he claims, while the political influence of the bourgeoisie has grown, budded, and bloomed. This leads to Leal's judgement of the post-revolutionary situation: the period since 1940 has stamped a question mark on the bureaucracy's claim to political hegemony, a question mark that grows larger with every passing year.

Leal compares the situation of the bureaucracy before and after 1940. Before this date it built its power on the weakness of both the bourgeoisie and the proletariat. The petty bourgeoisie backed it against big business; the peasants supported it because of agrarian reform. All this changed after the War. The bourgeoisie is no longer weak, and the ongoing fusion of finance capital and the state machine has cut down the independence of the bureaucracy. The petty-bourgeois and small capitalists, calling to the government in vain, are pushed to the wall by big business. That makes problems for the President, the chief umpire in the class struggle. To stay on top of the heap, the government bureaucracy now needs a pact with labour to revive mass support. This means more plums for the trade union bureaucracy, and that runs counter to the interests of finance capital, whose ability to move political levers is now greater than ever. Isn't the outcome obvious? Mounting headaches for the bureaucracy and an erosion of its political power.

The destruction of the liberal-oligarchic state in 1914, Leal continues, paved the way for a new type of state. This is the 'Boss State'. In chapter three he shows that the pre-revolutionary State was the instrument of a power bloc led by the *científicos* and semi-feudal *hacendados*. The new revolutionary State pushed both these classes from political power. Under the thumb of the political-military bureaucracy directing the Revolution, a new political coalition emerged comprising the national bourgeoisie, petty bourgeoisie, proletariat, and peasantry.

What is Leal's 'Boss State'? In this state the military-political bureaucracy arbitrates the conflicting interests of the classes in the new political coalition. The State is a semi-corporative mechanism: the social classes are organized in state controlled associations representing their interests. The class struggle no longer works itself out in the free play of independent associations of capitalists and workers, nor do the parties backed by these classes compete freely in the political arena. In political matters the government keeps the upper hand, and mainly represents the bureaucracy's interests. Marx's term for this exceptional state was 'bonapartism'.

Leal's point is that in Mexico from 1915 to 1940 the bonapartist state was progressive, but after 1940 regressive. Before 1940 the popular forces could advance their interests with the help of the military-political bureaucracy against the *científicos* and *hacendados*, against the forces of imperialism and feudalism. But after 1940 the bourgeois part of the new political coalition feasted at the government table while the popular forces looked for crumbs underneath. The power of the state kept growing, but even more so did the economic and political strength of the bourgeoisie. The overall result? Not the consolidation of the bureaucracy's political power, but its erosion.

The Consolidation of Bureaucratic Power

We now turn to the fourth interpretation of post-revolutionary Mexico mentioned at the beginning of the chapter. This is the thesis of bureaucratic consolidation, associated in the minds of Mexicans with the Socialist Popular Party (PPS). But it is also the thesis of an important segment of the Mexican left which still looks to the ruling PRI for leverage in moving the country toward socialism. Manuel López Gallo and his publishing house El Caballito are among the most articulate representatives of this group.

The Analysis of the Socialist Popular Party: The Socialist Popular Party (PPS), founded in 1960 you remember, was Lombardo Toledano's Popular Party (PP), baptized with a new name and given a new programme. But the word 'socialist' in its name and the Party's acceptance of Marxism-Leninism did not mean a move to the left. Instead, the reorganized Party ended by making its peace with the government; it has supported the PRI's presidential candidates ever since.

In the new programme adopted at its Third National Assembly in October 1960, the PPS gave its analysis of the Mexican political situation. The world correlation of forces no longer favoured imperialism. There had arisen the possibility of a Mexican road to socialism based on the public sector. Mexico was at a crossroads: either it must follow the capitalist road of the indigenous bourgeoisie allied to foreign capital, or it must take the non-capitalist road of spreading the public sector over the rest of the economy. The Party chose this second road in the struggle for economic independence, a people's democracy, and a redistribution of wealth.

In spite of official corruption and the role of the state bourgeoisie, the PPS argued, the democratic forces were regaining lost positions inside and outside the government. During the presidency of López Mateos (1958-64) the state sector so expanded that it became a match for the private sector. López Mateos reformed the electoral law by establishing 'party deputies'. This constitutional reform stopped short of the PPS's own demands for proportional representation, yet the Party was able to seat ten members in the 46th Congress. So the Party maintained that the initiative had passed from the state bourgeoisie to the country's popular forces.

This brought, we are told, a return to the goals of the Revolution and an increase in the state bureaucracy's power of manoeuvre. The government was once more answering the call of the masses. What did this mean? At the expense of the state bourgeoisie (bureaucrats who became capitalists) there was a consolidation of the power of the state bureaucracy (non-capitalist bureaucrats).

A Revised Marxist Analysis — Manuel López Gallo and el Caballito: This thesis is also favoured by that part of the Mexican left whose principal outlet is Manuel López Gallo's publishing house El Caballito. This house, by the way, is also a major publisher of works supporting the thesis of bureaucratic erosion!

López Gallo publishes the quarterly *Coyoacán*. This review takes a new look at Trotsky's legacy and aims at unifying the Mexican left around both socialist and nationalist objectives. Adolfo Gilly, author of *La revolución interrumpida* (1971), is the journal's editor. The thesis of bureaucratic consolidation is not a monopoly of the opportunists in the PPS.

In his *Economía y Política en la Historia de México* (1968), López Gallo argues that only since Alemán's administration has the President of Mexico become *uncontainable.* True, an aggressive local bourgeoisie allied to imperialism has cropped up; true, these two forces have become the economic beneficiaries of the post-revolutionary regimes. And yet, claims López Gallo, the powerful framework of the government, entwined with the sinews of bureaucracy and headed by the king-like President, has developed enormous political muscle. Although the capitalist and imperialist sectors are stronger than ever, so are the powers of the central political bureaucracy. What evidence does López Gallo give for this claim?

During the 1930s a President could still be removed before finishing his term; cabinets were often reshuffled or replaced. But since 1940 the President has become untouchable, and his ministers have entrenched themselves in power. There are no more rebellious generals like Cedillo or even Almazán, and the *caciques* have followed the *caudillos* into the album of historical curiosities.

The struggle for the presidential succession has lost its fire and spit. The campaign struggle begins in the year before the swearing in of a new President. To wage his electoral campaign Ávila Camacho resigned public office as early as January. But Alemán did not begin his campaign until June, and Ruiz Cortines waited until October to resign his cabinet post. López Mateos and Díaz Ordáz dawdled until November before launching their campaigns: why bother to start early when the winner's name was already known?

López Gallo points out that talented and ambitious elites can climb the ladder of success in government or business. Such safety valves take the steam out of the opposition, while co-option of leftist leaders weakens their party organizations. Several leading members of the Communist Party during Cárdenas' administration today hold important government posts. How, then, can a serious rival to the PRI emerge?

Mexico's elections run on a winner-take-all system, and everyone knows who the winner is going to be. Parties of the right and left join hands to push for a system of proportional representation, but the PRI has blocked these efforts. López Gallo rejoices over this oppositional failure, for he thinks that proportional representation would favour the right. Here is his argument:

the potentially revolutionary classes are politically illiterate, and large numbers of Mexicans get their politics from the pulpit or swallow the nonsense on radio and television. How would a Mexico with proportional representation have voted on the Cuban issue before the meeting of the Organization of American States? God only knows. But in Mexico *He* would have hardly favoured Fidel Castro. Says López Gallo: 'Thanks to the Revolution and its political instrument the PRI, our nation is not completely in the hands of reaction.'

The so-called political crisis expressed in the 1968 student massacre, he goes on, was not a crisis of the despotic powers of the presidency, but a failure of one president's leadership. Díaz Ordáz and his advisers bungled matters. Several times they could have reached an agreement with the student opposition: release of political prisoners jailed since the Great Railroad Strike of 1959, for example, would have calmed the roaring crowds.

Though Echeverría faced a similar problem on 10 June 1971, his lieutenants bungled the job, not he. So he tossed them out of key positions in the ruling party and government. Unlike the crisis of 1968, López Gallo concludes, the 1971 crisis was handled in a statesmanlike manner.

Supporting Arguments: We do not share López Gallo's provocative thesis of bureaucratic consolidation, but we think it an interesting hypothesis. For the sake of argument we will back up this thesis with some evidence of our own.

The government violence of 1968 helped launch the first urban guerrillas in Mexico, and this violence reached a climax in the middle of Echeverría's administration (1970-76). But then there was a decline in armed actions against the government which fell off sharply in 1975 and petered out in 1976. Echeverría made concessions that consolidated the bureaucracy's power.

The discovery of vast oil reserves off the Yucatan peninsula has strengthened the state sector against the local private sector. Although the state oil monopoly will continue depending on the technology and marketing services of the multinational corporations, the public sector now has a significant edge over local capitalists. The dependency of the Mexican bourgeois on the government oil monopoly should increase. The state bureaucracy now holds a trump card if private domestic capital forces its hand.

The consolidation of political power in the PRI goes on. This is clear from the election statistics of 1976 compared to the figures for the presidential elections of 1970 and 1964. In 1964 before the 'political crisis', 60 % of the *registered electorate* voted for the PRI. In 1970 the rage caused by the student massacre dropped this figure to 50%. But in 1976 it was up again to 60%. So in the 1970s Echeverría's strategy of dialogue and sops to the people regained the prestige lost by the PRI in the 1968 repression. This is a measure of the PRI's continuing strength.

Another measure is the percentage of the *total electorate* (registered and unregistered) voting for the ruling party during the past three presidential elections. In 1964 about 49% of the registered and unregistered electorate voted for the PRI. Despite the 'political crisis' beginning in 1968 this figure rose to 50% in 1970. In 1976 it jumped to 56%.

Of course the number of people who refused to vote also increased from 7.5 million in 1964 to 9 million in 1970 to almost 11 million in 1976. This raises the question: Which has increased more – the number who voted for the PRI or the number who stayed home? In fact the proportion of those who voted for the PRI to those who stayed at home has increased. It has increased consistently. Some sectors of the left point to the fact of increasing abstentions but clam up about the growing number who vote for the PRI. That is the fallacy of special pleading.

Most of the Mexican parties on the left have a semi-legal status, but the Socialist Popular Party (PPS) is legal: it can run candidates in the elections. Though subsidized by the government, the Party has a Marxist-Leninist outlook. If left-wing opposition to the PRI were on the rise, we might expect an increase in the vote for the PPS. But in successive elections the votes for it have fallen off.

Nearly everyone on the left claims that, in Mexico, election statistics are meaningless. Electoral fraud and strong-arm tactics are fairly common; during the late 1960s fraud probably grew. There were serious violations of electoral laws in Sonora (1967), Baja California (1968), and Yucatán (1969) – states where the right-wing National Action Party (PAN) claimed victory. The vote for the PAN was surely much larger than government released figures show. But the victim of electoral fraud was the right-wing PAN rather than the left-wing PPS. Is the PRI then stealing votes from the left?

The PRI's only serious rival for political power has been the bourgeois and restorationist PAN. A glance at the figures shows the PAN's growing strength.

Year	Votes for PAN in general elections
1946	68,000
1952	280,000
1958	700,000
1964	1,000,000
1970	2,000,000

In 25 years the PAN jacked up its representation of the active electorate from 3 to 14 %. What happens if we measure the popularity of the ruling party against its main opposition, the PAN? We see a decline in the PRI's popularity.

Is the PAN a threat to the PRI? In the 1976 elections the PAN split between traditional conservatives and new-line Christian Democrats who tried to take over the Party: it could not run a presidential candidate, and internal wounds bled away its strength. The PRI is once more without a serious rival.

Assessment

We have now considered all four of the interpretations of post-revolutionary Mexico outlined at the beginning of this discussion. These theses contradict one another; they cannot all be true. Let us decide between them.

Consider the first hypothesis, the thesis of bourgeois consolidation. It takes two forms: in the strong version the bourgeoisie seized political power before the Revolution of 1910-17, but in the weak version the bourgeoisie took power after the Revolution. The strong version claims that the bourgeoisie consolidated its power during a period of *state capitalism* between 1920 and 1940, while the weaker version says it did this during an epoch of *monopoly capitalism* from 1950 to 1970. We think that the strong version is really a weakling laid out on a shaky bed of evidence.

In our diagnosis of the Mexican Revolution we distinguished the state bourgeoisie from a state bureaucracy of well-paid salaried functionaries. Our diagnosis of the post-revolutionary period also relies on this distinction. Although there are no published figures on the incomes of the 'Revolutionary Family' and the sources of those incomes, by using our conceptual distinction we can reason about the nature of the 'Family'.

We must identify within the 'Family' the state bourgeoisie and the state bureaucracy. Those who belong to the state bourgeoisie draw the *bulk* of their income in the form of interest, dividends, profits, and rent — most of their money springs from capital investments. But state bureaucrats get the *biggest* part of their income through gains from public offices: selling privileges to the rich, bribes to do or not to do their duty, dipping into the honey pot of public funds. Salaries, however, are their main source of revenue.

Now we have to decide just how rich a state bureaucrat can become and still remain a bureaucrat. Remember the old Hegelian principle of the transition from quantity to quality? If you get enough of something it finally becomes not just more of the same thing, but something else entirely. And that's the way it is with state bureaucrats in our conceptual framework: if they manage to pile up enough wealth, one morning they wake up to find themselves transformed into state bourgeois.

Here is the criterion: using as our index the pre-devalued peso of 1976 at 12.50 pesos to the U.S. dollar, we say that a state bureaucrat can become a millionaire in office and still remain a bureaucrat. He must pile up much more than a million pesos to turn into a state bourgeois. Why is this so?

Let us consider that great public servant, Sr. Fulano de Tal (the anonymous 'Mr. Smith'), who owns assets of 2 million pesos, and we will see that even he has not made it into the state bourgeoisie. Let us say that his house in the federal capital, with the furniture thrown in, has a market value of 1 million pesos. And then there is *'La Chingada'* — his weekend *quinta* in Cuernavaca, modestly valued at 450,000 pesos. His used automobile has a market value of 50,000 pesos. The remaining half-a-million is invested capital yielding, let us say, a maximum return of 15%. And his income from public office, to use Aguilar's own estimates in a footnote to chapter three of *La burguesía, la oligarquía y el Estado*, will reach 'as high as 50 thousand pesos monthly'. That comes to an annual salary of 600,000 pesos. So his total capital of 500,000 pesos is less than his annual salary. Even if the rate of interest were 100%, Sr. Fulano would not qualify as a member of the state bourgeoisie. He could not live off his meagre rents in the style he has learned to love.

What threshold must ambitious old Fulano finally cross to enter the other class? Let us suppose that his assets are 5 million pesos. His total capital, we may say, is then 3,500,000 pesos. At 15% the annual yield of this capital will be 525,000 pesos. Our would-be state bourgeois is still just a bureaucrat! He will have to earn another 75,000 pesos from an extra capital of half a million pesos to reach the threshold of bourgeoisdom. To be sure of qualifying he must have assets of at least 6 million pesos.

The big question is this: How many members of the 'Revolutionary Family' had amassed assets before 1976 of 6 million pesos or more? And what was the proportion of these multi-millionaires to the other members of the 'Revolutionary Family'?

Again let us look at Aguilar's data designed to prove a bourgeoisie in power. He offers two lists of the multi-millionaires within the 'Revolutionary Family'. The first, covering the years from 1920 to 1946, runs through 25 names: Obregón, Calles, Torreblanca, Pani, Saenz, Portes Gil, Rodríguez, Cruz, Manzo, Platt, Amaro, León, Almazán, Alesio Robles, Soto Reyes, Ávila Camacho, Maximino Camacho, Eduardo Suárez, Ortiz Garza, Xavier Gaxiola, Ezequiel Padilla, Marte Gómez, Véjar Vázquez, Evaristo Araiza, and León Salinas. But these new bourgeois had to become millionaires before becoming multi-millionaires. That took time so that only toward the end of this period, precisely under Ávila Camacho, was it likely that all reached this pinnacle. Since Camacho's administration belongs to the post-revolutionary period, Aguilar's first list is evidence at best for bourgeois supremacy after 1940.

The second list, covering the period after World War II, is more ambitious. Here we have the names of 30 multi-millionaires in office during the presidency of Miguel Alemán alone. Aguilar claims that this list grew longer during every following administration, but he offers no evidence. His data for the 1946-52 period is all the evidence he gives for his thesis. But this period, the most corrupt in Mexican history, is well described by the *políticos'* slogan: 'Alemán led and we followed'. The extent of corruption under him staggered even the Mexican imagination.

What do Aguilar's figures actually prove about Alemán's administration? Within the circle of the top 100 bureaucrats, the state bourgeois could not have prevailed. For the state bourgeoisie to get the upper hand, the 'Revolutionary Family' at the top must have contained less than 60 people. But it surely embraced more than that. Let us see why.

Aguilar's ideas about the size of the 'Revolutionary Family' come from his judgment of the political importance of the family's different sectors. In 1972 he says that, at the top of the bureaucratic pyramid, there were probably between 6,000 and 10,000 people. For the presidency of Miguel Alemán twenty years earlier we should take the smaller of these two figures. But within this group of 6,000 probably no more than 600 had 'significant influence' inside the state machine. And within this privileged group again, says Aguilar, perhaps no more than 100 to 200 in the entire nation held the key positions in the President's inner circle.

For the sake of argument let us suppose that Aguilar's 30 multi-millionaires of the 1946-52 administration *all* belonged to this privileged circle. *State bureaucrats would still have outnumbered them three to one.*

The proportion of state bureaucrats to state bourgeois in the president's inner circle is only one possible index. Consider another: the cabinets during the last three presidencies from López Mateos to Echeverría. It is clear that professional bureaucrats far outnumbered the state bourgeois. This still holds for the present cabinet under López Portillo.

We think that our arguments deal mortal blows to the thesis of bourgeois consolidation. But don't they also crush the second thesis of bourgeois ascendancy? The state bourgeois were outnumbered more than three to one under Alemán in the most corrupt regime of the post-revolutionary period. So even this classic example fails to prove bourgeois ascendancy: the bourgeoisie has yet to dominate the government from within.

Do they control it from outside? Not in the Mexican one-party system in which the PRI operates as a kind of mafia, permitting only nominal opposition from the PAN, a mere shadow of a real bourgeois party. Mexico is not the United Kingdom, where a Labour Party government surely does not imply that the bourgeoisie is no longer the dominant class politically. The substance of 'rule' is a function of personnel or formal office-holders, as in Mexico, only where these are independent of other classes. Only if the PAN were to become a strong bourgeois party, in turn backed by the dominant role of the bourgeoisie in economic life, would business interests in Mexico be in a position to determine the substance and outcome of the PRI's own policies.

The various themes of a bourgeois political revolution in Mexico do not hold up. To Aguilar and the Communists, we can add the PMT and *Punto Crítico*. Did these four groups go astray by doing Marxist analysis in a doctrinaire way? Marxism, a useful instrument for interpreting history, easily slips into oversimplifications. Perhaps these groups, in their eagerness to prove that 'the state is but a committee for managing the common affairs of the entire bourgeois class' (Marx), have stumbled into the aforementioned fallacy of special pleading.

Aguilar has done the left a service by marshalling data, but it doesn't prove what he thinks it does: his figures really only support the thesis of bureaucratic erosion. His figures show that the size of the state bourgeoisie is increasing at the expense of the state bureaucracy. As that happens the influence of the bureaucrats *must* decline.

As for the adherents of the thesis of bureaucratic consolidation, they are up against a tremendous fact: rising participation by the bourgeoisie in political power. What is their defence? Mere denial that this growing participation matters. By 1970, these analysts point out, the assets of the public sector matched those of indigenous private enterprise.

But these reassurances sound like whistling in the dark. Experts agree that the foreign sector of multinationals is growing at the fastest rate of all. Add this foreign sector to the local private sector and they tower over the public* sector — Goliath's sword faces David's slingshot.

We can see the growing weight of foreigners in Mexico's affairs by considering the government's rising foreign debt. According to the PMT's report on the national economy in the Mexican daily *Unomásuno* (27 November 1977), this debt is out of hand. In 1977, 36% of the government's annual expenditures were covered by loans. The foreign debt was approaching 35 billion dollars. How much money is that? It represents 85% of Mexico's gross national product; it means that every Mexican adult owes 1,000 dollars to foreign creditors. Before the devaluations of 1976, the multinationals pumped capital out of the country at a rate of 2.34 dollars for each dollar invested, but by 1977 they were siphoning off at least twice that much. Even the state oil corporation was operating at a deficit, in spite of stepped up exports.

The evidence amassed by Aguilar and the PCM against the multinationals, thrown in with the PMT's report, smothers López Gallo's thesis of bureaucratic consolidation. All this evidence supports the hypothesis of *an erosion of bureaucratic power*.

We think this thesis stands out as the strongest of the four interpretations considered. And so our analysis of the Mexican political system converges on the thesis of the revolutionary-nationalist sector of the Mexican left: the Popular Party of Lombardo Toledano *before* its transformation into the weak-kneed PPS, the youthful Socialist Workers' Party (PST), and the Democratic Tendency led by Rafael Galván in the labour movement. Does that mean we also favour a strategy of alliance with revolutionary elements within the PRI government to stop the erosion of public power?

It means nothing of the kind.

Our acceptance of the thesis of bureaucratic erosion does not commit us to any strategy for revolution. Choice of a revolutionary strategy depends on more than a structural analysis of the Mexican political reality; it must also rest on a conjunctural investigation of the present correlation of social forces. We have not made that investigation. We are not committed here to any of the strategies proposed by the Mexican left.

6. The Bureaucratic Class

In our analysis the Mexican Revolution represents a step forward toward a post-capitalist order because, while it nurtured capitalism, it kept the bourgeoisie from capturing political power. Although overcoming feudal survivals was certainly a major accomplishment, the unique feature of the Mexican Revolution was the perpetuation in political power of a new ruling class — the bureaucracy. It was this class that administered a thoroughgoing agrarian reform and also manoeuvred to gain some independence from foreign economic interests. The final question is why it should be considered a class separate from the bourgeoisie.

The Bureaucracy as a Fourth 'Great Class'

For Marx land, capital, and labour power are the three factors of production under capitalism. But from conservatives like Alfred Marshall (*Principles of Economics*) to collectivists like Mikhail Bakunin (*Statism and Anarchy*) economists have found a fourth factor of production called 'organization', 'education', 'know-how', or 'science'. Are there hints in Marx's writing that there may be a fourth factor of production?

In *Capital* I:XIII-XIV, Marx writes as if there is a fourth factor called 'organization' or 'co-operation'. When several labourers work together in a single process or in different but connected processes, they 'co-operate'. You might dig a ditch alone, or you might dig it with ten others in simple co-operation. Marx traces the historical evolution from simple co-operation to combined labour on a large scale in the capitalist factory.

'All labour in which many individuals co-operate requires a commanding will to co-ordinate and unify the process, requires functions which apply not to partial operations but to the total acitivity of the workshop, much as that of an orchestra conductor,' writes Marx in *Capital* III:XXIII. An orchestra conductor need not own the instruments of the orchestra. The organizational work of supervising or orchestrating production falls to hired managers. 'The capitalist mode of production has brought matters to a point where the work of supervision, entirely divorced from the ownership of capital, is always readily obtainable. It has, therefore, come to be useless for the capitalist to perform it himself.' There is also Marx's insights that 'it is not the industrial capitalist, but the industrial managers who are "the soul of our industrial system".'

In *Capital* I:XIV, Marx shows that co-operation based on the division of labour is also expressed as technology or applied science. Long ago, intelligence in production was the property of the independent artisan. The cabinet-makers could do more than pound a hammer; they could calculate and design, and their sharpening intelligence made them great craftsmen. But in modern times this intelligence passes from the detail labourers into the machinery they tend. The new division of labour separates the labourers from the intelligence or science congealed in the instruments of production. Science passes into the hands of professional investigators, and the separation 'is completed in modern industry, which makes science a productive factor distinct from labour.'

In the final chapter of *Capital* III, Marx explains that ownership of three factors of production defines the great classes of modern society: 'The owners merely of labour-power, owners of capital, and landowners, whose respective sources of income are wages, profit and ground rent, in other words, wage-labourers, capitalists and landowners, make up the three big classes of modern society based upon the capitalist mode of production.' But we saw that there is a fourth factor of 'organization', 'education' or 'science'. Are the managers, owning a factor of production called 'organization', a separate class? Does this class include scientific workers, developing this fourth factor expressed as science? Is education or knowledge the basis of a new class?

In *Capital* I:XIV section five, Marx approvingly cites an English writer as follows: 'The man of knowledge and the productive labourer come to be widely divided from each other, and knowledge instead of remaining the handmaid of labour in the hand of the labourer to increase his productive powers . . . has almost everywhere arrayed itself against labour.' Scientists and managers earn high salaries for organizing wage slavery in the factories and designing monster machines for the labourer to run forever, like Sisyphus pushing his rock. It seems that we have another great class based on a fourth factor of production, a class of administrators, scientists, and professionals — the brain workers.

Marx himself never draws this conclusion. He says in *Capital* III:XXVII that the brain workers are merely skilled labourers getting wages. But we ourselves must draw the conclusion at once: living a century after Marx, we can see that there is another great class based on ownership of a fourth factor. We can call this organizational class the bureaucracy.

Bureaucrats draw income and power from their education and office. They are brain workers who sell services for an annual salary, while the manual workers sell labour-power for wages paid by the hour, day or week. The bureaucrats live off surplus value squeezed out of the manual workers. They are exploiters.

Bureaucrats and Petty Bureaucrats

Do these salary earners make up a single class? No, we must distinguish
between two classes, the petty bureaucracy and the bureaucracy, just as
Engels separated the petty bourgeoisie from the bourgeoisie. In 1851 in the
first and final chapters of *Germany: Revolution and Counter-revolution*,
Engels treats the petty bourgeoisie not as a sub-class of the bourgeoisie, but
as a separate class. He repeated the distinction in his article on 'Marx and the
Neue Rheinische Zeitung' as late as 1884 — clearly, he held this view all his
life. In the first chapter of his work on the German Revolution, he gives a
reason for considering the petty bourgeoisie separately: 'Its *intermediate
position* between the class of larger capitalists, traders and manufacturers —
the bourgeoisie properly so-called — and the proletarian class *determines its
character*' (italics ours). Politically, the petty bourgeoisie is dizzy and anxious,
swinging now this way and now that way in revolutions; economically, it
is dependent because of its small means.

Neither Marx nor Engels explains *how* the petty bourgeois differs from the
bourgeois. We can hardly expect our two pioneers in theory to do everything
for us, and so we must supply a criterion ourselves. Here it is: the petty
bourgeois draw the bulk of their income from their own labour rather than
from the labour of others. A carpenter working with an apprentice is a petty
bourgeois.

In the same way we distinguish between the petty bureaucracy and the
bureaucracy. The petty bureaucrats earn less from the indirect exploitation
of the people who obey them than from the value of their services to a
company, school or government. The bureaucrats on the other hand, earn
more from exploiting their subordinates than from the value of their services.

Big bureaucrats and petty bureaucrats alike are 'functionaries'. But only
the big bureaucrats — by their rank and station in the overall system of
bureaucratic exploitation — make up a fourth 'great class'. We can begin a
series of examples of this difference by pointing to government, for it also
takes part in production: the state machinery performs a number of economic services, including enforcement of industrial discipline and making
workers stick to labour contracts. In government the big bureaucrats are the
president, his cabinet, and the governors of states. Members of state con-
gresses and municipal government, along with most other public officials,
belong to the petty bureaucracy. In the military, generals and colonels make
up the bureaucracy, junior officers the petty bureaucracy. State education
trains people to serve industry: in education the presidents, vice-presidents,
deans of colleges and principals of high schools are big bureaucrats, while lower
officials in the administration and the teachers belong to the petty bureaucracy.

Our second example is business itself. In this case the bureaucrats are the
top executives of the great corporations, managers of different departments,
branch and plant directors, and middle executives generally. In contrast to this
group, the junior executives, production engineers, scientific workers, and

plant foremen belong to a different class, the petty bureaucracy.

In organized labour we can say that the presidents, vice-presidents, secretaries, and treasurers of the main unions make up the bureaucracy; while the union organizers and business secretaries of the local unions belong to the petty bureaucracy.

We can see from this list that membership in the political, military, educational, business, and labour bureaucracies calls for orchestrating and organizing large numbers of people. The most responsible jobs go to the bureaucrats; lower level jobs are for petty bureaucrats; and the two sectors cannot be conceived of as belonging to the same class.

The bureaucrats often follow an alliance with the bourgeoisie, or in socialist societies they may themselves be the economically dominant class. The petty bureaucrats behave like the petty bourgeoisie, for they can rarely push for an independent programme. They too swing back and forth between political extremes, from tailing after the imperialist bourgeoisie to liberal support for a rising bureaucratic class challenging big business, to radical demands as soon as the bureaucracy has taken over, to fear and hatred of the proletariat when it tries to move out on its own. Economically the petty bureaucrats are caught in a vice between the bureaucracy and the proletariat.

The Separation of Political and Economic Power: The Bonapartist State

In this model there may be more than one ruling class. According to Marx the ruling class has economic power: it owns the means of production (land and factories); it takes the bulk of the surplus product for itself; and it makes the key decisions in the economy on wages, investments, and prices. Yet this class may or may not be the governing class. It may assign this job to others, or it may have to share political power: control of the state, the army, and the police. Throughout most of history the class that rules economically also rules politically, but there have been exceptions.

Consider the example of the French government in the 19th century. In mid-century Marx described that government as follows: 'This executive power with its enormous bureaucratic and military organization, with its ingenious State machinery embracing wide strata, with a host of officials numbering half a million besides an army of another half million, this appalling parasitic body, which enmeshes French society like a net and chokes all its pores, sprang up in the days of the absolute monarchy' (*18th Brumaire of Louis Bonaparte*, VII). The monarch, Louis XVI, lost his head trying to retain control of the State machine: in the Revolution of 1789-92 the bourgeoisie took the government from him. Next, in the Revolution of 1799-1804, Napoleon's military bureaucracy wrenched it from the bourgeoisie.

Then in 1814 a political counter-revolution restored it to the landowners. In 1830 the bankers recaptured the government, only to lose it in the Revolution of 1848-51 to Louis Bonaparte's military-bureaucratic class. Not until the Revolution of 1870-71 did the bourgeoisie again seize control of the State machine. 'All revolutions perfected this machine instead of smashing it,' said Marx (in the *18th Brumaire*, VII). 'The parties that struggled in turn for domination looked upon the possession of this huge State structure as the principal spoils of the victor.' And so in France after 1789 there were many political revolutions, but only one social revolution: feudalism disappeared under the rising tide of capitalism.

A political revolution occurs when a new social class seizes political power. What is political power? It is the ability to make other people do what you want, whether they want to or not. In *The State and Revolution* Lenin put it bluntly: 'A standing army and the police are the chief instruments of State power' (I:2). You have to obey the man at the door with a gun.

From Mexico's Francisco I. Madero (d. 1913) to Chile's Salvador Allende (d. 1973), revolutionaries have often deceived themselves about this. Both Madero and Allende arrived at the presidency, but neither controlled the regular army. So neither had captured the government for his class; a political revolution had only begun. Madero represented the indigenous businessmen who hated Mexico's creaking feudalism, while Allende was the leader of a Chilean proletariat craving socialism. In both political struggles, the old ruling class held the loyalty of the army, and when it saw a social revolution brewing the generals killed the president and seized the government. As we saw much earlier on in this book, political power grows out of the barrel of a gun.

In the West, the corporate rich have economic power, but a good chunk of the political power they now share with a bureaucratic class. Since the big bureaucrats in government are usually allied to the corporate owners and managers, big business has its way with the state. And big money can often control parliaments through financing the political campaigns of senators, lobbying in the halls of congress, and even bribing the people's representatives to pass legislation favouring business interests. 'The democratic republic officially knows nothing any more of property distinctions,' wrote Engels in 1884. 'In it wealth exercises its power indirectly, but all the more surely. On the one hand, in the form of direct corruption of officials, of which America provides the classical example; on the other hand, in the form of an alliance between government and the Stock Exchange' (*Origin of the Family*, IX).

In the Communist countries, bureaucratic and petty bureaucratic classes control both the economy and the state. Even revolutionaries admit that in the Soviet Union the bureaucrats take a part of the surplus product through higher salaries. The humane character of these societies lies in their economic planning to meet the needs of the masses for food, clothing, housing, medicine, education, employment, public transit, and clean air in the cities.

But of the 162 countries on our planet most are in the Third World. In Third World countries there is usually a split between economic power and political power. One class rules economically and another rules politically. These classes may or may not be allied, though they often work together to preserve the economic system. Most of the Third World countries have capitalist economies, and the economically ruling class is made up of businessmen. But these countries are ruled politically by bureaucratic classes: one-party elites, army dictatorships, or some other bureaucratic political formation. The military bureaucracies or single-party governments don't necessarily take orders from businessmen.

Marx and Engels had already begun to theorize about this split between economic and political power with their concept of the bonapartist state. In the last chapter of his *Origin of the Family* (1884), Engels sets forth their theory of the state in a famous paragraph:

> It is, as a rule, the most powerful, economically dominant class which, through the medium of the State, becomes also the politically dominant class . . . . Thus the State of antiquity was above all the State of the slave owners for the purpose of holding down the slaves, as the feudal State was the organ of the nobility for holding down the peasant serfs and bondsmen, and the modern representative State is an instrument of exploitation of wage-labour by capital. By way of exception, however, periods occur in which the warring classes balance each other so nearly that the State power, as ostensible mediator, acquires for the moment a certain degree of independence . . . . Such was the Bonapartism of the First, and still more of the Second French Empire, which played off the proletariat against the bourgeosie and the bourgeoisie against the proletariat. The latest performance of this kind, in which ruler and ruled appear equally ridiculous, is the new German Empire of the Bismarck nation: here capitalists and workers are balanced against each other . . . .

The bonapartist state was a huge military-bureaucratic machine that raised itself above the proletariat and the bourgeoisie to govern in its own interest. The bourgeoisie remained the economically dominant class, but in order to save its purse it gave up the crown. The bureaucrats had the state to themselves.

In the passage above, Engels considered bonapartism exceptional, but a decade later he wondered if it might not be the rule. In his 1892 Introduction to *Socialism: Utopian and Scientific*, he says that 'It seems a law of historical development that the bouregeoisie can in no European country get hold of political power — at least for any length of time — in the same exclusive way in which the feudal aristocracy kept hold of it during the Middle Ages. Even in France, where feudalism was completely extinguished, the bourgeoisie as a whole has held full possession of the Government for very short periods only.'

During the 20th century in Third World capitalist countries, where the bourgeoisie is even weaker than in Europe, it has been difficult for the businessmen to capture political power at all. The indigenous bourgeoisies of Africa are politically weak, and many governments are taking over important sectors of the economy. At the time of writing (1978-79) the following African governments have at one time or another launched offensives against capitalism: Ethiopia, People's Republic of the Congo, Somalia, Egypt, Tanzania, Guinea, Libya, Benin (formerly Dahomey), Ghana, Madagascar, Sao Tomé, and Algeria. And others are going socialist through Marxist revolutions-from-below: Mozambique, Angola, Guinea-Bissau, the Cape Verde Islands.

Elsewhere in Africa the businessmen — often foreigners — still own the factories, banks, mines, and stores. They go on producing for profit, with all the misery that brings to the popular classes in underdeveloped societies: mass unemployment, bottomless poverty, continuing illiteracy, disease in the countryside.

In Latin America the situation is even worse: 25 countries are suffering the horrors of dependent capitalism. But even here the bourgeoisie usually does not control the government directly; it is in the hands of a military-bureaucratic class.

In most of the 125 countries of the Third World there is a split between the economic and political power: capitalist economies are governed by bureaucratic political formations. This opens the possibility, no matter how remote, of socialist revolutions-from-above. In 1967, for example, President Julius Nyerere of Tanzania decided in the Arusha Declaration that his ruling party (TANU) must build socialism. Since then the TANU party has pushed state ownership in banking, industry, and commerce; co-operative (*ujamaa*) villages have appeared by the thousands; and the education system is turning toward socialist goals.

The concept of a split between economic and political power surprises people under the influence of classical Marxism; they think that the economically dominant class must normally control the government. The source of that idea is the famous formulation in the *Communist Manifesto*: 'The executive of the modern State is but a committee for managing the common affairs of the entire bourgeoisie.' But when Marx and Engels wrote this in 1848 most European states were feudal; only in England and France had the bourgeoisie captured political power. In England little more than a million people had the vote, while in France only two hundred thousand had it — these were the propertied classes. In 1848 the tiny 'watchdog state' was indeed a committee for managing the affairs of the bourgeoisie in these two countries.

By the end of the 19th century the situation had become more complicated, as Engels' later writings on the state showed. And during the 20th century the liberal 'watchdog state' of the bourgeois democracies in Europe and North America disappeared. For the last 75 years the state has grown ever larger, a giant octopus whose bureaucratic tentacles reach into every corner of modern society. Huge bureacracies for administration, health, education, welfare, and war have spread over the developed countries, nor is the end of their growth in sight. In 1947 the federal bureaucracy of the USA had 3.5 million employees; by 1970 it had 14.5 million.

The steady growth of bureaucratic classes in 20th century society has complicated the analysis of the state. As we write, of the 162 governments in our world, 74 show no signs of traditional bourgeois democracy. Either these governments have pushed aside all political parties or they are run on a one-party system. There are no elections for the big money to manipulate, and the bourgeoisie is cut off from direct political power. So today in almost half the nations a political or military bureaucracy controls the government. In many of these countries, especially the communist states, the bureaucracy also runs the economy. But, in the rest, private enterprise controls the land and the factories, producing raw materials for export or cars and other luxury goods for a minority of the people, while huge masses lack jobs, schools, doctors, and food for their families. In these countries the state must spend more on arms than on education. Such governments listen nervously to the time bomb ticking under the nation and crank out anti-communist ideologies promising 'national security' to their supporters. History teaches us that they are whistling in the dark.

PART 2
The Continental Scope
of the Revolution

7. The American Popular Revolutionary Alliance

In our analysis the Mexican Revolution represents a step forward toward a post-capitalist order because, while it nurtured capitalism it kept the bourgeoisie from capturing political power. Under the influence of this experience the Guatemalan Revolution (1944-54) and the Bolivian Revolution (1952-64) achieved roughly similar results. But as the Mexican experience took root elsewhere it also became increasingly radicalized. In more economically developed countries, in Argentina and Cuba, the internationalization of the Revolution constituted a blow not so much against the remnants of feudalism in the countryside as against the bourgeoisie in positions of political power. And it had important repercussions on Mexico itself, contributing to a spate of guerrilla movements in the '60s influenced by the Cuban example.

Spreading the Principles of the Revolution

The Mexican Revolution turned Mexico City into a centre for subversion throughout the New World. The former capital of the Aztecs became a revolutionary fulcrum for national liberation movements against U.S. imperialism. During the 20th century Mexico City spread the ideas of the Mexican Revolution far and wide, just as Paris had radiated the principles of the French Revolution during the 19th century. What Paris and the French Revolution were to Karl Marx in 1844-45 and again in 1848, Mexico City and the Mexican Revolution were to the Peruvian revolutionary Victor Raúl Haya de la Torre in 1923-24 and again in 1927-28, to Leon Trotsky from 1938-40 and, to a lesser extent, to Che Guevara and Fidel Castro during 1955 and 1956.

Later this Paris of the Latin American revolution became a haven for
political exiles from the Spanish Civil War and from Latin American dictatorships. Mexico was the only country in the Americas that did not recognize
or exchange ambassadors with the Franco government in Spain, just as she
was the only Latin American country besides Cuba to break diplomatic
relations with the military regime in Chile in 1973. From Nicaragua came
anti-Somoza political exiles and from the Dominican Republic came revolutionaries to plot the overthrow of the Trujillo dictatorship. With the
persecution of Haya de la Torre's Peruvian followers under the dictatorship
of Manuel Odría (1948-56), a new crop of exiles arrived from that country.
Guevara's future wife, Hilda Gadea, was among them. Che himself arrived
at the end of 1954 in the company of exiles fleeing from the CIA financed
military coup in Guatemala. Fidel Castro and a group of Cuban exiles from
Fulgencio Batista's dictatorship came in 1955. With the fall of Juan
Domingo Perón in September 1955 Argentine political exiles began arriving
in Mexico City, as they were to do again two decades later to escape the
paramilitary terror launched against leftists after Perón's death in July 1974.
And during the '70s a new wave of political refugees flowed in from the
repressive regimes in Brazil, Bolivia, Chile and Uruguay.

It was mainly as a haven for political exiles that Mexico City helped spread
the principles of the Mexican Revolution throughout Latin America. Thus it
was not a Mexican who took the initiative in internationalizing the Revolution. In Mexico City the exile, Haya de la Torre, founded a Latin American
international called the American Popular Revolutionary Alliance (APRA).
Founded in 1924 under the influence of both the Mexican and Russian
Revolutions, APRA focused on the recovery and defence of the national
sovereignty of the Latin American countries held down by U.S. imperialism.

The APRA began as a Latin American anti-imperialist party with an
international executive committee. Its provisional headquarters were in
London until Haya, in his capacity as secretary-general, had them shifted
to Berlin in 1929. But it virtually ceased to function as a continental party
once he returned to his native Peru to organize the Peruvian Aprista Party
(PAP) and to compete in the national elections of 1931. Subsequently the
APRA came to consist of a family of national parties bound together no
longer by a centralized administrative apparatus, but by fraternal ties among
the parties themselves.

The origins of this new APRA can be traced to the national sections of
the original APRA which developed into separate and independent political
parties. Among these were the Mexican, Guatemalen, Costa Rican, Cuban,
Haitian, Peruvian, Bolivian, Chilean, and Argentine sections. Several of the
resulting parties have achieved government power: some have captured the
presidency; others have dominated the legislature (as did Haya's own Aprista
Party in Peru). Some have governed for long periods: the Cuban Revolutionary Party (PRC), the Guatemalan Revolutionary Party (PR), the Revolutionary Nationalist Movement (MNR) in Bolivia, Democratic Action (AD) in
Venezuela, the National Liberation Party (PLN) of Costa Rica, and the

Democratic Popular Party (PPD) of Puerto Rico. Among less successful APRA-type parties were Juan Bosch's Dominican Revolutionary Party (PRD), and the Cuban People's Party (PPC) which produced Fidel Castro and his July 26 Movement.

In some cases Haya's followers organized these parties directly; in others, they arose indirectly from mergers with non-Aprista groups, as did the Cuban Revolutionary Party. But several radical and self-styled liberal parties have converged on Aprista principles. Among these the most important have been the Radical Party (PR) in Chile, the Liberal Party (PL) in Honduras, and the Independent Liberal Party (PLI) in Nicaragua. During the late '30s the dissident youth sector of the Radical Party in Argentina, calling itself the Radical Orientation Forces of the Argentine Youth (FORJA), adopted an essentially Aprista programme. Haya's influence was also visible in the new Mexican political machine, the National Revolutionary Party (PNR), organized by President Calles in 1929 as a means of defending and insti-tutionalizing the Mexican Revolution. In 1938 President Cárdenas re-organized and renamed it the Party of the Mexican Revolution (PRM); in 1947 President Alemán gave it its final form and name — Institutional Revolutionary Party (PRI). It is still a party of the APRA type.

Haya de la Torre's 'Anti-Imperialism and the APRA'

The export of the Mexican Revolution was first and foremost the work of Haya de la Torre. His experience of the Mexican Revolution and its lessons became the basis for his analysis of Latin American social conditions and his programme for changing Latin societies. Haya explained and developed this programme in his major work, *Anti-Imperialism and the APRA*, written in Mexico City in 1928 and first published in Santiago de Chile in 1936.

In view of the Mexican Revolution, he tells us, the history of the political and economic relations between Latin America and the United States led him to the following conclusions. First, the governing classes in Latin America, made up of landowners, the import-export bourgeoisie, and their political representatives in power, were allies of Yankee imperialism — a reference to the *hacendados* and *científicos* during the regime of Porfirio Díaz. Second, these classes held power through a policy of concessions, loans, and joint business ventures with U.S.-based foreign corporations. Third, their alliance with foreign interests had unfortunate results: the natural resources of the Latin American countries were mortgaged or sold; the workers and peasants suffered brutal exploitation. In most Latin American countries there had been an erosion of national sovereignty and in some countries its outright loss: Panama, Nicaragua, Cuba, and the Dominican Republic.

To generalize, the Latin American republics combined colonial capitalism with feudal or semi-feudal economies. The dominant mode of production, according to Haya, was colonial capitalism. In Mexico during the *Porfiriato*, foreign interests supported by semi-feudal landowners dominated the economy; the foreign interests found representatives in the *científicos*, allied to the local *hacendados*. This pattern or a similar one, Haya argued, was also evident in his own country Peru; and throughout Latin America appeared its outline, either clearly or in shadowy form.

In the original APRA Programme there were five points. First, the main enemy of the Latin American peoples was Yankee imperialism; in other words, the basic task was the organization of a united front for the defence and recovery of national soverignty. Second, the Mexican Revolution showed that to overcome U.S. imperialism Latin America must achieve political unification through a federation of states patterned on that of North America. As allies of U.S. interests, the oligarchies in each country blocked political unification. How can Latin Americans overthrow their oligarchies? For that purpose they need revolutionary parties of the oppressed classes led by the workers. Third, to overcome imperialism, Latin America must achieve economic independence. That meant nationalization of land and industry. The United States bitterly opposed this step: the Mexican government put off nationalizing the petroleum industry until 1938. Fourth, the political unity and economic independence of Latin America require the internationalization of the Panama Canal. And fifth, Latin America's political unification and economic independence depend on a policy of solidarity with all the oppressed classes and peoples of the world.

The Programme ended with a three-point slogan summing up its most important features: 'Against Imperialism! For the Political Unity of Latin America! For the Realization of Social Justice!' What is social justice? Haya explains this concept in chapter three of *Anti-Imperialism and the APRA*. The nationalization of wealth is an anti-imperialist strategy first, and then a means of social justice. Imperialism gets it wealth through holding down the Latin American peoples as nations, and their workers as exploited classes; so their first defensive act must be nationalization. Then this wealth must go to those who work and increase it for the common good. Thus there were two steps in the APRA's original nationalization plan: first, the expropriation of the colonial capitalists and feudal landlords by the state; second, the redistribution of this wealth for the benefit of the direct producers. The first step signified economic independence; the second, social justice.

The Mexican Revolution suggested to Haya the three points of the original APRA Programme slogan. But will the interests of North American imperialism willingly allow Latin American revolutionaries to recover their national sovereignty? Certainly not. In chapter four of *Anti-Imperialism and the APRA*, Haya claims that 'The Mexican Revolution would have been perhaps the most advanced revolution of the epoch, if it had not come up against imperialist pressure.' Mexico did not lack revolutionary energy, but at the gates of the most powerful nation on earth she went as far as she could go alone: 'No isolated country of Indo-America could have gone any further; that is the first lesson that the Mexican Revolution offers us.' Nor should we forget, Haya warns, that the limitations and failures of this great revolution flow mainly from outside causes: revolutionary unpreparedness in other countries and the absence of a united front against U.S. imperialism. In the defence of national sovereignty no country can win alone; isolated Mexico cries out for a Latin American party on a continental scale.

Haya warned against bourgeois distortions of the Mexican model. If the state encourages the growth of an indigenous bourgeoisie, as in Mexico, then it will again fall under the imperialists' sway. In Latin America no form of domestic capitalism can hope to escape imperialist domination. On this point the Mexican Revolution offered Haya a valuable lesson: 'The lack of a scientific and economic organization of the state,' he wrote in chapter eight, '. . . has facilitated the preponderance of the middle class in post-revolutionary Mexico; ideologically, politically and economically, the Mexican Revolution in practice has not used the middle classes, but they have used the Revolution.' Thus the 'petty bourgeois illness' of the Mexican Revolution comes from not having taken preventive measures in time. What are those preventive measures? The organization of production along socialist and co-operative lines.

For the post-revolutionary struggle against imperialism, Haya expanded his original programme to include the strategy of the anti-imperialist state. We can sum up this strategy as follows. The economically backward countries lack capital for development, and that means they must make deals with imperialism. Since local businessmen are no match for their counterparts in the imperialist metropolis, the anti-imperialist state is needed to defend their interests as well as the national patrimony, and to become their bargaining agent with foreign capitalists. Private companies or isolated individuals lack the power to restrain imperialism's might. Only the anti-imperialist state can do that.

What will this state be like? It will be modelled on the principles of the Mexican Revolution, Haya tells us in chapter seven. The anti-imperialist state will begin by favouring the interests of the most oppressed class: first, those of the peasants, next those of the industrial workers, and only then those of the indigenous capitalists. What happens when this order is inverted? In Mexico even in the '20s that partly occurred. Such an inversion leads to the emergence of a bourgeois state, including the restoration of imperialism.

The new state will be a form of state capitalism dominated by a multi-class party of the oppressed classes; it will be a transitional step toward a socialist society. Only where the industrial proletariat has grown strong, only where capitalism flourishes, Haya argued, can the free enterprise system be abolished. So, in Latin America, the struggle for socialism is premature. This means that national liberation can occur only through building a social organization which shares features of both capitalism and socialism – a third system. The old colonial-type state must be replaced by a new anti-imperialist one ready to nationalize the foreign sector and defeudalize the local economy.

Haya's interpretation of Latin American society and his anti-imperialist programme became the basis of Aprismo — the politics and strategy of the APRA. Aprismo adapted Marxist thought to Latin American social and political conditions. Aprismo was also important for bringing Marxist analysis to the experience and lessons of the Mexican Revolution. Aprismo represented a Mexicanized application of Marxism aimed at spreading the Revolution throughout Latin America, aimed at making new revolutions on the Mexican model. The orignial Marxist-Leninist strategy was found inapplicable to Latin America: a one-class party and a dictatorship of the proletariat did not fit conditions of backwardness and dependency. Aprismo faced a tiny proletariat, and middle sectors that also suffered from imperialism and were potentially revolutionary. In that situation the Mexican Revolution rather than the Bolshevik Revolution seemed the pattern for revolutionary change.

The Revolutionary Progeny of Aprismo

Usually this judgment was well founded. In the Western Hemisphere the most important revolutions to follow the Mexican were the revolutions in Guatemala (1944-54), Bolivia (1952-64), and Cuba (1956-61). These three were the flowers of Aprismo, fertilized by its strategy of the anti-imperialist state and by the example of the Mexican Revolution. Each went beyond its immediate forerunner in radicalization, as if gaining momentum by what went before. These successive revolutions moved ever faster in carrying out their agrarian reforms and nationalizing foreign and local monopolies.

Guatemala Versus the United Fruit Company

Though the Guatemalan Revolution did not return the lands taken from the Indian communities, its Agrarian Law of June 1952 was more radical than Article 27 of the Mexican Constitution. First, the Guatemalan law fixed a limit on the lands anyone could hold — 223 acres. The government could take over any land beyond this figure and give it to the peasants. The Mexican agrarian reform, in contrast, had left the governments in each state to fix such limits; they were set high or low according not only to the fertility of the land, but also to the pressures of local *hacendados*. Second, the Guatemalan reform said that the landowners' 1952 valuations of their lands for tax purposes would decide its value for compensation. Everyone knew that the landowners' valuations were below the lands' market value. By contrast, Mexico's Article 27 did not tell how to decide the value of lands taken over by the state governments. Third, the Guatemalan reform provided that all expropriated lands must go to poor or landless peasants. But Article 27 had loopholes allowing landowners to sell to friends or relatives any properties larger than the maximum fixed by state laws; such sales were a strategem for keeping the properties intact, for in the extended family the land belonged on paper to fifty cousins but in fact to the old *hacendado*. Fourth, the Guatemalan reform was to be carried out by agrarian committees made up of peasants, and that ensured that they would get justice. By contrast, Article 27 said that only local governments could take over land. Landowners knew how to put pressure on those governments to slow down the reform.

During his three-year term as President (1917-20) Carranza only redistributed 400,000 acres; while in Guatemala, during the two-year period

(1952-54) between the law's passage and Arbenz's overthrow by the CIA-run coup, the redistribution reached a whopping 1,500,000 acres. The speedy carrying through ot the Guatemalan Agrarian Law shows its radicalization compared to the Mexican.

As for the nationalization of foreign enterprises, the largest in Guatemala was the United Fruit Company, also the largest landowner. The government went after its lands first. The Company's expropriated lands made up a third of all those taken over by the government.

But what about the long-run effect of the Mexican agrarian reform (1917-40)? What about Cárdenas' nationalization of the foreign oil companies in 1938? Weren't these reforms more far-reaching than those in Guatemala? In this respect the two revolutions are not comparable, if only because the Mexican Revolution survived the various coups aimed at overthrowing it.

Bolivia's Agrarian Reform and Nationalization of the Tin Mines
The Bolivian Revolution launched its Agrarian Reform Law in 1953. Unpaid labour, debt peonage, and all forms of serfdom were abolished. The landlords had allowed peasants to till tiny plots for themselves; the new Law gave these plots to the peasants as their property. The peasants had also worked the landlords' estates for them, and the law now promised the peasants part of those lands. Despite the slowness in redistributing the estates, the Bolivian agrarian reform compares favourably with the Mexican.

The lands to be expropriated in Bolivia were *latifundia*, large properties worked by ancient methods; landlords took the bulk of the surplus as labour rents rather than profits from invested capital. The few big farms investing in machinery, fertilizer, and seeds were safe from the reform. The Law exempted the modern farms in the department of Santa Cruz and the grazing lands of the Beni. There was another loophole: if the land surface prevented the use of machines, the owners could keep tracts of land provided that they or their families cultivated them. Though the National Service of Agrarian Reform had a Mexican advisor, Edmundo Flores, lands were usually redistributed as private plots instead of to co-operatives or Mexican-type *ejidos*. The Agrarian Law stated that peasant unions must take part in carrying out the reform, an advance over Article 27 of the Mexican Constitution.

As in Mexico, agrarian reform in Bolivia was due mainly to Indian initiative. The government was presented with a *fait accompli* and felt obliged to legalize Indian seizures of the land. By 1963 almost 10,000,000 acres had been distributed at the rate of 1,000,000 acres a year. That compares favourably with the Mexican reform: from 1917 to 1928 the Mexicans only distributed 11,000,000 acres in their huge country. Since in Bolivia both the arable land and the peasant population were several times smaller, its reform moved relatively faster.

Bolivia nationalized the tin mines and established workers' self-management, steps which marked a great advance over the Mexican Revolution. Mining was the source of 80% of Bolivia's foreign exchange; it was the main source of the State's revenue. In 1952 a few months after the seizure of power and a year before the Agrarian Reform Law, the revolutionary government nationalized the tin mines, the largest of which, the Patiño-owned ones, had been incorporated in the United States. By contrast, the Mexican Revolution had to wait three decades before the final nationalization of the railroads (1937) and the take-over of the foreign oil companies (1938).

Who administered the nationalized tin mines? A government-created public enterprise, the Bolivian Mining Corporation (COMIBOL), under seven national directors, two of them selected by the miners' union (FSTMB). In the mines there was also a system of workers' control. The miners could veto any management decisions they considered against their interests. To enforce workers' control, they organized militias under the nominal direction of the government, but under the actual command of the miners' union.

By contrast, in Mexico the experiment in workers' self-management was all too brief. In May 1938 President Cárdenas turned the nationalized railroads over to the Railway Workers Union. That same year he turned over the oil companies, reorganized in the government-owned Mexico Petroleum Company, to the Petroleum Workers Union. But these measures were short-lived. In 1940, under President Ávila Camacho, workers' self-management came to an end in these industries — they reverted to government administration as did the Bolivian mines in 1961.

Cuba: The First Liberated Territory of the Americas

The Cuban Revolution went furthest in applying the Mexican model of an agrarian and anti-imperialist national revolution. This was true of its Aprista stage, before the July 26 Movement dissolved in June 1961 in favour of the post-Aprista Integrated Revolutionary Organizations (ORI). Already in the Sierra Maestra the Rebel Army had proclaimed an agrarian law that turned over the land and cattle of the *hacendados* to the peasants. Like the Guatemalan agrarian reform, the Cuban one of May 1959 fixed a limit to the lands a person could own. This limit was set much higher than in Guatemala: 1,000 acres; and for estates of high productivity, 3,300 acres. Still, like the Bolivian Law, the Cuban abolished all absentee income in rents, while going further than the Bolivian to declare all lands occupied by tenants, sharecroppers and squatters to be the property of those who cultivated them. The revolutionary government would expropriate these lands from the big owners: they would get compensation through state bonds redeemable in twenty years, paying an annual interest of four and one-half per cent. As in Guatemala, the recorded tax declarations of the owners decided the value of these lands.

By June 1961 about a million acres had gone to small peasants in lots of from 66 to 165 acres — a pace slower than Guatemala's in 1952-54. But the Cuban agrarian reform advanced beyond its forerunners with its provision of medium-size farms for the landless, instead of the postage-stamp plots of less than ten acres distributed in Guatemala and Bolivia. More important than the distribution of lands in medium-sized plots was the development of the public and co-operative sectors. By 1961 the government had seized almost half the land and transferred it to those sectors; the bulk of this land went into state farms with mechanized agriculture and economies of scale. These advantages meant that the nationalized land would not revert to private property. Here the Cuban Revolution far surpassed the Guatemalan and the Bolivian.

The most spectacular achievement of the Cuban Revolution (1956-61) was, as in Bolivia, its nationalization laws against local and foreign enterprises. Fidel Castro, threatened by a U.S. embargo on Cuban sugar imports, declared in June 1960 that 'if they take away our sugar quota pound by pound, we will take away their sugar mills one by one'. In July the threatened embargo came to pass, and the Cuban Council of Ministers authorized Fidel to nationa-lize U.S. sugar properties on the island. The United States followed the sugar embargo with an oil, arms, and tourist embargo. So in August the first nationalization act took over the 36 U.S. sugar mills, all U.S.-owned utilities, and the U.S. oil companies and refineries: there would be no indemnification until the embargoes were lifted. In September came the nationalization of Cuban branches of U.S. banks. In October a law nationalized all the banks and 382 of the largest businesses — both local and foreign. Together the first industrialization wave in the summer of 1960 and the second in the autumn swept 80% of Cuba's industrial capacity from the hands of private owners.

These developments were followed by an urban land reform. Just as the Agrarian Reform Law of May 1959 had hit the rural landlords, so the Urban Reform Law of October 1960 undermined the city landlords. The new law annulled all rental contracts, expropriated all absentee landlords, and turned their tenants into owners-to-be of their dwellings. Rent payments to the government became mortgage payments. The government would compensate landlords a maximum of 600 pesos (U.S. $ 600) monthly until their dwellings became the property of their former tenants.

The main beneficiaries of the Cuban economy were still the expropriated landowners and businessmen: they went on pocketing the bulk of the privately distributed economic surplus in the form of interest payments on government bonds. But what was the nature of their capital? It was no longer means of production and real estate; it was entirely financial and divorced from the centres of economic decision-making. The immediate outcome was a system of state capitalism. Cuba became the first nation in the Western Hemisphere to fulfill the conditions of Haya's anti-imperialist state; such a state was basic to his Third Position between capitalism and socialism. Though Cuba would later pass into the socialist camp, what made this transition possible was the Aprista Programme of the July 26 Movement pushed through between January 1959 and June 1961.

The APRA's Post-revolutionary Ideology

Except for the first Cuban Revolution of 1933-34, these Mexican-type explosions occurred in the aftermath of World War Two, just as the APRA's original militancy declined. The corresponding parties most closely identified with these later revolutions – the Revolutionary Party in Guatemala, the Revolutionary Nationalist Movement in Bolivia, and the Cuban People's Party, a breakaway from the Cuban Revolutionary Party – were all latecomers on the historical stage. These three parties, not organized until the '40s, were still in their revolutionary phase when the established Aprista parties had begun to backslide. Cuba is a case in point, where as many as four different APRA-type parties succeeded one another after the earlier ones gave way to corruption: first, the ABC then the Cuban Revolutionary Party, followed by the Cuban People's Party and, finally, Fidel Castro's July 26 Movement.

Although most of the APRA parties ended by giving up their anti-imperialism for a compromise with Yankee corporate interests and local bourgeoisies, they did not all do this at once, nor even during the same decade. Cuba's first successful Aprista party, the Cuban Revolutionary Party, was organized in 1934. After it got a majority in congress in 1944 it followed the same general course as did Haya's own Peruvian Aprista Party. It was the older mostly pre-World War Two parties that were the first to abandon the APRA's original strategy against imperialism and the semi-feudal *hacendados*. This unholy alliance seemed too formidable to overcome with the strategy of a multi-class party limited to the workers, peasants, and middle sectors. It was also necessary, or so the Apristas believed, to get the support of the local bourgeoisie. As a result of this shift in policy, the bourgeoisie gained increasing influence over the various Aprista parties.

A number of circumstances dictated the APRA's change of line. President Roosevelt's New Deal and Good Neighbour Policy, the fascist menace in Europe, and the democratic alliance against the Axis powers during World War Two – these events softened the critique of Yankee imperialism. The APRA favoured a new strategy based on co-operation between the democratic 'left' in the U.S.A. and that in Latin America. It reinterpreted its earlier nationalization policy to mean state control rather than seizure of foreign interests; this convergence on the New Deal brought a reconsideration of the value of so-called bourgeois democracy. Thus the APRA's original slogan 'Against Imperialism! For the Political Unity of Latin America! For the Realization of Social Justice!' was replaced by the three principles of the Chinese Kuomintang: 'Nationalism, Democracy, and Welfare!'

Beginning in the early '40s the APRA's new formula of 'Democratic Inter-Americanism without Imperialism' was the proposed basis for relations with the U.S.A. Underlying this slogan was the APRA's belief that the Good Neighbour Policy was bearing fruit, that economic imperialism was losing its political arm. The APRA thought that the State Department was no longer giving unconditional protection to U.S. investments in Latin America. Haya went so far as to justify U.S. military intervention to defend democratic governments hit by army coups. The Cold War brought the APRA to accept Yankee 'democratic imperialism' as preferable to alleged Soviet totalitarianism. The Cold War deflated the menace of U.S. intervention by inflating the dangers of communist subversion. The influence of the Cold War on the APRA is evident in Haya's later book, *Thirty Years of Aprismo* (Mexico,

1956), completed in Lima during diplomatic asylum in the Colombian embassy. To the two enemies of the early APRA, imperialism and feudalism, Haya added a third: International Communism.

The early development of the APRA runs from its foundation in Mexico in 1924 up to the beginning of its detente with Yankee 'democratic imperialism' during World War Two. This development paralleled the carrying out of the Mexican Revolution by Presidents Obregón, Calles, and Cárdenas (1920-40). After a brief transition period under President Ávila Camacho (1940-46), the Mexican Revolution was frozen by President Alemán (1946-52). A state bourgeoisie, as we have seen, emerged within the government; a national bourgeoisie had already sprung from the ranks of the ruling party (PNR-PRM-PRI). The APRA, and the Aprista parties it fathered during the 30s, went through a similar evolution. By 1947 the Peruvian Aprista Party had abandoned its early militancy for an equivalent of Alemanism, as had the Cuban Revolutionary Party. Under the influence of the Cold War the Radical Party in Chile also shifted to the right, as did most of the other APRA-type parties on the continent. Just as the Mexican Revolution of 1910-40 gave way to a post-revolutionary regime typified by Alemán and his current in the PRI, so the APRA evolved through two stages: an early revolutionary phase insprired by the Mexican revolutionaries, Villa, Zapata, Obregón, Cárdenas; and a reformist phase corresponding to the Mexican developments after 1940.

The Generational Gap: The Emergence of a New Revolutionary Left

The universal tendency for APRA-type parties to go 'soft' on imperialism encouraged a policy of conciliation toward local oligarchies. The widespread corruption within the leadership of the Cuban Revolutionary Party during its years in power from 1944 to 1952, when it was deposed by Batista's military coup, is a case in point. A generational gap was emerging between the older Apristas, who had sold out to the vested interests, and the young militants in the movement. Initially, the ground swell of rebellion by the Aprista youth was contained through the organization of a semi-clandestine military brigade known as the Caribbean Legion. Later, a series of left-wing splits developed: the militants were expelled and denied a place of influence in their parties. The leftist faction wanted to revive the revolutionary spirit and push their parties toward socialist objectives.

The Caribbean Legion
Under the umbrella of the Good Neighbour Policy the Caribbean Legion was organized in 1947 with its first headquarters in Cuba. Recruited mainly from Aprista youth and political exiles from the Caribbean nations, the Legion's mission was to overthrow local dictators and re-establish democracy. In 1947 it organized its first abortive invasion of Trujillo's tyranny in the Dominican

Republic. In a letter dated 26 August 1956 to the director of the Cuban journal *Bohemia*, Fidel Castro recalled how he had enlisted in that expedition from Cuba and for 'three months lived out-of-doors on a sandy key waiting for the signal to embark' — a preview of his own Caribbean legion organized in Mexico and launched against Batista in November 1956.

In 1948 Costa Rica became the Legion's base for operations. With military aid from President Juan Jóse Arévalo of Guatemala and the participation of Aprista exiles, the Legion helped overthrow the President of Costa Rica who had refused to step down after defeat at the polls. In December 1948 the Legion received international attention: the Organization of American States (OAS) decided that Costa Rica must disband the Legion, for it stood accused of plotting the overthrow of dictatorships in other 'banana republics', in Venezuala and in the Dominican Republic. Later the Legion shifted its headquarters and training base to Guatemala, where an APRA-type revolution was taking place. But the Arbenz regime fell in 1954, and Costa Rica again became the base for the Legion's revolutionary activities. It aimed at the Somoza dictatorship in neighbouring Nicaragua and plotted the overthrow of Batista in Cuba. Pepe Figueres, the head of Costa Rica's National Liberation Party (PLN) and an associate of Haya de la Torre, used his presidential office to give money and guns to Cuban exiles trained by the Legion in the Costa Rican mountains. Thus young Aprista revolutionaries fought and died while the older generation turned reformist.

The Cuban People's Party
The first major split within an APRA-type party occurred in the Cuban Revolutionary Party (*Auténtico*). In 1947 Eduardo Chibás tried to revive the party's original programme which led to a rupture and to the founding of the breakaway Cuban People's Party (*Ortodoxo*). Although the emphasis of the new party was against moral corruption in government, the *Ortodoxos* also revived the original anti-imperialist programme of the APRA. It was this reformed APRA-type party that attracted Fidel Castro and later nominated him as its candidate in the congressional elections scheduled for June 1952. If it had not been for Batista's coup of 10 March 1952, Castro might have become one of the party's top leaders in congress. Instead, he was eventually to lead a split within the breakaway party because of differences with the leadership on how to respond to the coup.

The Popular Party (Mexico)
The next party to undergo a major split was the Mexican ruling party itself, the PRI. In 1936 Lombardo Toledano, with President Cárdenas' help, had founded the Confederation of Mexican Workers (CTM); he led the labour central into the World Federation of Trade Unions (WFTU) dominated by the communists. But as the Cold War broke upon the world in 1947, Toledano was expelled from the CTM which then abandoned the red WFTU to align itself with the United States' AFL-CIO. The next year Toledano and the left wing of the ruling PRI withdrew from the party to found the Popular

Party, later renamed the Popular Socialist Party (PPS). As the rebel PRI it tried to carry forward the work of the Revolution which Cárdenas' successors had either neglected or rejected.

At the same time, a new labour organization emerged, the General Union of Mexican Workers and Peasants (UGOCM), also Marxist in tendency and working with Toledano's PPS. To this rival of the official CTM the government denied legal status and recognition in negotiating collective agreements. But in the countryside the UGOCM played a considerable role in mobilizing mass support for the *ejidos* and in stepping up the agrarian reform. In 1961 the UGOCM also helped organize the Movement of National Liberation (MLN) that called for solidarity with the Cuban Revolution and pushed for nationalization of industry at home.

The first guerrilla *foco* in Mexico sprang from the ranks of the UGOCM, but it was promptly denounced by the PPS. Its leader was the rural schoolteacher, Arturo Gámiz. He joined the PPS in 1956, organized a youth section of the party in the town of Adolfo López Mateos in Chihuahua, and finally became the head of the local UGOCM in the region that includes the city of Madero. The other leader of the *foco*, the rural doctor Pablo Gómez, was also an activist in both parties in the state of Chihuahua. Gámiz's group, mostly of young peasants, began armed actions in February 1964. Then it made international news with its Castro-like attack on the barracks of the city of Madero on 23 September 1965.

The July 26 Movement (Cuba)
The model for these guerrilla movements was the split in the Cuban People's Party which led to the organization of the July 26 Movement in commemoration of Fidel's assault on the Moncada Barracks. This first rupture within a reformed APRA-type party in 1956 was followed by similar splits in Venezuela's Democratic Action (AD) and in the Peruvian Aprista Party in 1960. The youth sectors withdrew to organize rival movements; they finally created insurrectionary *focos* of their own. The exception was Bolivia. There the division had its roots in the Bolivian Labour Central (COB). The ruling Revolutionary Nationalist Movement expelled the COB's leader, Juan Lechín, in the same way that the PRI-dominated CTM had kicked out Lombardo Toledano in Mexico.

The Cuban People's Party split over how to answer Batista's coup in March 1952. Some of the party's leaders began flirting with revolution, importing arms and bullets, and giving military instruction to the rank-and-file. Others chose to parley with the regime, playing for time. The quarrels within the leadership undermined the chances of any action against Batista, so Fidel Castro organized his own group from the party's youth. Without consulting the official leaders, this group launched armed actions against the dictatorship. Castro's attack on the Moncada Barracks in Santiago de Cuba came on 26 July 1953. The insurrection failed and its cadres were shot or imprisoned. Freed by an amnesty in 1955, the survivors went into exile in Mexico; Fidel reorganized them as the first cadres of his July 26 Revolutionary Movement. This movement was designed to be the revolutionary apparatus of the Cuban People's Party, and its line got unanimous approval at the Congress of Orthodox Party Militants on 16 August 1955. But the Party's top leaders had already agreed to the outcome of the national elections of November 1954, by which Batista legitimized his dictatorship; so they refused to support the armed actions approved at the Congress.

This cold shoulder from the leadership, Castro explained in a statement dated 19 March 1956, led to his split with the party in March. But he declared that the July 26 Movement was not different from the Orthodox political current: it represented the rank-and-file against an old guard refusing to obey the decisions of the Party's Congress. Thus a 'Rebel Orthodoxy' emerged out of the Cuban People's Party. The rebel tendency was still committed to an APRA-type programme based on political sovereignty, economic independence, and social justice. Though the July 26 Movement was later to converge on Marxism-Leninism, it did so only after an internal struggle against its own right wing.

The Movement of the Revolutionary Left (Venezuela)

On the heels of the Cuban insurrectionary struggle against Batista came a similar struggle against Pérez Jiménez in Venezuela. For ten years the Venezuelan dictator had ruled the country with an iron hand, but a popular uprising in the capital finally overthrew him in January 1958. Like Batista, Pérez had tried to legitimize his military dictatorship by holding a plebiscite in December 1957: 85% of the electorate had allegedly voted for him. The next month in Caracas the students at the national university began several days of rioting against the electoral fraud. Then came a general strike, called by an underground group known as the Patriotic Junta. Fabricio Ojeda, president of a coalition of all the banned parties, had conceived this group six months before. The junta included the following parties dedicated to overthrowing the dictatorship: the Aprista party known as Democratic Action (AD), Ojeda's own Democratic Republican Union (URD), the Christian Democrats (PDC), and the Communist Party. Supported by armed brigades of the CP, the general strike paralyzed the capital. Pressure from elements in the armed forces and two days of street fighting caused Pérez Jiménez to flee the country on January 23.

The Patriotic Junta lacked the arms to seize power: a five-man military junta under the navy's chief, Rear Admiral Wolfgang Larrazábal, pushed it aside. In the elections of December 1958 he was the candidate of Ojeda's URD supported by the Communist Party. But Democratic Action's Rómulo Betancourt won the elections. Like Haya de la Torre, he had evolved into a partisan of 'democratic capitalism'; he opposed both 'Soviet totalitarianism' and 'Castro Communism'. He soon repressed Castro's disciples with violence.

That was the background of the first big split in AD, Venezuela's ruling Aprista party. In April 1960 a youth conference in Maracaibo, meeting against

143

party instructions, voted to split with the party's leadership and organize an independent movement. The new organization, calling itself Left Democratic Action, then changed its name to the Movement of the Revolutionary Left (MIR).

At a national conference held in July 1960, the MIR charted a new political course independent of the APRA. The MIR defined itself as a Marxist party; that was its rationale for a complete break with Betancourt's Democratic Action. The MIR took with it 14 out of 73 deputies in Congress, many rank-and-file members of the party, and the youth sector. The government hit back with everything it had: on October 20 it arrested six MIR leaders for subversion. That set off a cycle of demonstrations against the government, met by repression, followed by larger demonstrations. Finally in November 1960 the MIR abandoned its original constitutional alternative in favour of a combined general strike and insurrection. It failed. Then the MIR prepared for a long guerrilla struggle in the countryside. When in 1962 the Communist Party played its hand with guerrillas, the MIR followed suit.

The Rebel APRA (Peru)

The Peruvian APRA suffered a similar split. In October 1959 at the party's Fourth National Convention, Luis de la Puente presented a motion critical of the official leadership: his group thought the leadership was opportunist. The party suspended some members of his group and expelled others. De la Puente's group wanted to defend itself and to revive the party's original militancy. So on October 12 it organized the Aprista Committee for Defence of Principles and Internal Democracy, later known as the Rebel Aprista Committee. When reforming the party from within seemed hopeless, the Committee split off to become the Rebel APRA. This first formal split between the party's left and right happened in November 1960.

Slowly the Rebel APRA decided that any connection with the parent organization was a liability. So the rebels changed their name to the Movement of the Revolutionary Left (MIR). They followed the example of the Venezuelan MIR and adopted the politics and strategy of revolutionary Marxism. In July 1964 the Peruvian MIR published its policy document, *Our Position in the Light of the World Revolution,* calling for guerrilla warfare. Basing itself on the example of Fidel's July 26 Movement, the Peruvian MIR prepared to carry the struggle into the countryside. In June 1965 it launched three *focos* in the north, centre, and south; but the regular army defeated these guerrilla units one by one.

By January 1966 the MIR guerrillas were routed, but the insurrection had impressed the Peruvian military. The situation of the masses was critical, and in October 1968 the army launched a national revolution of its own. The young colonels who had fought the guerrillas ended by carrying out an agrarian reform similar to that projected by the Rebel APRA. (The Peruvian Congress had rejected this project back in 1961).

The Revolutionary Party of the National Left (Bolivia)
What was the background of the split in Bolivia's Revolutionary Nationalist Movement (MNR)? On 9 April 1952 a popular-based armed insurrection in La Paz overthrew the reactionary military junta of General Hugo Ballivián. The leadership of the MNR started the insurrection, but it also relied on General Antonio Seleme, Chief of the National Guard. On the second day, as street fighting continued and the insurrection seemed to fade, General Seleme took refuge in the Chilean Embassy. But the miners arrived with dynamite to win the struggle, and the MNR alone reaped the fruits of the uprising.

The new government launched an anti-imperialist and anti-oligarchical campaign that made Bolivia the most advanced Mexican-style revolution on the continent. As stated earlier in this chapter, in 1952 the government nationalized the tin mines; in 1953 an agrarian reform law abolished feudalism. But the MNR's leadership later challenged the co-government status of the Bolivian Labour Central (COB) that ran the mines and took part in the cabinet. Workers' self-management worried the right wing of the MNR; these leaders saw the miners as a brake on economic progress. Victor Paz Estenssoro, the party's leader, defined the chief goal of the revolution as economic development.

The party's leaders did not see the future of Bolivia in tin. They planned to develop agriculture and oil in Eastern Bolivia. But where could they get investment capital for their project? During Paz's second term as president (1960-64) he modernized the mining industry to get foreign exchange for developing the east. Bolivia was to leap beyond tin production into a diversified economy.

The MNR's right wing planned to modernize the mining industry by imposing drastic measures: lay-offs in unproductive mines, a slash in the miners' wages, new technology cutting back the work force, and the end of workers' control. This policy struck hard at the miners' organization, and Paz had to break the Bolivian Labour Central (COB). So he campaigned against the MNR's left wing and the miners' union as counter-revolutionary, then conjured up the spectre of communist subversion.

As the struggle heated up through 1963-64, the left lost its grip first on the government, then on the party. In April 1964 the MNR's Ninth National Convention expelled the party's left wing and the COB's Juan Lechín (elected Vice-President of Bolivia in 1960). With COB cadres Lechín then organized a Rebel MNR, the Revolut onary Party of the National Left (PRIN). But the PRIN differed from the Venezuelan and Peruvian MIRs: it did not break with the multi-class tradition of the early APRA; instead it reaffirmed the MNR's original programme against the party's right wing.

The Mexican Revolutionary Heritage

The divisions in the APRA reflected the divisions within the Mexican revolutionary heritage. They reproduced the split within the Mexican revolutionary forces in 1914. The dictator Huerta was overthrown. Then it seemed that Carranza would betray the demands for agrarian reform. So, in November 1914 at the Convention of Aguascalientes, there was a split between the right and left wings of the Constitutionalist movement. Under Villa's influence, the Convention declared itself independent of Carranza's liberal government and in favour of a radical solution of its own. The outcome was civil war: on the one hand, the Constitutionalist forces of Carranza; on the other hand, the peasant armies of Villa and Zapata. Though Zapata's armed struggle ended with his death five years later, his agrarian reform was finally carried through by Obregón, Calles and Cárdenas. Zapata so aroused the peasants that he achieved posthumous triumphs: the rural masses forced the government to redistribute the land.

Carranza's tradition of revolutionary nationalism survived in the post-World War Two APRA parties, while Villa's and Zapata's programme of Land and Liberty reappeared in the left-wing splits from the APRA in the late '50s and early '60s. The early APRA managed to hold these two traditions in balance, but the post-World War Two history of the Aprista parties is that of one split after another: the right wings followed the pattern of Carranza's struggle against the Revolutionary Convention; the left wings revived the agrarian reforms and work of Emiliano Zapata.

The Cuban Agrarian Reform followed the model established by the Revolutionary Convention in Morelos (1915). The Cubans expropriated local capitalist farms with compensation, but foreigners' lands without compensation because of their hostility to the Revolution. Though in 1959 Cuba's first agrarian reform chose for expropriation lands larger than those seized in Morelos, in 1963 the second reform lowered the limit to 165 acres.

Neither Democratic Action in Venezuela nor Haya de la Torre's party in Peru favoured agrarian reforms based on the Zapatista model. Only in Bolivia and Cuba were such reforms evident. But in Bolivia the parcelling out of land neither touched the big cattle ranches of Santa Cruz nor developed the collectivizing tendency of the Mexican *ejidos*. Only in Cuba did Zapata's programme fully bloom, and that makes Fidel Castro his greatest heir. Who were Zapata's other heirs? In Latin America the rebel APRAs, especially the Venezuelan and Peruvian MIRs – partly influenced by the Cuban example. And so the seeds sown by the Mexican Revolution's greatest hero, Emiliano Zapata, budded in Mexico but reached full blossom in neighbouring Cuba, 'the first liberated territory of the Americas'.

Fidel Castro, during the years in which he headed the July 26 Movement, was unquestionably the most important single heir of the APRA's original anti-imperialist programme. But between him and Haya another *caudillo* was to raise the banner of revolutionary nationalism that Haya had betrayed. That was Argentina's Juan Domingo Perón.

8. Military-Populist Regimes in Latin America

The ultimate destiny of the Mexican Revolution was to overflow its national boundaries and to serve as a catalyst for similar revolutionary movements throughout Latin America. In effect, the Mexican Revolution was not just a national event but, like the Bolshevik Revolution, had international repercussions.

The legacy of the Revolution was carried forward by two major political currents. The first, as we have seen in the previous chapter, under the leadership of Haya de la Torre, expanded southward through Central America, the Caribbean and the Andean countries to his own native Peru. These were the direct heirs of the Revolution. The APRA's influence finally reached the continent's sub-equatorial eastern seaboard, but it was only feebly felt there. When a new wave of revolutions was launched from Argentina by Juan Domingo Perón, it was more influenced by nationalist tendencies within his own country than by Haya or the APRA. Unlike the first wave, it barely reached beyond the country of its origin. But it did set off a chain reaction in the relations between the military and popular forces which was felt as far northward as Peru, in the national revolution of 1968 and the Peruvian-type military regimes that followed in Bolivia and Panama. These indirect heirs of the Revolution picked up the torch which the APRA had abandoned.

The Nature of Military Populist Regimes

Prior to World War Two military coups in Latin America, almost without exception, were politically regressive. The professional military, as in Mexico under Díaz, represented at best a static social force, while military interventins were typically holding actions in response to emerging popular parties. That is no longer the case. In several instances influential sectors of the armed forces have either turned toward a populist ideology or generated one of their own. The two most noteworthy examples are the Argentine military coup of 1943, which fathered the Peronist Movement, and the Peruvian military coup and resulting social transformation of 1968-75. The general thrust of these two national revolutions and their respective progeny was against both imperialism and the local oligarchies.

147

Increasingly, the armed forces in Latin America are being officered by men from the urban middle classes — the petty bourgeoisie and petty bureaucracy — who are responsive to their countries' underdeveloped and dependent condition. Although indoctrinated with a conservative nationalism in the military academies or with a pro-imperialist ideology in U.S. training centres, they have also responded positively to revolutionary nationalist currents instilled by progressive forces in their own countries. This was true not only of Colonel Perón in Argentina, but also of Colonel Juan Velasco Alvarado in Peru and of the younger generation of officers in several other Latin American countries.

The convergence of military nationalism and the populist currents typified by the Mexican Revolution and the APRA has given birth to the political phenomenon known as military populism. How does it differ from the APRA's own populism which helped to diffuse the principles of the Mexican Revolution?

The Aprista parties on the continent have been dominated by civilians, while the Mexican Revolution itself was led by civilians who, only after several years of fighting, rose to the rank of revolutionary generals. Quite different were the military-populist regimes beginning with the Argentine national revolution of 1943-55. That revolution was the work of professional soldiers; and it took the form initially of a military coup rather than a popular or mass insurrection. That was also the pattern followed by the Peruvian national revolution of 1968-75 and its successors. Further, these second-stage national revolutionary struggles against the landed oligarchies and imperialism were not inspired by the Mexican example; they converged upon it. Rather than diffusing the ideology of the Mexican Revolution, which they radiated only very faintly, they diffused the principles of their own national revolutions which happened to resemble the Mexican. Similar objectives were achieved, but by different means.

The Argentine National Revolution and its Philosophy

The APRA had degenerated into a liberal movement making concessions to imperialism and the local oligarchies. From the APRA's ageing shoulders the continent's anti-imperialist mantle fell upon the young Peronist Movement in Argentina. This movement, a by-product of the military coup of June 1943, was only indirectly influenced by the APRA. However, its distinguishing feature was the populist philosophy known as the Third Position.

The Influence of Aprismo on Peronism
Peronism shared common ground with the early APRA. Haya's programme contained sketches of several Peronist ideas: the concept of a Third Position between capitalism and socialism, and the three pillars of Political Sovereignty, Economic Independence, and Social Justice. In Peron's programme political sovereignty meant the struggle against imperialism and the struggle for Latin

American unity. Economic independence stood for a policy of nationalizing foreign industries and ending foreign controls. How did Perón think of social justice? Briefly, as the redistribution of the national income through profit-sharing and a minimum wage; and the redistribution of economic power through farm and factory co-operatives managed by the workers. Though the wording of the two programmes was different, the content was roughly the same. And there were other similarities between Peronism and Aprismo. In a circular letter dated 28 July 1953, the General Secretary of the Peruvian Aprista Party commented on the parallelism: 'In its support of continental unity and its anti-imperialist position, Peronism shows features coincident with Aprismo; likewise, in its tendency to constitute a party based on a united front.'

These similarities tempt us to search for the historical origins of Peronism in the early APRA. Is there more than a formal convergence linking the two movements?

In the Introduction to his translation of Haya de la Torre's political writings, *Aprismo: the Ideas and Doctrines of Victor Raúl Haya de la Torre* (1973) Robert Alexander claims to discover a direct influence on Peronism. He infers this influence from Perón's own statements. Before Perón got into politics he read Haya's writings, kept Haya's books for reference, and studied Haya's arguments for Latin American political unity.

The APRA's influence on Peronism, nevertheless, was probably more indirect than direct. In 1935 Arturo Jauretche organized young dissidents in the Radical Party into the Radical Orientation Forces of the Argentine Youth (FORJA). This group took over Haya's ideas, adapting them to Argentine social conditions. Through speeches, conferences, books and essays, FORJA spread its views on anti-imperialism, economic independence from Britain, the local oligarchy as an agent of foreigners, and the need for Argentine neutrality in European wars. As early as 1936 FORJA summed up its political objectives under the slogan of 'Popular Sovereignty, Economic Emancipation, and the Dominion of Social Justice' — almost the same words to appear later on Perón's political banner. In December 1945 FORJA dissolved to merge with the new Peronist political organization.

What was FORJA's relationship to the APRA? In the opening section of *FORJA and the Infamous Decade* (Buenos Aires, 1962), Jauretche testifies to Haya's influence in shaping FORJA's political outlook. Again, in a section about university reform and the APRA, he says that 'the influence of the APRA was more than anything the result of its general analysis of the phenomenon of imperialism'. Article One of FORJA's first public statement (29 June 1935) declared that the historical processes in Argentina and Latin America 'reveal the existence of a permanent struggle by the people for popular sovereignty against the oligarchies, as agents of imperialism's economic, political and cultural penetration'. This APRA-like formulation recalls passages from Haya's early writings. When Perón's budding movement took in FORJA's militants, there was a rise in the indirect influence of APRA on Peronist politics.

Among the members of FORJA one, in particular, exercised a deep personal and intellectual influence on Perón. This was Raul Scalabrini Ortiz, whose revisionist interpretation of Argentine history gave precedence to the role of indigenous elements from the interior over the liberal, cosmopolitan and Europeanizing influence of the port city of Buenos Aires. His analysis of British imperialism in the River Plate and of the obstructive role of British economic interests was regarded by Perón as a major contribution to Argentine nationalism. In *Perón: As He Is,* a book of political dialogues between Perón and his appointed biographer, the Spanish historian Enrique Pavón Pereyra, Scalabrini is said to personify the best civic tradition of the Argentinians. In a chapter entitled 'The Legacy of History', Perón pays further tribute to him: 'I am particularly indebted to his germinal ideas incorporated in my own *Force is the Right of Beasts* and *The Country's Betrayers.* He exercised, in a manner, the first moral chair of the Republic and, when his turn came to leave this world, he made me the trustee of his political testament.' It is sometimes claimed that the principal influence on Perón came from Mussolini and Italian fascism. On the contrary, it was Scalabrini's native brand of nationalism that had the more profound effect.

The Third Position
The first statement of Perón's Third Position was presented under the title *Peronist Doctrine* (Buenos Aires, 1947), within a year of beginning his first presidency. During the last two centuries, he observes in chapter one, the world has evolved through two great stages: the evolutionary cycle initiated by the French Revolution, and the new evolutionary cycle beginning with the Russian Bolshevik Revolution. The first period put an end to rule by the aristocracy and gave birth to governments by the bourgeoisie. The second upset a bourgeois government and opened the way for rule by the proletariat. The economic, social and political problem posed by this latest evolutionary cycle is precisely *how* the workers will achieve power. A revolution by violent means is imperative, Perón claims, only when an oligarchical class deprives the workers of their rights and there is no other method of making one. Otherwise, 'the State must search for an equilibrium that will permit a political or peaceful evolution'. For Perón, the problem is how to overcome capitalist oppression without falling victim to a new tyranny by a proletariat bent on avenging itself for past injuries.

Political movements and socio-economic systems, he argues in the same chapter, follow a pendulum-like course between extremes. Today these extremes are individualism — the best State is that which governs least — and collectivism, or the supremacy of the State over individual interests. Neither extreme is capable of enduring: 'Historically, the most stable human organization seems to have occupied a middle ground.' Thus Perón opts for a position of equilibrium, a third position between extremes: 'That is to say, our position would be centrist, a position in which the State does not tyrannize over man, and man does not abuse the State.'

On May Day 1950, in a message to the Argentine Congress, Perón first applied the term 'Third Position' to characterize his political philosophy. The term 'justicialist', a neologism of justice and socialist, was also used: 'Placing things where they belong, individual capital and property as social functions, our economy ceased to be individualistic without becoming collectivistic, thus situating itself in a just mean that permits us to qualify it as justicialist.'

This position had its roots in a number of discrepant sources. Two decades earlier we find it sketched in Haya's *Anti-Imperialism and the APRA*. In addition, it was part of the heritage of European fascism. President Lazaro Cárdenas of Mexico was known to have articulated a similar philosophy. It was also the political doctrine of the ecclesiastical hierarchy in Latin America.

President Cárdenas incorporated it in his 1934 electoral campaign. In his speech for state intervention and the Six Year Plan of his party, he declared: 'The Mexican Revolution stands opposed to individualistic liberalism because our people do not want the sources of wealth and the means of production to be controlled by the egoism of individuals; to State communism because our people to not want a system that deprives them of the fruits of their labour or substitutes the State boss for the individual master.' Again, 'In Mexico we are trying to destroy by revolutionary action the regime of individual exploitation, not in order to fall under the exploitation of the State, but to turn over the sources of wealth and the means of production to organized workers' collectives.'

The concept of a Third Position is also part of Church doctrine. It reaches back to the papal encyclicals of Pope Pius XI, 'Quadragesimo Anno' (1931), and Pope Leo XIII, 'Rerum Novarum' (1891). The Catholic influence prompted Perón to distinguish his national socialism from the Aryan variety in Nazi Germany. His preferred term was 'Christian National Socialism'. That Perón used the term socialism at all is instructive. Cárdenas also did: in the struggle against the Mexican oligarchy when he was trying to whip up mass support and steal the left's thunder. Since the 1968 coup in Peru, the military junta has also called itself socialist, while launching an anti-imperialist national revolution in the tradition of the early APRA and the Mexican Revolution.

Perón's Third Position had important results for both Argentine domestic and foreign policy. At home the Third Position steered between the private and public sectors of the economy to favour co-operative ownership. It also pushed for a new kind of political representation: in the federal and provincial governments organized labour would get influence to offset the interests of big business. Internationally, the Third Position stood for a bloc of non-aligned nations against both Soviet and Yankee imperialism. This meant efforts to offset Yankee interests in the Hemisphere by approaching communist governments through recognition and trade.

Domestically, the Third Position pursued a course between the traditional right and the Marxist left. Perón worked to build a military-labour coalition as the backbone of his regime. He began by first overthrowing a civilian government, next restoring elections, and then winning presidential office as a military hero with labour support. The pattern followed was remarkably similar to that of General Obregón in Mexico. In 1920 Obregón overthrew

Carranza and then got himself elected with the help of two forces: the Mexican Labour Party of Luis Morones and a radical offshoot of the Constitutionalist Liberal Party headed by General Benjamin Hill. In 1946 Perón won the election in a similar way. His support came from the newly organized Labour Party and from a split-off of the Radical Civic Union under his running-mate, Hortensio. Quijano.

The first Peronist government helped to organize about 2,000 co-operatives with almost 1,000,000 members. The State banks aided them with big credits. The State sector favoured them in distributing scarce goods, farm machinery, and other inputs. In 1951 the government announced a long-range plan for developing production in the countryside: animal raising and food growing would be run co-operatively; commerce in food, meat, and dairy products would pass from the State to the co-operatives.

In November 1951 Perón announced that the old political forms would pass away and the executive and legislature would represent the people's organizations according to their weight in production. The government was moving toward a new syndicalist State. Labour was to have a big share in running the life of the nation, including management of production, exchange, and distribution. In December, the province of Chaco adopted a new constitution, under which 30,000 members of the trade union organizations chose half the legislature and 200,000 voters chose the other half. But structural reforms like these almost stopped during Perón's second term. His radical wife, Evita, died in 1952. Then elements in the military and the oligarchy mobilized opposition to Perón's government and slowed the Argentine revolution to a crawl. They sent the revolution reeling backward after the military overthrew Perón in 1955.

In the early '40s Peronism emerged at a critical moment in the history of the Latin American revolution. The APRA was softening its critique of Yankee imperialism; Haya was brandishing his new slogan of 'Democratic Inter-Americanism without Imperialism'; the democratic left in Latin America was calling for co-operation with that in the United States. As the APRA's turn to the right sharpened, Peronism burst upon the continent as a powerful anti-imperialist movement.

The APRA courted the Democratic Party in the U.S.A. Such an alliance never tempted Perón because of his open sympathy for the Axis powers as an emergent Third Force in Western Europe. He never thought that traditional democracy offered an effective strategy against imperialism and the oligarchies, but Nazi-Fascism's defeat in war later made him shift to a democratic ideology. This is the paradox: because Perón's Axis sympathies kept Argentina neutral during World War Two, Haya de la Torre censured the 'political cancer' of Peronism; yet while the APRA was betraying the anti-imperialist movement, the 'fascist' Perón was reviving it in the Southern Cone.

In *Latin America: Now or Never* (Montevideo, 1967) Perón boasted that twenty years earlier his government had first launched the idea of a Third Position, the strategy today defended by so many countries in the Third World. Since then, Mao in Asia, Nasser in Africa, even De Gaulle in Europe,

have become advocates of a neutral bloc of nations, a bloc opposed to both
Yankee capitalism and Soviet communism – both imperialist systems according
to Perón. Fascist Italy and Nazi Germany also had opposed traditional capitalism and Soviet communism back in the period between the two World
Wars. That was what led Perón to include them as the leaders of a bloc of
powers representing the Third Position. In his perspective, the APRA and
European fascism shared a common ground.

Throughout the Hemisphere the Peronist regime pursued a foreign policy
aimed at buttressing every national revolution against U.S. imperialism. The
Aprista parties in Latin America did less to defend the Guatemalan Revolution than did the Argentine government under Perón. In a March 1969
interview with the authors, Guatemala's ex-President Juan José Arévalo
confessed this truth: only secret arms shipments from Perón to Guatemala
kept the revolutionary movement from going under during Arévalo's term of
office (1945-1950). Later Perón sent arms to Arévalo's successor, President
Jacobo Arbenz (1950-54). Only two Latin American governments refused to
vote with the U.S.A. against the alleged intervention of world communism
in the Guatemalan Revolution: Mexico and Argentina. In March 1954 at the
10th Inter-American Conference in Caracas John Foster Dulles, the then U.S.
Secretary of State, presented the motion for solidarity against Soviet communism in Guatemala. It was the first thunder from the storm clouds
gathering over the populist revolution there. In June the storm broke, as a
CIA-financed invasion washed away Arbenz's elected regime.

Earlier, in 1951 at the fourth reunion of the Chancellors of American
States in Washington D.C., Perón's government voted against the creation of
a Pan-American army to defend the Hemisphere against international communism. Its only support was from the Mexican and Guatemalan governments. On other issues the Peronist government stood alone: it refused to
ratify the charter of the new Organization of American States (OAS), and it
resisted the siren song of the lending agencies dominated by the United
States – the World Bank and the International Monetary Fund.

Who took the first steps toward a Latin American common market to lay
the basis for political unity on the continent? Not the reformist leaders of the
main Aprista parties, but Juan Domingo Perón. In February 1953 he signed a
bilateral pact with Chile, in August with Paraguay, and in December with
Ecuador. In 1954 the Bolivian government announced its support for Perón's
economic union. Resistance to Yankee economic penetration of Latin America
had passed from the Aprista parties to the Peronist Movement in Argentina
and its sympathizers in other countries.

Haya was replaced by Perón as the spokesman for anti-imperialism in
Latin America. Perón revived the international principles of the Mexican
Revolution just as the revolutionary current in Mexico's ruling party was
being damned up by Miguel Alemán (1946-52). As the APRA betrayed its
earlier militancy, so did its Mexican counterpart. The Mexican ruling party,
PRI, rebuilt by Alemán, sought an accommodation with the Yankee colossus.

Toward the end of World War Two the APRA had begun to turn away

153

from its old Programme; in the same way the Peronist Movement in power ended by adjusting to U.S. imperialism. In the middle of Perón's second administration (July 1953), the Argentine Congress passed a law guaranteeing foreign investments. In 1955 Peron signed, with a subsidiary of Standard Oil, an agreement for finding and drilling oil in Patagonia. What saved the Peronist Movement from the APRA's fate? In September 1955 a rightist military coup drove Perón into exile and forced him to reaffirm the original militancy of his movement.

The National Marxism of the Peronist Left Wing

After the coup Perón did not move to the right with most of the Aprista parties on the continent; the Peronist Movement looked for a way to live with the revolutionary currents in its own ranks. While during the '60s internal feuds ripped open the main Aprista parties to throw up Rebel APRAs, the Peronist Movement fathered a revolutionary tendency that flourished alongside the party's right wing. This went on for twenty years. Peronism regained power in May 1973; Perón died in July 1974. Two months later Peronism's left wing, under Montoneros leadership supported by 200,000 Peronist Youth, declared war on Isabel Perón's government. By supporting police and paramilitary repression, the official leadership finally forced a split with the Movement's revolutionary Marxist tendency.

If the APRA was the first successful linking of Marxist currents and Latin nationalism, Peronism was the second. The early Haya worked out a variant of Latin American or national Marxism, clearly identifying with the Marxist political tradition. Not so Perón: his background shows the influence of German National Socialism and Italian Fascism in the formulation of his Third Position. But Peronism did not have to wait for the internationalization of the Cuban Revolution to get Marxist support. While Marxism came to the APRA from within, it converged on Peronism from without.

This convergence took three forms. First, a Trotskyist splinter-group disobeyed the Fourth International in order to favour Argentine neutrality during World War Two. Led by Jorge Abelardo Ramos, it stopped short of joining the Peronist Party, but did offer Perón its support. Second, a year later in 1947, a group of communists supported the new Peronist regime elected with the help of the first labour party in Argentina that was independent and nationalist. Led by Rodolfo Puiggrós, they joined the Peronist Party as the only revolutionary force in Argentina that carried any weight. Third, in 1949 a group of socialists broke with their party and supported the Peronist regime. Led by Enrique Dickman, they merged with the Peronist Movement without actually joining the Peronist Party.

The national Marxism spread by these three groups differed from that of the socialist and communist parties who drank their wisdom from European fountains. This national Marxism adapted itself to Argentine interests and traditions; it ignored doctrinaire, abstract or ideal possibilities. What prompted the organization of a national left in keeping with the historical realities of the Argentine working class? The rank and file's rejection of the established

Marxist parties for abandoning the politics of neutrality during World War Two.

Within the Peronist Movement the Marxist-Leninist cadres, offering critical support from inside, helped build a left wing. This tendency, growing in power and influence, was known as 'labour Peronism', 'hard-core Peronism' or 'revolutionary Peronism'. It caught the nation's attention by organizing a bloc of labour deputies. These deputies were attracted by the militancy of John William Cooke. Somehow Cooke had mixed Marx with Perón, and his brew was spiced with the currents of national Marxism inside the Peronist Movement.

The Peruvian National Revolution

The influence of Peronism, unlike that of Haya's APRA, took the form of a chain reaction rather than the organized diffusion of a revolutionary ideology. It was the first act of a drama that helped to establish a new climate in the relations between sectors of the military and the popular forces in each country. The second act of this drama begins in Peru. There a military coup also set about reorganizing the country's destiny.

In Peru Colonel Juan Velasco began where Perón left off. Just as Fidel Castro went beyond Haya in radicalizing the APRA's policies of progressive nationalization, so Velasco surpassed Perón in radicalizing the military-populist model of revolution. First, Velasco did not see the Third Position as a static point between capitalism and collectivism; he saw it as a dynamic centre moving toward socialism. Second, he went beyond Perón to build agricultural co-operatives on a national scale and to develop industrial co-operatives as partners of private capital. Under Perón co-operativization crawled along, but Velasco kicked it rapidly forward. If Perón appears to have followed Obregón's footsteps, then Velasco seems inspired by Cárdenas' example. Not Obregón but Cárdenas smashed the semi-feudal system of land tenure in Mexico, and not Perón but Velasco launched and completed an agrarian reform of the Mexican type.

These were not the only differences between the Argentine and Peruvian national revolutions. Perón's reforms incorporated elements of Italian Fascism and the Spanish Falange, while Velasco's reforms show the influence of Yugoslav and Algerian experiments with workers' self-management.

In spite of the differences, Perón's and Velasco's regimes show even greater similarities. Both of them spurned the civilian traditions of the APRA and had military origins. The APRA-type parties launched their revolutions from below backed by a mass political movement. Perón and Velasco started their revolutions from above with military coups, then mobilized support from the masses.

At first nobody knew where the Peruvian military junta was heading. On 3 October 1968 the junta overthrew a populist party, and the Peruvian Apristas called the colonels undemocratic and reactionary. But a week later the junta annulled an agreement with a Jersey Standard Oil subsidiary (IPC), a contract underwritten by overthrown President Fernando Belaúnde. The junta sent troops to seize, without compensation, the IPC's lands and plant at La Brea and Pariñas. What was the meaning of this dramatic act?

By the Act of Talara, Belaúnde's Popular Action (AP) government had agreed to cancel IPC's debt of $ 144,000,000 in back taxes and to forget another $ 830,000,000 dollars owed the government for oil taken out illegally. The agreement meant a loss of one billion dollars to the nation – a sum equal to the government's annual budget! In return the government got the company's lands at Talara, but not its refinery. No wonder the government tried to hide the terms of the agreement from the public.

The military stepped in to nationalize IPC's refinery along with its other holdings. That put an end to Peru's largest foreign monopoly in the production and sale of oil, and triggered off a diplomatic battle with the U.S. government. This shaped the development of the Revolution. The properties of IPC went to the government-owned PETROPERU to make it the biggest oil producer in the country. But the new government announced that it had acted under exceptional circumstances, that the oil seizure would not open a barrage of expropriations aimed at other companies. This move calmed the international monopolies, and foreign oil companies later beefed up investments in Peru with the help of government concessions.

But the junta had embarked on a new course of revolutionary nationalism. That was clear from its radical agrarian reform law of June 1969. Back in 1964 an Aprista Congress had passed a moderate agrarian reform, but by 1968 had redistributed only 1,500,000 acres. And the revolutionary junta? Within five years of its agrarian law, it had redistributed 11,000,000 acres.

This record equalled that set by the Mexican agrarian reform from 1917 to 1928, but in half the time. It beat the performance of the main APRA-type parties that took the Mexican agrarian reform for a starting-point. Furthermore it was the only reform to go beyond the Mexican in favouring co-operatives: to them went 97% of the redistributed land in lots of between 10,000 and 30,000 acres. It struck down the modern bourgeois sector of the agrarian economy; it took over all agro-industrial enterprises, *about 60% of them foreign owned*. Thus, like the Cuban agrarian reform, the Peruvian stood up and faced down imperialism.

The seizure of the oil refinery of Talara was only the first step along the road of nationalization. Soon there came a restructuring of the economy: the Agrarian Reform Act of 1969, the General Law of Industries of July 1970, and the Law of the Industrial Community of September 1970. The new laws governing industry aimed to force the capitalist sector of the economy into the role of junior partner. The General Law incorporated within the State sector all industries making basic inputs, capital goods, and industrial technology. By February 1974, 29 big enterprises were nationalized, raising the State's share in manufacturing from 1.5% to 20%. All companies dominated by foreign capital were 'Peruvianized'. For companies with foreign and domestic capital, the law set a limit of 50% foreign ownership. For companies dominated entirely by foreigners, it ordered foreign ownership to drop to 30%.

What was the law creating industrial communities? This concerned all indigenous enterprises with either at least five workers or a gross income of more than 1,000,000 soles (U.S. $ 23,000) a year. Over a twenty-year period these firms would have to introduce profit-sharing and workers' participation in ownership, slowly lowering private capital to 50% of the total. In these enterprises the workers would become co-owners and co-managers. By May 1974 there were from 3,000 to 4,000 industrial communities representing 200,000 workers. Co-operative property combined with private capital — this was a unique economic form. It soon extended beyond industry, and there appeared communities in mining, fishing, and telecommunications. The industrial communities, along with the co-operatives in agriculture, made the co-operative sector a powerful force in the economy. It and the State sector both competed with the private sector.

The regime encouraged other forms of public and semi-public property. In April 1974 a Law of Enterprises of Social Property aimed to develop industrial co-operatives owned and managed by the workers alone. In Yugoslavia to form producers' co-operatives the government took over factories and gave them to the workers, but the new law in Peru aimed to found new enterprises. The law provided that any person or group might found a co-operative: if his or her proposal met with approval from the authorities they would finance the co-operative through State loans or by floating special bonds. Who were the authorities charged with this task? The National Commission of Social Property, the Finance Development Corporation, and the National Fund of Social Property.

The Law outlined promotional means for favouring social property over the State sector: preferential treatment in getting low-interest loans from national banks; preferential treatment in obtaining technical help from the State; essential inputs given by the State from government industries; and commercial outlets provided by the State. In other words, the Law meant this co-operative sector to some day dominate the economy.

On 28 July 1973 President Velasco made public the government's plan for restructuring the economy. The project favoured a pluralistic economy with four sectors: first, the sector of social property, eventually to become the dominant one; next, the State sector, occupying the commanding heights of the economy; then, the sector of industrial and other labour communities; and finally, the private sector, dominated by capitalist entrepreneurs, partnerships and corporations, but also including people working for themselves, like artisans and shopkeepers. Clearly the junta had chosen a Third Position favouring State and co-operative forms of property over capitalist enterprise. Three weeks earlier, on July 4, the President had clarified the government's position: 'It is not true that the Peruvian Revolution . . . has from the beginning followed a "path equidistant from capitalism and socialism". What we have rejected, besides capitalism, is communism which, in our judgment, is fundamentally different from socialism . . . . Our Revolution is already enriching the revolutionary tradition of contemporary socialism, but from a perspective entirely Peruvian and national, which imitates nothing nor mechanically borrows from other revolutionary processes distinct from ours.'

The following year in a press interview, the President revealed the *Plan Inca*, the junta's programme for structural reforms. The revolutionary officers had drafted it before the coup in 1968, keeping the plan secret until 1974 for tactical reasons; they needed time to neutralize potential enemies of the Revolution. The *Plan Inca* spoke of a 'nationalist, independent, and humanist' Revolution. This was interpreted in language like Perón's, in terms of political sovereignty, economic independence, and social justice. The Plan was a 31-point programme. It analysed the major problem areas of Peruvian society, formulated a strategy for dealing with each situation, and proposed a series of tactics for carrying out each strategy. One objective was the expropriation of the oil; another was agrarian reform; another was the project for reforming business enterprises. The junta's actions roughly followed the points listed in the Plan.

Like the Peronist movement in Argentina and like the APRA itself, the Peruvian military junta subsequently developed a counter-revolutionary thrust. Within a year of the publication of the *Plan Inca* President Velasco was deposed, after which the military junta began perceptibly to undermine his reforms. The project to found a new sector of social property never materialized, while the sector of industrial and labour communities was deliberately scuttled in favour of the private sector. In short, the Peruvian National Revolution of 1968-75 ended in much the same way as the Mexican Revolution of 1910-40: once the bureaucratic class had effectively institutionalized its political power, it reached an accommodation with the private sector which would not rock the boat by pushing the country toward a socialist transformation.

The Bolivian Revolution Takes a Peruvian Turn

Nonetheless, like the Cuban Revolution, the thunder of the 1968 Peruvian Revolution has echoed across the continent. In Bolivia, less than a year later, there was a military-type revolution inspired by the Peruvian example. It overthrew the government of Siles Salinas. Who was Siles? He had served as Vice-President under General Réné Barrientos; a helicopter crash killed the general in April 1969, and Siles took over. But on September 26 a nationalist-led coalition of officers toppled his civilian government.

The coup had the support of three sectors of the military. First, there was the pro-imperialist sector made up of followers of the late General Barrientos. Most of the army's officers belonged to this pro-Yankee sector; the prospect of losing status under the civilian government of Siles Salinas prompted them to enter into a coalition with the moderate nationalist sector. Second, there was the moderate nationalist sector led by General Alfredo Ovando Candia, made up of pro-MNR officers hoping to return the party to power. These officers planned to replace the party's civilian leadership with military men. Ovando formed the new government, and he kept the pro-imperialist sector from playing the large role it had expected. Third, there was the revolutionary nationalist sector. This was the 'Peruvianizing' group under General Juan José Torres, whose pro-MNR officers hoped to restore the party to power and to revive its anti-imperialist programme. These officers believed the party's civilian leaders had betrayed it.

A document called *The Revolutionary Mandate of the National Armed Forces* was drawn up by the coup's main leaders, General Ovando as the army's commander in chief and General Torres as the army's chief of staff. Referring to the revival of the dead Che Guevara's National Liberation Army (ELN), the army document called for 'a rapid and profound transformation of the economic, social and political structure face to face with the dependence, poverty, disorientation and Vietnamization of Bolivia in a new and sterile fratricidal immolation'. The document declared that Siles' government 'was pseudo-democratic' and 'anti-national', infiltrated by the oligarchy, and dependent on reactionary right-wing forces. The government 'was disqualified to lead the national struggle against the terrorist adventure of the ELN and against backwardness and dependence'. Like its Peruvian cousin, the Bolivian coup aimed to cure a sick social organism: this did not mean suppression of the symptoms of society's discontent; it meant cutting away the causes.

That called for a revival of the MNR's old militancy against imperialism, based on a programme of political sovereignty, economic independence, and social justice. In common with the Peruvian model, Ovando's regime adopted a Third Position. According to the army's revolutionary mandate: 'The development of a country which, like Bolivia, belongs to the area of misery and dependence cannot be based exclusively on a capitalist system nor exclusively on a socialist one; it must be based on a national revolutionary model in which State property, social, co-operative and communal ownership of the means of production co-exist with private property.'

Ovando's cabinet included Marcelo Quiroga Santa Cruz as Minister of Mines and Petroleum, and Alberto Bailey Gutiérrez as Minister of Information, both known for their criticism of Barrientos' pro-imperialist policies and for their defence of Bolivia's natural resources. The first act of the new government was to abolish the Petroleum Code. The Code sprang from the MNR's early administration in 1955 and provided opportunities for foreign capital to exploit the country's sub-soil. Next came the abolition of the Law of State Security which had choked off democratic freedoms. Then came the abolition of Barrientos' anti-labour decrees against the Bolivian Labour Central (COB). Within a month of the coup the government nationalized the largest oil monopoly in the country, Bolivian Gulf Oil Company: General Torres' troops seized its plant and offices. In the following months Ovando's regime built state refineries and a state monopoly for selling mineral resources.

The United States imposed an economic blockade on Bolivia's petroleum exports. That, plus pressure from the State Department, forced Marcelo Quiroga out of the government in March 1970. In May pro-imperialist army officers carried out repressive acts against the revived COB. Alberto Bailey, protesting a wave of government censorship, resigned as Minister of Information; General Torres lost his post as chief of staff of the armed forces. All this set the stage for a right-wing military coup by the pro-imperialist sector of the army. Its new commander in chief, General Rogelio Miranda, waited for his cue.

On 4 October 1970 he pushed Ovando from the stage and struggled to form a new government. But General Torres and the army's anti-imperialist sector defied the military junta and called for support from the miners' COB. The miners paralyzed the capital with a general strike that helped bring down the reactionary interim regime. The military was tearing itself apart. Its right wing decided on a strategic retreat, while its left wing took the presidency and organized a government. This government turned sharply to the left. Under Torres' regime a Soviet-type popular assembly was established on May Day 1971.

The Torres government faced increasingly right-wing opposition in the following months. In January 1971 the first abortive military coup occurred under Colonel Hugo Banzer. The United States was hostile, and in exile the right-wing officers sharpened their teeth. In August, Banzer returned to Bolivia to overthrow the Torres government. For almost two years the nation had benefited from revolutionary nationalist regimes patterned on the Peruvian model.

The Panamanian Revolution

Panama was the second country to fall under the influence of the Peruvian example. Coups and counter-coups sent Panama spinning into the wake of the Peruvian Revolution. It all began on 11 October 1968, with a coup by the National Guard's Commander, Omar Torrijos, against the 11 day old government of the elected President, Dr. Arnulfo Arias. What was the aim of the coup? Its supporters said they were fighting corruption and nepotism in government, but the National Guard was obviously angered by the President's decision to retire some of its officers.

At first the new Torrijos regime looked like just another Caribbean dictatorship. The government arrested the political opposition and launched a campaign against guerrillas and communists. On the pretext that the universities were bases for urban guerrillas, the government closed them in December 1968. In February 1969 a government decree smothered civil liberties and dissolved all political parties. The Panamanian National Assembly was sent packing; the government took over the courts. The Torrijos dictatorship had raped the Constitution, so the entire left prepared to fight it.

But Torrijos was soon to surprise the left. By the end of 1969 it became clear that the ruling junta was divided, that there was a struggle over which direction the country's development should take. Who would win this internal struggle, Torrijos' nationalist officers or the pro-imperialist colonels? On

15 December 1969 a CIA-backed coup installed a provisional president. The coup's leaders charged Torrijos with being 'soft' on communism! They spread rumours that Torrijos had once been a member of the Panamanian People's Party (the name of the local communist party). Everyone knew that Torrijos' second in command, Colonel Boris Martínez, had been a leader of the communist youth during his student days. The day after this CIA-supported coup, Torrijos rushed back from a Mexican vacation to take charge of loyal units. He smashed the coup: the nationalist sector of the armed forces gained control and purged the pro-Yankee elements behind the conspiracy.

What is Panama's armed force, the National Guard? Compared to other military forces in Latin America, the Guard is a recent creation, organized and trained by the Pentagon in 1953. Unlike the older caste armies run by senior officers from the oligarchy, the Guard was officered by men drawn from the middle sectors of Panamanian society. Many of these sympathized with Peru's new nationalist military regime. Several of Torrijos' colleagues had been to the Centre for Higher Military Studies (CAEM) in Lima, where they attended lectures by representatives of the nationalist sector of the armed forces — before the revolutionary coup. One of these lecturers was Colonel Velasco, destined to become leader of the Peruvian Revolution. And so the Peruvianist group within the Panamanian National Guard was spurred into action by the CIA-supported coup. The Peruvianists took a left turn in December 1969 by purging CIA agents and pro-Yankee officers.

Later Torrijos and his men looked for support among the middle and lower classes against the local oligarchy linked to U.S. interests. In January 1970 Torrijos appointed Juan Antonio Tack as Foreign Minister, a man known for his anti-imperialist views. In August an amnesty for political prisoners brought the release of representatives of the leftist organizations in Panama. The government recognized the National Labour Centre, organized to offset the labour central controlled by the United States' AFL-CIO. Peasant unions were allowed to go into action; land seizures were legalized with no compensation for big owners. Student organizations revived with government encouragement. By the middle of 1970 there was a widening chasm between two groups: on one side, the Panamanian oligarchy backed by the United States; on the other side, the military government. On 12 September 1970, Torrijos took a big step forward. He announced his determination to end U.S. occupation of his country; he called for the end of all past treaties and for a new one recognizing Panama's total control of the Canal Zone.

In a letter to Senator Edward Kennedy published in the newspaper *Estrella de Panama* in July 1970, Torrijos noted how the Panamanian oligarchy, using himself as their unwitting tool, had repressed popular-based movements. The oligarchy had not only used Torrijos personally, but also the National Guard to defend its vested interests through continued represssion. Only after many years, said Torrijos, had he become aware of the oligarchy's cynicism and of the possibility of improving the living conditions of his people.

Then he realized the importance of a new kind of military mentality — that shown in the Peruvian armed forces. He considered himself a representative of the new military mind. Five years later in an interview published in the Mexican daily *El Dia* (6 July 1975), he reaffirmed this conviction:

> A new type of military is emerging in Latin America; and it is emerging because the armed forces have become tired of being the instrument used to correct the mistakes of politicians. Many years ago the Mexican armed forces constituted an example. Today, we have examples of Peru, Panama, and Cuba. And a boiling point has been reached in other armed forces which no longer wish to be used to repress the rebellion of their peoples . . . . The armed forces that are still instruments of the oligarchy suffer internally. This happened in Panama. We were instruments but are no longer so: and, not being so, the people now holds us in high esteem. We have, indeed, designed an organization for war, but . . . against hunger, against injustice, against illiteracy and against the unequal distribution of goods in our country. This is the new attitude, the new mentality, the new philosophy that is flourishing among the new generation of military men in Latin America.

Juan Bosch's 'Dictatorship with Popular Backing'

Among the first to be persuaded by the Peruvian model was Juan Bosch, former president of the Dominican Republic and leader of the Dominican Revolutionary Party (PRD). In his book *The First Step: Dictatorship with Popular Backing* (1970), he criticized the system of representative democracy in Latin America as an instument of the oligarchies in blocking social change. His own project for a dictatorship with popular support worked differently. First it would nationalize foreign business interests. Next it would nationalize the big estates and give them to the peasants to run through co-operatives. Then it would nationalize the banks, allowing the employees to administer them as social property. And finally, it would nationalize the export-import trade: the State would supervise workers' administration of this branch of the economy, and share in the profits.

Bosch's popular-backed dictatorship would not expropriate the local bourgeoisie. But it would prevent private enterprise from becoming the economically dominant sector, and would cut off the businessmen from political power. Thus, Bosch adhered to the APRA's original programme, including its project of an anti-imperialist state. But he turned away from the electoral road as an unworkable strategy for fighting both the oligarchy and imperialism.

In a Santo Domingo interview on May Day 1971, Bosch explained to Uruguayan journalist, Carlos Maria Gutiérrez, how his project for a popular-based dictatorship rested on his theory of the Latin American revolution. A developing national bourgeoisie would not push the revolution down a bourgeois-democratic road; rather the revolution would pursue a military-nationalist trajectory under the leadership of the 'national petty bourgeoise'.

What was the sociological make-up of this class? Bosch said that it included the bureaucracy of salaried employees as well as the old middle class of people working for themselves. He saw it as the driving force of the Peruvian and Bolivian national revolutions of 1968 and 1969. As soon as the Latin American businessmen get economic and political influence, he warned, they turn into allies of imperialism: 'Their purpose is to do business, and they do better business with those who have the most business.'

Bosch assumed that the U.S. State Department would never allow another popular explosion of the Mexican type, such as the Dominican Revolution of April 1965 crushed by Yankee marines. From now on, he claimed, Latin American revolutionaries must rely mainly on the 'petty bourgeoisie' in the armed forces. This class once hoped to become part of the national bourgeoisie, but now sees this option closed to it. Its only hope for improvement, Bosch argued, is to build an alliance with the working class and the unemployed. Then it can try to seize power without the oligarchy. Bosch thought that the Peruvian model avoided the predicament of the Mexican Revolution: in Mexico the petty-bourgeois leadership had helped the bourgeoisie to grow and link up with foreign interests until the economy again became dependent on U.S. imperialism. But Bosch was over-optimistic. The Peruvian national revolution, like the Argentine national revolution before it, has since gone the way of the APRA and the Mexican Revolution after 1940.

9. Mexico in the Revolutionary Spectrum

The example set by the Mexican Revolution has influenced all Latin America. The APRA was a lighthouse beaming that influence everwhere, while Peronist-type regimes radiated it only faintly. At the same time revolutions in other parts of the world converged on the Mexican model. It was not that they were influenced by the Mexican Revolution, but that conditions in those countries were sufficiently similar to those in pre-revolutionary Mexico to have elicited a similar response. One such example was Colonel Nasser's revolution in Egypt.

We have seen the direct and indirect influence of the Mexican Revolution. We must now explore its meaning as a model of social change. Mexico does not provide the only model of political revolution on the continent. How, then, does the Mexican model compare with its principal rivals on the left and on the right, which also have transferred political power to the military or civilian sectors of the bureaucratic class?

The Uniqueness of the Mexican Model

Most social analysts see the principal contribution of the Mexican Revolution in its anti-feudal restructuring of property relations in the countryside. Although overcoming feudal survivals was certainly a major accomplishment, the unique feature of the Mexican example was the bureaucratic political revolution that launched a throughgoing agrarian reform and also manoeuvred to gain some independence from imperialism. With the exception of Cuba, other Latin revolutions — directly or indirectly influenced by the Mexican example — have been content to displace the landed oligarchy from political power, while increasing the relative weight of the national bourgeoisie in economic matters.

Let us see why the importance of Mexico's struggle against feudalism is limited. Outside Mexico there were few imitators of the agrarian revolts of Villa and Zapata — spontaneous movements from below. Only in Bolivia was agrarian reform virtually forced on the revolutionary government by the Cochabamba villagers' revolt. More often it was a result of calculated restructuring from above, whether by a revolutionary movement in power as in Cuba or by reformist political parties as in Peru and Venezuela. In Cuba agricultural production had long been capitalist farming; its agrarian reform was thus anti-capitalist rather than anti-feudal. The Bolivian Revolution (1952-64) was the only one that destroyed a huge feudal system: in the countryside there was debt-peonage and semi-serfdom; estates larger than 2,500 acres, too big to work efficiently, covered 90% of the national territory. The bulk of the domestic surplus, not including mining, came from agricultural methods dating back to the feudal epoch.

Elsewhere in Latin America what overcame feudalism was the impact of imperialism: absentee landowners became an urban bourgeoisie associated with foreign capital. Though agriculture continued on a semi-feudal basis, landowners did not invest in the countryside but in banking, commerce, and industry. These owners drew more and more revenue from their capitalist investments. During the '50s the bulk of the oligarchy's revenue ceased to derive from the land, and the dominant mode of production became capitalist. In the settler colonies along the continent's eastern seaboard, the transition to capitalism was a little more complicated: in the countryside Argentina, Uruguay, Brazil, and Colombia saw the birth of an independent class of capitalist farmers; in the cities an indigenous bourgeoisie emerged from the petty bourgeoisie as well as from the absentee landowners above.

The post-World War Two agrarian reforms did not make bourgeois social revolutions in Latin America. The reforms merely completed those social revolutions. Nor did APRA-type revolutions, like the Bolivian (1952-64), hurl from political power a feudal landed oligarchy. What fell was a new oligarchy with bourgeois interests.

What had happened in Latin America? The main enemy of the working class and its populist allies had changed. That enemy was no longer feudalism; the enemy was imperialism and its local associates, increasingly bourgeois entrepreneurs. Haya de la Torre had foreseen this development in APRA's first programme in 1924. What he had not foreseen was the eventual betrayal of that programme by the later APRA: its national sections sought a way to live with imperialism in the interests of 'development'.

From the theoretical standpoint, the important common denominator of the Mexican Revolution and its revolutionary successors is a bureaucratic political revolution, nationalist in character and aimed at imperialism.

The Mexican model of revolutionary nationalism is broad enough to cover both its Cardenist and post-Cardenist developments. The Revolution was a prelude to a series of anti-imperialist national revolutions on the continent, while it forecast what might happen to them once institutionalized (usually the bourgeoisie penetrated these anti-imperialist alliances). Just as the Chinese Kuomintang changed from a bloc of three classes into a party of four classes including the bourgeoisie, so did the Mexican PRI (unofficially), and so did the APRA. How did this change come about? The example of the PRI is instructive, for its structure was designed to exclude the bourgeoisie and keep it from capturing the party.

The PRI recruits only from the Confederation of Mexican Workers (CTM), the National Peasant Confederation (CNC), and the National Confederation of Popular Organizations (CNOP). The CNOP is made up of the middle sectors, including the petty bourgeoisie and the salaried and professional employees. So there was no way the bourgeoisie could legally enter the party. But nothing prevented members of the petty bourgeoisie from rising to the status of capitalists; nothing stopped political bureaucrats from enriching themselves in office to become a state bourgeoisie (state employees drawing more from personal investments than from salaries).

The PRI placed tougher restrictions on membership than any Aprista party based on the Mexican model. If the bourgeoisie could become a rival for leadership within the PRI, even more could it dominate the other multi-class parties. If only the Mexican ruling party (PNR-PRM-PRI) had thrown emergent bourgeois from its ranks as well as keeping them from joining up, it might have preserved the bloc of three classes. The transformation of Cárdenas' PRM into Alemán's PRI became the pattern for most Aprista parties on the continent. Unlike the PRI they had loose membership qualifications and went further in betraying their anti-imperialist slogans. Somehow anti-imperialism lingers on in Mexico's bureaucratic regime.

The Mainstream of the Latin American Revolution

During the '60s Marxists expected the Cuban socialist model to replace the Mexican populist one. This expectation was not fulfilled, for Mexico still represents the mainstream of Latin American revolutions. For a time Cuba's social revolution was the main rival of a Mexican-type political revolution but, beginning with the Brazilian military's 5th Institutional Act of December 1968, Brazil became the principal rival. There a military-bureaucratic class seized the government and pushed the bourgeoisie aside. This was a politically revolutionary act. But the bureaucracy reacted economically by opening the door to American capital. This — as well as its repression of nationalist and socialist tendencies and its physical elimination of much of the Brazilian left — meant that it played a counter-revolutionary role.

Unlike the stereotype of Latin American juntas led by generals who are themselves landowners or connected by family ties to the local bourgeoisie, the new repressive regimes patterned on the Brazilian model have been led by soldiers with modest means. Their main source of income consists of salaries they receive for professional services. When they take over politically, they do so in the interests of the bureaucratic class to which they belong rather than as political dependents of the economically dominant class of property holders. In order to avoid confusion we are forced to say, within a Marxist framework, that these generals have made a political revolution even though they are ideologically and economically reactionary. Although they have brutally suppressed the left-wing parties striving for socialism, objectively they have also transferred political power from a class of property owners to the military sector of the new bureaucratic class. Contrary to conventional Marxism, a bureaucratic political revolution may take a military-repressive form.

In the '70s oppressive regimes appeared, partly under Brazilian influence, in Bolivia, Uruguay, Chile, and Argentina. A new military repressive axis, propped up by alliances with global corporations, arose to challenge the populist bloc that includes Mexico, Peru, and Panama. What is the advantage of this Mexican-type bloc? It represents a middle way between Cuban revolutionary socialism and Brazilian bureaucratic capitalism. In other words, only the Mexican type has balanced the interests of foreign corporations against those of organized labour and the national bourgeoisie. The dozen variants of a bureaucratic political revolution on the continent together overshadow the bourgeois democracies: Colombia, Venezuela, Costa Rica.

As Trotsky noted during his Mexican exile, in Latin America the pressures of foreign capital together with the weakness of the local bourgeoisie and the rapid growth of a proletariat undermine democracy in favour of bonapartist regimes. In an article on 'Workers' Administration in Nationalized Industry' published in the *Socialist Appeal*, 25 June 1938, Trotsky distinguished bonapartist regimes of the classical European type from those typical of underdeveloped countries. The classical variant, described by Marx in his *Eighteenth Brumaire* (1951), emerges when neither the bourgeoisie nor the proletariat is strong enough to rule. This provides the state bureaucracy with a chance to play off each against the other in order to rule independently of both. But in underdeveloped countries Trotsky noted the presence of another power: foreign capital or the imperialist bourgeoisie, which smothers the indigenous businessmen. Under such conditions the bureaucracy can rule independently only by balancing the interests of foreign capital against those of organized labour; the bureaucracy then claims to represent national interests. But the balancing act is much too hard for it. 'In reality', says Trotsky, 'it can govern either by converting itself into an instrument of foreign capital and shackling the proletariat with the chains of a police dictatorship or by manoeuvring with the proletariat and making concessions, thus enjoying the possibility of a certain independence with respect to foreign capitalists.' The Mexican government under Cárdenas, he believed, had chosen the second kind of alliance.

Trotsky contrasted two main types of bonapartist (in our terms, bureaucratic) regimes in Latin America: a military-police dictatorship making the government bureaucracy an ally of imperialism, and a revolutionary nationalist regime buttressed by an alliance with the working class. He overlooked a third possibility. The bureaucracy may balance the interests of foreign capital against those of the working class in order to develop the weak local bourgeoisie. This is what really happened in Mexico.

Trotsky made a mistake when he denied that a populist coalition could last: in Mexico one endures to this day. Trotsky also erred in seeing the Cárdenas government as allied mainly to organized labour. True, that government favoured the interests of labour over those of foreign capital; but apart from oil, railways, and some big farms, Cárdenas tolerated imperialism in the Mexican economy. And under his administration the weak local bourgeoisie gained strength.

There is a subtle distinction between the following forms of rule: a bureaucratic political regime strengthening the local bourgeoisie, and a bourgeois-democratic government in which business interests hold sway. An example of the first form is Mexico: under Cárdenas' bureaucratic regime the local bourgeoisie gained ground at the expense of foreign interests; his bureaucratic successors encouraged foreign investments, resulting in a new dependency that made the bourgeoisie a servant of U.S. imperialism. The second form appeared in Costa Rica and Venezuela, where popular insurrections opened the door for Mexican-type parties to enter power; there the local bourgeoisie got the same stimulus and it led to similar results. But there was an important difference. In those countries bourgeois influence so penetrated the Aprista parties that they never enjoyed the autonomy of the Mexican PRI. The evidence shows that indigenous capital directly or indirectly dominated those populist coalitions. The revolutions in Costa Rica (1948) and Venezuela (1958) were basically bourgeois-democratic. They resembled an arrested Mexican-style revolution at the stage achieved by Madero in 1913 or, preferably, by Carranza in 1920.

Political and Social Alternatives

The destiny of the Mexican Revolution and its imitators on the continent was to issue in a bureaucratic political revolution. The outcome might take one of three forms, depending on the choice of allies. It might take the form of a socializing tendency by a political bureaucracy allied to both organized labour and the peasantry. It might take the form of a popular nationalist regime based on a multi-class alliance including the national bourgeoisie as the principal associate of the bureaucratic class. Or it might take the form of a military repressive order allied to foreign interests.

Only Bolivia has experimented with all three. It experienced the socializing tendency during Paz Estenssoro's initial government (1952-56): the miners and their militia were the main ally and partner of the political bureaucracy in power. A second strategy came into play during the MNR's subsequent administrations (1956-64). The government undermined labour's power, while remodelling the economy with U.S. aid. The political revolution shifted from a socialist course to a populist compromise, and the regime revived the army. Then under Barrientos' dictatorship (1964-66) the government moved further to the right, wrecking unions and militias. Barrientos had himself elected President and ruled with a semblance of legitimacy (1966-69); the populist alliance narrowed to the military bureaucracy, the peasants, and a section of the national bourgeoisie. Under Ovando and Torres the pendulum briefly swung back to the socializing tendency of the Revolution (1969-71). In 1971 a right-wing military coup against Torres brought on the third strategy. The military built an alliance with foreign capital, freezing out both labour and the peasants. Bolivia became a military repressive dictatorship opposed both to the national bourgeoisie and to organized labour.

The most important ideological influence in promoting political revolutions in Latin America stems from the Mexican Revolution. But it is not, the only ideology shaping such revolutions: there have been recent challenges from both the left and the right. On the left, the revolutionary socialist model spread by the Cuban revolutionaries had the advantage of displacing the bourgeoisie from economic as well as political power. The bourgeoisie ceased to take the lion's share of the economic surplus; that passed to the petty bureaucracy. The only class that can challenge the petty bureaucracy's monopoly of both political and economic power is its main ally, organized labour. On the right, the Brazilian coup-within-a-coup of December 1968 is the pattern for military repressive regimes. Such regimes contribute to propping up the military bureaucracy's rule through an alliance with the foreign bourgeoisie. This solution means increasing dependency on foreign capital, bribery of government personnel, and kick-backs from the giant corporations. That arouses hostility in the population, but the bureaucracy can hold power through sheer force. Under military repressive regimes neither organized labour nor the local bourgeoisie represent major threats to the bureaucracy: its systematic repression chokes off every whisper of opposition.

The Cuban challenge, dominating the international headlines during the '60s, is familiar. Just as Haya internationalized the Mexican Revolution, so Guevara led in spreading the Cuban example. Political (but armed) organizations similar to July 26 Movement were founded in Venezuela, Peru, and Guatemala. But unlike the APRA's steady shift to the right, these Cuban inspired movements moved off to the extreme left: they cut their ties with the major populist parties; they lost their mass base; and they disappeared in an unequal struggle with the armed state. These failures partly explain why the Cuban Revolution is isolated from the political mainstream. Imperialist pressures on Latin American governments also account for Cuba's isolation: the revolution remains the only example of its kind on the continent.

Military Fascism in Latin America?

During the '70s the principal rival of Mexican-type revolutions became the military repressive model. Brazil replaced Cuba as the main subversive influence on the Latin American military. The question is whether to characterize Brazilian-type regimes as 'military-fascist'. Political sociologists and students of contemporary revolutions look upon this label with scepticism. In academic usage the term 'fascist' usually suggests political counter-revolution rather than revolution, while scholars restrict its meaning to its Italian origins. Some use it for the features common to Italian Fascism and German Nazism.

Several ingredients are found in both the classical Italian and German models of fascism. First, a political party of the old petty-bourgeois and new middle classes held a monopoly of government power; this party, demagogically oriented, achieved a mass following. Second, there was an important industrial complex controlled by a dynamic native bourgeoisie. Third, a nationalist ideology, hostile to both communism and liberal democracy, promoted economic development, while warning against dependency on the major imperialist powers. Fourth, a pact between the new middle class and the bourgeoisie resulted in the bureaucracy getting a monopoly of political power if it would guard the existing social order and keep the native capitalist sector dominant. None of these features appears in the new military regimes in Brazil, Bolivia, Chile, Uruguay, and Argentina. The reason for calling them fascist lies elsewhere.

In the Great Act of Anti-fascist Unity celebrated in Mexico City's Alameda Theatre on 11 May 1975, the ex-rector of the Autonomous National University, Pablo González Casanova, underlined some of the differences between the fascisms of today and yesterday. In the '30s fascism had an ideological appeal, but today its lies are obvious to most people, and it can no longer talk of a superior race. Thus it lacks the support of a political party with a mass base; it can survive only through brute force. In the '30s fascism's Rome-Berlin-Tokyo axis was centred in industrial nations. That made it a powerful force in world politics; but today it has influence only in the underdeveloped countries, especially in Latin America. In the '30s fascism could claim to serve national interests, to raise the standard of living at the expense of less developed nations — a form of 'peoples' imperialism'. It can no longer claim to do this: in underdeveloped Latin America it is dependent on foreign interests, it exists in a neo-colonial relationship to the Western powers, and its principal beneficiaries are the U.S. global corporations.

Finally, González Casanova pointed to the transformation in world socialism. In the '30s backward Russia, an isolated socialist country, was struggling to develop itself with terrorist methods. Today's socialist countries are found all around the globe. They include industrial nations backed by Soviet technology, a billion people in rapidly developing China, and revolutionary centres like Cuba. These peoples now enjoy a standard of living and a measure of personal freedom that seemed impossible during the '30s. This means that fascism's anti-communist ideology no longer carries the conviction it used to.

In this view Latin American fascism is a caricature of its classical European origins. But this is the only way it could survive and still represent the common denominator of its classical and colonial variants — that denominator being neither a party nor ideology, but a bureaucratic political revolution that smashes organized labour and leftist parties as a concession first to imperialism, and then to the bourgeois and landed oligarchies pushed from political power.

We can trace the origins of this underdeveloped fascism, lacking a strong party and native bourgeoisie, back to Franco's Spain. Franco was not a member of the Spanish Falange of José Antonio Primo de Rivera. To destroy the Falange's independence, Franco fought its leadership and brought it under military control. His first step in this struggle came in April 1937 with a decree unifying two bitter rivals in the conservative camp, the monarchist old right representing the landed oligarchy, and the fascist new right representing the old and new middle classes. This meant a fusion of two groups: the monarchist Traditionalist Communion (*Requeté*), and the Spanish Falange.

The new party was called the Traditionalist Spanish Falange (FET), and Franco made himself its supreme leader. This manoeuvre of the high military command met resistance from Manuel Hedilla, leader of the original autonomous Falange, who refused a top post in the reorganized party. He told his followers to resist the unification decree and Franco's bid for political leadership. A military tribunal condemned Hedilla to death, but his sentence was commuted to life imprisonment. During this power struggle the Nazi ambassador to Franco's government openly supported Hedilla. Nazi Germany had granted military aid to Franco on certain conditions; one stated even before the fall of Madrid that the Falange must have a monopoly of political power.

The Falange had hoped to use General Franco to attain its political ends, but it had reckoned without the general's own plans. With the banning of the autonomous Flanage in 1937, the struggle between it and Franco really began. The Civil War ended and Franco made his next move: he purged the Falangist old guard from the reorganized party, then appointed his brother-in-law to keep watch over the party's remains. Was the new government's Falange still a fascist party? It included the fascists, but only as backseat drivers in a military government. For this government, fascism was not an end but a means; the fascist Falange was the political arm of the military high command.

Over the next two decades this bastard Falange slowly lost the little influence it had within the Franco regime. Thus in 1957 the Minister of Housing revealed a survey showing that Falangist representation in the main government posts had dwindled to 5%. The Falange could count on only two of sixteen ministries and one of seventeen sub-secretaries. In December 1966 ratification of the Organic Law of the State was the final blow: the law dropped the Falange from the legal machinery of the government, and it became a marginal political force. This development reduced the influence of the classical Italian and German fascisms to a minimum in Spain, though Franco's dictatorship continued to be a model of military fascism. It was this later development of *franquismo* that contributed most to shaping the military repressive regimes in Latin America during the '70s.

For dogmatic Marxists, the alternatives to a Mexican-type populist regime take the form of a dilemma: fascism or socialism. Both receive a doctrinaire interpretation which overlooks their common denominator. For these Marxists fascism is defined within a European context as the most open, brutal, and reactionary dictatorship of finance capital; socialism is conceived as a classless society established through a dictatorship of the proletariat. But the societies, labelled by the terms fascism and socialism, are not reflected in these definitions.

Contrary to these doctrinaire interpretations, neither the fascist regimes in Italy and Germany nor their military caricatures in Latin America have achieved political power for the bourgeoisie. Nor has Cuba and its bedfellows in Eastern Europe made the proletariat the main beneficiary of a new economic order. The doctrinaire interpretations are simplistic and exaggerated. Military fascism has assured the political sovereignty of the bureaucratic class, but by destroying its popular base. And socialism has turned the petty bureaucracy in Cuba, not Marx's proletariat, into the main beneficiary of a post-capitalist economic order.

An Analysis of Military—Repressive Regimes

Marxist judgments miss the revolutionary character of military fascism. True, such regimes are bascially counter-revolutionary in denationalizing the economy, in subjecting their people to more dependency and imperialist exploitation, and in destroying the political parties of the left. But the displacement of the bourgeoisie from political power by the professional military is still a revolutionary act. Fascist regimes have usually come as a reaction to strong socialist and communist movements, but the fascists' price for crushing the left has been the displacement of the traditional right from control of the State. What Marxists rarely see is that the losers under fascism include both the proletariat and the local bourgeoisie.

Among the better Marxist interpretations of the new military regimes in Latin America is João Quartim's *Dictatorship and Armed Struggle in Brazil* (London, 1971). The most striking feature of Brazil's society since the 1964 coup, he thinks, is its dual character: a militarized bureaucracy monopolizes political power, while the global corporations and their Brazilian associates make the important economic decisions. This oligarchic bloc has made a 'pact of dependence' to assign control of heavy industry and consumer durables to the foreign corporations, light industry to their Brazilian associates, and infrastructural investments to the state sector. At the same time, there is political rule by a bureaucracy of military officers and technocrats. The Brazilian generals may represent the economic interests of the foreign bourgeoisie and its local associates, but they also govern in their own interests and those of the state sector.

According to Quartim, there are several factors supporting the divorce between bourgeois economic power and bureaucratic political power. First, the foreign economic interests have their main residence abroad, and that strenthens the political hand of the military at home. Second, the economic role of state capital increases the political independence of the military, and state control of the economic infrastructure builds up the military's power. Though the military have supported denationalization of the economy, this process has hurt the indigenous private sector, not the state sector. Denationalization does not mean destatificátion; it means local enterprises under foreign control while destatification means returning state enterprises to the private sector. Third, the congenital weakness of the political parties and the congressional system has strengthened the military's hand against the moneyed interests. The big money continues to pressure both congress and parties, at least indirectly, but big political decisions are made elsewhere. The politicians are little more than figureheads, and the local businessmen are down in the audience with the other classes, watching the military play its part to the end.

Quartim's analysis stood up five years later. On 10 April 1976 Jonathan Kandell, a correspondent of *The New York Times*, noticed that the Brazilian state controlled 50% of the economy, not only energy, transportation, communication and basic industry, but also increasingly manufacturing. He compared the level of state control with that achieved during Perón's revolution in Argentina and with that in Peru under the new military junta. The United States' Secretary of State was worried about Brazil's creeping socialism, while the newspaper *O Estado de São Paulo* trumpeted fearfully: 'During the last ten years there has been an escalation of state interventionism without precedent in the country's history — comparable only to that in the socialist countries.'

Quartim's analysis applies with some force also to the Bolivian military regime and, to a lesser extent, to the Chilean and Uruguayan dictatorships. Their greatest weakness, according to this analysis, is their anti-national posture and dependence on U.S. imperialism, for this sparks resistance from nationalist sectors in the armed forces. In Brazil the succession crisis of September 1969 resulted in a new compromise that forced the nationalists to wait for a better moment. They are biding their time, but the moment cannot be put off forever. As Quartim acknowledged, the crucial question is 'whether Brazilian state capital will remain as a complement to foreign capital, providing only for infrastructural development, or develop to replace foreign capital . . . .' Obviously the need for military nationalism is even greater in Chile, where the junta went beyond denationalization to destatification.

Conclusion

In this perspective most Marxists err in stressing the instability of populist or nationalist regimes of the Mexican type. Military repressive governments are far more unstable. They face a dilemma: either populism or socialism.

The socialist variant of a bureaucratic political revolution is the most stable of all. In Cuba the Revolution is irreversible internally, because it is based on corresponding economic revolution; it could be overthrown, but only by foreign intervention. There a multi-class populist road is no longer open, much less a military repressive one. Cuba does not face the dilemmas that erode the variants of a bureaucratic political revolution in Mexico or Brazil.

These are the main rivals for political power in Latin America today. Both oligarchic and bourgeois democratic regimes have fallen before political revolutions in Mexico and the other leading Latin American republics. In South America only Colombia and Venezuela, representing the old bourgeois political system, are holding out. Their days are numbered.

PART 111
The Mexican Revolutionary Process

10. Cycles of the Mexican Revolution

'Epochs in the history of society,' says Marx, 'are no more separated from each other by hard and fast lines of demarcation than are geological epochs.' On a world scale the transition from the feudal to the capitalist epoch developed slowly, sparked occasional violence, and dragged on for centuries. The bourgeois revolution was a process starting in the Middle Ages with the emergence of the towns, the cradle of the manufacturing class. It swelled in wave after wave, each stronger than the last, and washed against the feudal fortress. In the leading countries of Western Europe, the feudal political forms crumbled away.

In most countries the revolutionary movement broke out again and again without success; it often made a breach in feudalism, then interrupted itself to return to its starting point. It was only through many starts and stops, say Marx and Engels, that the bourgeoisie gradually abolished the feudal political structures.

Marx and Engels also point out that the great revolution in 17th century England, though it broke the political bonds of feudalism, ended in compromise between the bourgeoisie and a fraction of the nobility in 1689. This aristocratic fraction then governed England in the interests of the bourgeoisie. For a century the compromise underwent gradual changes in favour of the bourgeoisie and, in the revolution of 1832, the industrialists momentarily won political power.

The year 1789 opened a series of revolutions in France. For a century, political revolutions swelled up in Paris and burst over the nation like a shower of stars. In 1789 the August 4th Decrees, stripping the feudal Church of its lands, also began a long social revolution — the transfer of the bulk of the surplus product from the feudal lords to the greedy bourgeoisie. In the

coming years emigré aristocrats watched from Coblenz as revolutionaries confiscated their holdings and sold them to the business world. Both Robespierre
and Napoleon kept up this plunder.

What means did the bourgeoisie use to fight the landowning aristocracy for
the surplus product? In part three of *The Civil War in France*, Marx gave the
answer: 'the centralized state power'. In 1789 there remained 'all manner of
medieval rubbish, seigneurial rights, local privileges, municipal and guild monopolies and provincial constitutions. The gigantic broom of the French Revolution of the 18th century swept away all these relics of bygone times.' After
the bourgeoisie nailed down its political power in 1792, it pushed the revolution beyond French borders. A new political revolution in 1799 brought
Napoleon's military bureaucracy to power, and it fixed the gains of the
creeping bourgeois social revolution in three legal Codes and pushed French
influence across Europe.

During the period from 1789 to 1814 the bourgeois social revolution was
launched on its long course toward victory. Marx describes this great
beginning in the opening pages of *The Eighteenth Brumaire*:

> Danton, Robespierre, St. Just, Napoleon, the heroes as well as the
> parties and the masses of the old French Revolution performed . . . the
> task of unchaining and setting up modern bourgeois society. The first
> ones knocked the feudal basis to pieces and mowed off the feudal
> heads which had grown on it. The other [Napoleon] created inside
> France the conditions under which alone free competition could be
> developed.

In 1814 a political counter-revolution restored the old landowners to
power under the Bourbons, and the bourgeois social revolution went into
reverse. Some returning emigrés got their lands back, and in 1825 others
received compensation.

'The Revolution of 1830,' Marx wrote in part three of *The Civil War in
France*, 'resulted in the transfer of government from the landlords to the
capitalists.' Through Louis Philippe, the 'bourgeois king', the bankers began
to rule; and this revived the bourgeois social revolution. In 1839 France had
600 steam engines, by 1847 it had almost 5,000. But as late as 1844 agriculture still accounted for 73% of the national product, and on the land pre-
capitalist forms of production like sharecropping were more common than
agribusiness.

In the political revolution of 1848 to 1851 the weak industrial bourgeoisie
seized the government but could not hold it: Louis Bonaparte's bureaucratic
caste ruled for 20 years, while French industrialization crawled ahead. Then
in the political upheavals of 1870 to 1871 the bourgeoisie again grabbed for
power and this time came out on top. The business class retained political
power, industrial development surged forward, and the bourgeoisie eventually
completed its social revolution by liquidating the survivals of pre-capitalist
production in the countryside.

In Russia the bourgeois revolution that began in 1905 was also interrupted but revived in February 1917; a post-bourgeois revolution brought it to fruition; capitalism triumphed under NEP-men and kulaks until 1929 when Stalin initiated the Five Year Plan.

In 'Notes of a Publicist', an article of 6 March 1910, Lenin discusses 'the bourgeois-democratic revolution's *culmination*'. What interests him is not 'a particular revolution, one of the bourgeois revolutions, one of the waves that batters the old regime but does not destroy it, does not remove the soil that generates later bourgeois revolutions', as happened in 1789, 1830, or 1848. More important is the concept of the revolution's completion: 'it means the fulfilment of the objective historical tasks of the bourgeois revolution, its "culmination", in other words, the washing away of the very soil capable of generating a bourgeois revolution, the culmination of the entire cycle of bourgeois revolutions. In this sense, for example, the bourgeois-democratic revolution in France began in 1789 but culminated only in 1871.' Among interpretations of Mexico's history, Lenin's notion has sparked sharp debate; in different ways Marxist historians apply his concept of *the culmination of a nation's entire cycle of revolutions.*

To understand the destiny of the Mexican Revolution, its results and prospects, we must know if it is an ongoing process or if it has come to an end. Is there a temporary interruption? These questions seem simple enough, but their answers hinge on the nature of the revolutionary cycle. Was the Revolution that began with Madero's struggle against Díaz in 1910 an independent eruption of the Mexican masses or was it a link in a chain of eruptions going back to the Independence War of 1810? There are interpreters who fix the dates of the Mexican Revolution as 1910 to 1917, while others stretch it from 1910 to 1940. Some see the Revolution as the last link in a cycle of bourgeois-democratic revolutions; for others it is the first link in a new cycle of post-bourgeois revolutions. Could it be a combined revolution marking the end of one revolutionary cycle and the beginning of another?

The popular explosion of 1910 means different things to Mexico's political parties. The governing Institutional Revolutionary Party (PRI) still strikes the old optimistic note on its ideological lyre: there is an ongoing, continuing, uninterrupted national revolution. For decades the Communist Party (PCM), now re-organized as the Unified Socialist Party of Mexico (PSUM), shared with other sectors of the Mexican left the thesis of an unfinished bourgeois revolution, but in 1960 the communists sounded a pessimistic note when they announced that the Revolution had ended. Between the bright official note and the discordant revolutionary tone sounds an arpeggio of interpretations.

Today the left is more divided than ever in its assessment of the Mexican Revolution: a new interpretation by its revolutionary nationalist wing has emerged. On this view, 1910 marked the beginning of another revolutionary cycle — a cycle of unfinished post-bourgeois revolutions. The main variants of this latest interpretation agree that in 1910 a new cycle of revolution began that shook off bourgeois political control; but the interpreters differ over the periodization of the post-bourgeois cycle. We must examine each view. We begin with their common source in the communists' post-1960 interpretation of the Mexican Revolution.

The Bourgeois Revolutionary Cycle

The PCM popularized the thesis of a cycle of bourgeois revolutions beginning with the War of Independence in 1810; the party borrowed this theoretical coin from two Soviet historians, M.S. Alperovich and B.T. Rudenko. These Soviet scholars analysed both the concept of an interrupted revolution and the notion of a revolutionary cycle by separating the narrow from the broad meaning of 'revolution'. In the epilogue of their book on North American intervention in the Revolution they based their distinction on the words we cited from Lenin's 'Notes of a Publicist'.[1] In the narrow sense, a revolution is a single attack on the conditions that block progress but, in a broad sense, the revolution is the completion of the entire historical cycle of attacks: it is the elimination of the causes that repeatedly generate revolutionary movements.

With this distinction, the Soviet historians argue that, in a narrow sense, the Mexican Revolution of 1910 came to an end with the 1917 Constitution. They also argue that this revolution 'represents only a particular stage of the bourgeois revolution in the broadest sense, which began in Mexico before 1910 and is still unfinished.' What proved influential was not their dating but the concept of a cycle of bourgeois revolutions in Mexico.

Next the Soviet historians pick out the stages of the bourgeois revolution launched in 1910. They see a brief ebb of the revolutionary tide from 1917 to 1920 during Carranza's presidency, followed by a new revolutionary flow from 1920 to 1928 under ambitious Presidents Obregón and Calles. There was a second interruption of the revolution between 1928 and 1934: during this period puppet governments manipulated by rich old ex-President Calles broke diplomatic relations with the Soviet Union and made concessions to United States business interests. When the energetic Cárdenas assumed command in 1934 the revolution again surged forward, but in 1940 another interruption occurred as a non-revolutionary recession set in. This downturn lasted through the government of incorruptible Ruiz Cortines to 1958, when Alperovich and Rudenko published their study.

The influence of these Soviet historians on the PCM's evaluation of the Mexican Revolution shows up in a 1971 work by Arnaldo Martínez Verdugo, the party's secretary since 1960. He argues that 'the cycle of bourgeois democratic revolutions in Mexico has ended. This cycle covered the period from the War of Independence with its partially bourgeois tasks, the Reform that was also a bourgeois revolution, the revolution of 1910 to 1917, and ended with the structural reforms of 1935 to 1939.' He concludes that the Mexican Revolution, regularly interrupted and often revived, had by 1940 run down for good.

Professor Enrique Semo, an innovative historian on the PCM's Central

177

Committee, makes a bow to the Soviet twosome in a 1975 essay on the cycle of revolutions in Mexico. What common element does Semo find in the War of Independence against Spain from 1810 to 1821, the Juárez reforms and war of national liberation against the French from 1857 to 1867, and the third upsurge of bourgeois revolutions in Mexico from 1910 to 1917? Answer: the common objective of a bourgeois political and social transformation to bring to an end feudal residues such as debt peonage. But for this communist veteran of campus violence, the cycle of bourgeois revolutions spinning through the 19th century from 1810 onward did not grind to a stop in 1917. There was a fourth revolutionary whirl that swept away the semi-feudal mode of production in the countryside: from 1935 to 1939 the structural reforms of President Cárdenas set the stage for the industrialization of Mexico.

For Semo the cycle of bourgeois revolutions in Mexico resembles the cycle in France. There, in order to reach its objectives, 'the most profound bourgeois-democratic revolution in history (1789) needed four other assaults in 1792, 1830, 1848, and 1870.' In this perspective the Mexican Revolution of 1910 to 1917 and the structural reforms under Cárdenas appear as final links in an earlier chain of bourgeois democratic revolutions. Even though the Cardenist reforms of 1935 to 1939 expressed tendencies surging beyond a bourgeois framework, the Mexican upheaval was not the start of a new people's democratic revolution.

Our scholar-activist concludes that the cycle of bourgeois revolutions ended in 1940. At this point 'my conception differs from that . . . of Alperovich and Rudenko, who thought that the cycle of bourgeois revolutions has not yet finished, since its historic tasks have not been fully resolved.' For Semo that is normal since the bourgeoisie surrenders to the past in order to build dykes against coming storms. On the international horizon loom the clouds of revolutionary socialism; in every country the proletariat raises its fist. No wonder the bourgeoisie shrinks from the democratic revolution! The coming revolution led by the working class will establish democracy by replacing the bourgeois order with socialism.

Our Marxist professor's interpretation also differs from that of the Russians in the following way. He does not see the period from 1920 to 1928 as a revolutionary upsurge like that of the Cardenist period, for he finds only one interruption of the revolutionary flow that began in 1910. This interruption lasted from 1917 to 1935. The Soviet historians recognize two interruptions: one from 1917 to 1920 and another from 1928 to 1934.

The first formulations of a Mexican bourgeois revolutionary cycle Semo traces to 1960; in that year the PCM held its 13th Congress and sounded the cry for a new revolution. The party picked up the cycle concept from the two Soviet historians, but there is another, even earlier source – the interpretation by Lombardo Toledano. This labour intellectual's Popular Party (PP), a left-wing split from the PRI, was the only legally registered Marxist-Leninist party in Mexico from 1948 to 1979. Lombardo Toledano delivered his ninth annual report to the Popular Party in the spring of 1955 with habitual wit and fire. He described the Mexican Revolution as 'uninterrupted' from 1810 to the present — but he also separated four discontinuous stages in it.

The Mexican Revolution first launched in 1810 was a struggle for national independence. The second stage from 1850 to 1870 took in Juárez's liberal reform and a national liberation movement against the French. The third stage, the Revolution of 1910, was anti-feudal and democratic. The fourth stage, Lombardo predicted, will follow the backsliding by the pro-bourgeois regimes from 1946 to 1958, and it will set the revolution marching again, a people's democratic or 'new' revolution. But what description of the Revolution did this clever old Marxist really give his listeners? His uninterrupted, anti-feudal, democratic revolution against imperialism boils down to an interrupted revolution!

A year earlier in a lecture arranged by the Mexican Association of Journalists on 12 May 1954 Lombardo presented a sketch of this same thesis. The Mexican Revolution, he said, is a drama of national liberation in three great acts: the Revolution of Independence, the Revolution of the Reform, and the Revolution of 1910 — 'an anti-imperialist, anti-feudal, and democratic revolution'. But it is an unusual sort of bourgeois democratic revolution, he noted, for it does not imitate the 18th century European revolution as a disciple imitates a master. The Mexican cycle of revolutions is painted in colours all its own: it is a combined struggle against both feudalism and imperialism.

As a revolutionary holds the hand of a fellow traveller free to operate in public life, so the outcast PCM clung to the legal PP from 1948 to 1960. Valentín Campa, a communist survivor of Lecumberri federal penitentiary in Mexico City, later described the relation between the two parties during the period: the most sinister aspect of the PCM's political line was 'to make the party wag Lombardo's tail'. The PCM's top cadres knew Lombardo's interpretation of the Mexican Revolution. Was their left turn after 1960 a break with it?

Whatever the reasons for the PCM's post-1960 interpretation of the Revolution, it helped spread the concept of a cycle of bourgeois democratic revolutions in Mexico. In our view, communist Semo was right to argue that the Revolution of 1810 launched by Father Hidalgo was the first phase of a cycle of bourgeois revolutions. He was right to see the liberal Constitution of 1857 and Juárez's reforms as milestones along the road of the bourgeois cycle. He correctly pointed to the Revolution of 1910 as taking up the unfinished tasks of the democratic revolution. He accurately ended the cycle of bourgeois revolutions in 1940.

Yet, both before and after 1960, the PCM drew too simplistic a picture of the Revolution; the party's sketch left out the Mexican Revolution's combined character. The 1910 Revolution was both the final stage of a bourgeois revolutionary cycle and the beginning stage of a post-bourgeois cycle — the cycle leading to a socialist revolution.

The Communist Party has misunderstood the Mexican political situation.

Its interpretation implies that one must simply wait for a new revolutionary cycle or at most prepare for its arrival. Yet the post-bourgeois revolutionary cycle has already begun.

An Interrupted Peasant and Proletarian Revolution?

In Chapter Four we discussed Adolfo Gilly's interpretation of the class nature of the Mexican Revolution; now we turn to his analysis of the Mexican revolutionary process. We begin by recalling some of his basic concepts, and we add some details left out of our earlier presentation.

From his cell in Lecumberri Adolfo Gilly pondered the two Soviet historians' picture of the Mexican Revolution. He is an ex-militant of Posadas' Fourth International (International Secretariat), unique among the Internationals surviving from the 1953 split in world Trotskyism. The Posadists stand out among Trotskyists as those who understand how revolutionary Marxism can adapt itself to revolutionary nationalism.

Gilly spent his prison years studying the ebbs and flows of the Mexican revolutionary cycle. His starting point in *La revolución interrumpida* was Posadas' articles on the 'national revolutionary state' as a transitional stage between capitalism and socialism in the developing countries. The articles share two concepts with Lombardo Toledano's evaluation of the Mexican Revolution: a 'national revolutionary movement' and its corresponding 'state'. Posadas did not invent these concepts. At the Second Congress of the Communist International in 1920, the concepts appeared in the debate between the Hindu nationalist M.N. Roy and Lenin. For Lenin movements of national liberation in the Third World were 'national revolutionary' rather than 'bourgeois democratic'.

Gilly's analysis starts with a citation from Posadas.

> The Mexican Revolution has three phases. The first is that of Villa and Zapata, the second is that of Cárdenas, the third is one of continuation and completion. The revolution, interrupted since Cárdenas, is permanent. So far it has two ascending phases: that of Villa and Zapata who launched the land reform but were stopped; and that of Cárdenas who nationalized the principal means of production. The third phase must be the nationalization of all means of production and the distribution of all land to the peasants. That is the present stage . . . . The Mexican Revolution was begun and interrupted. We must insist on . . . continuing the Mexican Revolution until it is completed in a socialist revolution.

It is this sketch of a new stage of the Revolution that closely resembles Lombardo's picture.

In the introduction Gilly contrasts his 'interrupted revolution' with the most widely held conceptions of the Mexican Revolution. First, there is the

'bourgeois conception shared by opportunist and reformist socialism [PRI],
which holds that the Revolution from 1910 to the present is a continuous
process . . . that has perfected itself and slowly accomplished its objectives
under successive "governments of the revolution".' Second, there is the
'petty-bourgeois conception shared by centrist socialism [PCM], which holds
that the revolution of 1910 was a bourgeois democratic revolution that . . .
could not accomplish its objectives and is now exhausted, a cycle that has
closed, as a result of which it is imperative to make a "new revolution" that
has nothing to do with the past: some say a socialist revolution, others say a
popular and anti-imperialist one.' But the Mexican Revolution is neither an
unfinished bourgeois-democratic revolution nor a finished one. Gilly argues
that it is an interrupted proletarian and peasant revolution.

This is Gilly's interpretation: 'a proletarian and Marxist conception, which
says that the Mexican Revolution is an interrupted one . . . that developed
initially as an agrarian and anti-imperialist revolution, and acquired during its
course an empirically anti-capitalist character imposed on it from below — in
spite of its predominantly bourgeois and petty-bourgeois leadership.' But we
should not be misled by the Argentine's rhetoric: his own interpretation is no
more Marxist and proletarian than the others, and they are no more bourgeois or petty-bourgeois than his own.

He says that the Mexican Revolution has gone through two ascending
phases yet it still lacks a Marxist and proletarian party in the vanguard. The
first phase of land reform began in 1910 but was interrupted at the end of
the decade — Zapata fell in 1919 and Villa surrendered in 1920. For 14 years
the Revolution sputtered along out of gear. It roared forward in 1934 when
Cárdenas, the 'sphinx' who said little but did much, nationalized the principal
means of production. But this second phase was interrupted in 1940 and
could not advance its socialist aims. Today the Revolution has entered a third
phase catalysed by the 1968 student movement, by growing labour unrest,
and by peasant struggles in the early 1970s. The Mexican Revolution, our
Trotskyist claims, 'has begun its third ascent — starting not from zero but
where it was last interrupted — as a nationalist, proletarian, and socialist
revolution.'

Our revolutionary sums up the Revolution. It began with the Mexican
peasantry rising in arms to seize the land. This peasant insurrection raised a
question mark over bourgeois property rights. Though the peasantry lacked
leadership by a proletariat with party and programme, 'it generated and
encouraged a petty-bourgeois radical and socializing, national and anti-
imperialist wing that had a decisive effect on the first two ascending phases
(1910-20 and 1934-40).' Today this petty-bourgeois wing still carries tremendous political clout and, according to Gilly, serves as a bridge toward the
proletarian leadership forming at lower levels.

The Mexican peasant war, he goes on, differed from those in other epochs
because it was caught up in the proletarian world revolution, the social transformation of the 20th century. To understand the Mexican upheaval he
applies the theory of permanent revolution to the entire revolutionary cycle

in Mexico since 1910. The Mexican Revolution paved the way for the economic strengthening of the bourgeoisie but loosened the hold of that class on political power. The masses could not capture the government; the bourgeoisie could not govern for lack of support. To this day the Revolution has created neither a congress the business world can manipulate nor a presidency open to entrepreneurs. The bourgeoisie hardly feels safe with a government beyond its control, even though the State usually favours capital in its development programme. In favouring big business the State continues the policies of Porfirio Díaz. Before 1910 the bourgeoisie held sway in the economy and also called the shots in the National Palace – the State was already bourgeois. After 1910 the Revolution created a State representing the radicalized petty bourgeoisie and, through more than 50 years, this State has disguised its class character with revolutionary rhetoric.

Crucial for understanding Mexico's recent history is the role of the world proletarian revolution.

> When in November 1917 the proletarian revolution triumphed in Russia, the height of the peasant revolution in Mexico had already passed. But the Revolution had not ended. It was able to link up with the new stage of victorious proletarian revolutions. The emergence of the Soviet Union was a blow world capitalism has not recovered from . . . . It gave rise to dual power on a world scale. So the great Mexican peasant insurrection, though it could not triumph, did not die out . . . . The revolution erupted during the world juncture of two epochs: too early for it to pick up a proletarian leadership, too late for the bourgeoisie to bring it under control . . . . The revolution remained interrupted: it neither achieved its potentially socialist aims nor suffered a final defeat.

In the consciousness of Mexico's masses flickered the hope of continuing the Revolution. The early upheaval brought forth the embryo of a socialist revolution, says Gilly, which must finally grow to full stature. The Mexican Revolution is a combined revolution with a peasant origin and a proletarian outcome – someday!

In chapter nine of his book the Argentine revolutionary argues that Carranza's downfall resulted less from Obregón's rebellion than pressure from the insurgent masses. The mass struggles flowed against the foundations of Carranza's bourgeois regime and undermined his rule; the increasing pressure pushed Obregón into revolt. The historic role of the masses, says Gilly, required a bonapartist performance from the regime that followed. 'It determined that the Revolution, instead of concluding and closing with a stabilized capitalist regime resting on social and political foundations of its own, would be interrupted by a long and unstable bonapartist interregnum.' So a bourgeois social order was fastened onto a new political base no longer serving the bourgeoisie alone.

Gilly says that the first phase of the Mexican Revolution, running from

1910 to 1920, opened the doors for the bourgeoisie to pile up ever more riches. He claims that this phase left a few capitalist fingers grasping the political sceptre while simultaneously destabilizing the bourgeois regime. The foundation of Carranza's power, an alliance of the new national bourgeoisie with surviving sectors of the old financial oligarchy, was hammered apart by Obregón and his revolutionary nationalist officers. They represented the interests of another class, the radical petty bourgeoisie.

Carranza's civilian regime aimed to wipe out the revolutionary conquests of the masses. His murder in the mountains ended the last reactionary bourgeois regime trying to consolidate its power without popular support.

> For that reason the bourgeois Carranza, who emerged from the *Porfirista* oligarchy, and not the bourgeois Obregón, who came from the petty bourgeoisie, holds first place on the altars of the Mexican capitalist class which, half a century later, has not succeeded – and will never succeed – in doing what Carranza proposed but failed to achieve: end bourgeois dependency on the masses and close the cycle of the Mexican Revolution.

Obregón's alliance with the proletariat and peasantry brought government concessions to them that the upper classes could never approve; his revolutionary generals needed the masses for the struggle against the reactionary forces. Yet his generals also plundered the State and encouraged capitalist development by Mexican entrepreneurs. Gilly argues that the Obregonist model was bonapartist and that the revolutionary army was its political instrument. This model kept the bourgeoisie outside the halls of political power. This bonapartism survives to the present day because mass organizations support it.

Why do we stress Gilly's interpretation? He was among the first to conceive of the Mexican Revolution as other than bourgeois democratic. While the PCM argued that the Revolution of 1910 was the last phase of an earlier cycle of bourgeois revolutions, Gilly's thesis that the great upheaval began a new cycle of post-bourgeois revolutions stole a march on other Marxist interpreters.

The tall blond Argentine, now part of the faculty at the National Autonomous University of Mexico, defends his interpretation in influential circles. His widely read book is brilliant and provocative – with serious flaws. In chapter nine he seems to contradict himself. At one point he refers to Carranza's regime as an expression of a descending phase of the revolution: 'Another expression of the enduring power of the Mexican Revolution is the fact that, even in descent during this stage, the third bourgeois attempt to liquidate the Revolution and to confine it within classical bourgeois limits would collapse with Carranza.' At Ciudad Juárez, Madero made the first attempt by agreeing with Díaz to leave intact both the land tenure system and the dictator's own army; Huerta made the second attempt by overthrowing Madero and pounding at the revolutionary movement with violence;

Carranza's third attempt occurred during the descending phase. But a few pages later Gilly adds that, spurred forward by the triumph of the Russian Revolution, 'beginning in 1918 and especially in 1919 and 1920, the workers' movement underwent an intensive re-animation.' We ask: can there be a descent in the revolutionary tide and a re-animation of it at the same time?

This point shows how Gilly vacillated in his periodization of the Revolution. His periodization is too simple. In fact, the revolutionary tide that began in 1910 subsided in 1917. In 1920 the flow again moved forward but ran up against the dam of the *maximato* lasting from 1928 to 1934. Then it surged ahead until 1940.

Gilly wrongly speaks of a phase of revolutionary ascent from 1910 to 1920 embracing the brief descent under Carranza. A worse mistake: he includes in his phase of revolutionary decline from 1920 to 1934 the period of intense re-animation of the workers' struggle beginning in 1920.

Our Trotskyist historian errs in judging the class nature of both the pre-revolutionary regime before 1910 and the post-revolutionary regime after 1920. The liberal reforms of 1857 to 1867 failed to make the native bourgeoisie masters in their own house; the *Porfiriato* was not a triumph of the bourgeoisie. The bonapartist regime that followed Carranza in 1920 was not staffed by petty-bourgeois elements, and the new bourgeoisie did not govern through it: it was essentially a bureaucratic regime that played off the bourgeoisie against the proletariat.

Gilly misunderstands the combined character of the revolutionary process. The Revolution of 1910 did not begin with a peasant war. It first erupted as a combined bourgeois and proletarian revolution: the two streams of glowing revolutionary lava were reflected in the dreamy faces of Madero and Flores Magón. Next it exploded as a peasant insurrection under rampaging Villa and avenging Zapata. Then the molten flow congealed in Carranza's institutionalized bourgeois phase. A final burst of ash temporarily capped the revolutionary volcano with Obregón's new bureaucratic regime. In the next sections we explain these criticisms based on our interpretation of the new revolutionary cycle.

An Interrupted National Democratic Revolution?

During the early 1970s in the pages of *Solidaridad*, the journal of the Democratic Tendency of the Electrical Workers and of the Revolutionary Trade Union Movement, there appeared a new interpretation of the Mexican Revolution. Rafael Galván, the journal's founder, was until 1972 the general secretary of the independent Electrical Workers Union of the Mexican Republic. Then as the leader of the Democratic Tendency within the new amalgamated union of electrical workers, he carried on a running fight against the labour bosses within the government Confederation of Mexican Workers (CTM). Galván's life was in constant danger during his last years, but he managed to die a natural death.

A member of the Communist Youth in the early 1930s, he later came under the influence of the eloquent Lombardo Toledano. In 1938 he entered the official party and stayed inside even during its rightward turn in the 1940s. In 1948 many ex-communists poured into Lombardo's new Popular Party, but not Galván. During the 1950s and 1960s he stuck with the PRI. In 1976 the repression of his Democratic Tendency drove him into a front with his old comrades in the PCM, but he represented the left wing of the PRI to the end of his life.

In the late 1960s a new wave of popular insurgency accelerated by the student rebellion found theoretical expression in the pages of *Solidaridad*. From 1969 on, the articles in this third epoch of the journal are of special theoretical interest; in 1973 Rodolfo F. Peña published them under the title *Insurgencia obrera y nacionalismo revolucionario*. We assume that they represent Galván's views. In the labour militant's interpretation of the Mexican Revolution, two revolutionary traditions flow together. First, there is the Marxist-Leninist tendency in the labour movement with sources in the anarcho-syndicalism of the House of the World's Worker and in the anarcho-marxism of Ricardo Flores Magón and his journal *Regeneración*. Second, there is the revolutionary nationalist current springing from Madero's and Carranza's Constitutionalist Movement and flowing into the Cardenist left wing of the official party of the revolution. Flores Magón's influence shows up in Galván's cry for organizing workers outside the government CTM; Cárdenas' influence appears in Galván's decision to remain inside the governing PRI. The fusion of these two tendencies resulted in an uneasy alliance between revolutionary unionism and the Mexican state.

Lombardo Toledano shaped Galván's thinking. We have seen how Lombardo painted the Mexican Revolution as a people's democratic upheaval: national because anti-imperialist, and democratic because anti-feudal. It is a national revolution standing for the interests of a whole nation. It is a democratic revolution voicing the interests of the workers, peasants, shopkeepers, clerks, and Indians of Mexico. Galván also saw the Revolution this way. But in practice Lombardo's marriage of Marxism-Leninism and revolutionary nationalism relied on the Mexican state for support. By contrast Galván's synthesis stressed labour insurgency and the liberation of the workers by the workers themselves. Paradoxically, Lombardo's divorce from the state and its party meant he could not afford to deny it, while Galván's loyalty to state and party allowed him independent action.

For Galván the Mexican Revolution was above all a fight for national liberation from United States imperialism; it continues to be a revolution in the national interest. But what is the national interest? Mexico is split into capitalists and workers, into latifundists and peasants, into foreign mono-polies and small producers, into white elites and mestizo masses: the anta-gonistic interests of these social groups do not melt into a general interest. So *Solidaridad* defines the national interest as that of the majority, as the interest of the downtrodden classes. Only these classes have an interest in standing up to North American presidents, financiers, and corporate managers; only the

poor and exploited are driven to overcome Mexico's pitiful economic dependence. From this standpoint the Mexican Revolution does not look like a
struggle for bourgeois democracy, yet most of the Mexican left insists on
calling it a bourgeois revolution.

Galván and *Solidaridad* contrast their own interpretation of the Mexican
Revolution with the fashionable ones. They point out that the PRI stresses
the continuing nature of a revolution whose master strokes belong to the
past. And the future? The PRI argues that capital formation and bourgeois
enrichment are creeping toward a higher stage of 'social justice'. But the
PCM and other Marxist-Leninist parties, say Galván and his labour revolutionaries, stress the exhaustion of the revolution. The Mexican Revolution
of 1910 to 1940 mainly benefited the bourgeoisie. This revolution has run
out of strength; it limps along with no future. The communists say that the
workers need a new revolution: a proletarian socialist transformation.

Two contradictory accounts of the revolution? But they agree on funda-
mentals: 'for both of them the Mexican Revolution is an unquestionable and
accomplished result, though scorned by the one and praised by the other.'
For both, the revolution is a bourgeois revolution, though the PRI calls it by
another name.

Against these interpretations *Solidaridad* defends the thesis of a national
democratic revolution not yet finished. The journal slowly builds up its case.
First, 'a bourgeois revolution does not begin its institutional life . . . with the
juridical degradation of private property and its subordination to the collective interest.' Second, 'a revolution led by "bourgeoisified liberal landowners",
which is only a half-truth, does not constitutionally postulate either the distribution of land among the peasants or an agrarian reform.' Third, 'a bourgeois revolution does not bind itself by the kind of juridical institutions that
make up Mexican law, especially those that concern labour legislation and the
policy of nationalizations.' Fourth, 'the Mexican Revolution does not in any
way justify the present reconcentration of land . . . in the hands of new latifundists.' Fifth, 'the Mexican Revolution postulates a defensive nationalism,
the independence and not the growing dependence of its economy with
respect to U.S. monopolies.' Sixth, 'the Mexican Revolution does not justify
the free play of market forces, nor even an impossible "mixed system" in
which the private sector can do what it wants while the public sector is
limited to serving social needs.' Seventh, 'the Mexican Revolution does not
establish the nationalization of basic industry and social services as a means
of promoting a slowly developing and deformed national capitalism, but as a
means of controlling the economy as a whole and promoting social justice.'
And eighth, 'the historic backwardness of Mexico, its economic and social
conditions of a pre-capitalist and semi-colonial country, compelled it . . . to
take a non-capitalist road of development . . . with a vigorous State and the
formation of a revolutionary national and democratic regime.'

The Mexican Revolution, according to *Solidaridad*, did not have the
foundations for becoming either bourgeois or socialist. 'In the old Mexico,
still trapped in feudal formations without an internal market and with its

industrial production directed from abroad, the social classes . . . were not able to achieve their objectives or to acquire power for themselves. It was necessary then . . . to establish common objectives of national liberation.' In such a situation the State swayed high above the privileged classes and embodied the national interest. This explains the relative autonomy of the State after the revolution. And it also explains the sudden shift of the state from a capitalist road to a non-capitalist road of development and back again. In other words, it accounts for the interrupted course of the Revolution.

In an article in memory of the 50th anniversary of Lucio Blanco's death, the journal spells out the national and democratic character of the revolution. Hard-riding Blanco, a revolutionary general assassinated in 1922, belonged to the jacobin wing of the Constitutional Movement. Others in this left wing were General Francisco Mújica, Salvador Alvarado and Felipe Carrillo Puerto, the socialist governors of Yucatán. Adalberto Tejeda, the governor of Veracruz, also nestled in this wing, and so did General Heriberto Jara and President Lázaro Cárdenas. Such leaders made up a revolutionary nationalist current within the governments of the revolution and later the official party. *Solidaridad* traces the new wave of labour and peasant insurgency starting in the 1970s to the worker movements and land reforms authorized by Lucio Blanco and Francisco Mújica under the influence of Ricardo Flores Magón.

This article notes both the popular character and the interrupted course of the Mexican Revolution. The article observes that Lucio Blanco, like Francisco Mújica and Lázaro Cárdenas, was moving in a socialist direction; it concludes that 'the revolutionary nationalist experiment of 1934 to 1940 was moving toward socialism, but was interrupted by the international isolation of the Revolution.'

Other issues of *Solidaridad* tag the big interruption with different names: the 'degeneration' of the revolution, the revolution 'betrayed', and '30 years of counter-revolution'. One article, echoing Cárdenas' criticism of the 1946 'counter-revolutionary' amendments to the Constitution, snarls at the Alemanist regime as an 'open and blatantly counter-revolutionary government'.

Does this mean that the Revolution went into reverse? In many ways the popular classes indeed suffered setbacks. An article on the conspiratorial efforts by the PRI's right wing to establish a fascist-type dictatorship examines the implications:

> After Cárdenas the country was again placed on the capitalist road of development . . . . This political turn necessarily generated a change in the governing class. Instead of remaining a *bonapartist intermediate class* conditioned by the insufficient differentiation among the nation's social classes, it would become a *bureaucratic class* in the service of the dominant forces — imperialism and the nascent Mexican bourgeoisie allied to imperialism.

For Galván this is the main social question in Mexico: the antagonism between revolutionary nationalism and U.S. imperialism. Inside the country this antagonism shows up in the struggle between a people's democracy and an unpopular dictatorship.

The big gains of the Revolution remain; the Mexican Revolution 'simply stagnated, ceasing to advance.' The counter-revolution will last until another wave of popular insurgency drives the revolution forward. The 1968 student movement has already set the revolutionary current in motion, but the youth could not organize a resistance embracing workers and peasants. Yet their example brought the main social classes into action, especially the proletariat. Beginning in the early 1970s the workers led a new ascending phase of the Revolution.

To complete this sketch of *Solidaridad's* view of the Mexican Revolution we must consider the article on the organization of workers and peasants under President Cárdenas. The article outlines the main revolutionary cycles since 1910. The first revolutionary flow lasted until the end of the armed struggle and the Constitution of 1917. Then came the ebb tide: 'As the new post-revolutionary bourgeoisie consolidated and enriched itself through public office and its alliance with the vestiges of the Porfirian oligarchy, the national revolutionary tendency suffered setbacks.' This first interruption of the Revolution lasted until the 1930s when labour and popular insurgency helped raise Cárdenas to the presidency. But a second interruption in 1940 endured until 1970. Then the Democratic Tendency of the Electrical Workers emerged as the leader of a new wave of labour insurgency rising into the present.

Rafael Galván, in his March 1977 speech 'On the Unity of the Left', put the finishing touches on this sketch of the Revolution. The Mexican Revolution has passed through two ascending and two descending phases. The first ascending phase from 1910 to 1917 was interrupted by a descending phase running from 1917 to 1934. Then followed a new ascending phase from 1934 to 1940, interrupted by a second descending phase from 1940 to 1970. To explain these interruptions of the revolutionary flow Galván speaks of the combined character of the Mexican Revolution: 'national revolutions in backward countries invariably acquire a combined character: they are agrarian, nationalist, and anti-imperialist but cannot achieve their democratic goals without going further, without passing through a contradictory process of flows and ebbs toward a socio-economic transformation.' The Mexican Revolution of 1910 to 1917 belongs to the cycle of socialist revolutions that began in the world's backward areas. There the ties to international capitalism were weak. Galván notes that most of these revolutions stopped halfway; like the Mexican Revolution they suffered interruption and now wait for an upsurge in the world revolution.

This interpretation by Galván resembles that of Gilly. In fact, these two interpretations marched onto the theoretical stage simultaneously and startled each other by their mutual resemblance. The general director of *Solidaridad*, Francisco Martínez de la Vega, wrote a glowing tribute to Gilly's work — a recognition of its importance for his own journal. Later he invited Gilly to take part in the 'Homage to Rafael Galván' in a 1981 issue commemorating the dead leader's services to the working class.

However, despite the obvious resemblances between Galván's and Gilly's portrait of Mexico's interrupted revolution, the likeness is hardly perfect. We turn to the differences. First, the two interpretations examine the Díaz dictatorship — that gigantic Alcatraz imprisoning the Mexican masses for 30 years. What economic structure held up those grim walls? What socio-political power sat in the watchtowers? For Gilly the Porfirian bourgeoisie laid down the law, a despotic class driving ever more people into the capitalist mode of production. The Revolution broke the hold of these capitalists on the government. By contrast, Galván and *Solidaridad* see a crumbling baroque castle based on the feudal mode of production with foreign capitalist allies in ports and mines. The Revolution snatched the sceptre from feudal lords and comprador allies — it was anti-feudal and anti-imperialist.

Second, the two interpretations see different class contents in the revolutionary forces. For Gilly the Revolution whirled up as a peasant insurrection and later sucked in the petty bourgeoisie. But Galván and his friends see the Revolution as a combined insurrection with the peasants surging up inside to become the main force. As the star of revolution rose over Mexico its gravitational centre attracted all classes but two. The semi-feudal latifundists, blind with despair, turned their backs on the mighty light; the big bourgeoisie allied to imperialism ground its teeth in fear. The new national bourgeoisie fostered by the Revolution drifted toward the gravitational centre, but after the armed struggle was over this class fraction jumped out of orbit. The national bourgeoisie turned against the Revolution in order to stop its acceleration.

Third, the two interpretations both focus on the moment when the government replaced bearded old Carranza but then they dispute the class character of this bonapartist transitional regime. For Gilly the bonapartist regime represents the 'petty bourgeoisie', a class embracing shopkeepers and small entrepreneurs but also the new middle sectors of salaried workers in factory offices, government bureaus, university towers, law firms, bank windows, and commercial houses. By contrast, *Solidaridad* finds that the transitional regime represents a 'bureaucratic class'. This 'governing class' of political, military, and labour bureaucrats is allied sometimes with the popular classes, sometimes with the native and foreign bourgeoisie. So the State is a potential ally of workers and peasants.

Solidaridad's interpretation of the *Porfiriato* is better than Gilly's, for the Argentine's conceptual engine jumps the Marxist track and generates confusing smoke. In his first chapter he notices the survival of pre-capitalist and feudal production relations in the Mexican countryside but insists that debt peonage, the system holding sway on the land, was a form of wage labour: 'the peons were nothing but wage labourers, in spite of their miserable wages and minimal consumption of commodities available through the company store.' The peons' debts to the landlords passed from fathers to sons, and they had to stay on the land all their lives, like the cows and the fences. They often suffered the foreman's whip. Runaway peons were hunted down and slapped into the landlords' private jails. But Gilly thinks that these hangovers of serfdom pale before the payment of a daily wage, even when the landlord's currency functioned only on the hacienda.

Gilly is working with facts from the official 1910 census. Scholars agree on the importance of these data about peonage, but there are squabbles over its meaning. Let us see why Gilly has misunderstood it. As Marx analyses the class of wage labourers in chapter six of the first volume of *Capital*, there are two necessary conditions making up the definition of a proletarian: the worker must be paid in money functioning as a universal equivalent, and he or she must be free to sell their labour power to anybody. In a footnote Marx adds that Mexican peonage was not wage labour: 'In some countries, particularly in Mexico . . . slavery is hidden under the form of peonage. By means of advances repayable in labour . . . not only the individual labourer but also his family become the *de facto* property of other persons and their families.' So the peon's labour power was not really a commodity. To become a commodity, labour power must be marketable, but Gilly admits that the peon's labour power could be bought and sold only in exceptional cases.

The 1857 Constitution declared every Mexican free to accept any work chosen; it prohibited holding anyone a prisoner for civil debts. The peon was formally free, but the Constitution was abused and violated with impunity. If there was a nominal proletariat in the Mexican countryside, there were few real wage labourers in Marx's sense.

Gilly, relying on figures given by the Mexican economist José Luis Ceceña, claims that in 1910 foreigners owned 77% of the total invested capital in Mexico. Should we infer from this that foreign enclaves generated the bulk of the GNP or that capitalist enterprises employed most of the labour force and paid wages? No, we should remember what Marx said in chapter 47 of the third volume of *Capital*: 'the specific form in which unpaid surplus labour is pumped out of the producers determines the relationship of rulers to ruled as it grows out of production itself . . . upon this relationship is founded the entire economic formation of the community.' In 1910 two-thirds of the people lived and worked in the countryside, and roughly half of the labour force was trapped in debt peonage. There were also large numbers of share-croppers — another pre-capitalist form. Most of the surplus labour was pumped out under semi-feudal conditions. So we can say in Marx's words that debt peonage and sharecropping together revealed 'the innermost secret, the hidden basis of the entire social structure'. That is why the 1910 census data are so important. Gilly's conceptualization of the data distorts Mexican reality.

Solidaridad's interpretation is better than Gilly's in another way. The journal's interpretation does not swallow up the political-military bureaucracy in the petty bourgeoisie. In fact, the interests of the bureaucracy clash with the interests of the petty bourgeoisie and those of other social classes.

Yet *Solidaridad's* interpretation of the revolution as national democratic is sloppy. Like Lombardo's concept of a coming people's democratic revolution, the category lacks precision. For in every grand political coalition one class stands out as the leader. As *Solidaridad* surveys the 70 years of the

Mexican Revolution, it leaves us guessing about this historic question: which class headed the revolutionary bloc?

The Concept of a Bureaucratic Revolution

In the 1970s there arose another interpretation of the Mexican cataclysm as a combined revolution. It maintained that a political-military bureaucracy seized the reins of government while the capitalist class bent the economy to its will. So the State teeters on the tightrope of contradiction, because one elite wears the political crown and another carries the economic purse.

Starting in 1920 the political-military bureaucracy tightened its grip on the Mexican State, but after 1940 the bureaucratic engine began to run out of steam. As the bureaucracy helped capitalist development against workers and peasants, the economy grew dependent on foreign capital, and for 30 years the State's popular support was slowly eroded. Then in the 1970s came a turning point: the bureaucracy tried to get the upper hand again through a series of reforms. To sum up: from 1920 to 1940 a bureaucratic political revolution came off with flying colours but from 1940 to 1970 faced the rising threat of bourgeois counter-revolution. That thesis attracts some of the best brains on the Mexican left; they believe that the fate of the Revolution hangs in the balance. We don't want to bore you with a roster of names, but the claim is so important that we mention a few authors whose works are listed in our bibliography: Gastón García Cantú, Mario Huacuja, José Woldenberg, Juan Felipe Leal, Américo Saldívar, Rolando Cordera, Carlos Tello, Miguel Basáñez, Carlos Pereyra, and Luis Javier Garrido.

These political analysts are on the right track. We skip a description of their views because they have a common denominator with our own. Besides, their generalizations are hemmed in by short-run considerations, while their conceptualization of the political process lacks a theoretical framework. But there is one version of the bureaucratic thesis with a theoretical foundation: Salvador Carmona Amorós' *La economía mexicana y el nacionalismo revolucionario*. He misconceives the revolutionary process as uninterrupted since 1910 but rightly sees an earlier bourgeois revolutionary cycle ended by the Mexican Revolution.

What were the intellectual influences on Carmona? The national Marxism of Lombardo Toledano and the neo-Lombardism of Galván and the Democratic Tendency of the Electrical Workers. From these sources Carmona took theoretical material to build his own version of a continuing national revolution led by a bureaucratic elite.

Carmona, a militant in the PRI's left wing, builds his interpretation of the Revolution on a combination of neo-Marxist political economy and Latin American dependency theory. *La República*, the PRI's official organ, has published his views, and they receive support in official party circles. Carmona is the current editor of *La República*; several ex-communists sit on the editorial board: Alejandro Carrillo, Vicente Fuentes Díaz, Angel Olivo

Solís, and the associate editor, Raul Moreno Wonchee.

Carmona finds two cycles of revolution in Mexico: a bourgeois cycle that began with the Reform of 1857 and ended with the Revolution of 1910; and a post-bourgeois cycle starting with the Revolution of 1910 and still making progress. In chapter three he writes:

> The most extreme liberals of the Reform wanted to promote the capitalist system. But independent of human intentions, the developing productive forces during the last decades of the 19th century and the first decade of the 20th show that the dominant order in Mexico was not capitalism but a feudal system with overlapping slavery. In this system the feudal and slave-owning landlords made up the hegemonic social class, while the dominated class consisted of peons tied to the land — peons who were formally wage labourers but really semi-enslaved by debts.

The islands in this sea of debt peonage were ruled by foreigners; their investments did not push the country toward independent development. 'Foreign capital connived with the *Porfiriato* to fuel this dependent capitalist model, but the project was wrecked by the Revolution.'

The bourgeois revolutionary cycle went up in the smoke and fire of 1910; the national revolutionary cycle replaced it. This new cycle, Carmona admits, has also stimulated the private sector but only to develop Mexico's industry and to bring independence from foreign interests. 'The public sector is independent in its own decisions and management, for it is not under the thumb of native or foreign capital.' He believes the public sector will remain the motor of the nation's economy. The national revolutionary model has raised up a healthy private sector, and now its big task is 'the gradual or radical transformation of the boundaries between the private and public in favour of the public.' Carmona calls this process an 'uninterrupted' or 'continuous' remodelling of the social structure.

In the introduction to his book there is a sketch of 'the national revolutionary model'. The Mexican economy is more than a balanced mix of capitalist and socialist elements. 'The national revolutionary model is a complete and differentiated socio-economic formation, a specific and unique road of development different from capitalism, socialism, and the transition from one to the other.' What is the model's historic mission? To tear out the roots of underdevelopment and to raise up a just society.

This model fits three clashing sets of interests into one harmonious framework. Three squabbling social groups are made to march hand in hand toward the new society: the working class, the national bourgeoisie, and the national revolutionary bureaucracy in the lead. This tripartite State should lead beyond the national revolutionary model to a more advanced social formation — in the long run! What is this advanced social formation? Carmona is vague about the future, but he hints that it is a regime based on two groups: the working class and the national revolutionary bureaucracy.

In chapter three he finishes this sketch of the model. Historical development climbs the ladder of social formations: primitive communism, slavery, feudalism, capitalism. In the advanced countries the next rung of the ladder is socialism, but in Third World countries it is the national revolutionary model. To fuel economic development in a national revolutionary state, investments must flow into the public sector. In the private sector there is both native business and foreign capital, but the revolutionary State should mainly nationalize foreigners' holdings. The national revolutionary model suits poor semi-colonial countries that must escape the grip of foreign capital but have neither a strong bourgeoisie to whip them along the capitalist road nor a powerful proletariat to lead them to socialism. In this backwardness a new social group takes the place of Marx's bourgeoisie and proletariat: the national revolutionary bureaucracy commanding the State.

Marxist economists such as Oscar Lange and Paul Baran have written studies of transitional societies, and Carmona relies on these in distinguishing between the national revolutionary model and state capitalism. What is state capitalism for our PRI intellectual? It is neither a social formation nor a stage of capitalism but rather a strategy for growth! This strategy can work for different social formations: advanced capitalist societies, socialist states in a developmental take-off, and national revolutionary regimes.

Salvador Carmona maintains that the national revolutionary model is the only way for a poor backward country to get mass support for economic development. It is also the only way to keep the state bureaucracy from abusing its extraordinary powers. Abuse of those powers may bring a loss of popular backing, and without working class support the bureaucratic State must give way before native and foreign capital.

The main theses of the PRI thinker are clear enough, but it is time to subject him to the lash of criticism. This left-wing intellectual in the official party, dancing along in the enchanted shoes of theoretical innovation, has fallen into the mud of false consciousness. His Marxism gives off an aroma of apologetic ideology.

Carmona sees that, as in the capitalist system, there is a contradiction within the national revolutionary society between the forces and relations of production. But the antagonism between socialized production and private appropriation, he argues, is softened by public ownership of energy, transportation, communication, steel, chemicals, paper, mining, autos, cement, hemp, textiles, and wood. The contradiction is also softened by the absence of exploitation in the public sector. As this sector encroaches upon the private sector, he maintains, the bourgeoisie slowly disappears as a class. Such is the higher stage of society the national revolutionary model leads to — a stage usually called socialism. But, we must ask Carmona, how can the national revolutionary model qualify as an independent social formation? Under analysis it reduces to a transitional stage between capitalism and socialism.

The bourgeoisie owns land and factories but the bureaucrats running the national revolutionary state have no legal title to the means of production.

Yet these bureaucrats control the commanding heights of the economy: oil, energy, railways, telephones, banking, steel, textiles, paper, mines. Carmona says that the new form of property here is state-social — the public economic sector. He means that the bureaucrats collectively *control* the means of prodution but don't collectively *own* them; that is why he defines the bureaucracy as a social stratum and not a class. He follows Lange in distinguishing a primary mode of distribution based on owning the factors of production from a secondary mode of distribution based on non-productive services. Classes receive their incomes from production, but strata get their incomes through a secondary distribution of the national income. With this questionable distinction Carmona tries to pry a new interpretation out of his Marxoid theoretical matrix. But the distinction won't work. It severs unproductive workers in commerce and finance from membership in the working class, and it separates merchants and bankers from membership in the capitalist class. The interpretative birth is botched.

He falsely claims that the state bureaucracy does not exploit the working class. Of course the high salaries of top bureaucrats are still far below the incomes of captains of industry and big bankers, but who can believe that state enterprises are run in the public interest only and not the interests of their managers? Answer: the government of Mexico believes it; in the PRI it is an article of faith. This faith may explain Carmona's blind spot for the extraction of an economic surplus from public enterprises in the form of bureaucratic salaries. But even the Marxist economists he relies on suffer from a conceptual blindness that afflicts Carmona personally: none of them can identify as the extraction of an economic surplus from workers in the private sector a system of taxation providing high salaries for top bureaucrats and low wages for their clerical staffs. Even in countries like the U.S.S.R. where capitalist exploitation has disappeared, bureaucratic exploitation survives. The concept of bureaucratic exploitation is the key to actually existing socialism. Real socialism, not the idealization of it in official Marxist textbooks, is a class-stratified social formation.

In trying to figure out what Mexico's vaunted mixed economy is, Carmona is out of his depth as a Marxist. He stumbles into conceptualizing it as a social formation different from capitalism. He thinks that between the bourgeois order and the socialist order stands the national revolutionary model as a Third Position. But it is only nominally a third way, for what this so-called new model amounts to is a reformed capitalism with a big public sector: a bureaucratic political regime combined with a capitalist economy. Carmona confuses the non-capitalist road of development taken by puritanical President Cárdenas with the capitalist path pursued by corrupt President Alemán. Yet even Cárdenas' non-capitalist road could have led through a mainly capitalist economy on the way to socialism. The Third Position is a halfway house between capitalism and a new economic order — it is a transitional stage.

Carmona raises a wall between the bourgeois and post-bourgeois revolutionary cycles — they don't overlap. But his interpretation misses the mark, for he starts off from a wrong premise: the view that the Revolution of 1910 rolled up the bourgeois cycle of revolutions for good.

Carmona presents the post-bourgeois cycle as a 'permanent' or 'uninter-rupted' revolution. That is a slip into apologetic fiction, for the Mexican Revolution was nothing of the sort. Almost all versions of a bureaucratic political revolution recognize its interrupted character.

The Cycle of the Bureaucratic Revolution

We now give our own periodization of the bureaucratic cycle. We also trace its connection to the series of bourgeois democratic revolutions that started up the stairs of history in 1810, fighting a century of battles against Spanish viceroys, reactionary generals, French imperialists, native landlords, religious guerrillas, comprador swindlers, feudal bishops, and U.S. troops.

The bourgeois cycle that took off behind revolutionary priests in 1810 and pressed on to 1821 was a dress rehearsal for the War of Reform. From 1857 to 1867 the liberal reformers fought battles against die-hard bishops and French imperialists, clashes that foreshadowed the struggles of the Mexican Revolution of 1910 to 1920.

In Mexico and Latin America this bourgeois cycle differed from the liberal democratic revolutions arching through European history. For in our hemi-sphere the cycle combined a struggle against feudal institutions with wars for national independence.

In Mexico there were even more complicating factors: in the struggle against Spain, bourgeois and even petty bourgeois leadership was missing; and the bells of independence in 1821 were rung by semi-feudal *hacendados*. How did this War of Independence start? Two priests ignited the powder, and a mass insurrection exploded against both the Spanish crown and rich creoles. The priests' programme aimed to wipe out slavery and restore lands to Indian villages, but the revolutionary war spread and its aims expanded. Father Morelos planned to curb the Church's vast powers, stop compulsory tithing, redistribute big estates, and set up a democratic republican government. Morelos and the other priests who led their troops into battle were not bour-geois leaders; rather the bourgeois content of the Independence War shows up in its liberal programme. The priests fell one by one; Morelos smoked a cigar at his execution on 22 December 1815. The social content of the Revo-lution was buried with him, and its liberal programme bore first fruit during the bloody Reform of 1857 to 1867 and the Revolution of 1910 to 1920.

Father Morelos did not die in vain. The failed bourgeois revolution of 1810 to 1821 did free Mexico from colonial exploitation, kick out the Inquisition, and tribute paid by Indians, extinguish forced labour, abolish slavery for blacks, and undermine the tithe.

The bourgeois upheaval that ripped open Mexico from 1857 to 1867 was led by liberal landlords who could not bring an end to the Middle Ages. But they stripped the feudal Church of its lands, tamed the rebellious military chieftains, defeated French imperialism by a people's war, and forged a genuine nation-state. Their leader was the Zapotec Indian Benito Juárez.

After Juárez's work Mexico was a decrepit feudal castle with a cardboard republican facade: liberal, federal, and democratic. Juárez's successor, Díaz, interpreted 'democracy' to mean his re-election to the presidency every six years without fail!

The bourgeois revolution of 1910 to 1920 cost two million lives in a tiny society but failed to hammer it into a new shape. The Revolution did throw up powerful worker and peasant organizations – something new in Mexico – and during the coming decades they helped to tear down the feudal castle. Zapata's peasant war started the land reform stumbling forward, while bespectacled Carranza flapped through the political sky, weighed down with a Constitution declaring social change. For refusing to observe its radical clauses Carranza was soon shot down, and a revolutionary bureaucratic regime under pragmatic Obregón and swearing Calles spurred the land reform from a trot to a canter. Tireless Lázaro Cárdenas sent the reform galloping ahead while he seized the oil and railways for his country, talked up populist socialism, and created a base for industrialization. In the 1940s and 1950s bourgeois industrialists reaped the economic benefits of Cárdenas' populist reforms.

In Europe the cycle of bourgeois revolutions wound up with *la grande bourgeoisie* master of the situation: the new industrial and financial class had the economy under its thumb: merchants, bankers, entrepreneurs, and stockholders financed elections and manipulated parliaments. How did the bourgeois cycle in Mexico finish? The business class ruled the roost in economic matters but could not enter the halls of political power. Bankers and industrialists stood outside the national palace staring at rifle muzzles guarding the door. Inside sat *el presidente*, the nation's top bureaucrat. The bureaucracy's man shapes all of the laws, and the pitiful congress uses rubber stamps. In Mexico the bourgeoisie plays first fiddle only in the economy, while the bureaucracy governs with a rod of iron.

The bourgeoisie's efforts at political revolution, first with Juárez, then with Madero, and finally with Carranza, all miscarried. And who opened the doors to bourgeois ascendancy over the economy? The political-military bureaucracy wrenched open those doors during President Cárdenas' administration. Only after Cárdenas' land reform had smashed the semi-feudal and pre-capitalist rural production relations did the capitalist sector take possession of the field. The bourgeois cycle of revolutions came to an end in 1940 with the capitalists benefiting from the economy and the bureaucrats bossing the State.

During the final phase of the bourgeois cycle began the cycle of bureaucratic revolutions. The first phase started in 1920, an uprising against the bourgeoisie's last effort to hang onto the government of Mexico: Carranza tried to impose a puppet president on the country and paid with his life. This ascending bureaucratic phase made headway as the revolutionary generals under Presidents Obregón and Calles firmed up their political power. In 1928 the revolutionary energy was switched off. During this interruption Calles' governing *camarilla* acquired some traits of a new state bourgeoisie.

The first phase of the bureaucratic cycle was over.

In 1934 the revolutionary energy surged up and shot along the wires of President Cárdenas' political towers, powering new efforts to institutionalize bureaucratic dominance, this time in the form of a neo-corporatist state. Then came a short circuit in the revolutionary flow. From 1940 on, the Revolution flickered dimly as the bureaucrats went on the defensive: their main concern was the industrialization of Mexico at any cost. Many historians mislabel this period '30 years of counter-revolution'.

Between 1920 and 1940 two revolutionary cycles overlapped. Before 1920 the revolutionary generals represented peasant interests (Zapata, Villa) or the interests of small farmers and petty bourgeois (Obregón) under the leadership of men who stood for native capitalist development (Madero, Carranza). But from 1920 to 1928 the bulk of the Constitutionalist generals followed the Obregón-Calles tendency; they built up their political power while the weak business class came off second best. During the *maximato* of 1928 to 1934, the Calles group became a state bourgeoisie but could not gain the upper hand over the political-military bureaucracy. In 1935 that bureaucracy, seated on the galloping masses, rode the whirlwind and directed its course. Only after 1940 did the Mexican business elite manage to turn Cárdenas' modernizing reforms to its own account, driving a roaring trade in the economy, making big profits and gathering up the economic power. But the political power stayed in the hands of the weakening bureaucracy where it remains today.

Our periodization from 1920 to 1940 coincides with that of Anatoli Shulgovski. His research on the Cárdenas period broke with his colleagues' historical stereotype: most Soviet scholars analyse the Mexican upheaval as a bourgeois democratic revolution. Shulgovski agrees with them that the outcome of the Revolution after 1940 was a dominant capitalist mode of production. But he argues that the bourgeoisie was not the driving force behind Mexico's political and social transformation. The real force swept Obregón into the halls of power in 1920; the important historical agency in the Mexican Revolution is the bonapartist political and military bureaucracy.

Shulgovski argues that this new regime was relatively independent of both the bourgeoisie and the proletariat. During the *maximato* the regime snuggled up to business interests but under Cárdenas switched to a revolutionary democratic alliance with workers and peasants. In 1940 Mexico stood at the crossroads of its history; the bonapartist regime had to choose between three directions. There was the road the regime had once followed from 1920 to 1928, balancing the interests of the popular classes against the interests of the capitalist class. Another road — pursued from 1928 to 1934 — would incline the balance in favour of the bourgeoisie. Finally there was the road the government had been travelling since 1934: an alliance with workers and peasants.

After 1940 the bureaucrats in power left this non-capitalist road; adverse circumstances had changed the correlation of social forces. The Spanish Republic had fallen; the lights went out on the continent of Europe; the

Finns, Austrians, Hungarians, Romanians, and Germans hurled their minions upon the Soviet Union. In Mexico armed peasants settled down to till new corn patches, and newly organized workers relaxed inside undemocratic unions. So the bureaucratic regime again switched to collaboration with native business and foreign monopolies. But is this collaboration enough to make the Mexican Revolution in essence bourgeois democratic?

What are the advantages of our periodization? It stresses the reforms of Obregón and Calles as the key to understanding the class content of the new revolutionary cycle. And it recognizes that the '30 years of counter-revolution' undermining the reforms of President Cárdenas did not turn back the clock of history: the bourgeoisie are still barred from the presidential palace. Beginning in 1940 the erosion of bureaucratic power kept on for three decades, but a bureaucratic regime survives. In the new skyscrapers housing state ministries, the slogans of the Mexican Revolution hang over bureaucrats at their desks. Will the winds of history once more stir the masses and blow life into the old clichés?

The Mexican Revolution flows in the subterranean crevices of society. It feeds off Latin America's magnificent revolutionary tradition: 150 successful uprisings between Independence and the First World War, with Mexico making the big contribution. It is Mexico's spirit of resistance to 270 armed interventions — the victorious struggle for national survival.[2] It is the country's overlapping revolutionary cycles spanning centuries.

Is the Revolution really dead? It lives on in a squatter defending her shack, a student writing on walls, a worker breaking his machine, a peasant turning guerrilla, a teacher singing the Internationale, an Indian demanding land, a Jesuit organizing slum-dwellers. It is Rosario Ibarra disguised as a maid in Military Camp Number One looking in vain for 'disappeared' sons and emerging to stump the country with a cry for resistance. The Revolution is Mateo Zapata's refusing to surrender his father's bones to the government's Pantheon in exchange for two million pesos: 'You can have the bones for nothing when my peasants have land!' It is a people's priest freed from arresting officers by Torreon's citizens.

In the Mexico City subway a 15-year-old girl hurtles toward Vocational School Number Five, carrying a school pack containing Kovalson's manual on historical materialism: she dreams of the Revolution.

It is the magnetic future.

Notes

1. The full titles of works by authors criticized in this chapter are listed in Part III of the bibliography.
2. As the huge mural in the José Martí Cultural Centre in Mexico City explains, between 1800 and 1969 there were hundreds of foreign colonial and imperialist interventions in Latin America by Spanish, English, French, and especially United States forces. Mexico suffered

270 interventions, Latin America as a whole 784. This data was supplied to the Centre by Pablo Gonzalez-Casanova, former Rector of the National Autonomous University of Mexico and one of the nation's leading sociologists.

11. The Contradictory State and Post-Bonapartist Regime

What is the class character of the Mexican State? In Mexico the left agrees on the answer to that question but not on the interpretation of the political regime. If you ask each of the parties on the left about the State, the answers harmonize in a familiar chord: the State is bourgeois. What about the political regime supported by the state party, the hated 'PRI government'? The left's answers jangle in discord. The left's main representative, the Unified Socialist Party directed by cadres from the former Communist Party, believes that the PRI government is bourgeois. But the two other left-wing parties with any following, the Revolutionary Workers' Party and the Socialist Workers' Party, see the political regime as bonapartist.

What does the Mexican left understand by a 'bourgeois state'? A state that acts as an agent of the class that rules the economy – the bourgeoisie. And what is that which, according to some, stands at the helm of the bourgeois state – what is a 'bonapartist regime'? By such a regime the left understands a bureaucratic stratum that bars the business class from political power, stokes up capitalism to warm the bourgeoisie, and throws tasty sops to other classes – it is an authoritarian structure with law-makers jumping to obey the executive.

The left says that these definitions come from Marxist texts but gives no proof for its claim.

Is there a bourgeois state in Mexico? Is its government bourgeois? Or is it bonapartist? In answering these questions the Mexican left has gone astray. For if we stick to Marx's and Engels' usage, the Mexican State is not capitalist and the PRI government is neither bourgeois nor bonapartist. The Mexican left has not only misread the Marxist classics on bourgeois states and political regimes; it has also misunderstood Mexican society and the present correlation of social forces.

In our view, the Mexican State is a contradictory state of exception, and the official government of the Revolution is a post-bonapartist bureaucratic regime.

Why There Is No Bourgeois State in Mexico

The Mexican left thinks that its description of the state as bourgeois is based on the conditions of a bourgeois state according to Marx and Engels. But a capitalist state is not just a state in which the bourgeoisie holds the whip hand in the economy. If the bourgeoisie has control of the economy, argues the Mexican left, that is a sufficient condition for a capitalist state. For Marx and Engels it is only a necessary condition.

In *The Eighteenth Brumaire* Marx paints the French economy of 1851 in bourgeois colours – it is mainly capitalist. The bourgeoisie is the ruling class. In part one he says that the parties and masses of the Great French Revolution carried out the task of their time by unleashing modern bourgeois society. The Revolution of 1789 destroyed the feudal basis of the French economy, mowed off its aristocratic heads, and exported the Revolution throughout Western Europe. The Revolutions of 1830 and 1848 gave further pushes to bourgeois society, strengthening what Marx calls the 'new social formation'.

But in part four he notes that in the 1850s the bourgeoisie had become so divided against itself that 'its own interests demand its deliverance from the danger of its own rule; that in order to preserve its social power intact, its political power must be broken; that in order to save its purse, it must forfeit the crown; and the sword that is to safeguard it must at the same time be hung over its own head as a sword of Damocles.' The bourgeoisie remains the economically ruling class, but under Louis Bonaparte ceases to be the governing class. A new state emerges that for the time being is not bourgeois.

In part six Marx singles out the parliamentary republic as the only state form upholding the interests common to all bourgeois fractions. 'The parliamentary republic . . . was the unavoidable condition of their common rule, the sole form of state in which their general class interest subjected to itself both the claims of their particular factions and all the remaining classes of society.' He also describes the peculiar traits of a bourgeois regime: the executive is pushed and pulled about by a powerful parliament. Does this mean that the only form of bourgeois state is a republic? No, the bourgeois state may be a monarchy, but it must take a parliamentary form, as under ambitious King Louis-Philippe. Under the Orleanist 'bourgeois king' the bankers ruled, says Marx, and Louis' personal friend and prime minister preached to the other bourgeois fractions: 'Get rich!' To be bourgeois a parliament does not have to act in the special interest of every fraction of the capitalist class, but it must be led by some part of the bourgeoisie. Without a bourgeois government there can be no bourgeois state.

In part seven Marx returns to this point. He says that the Orleanist monarchy and the parliamentary republic were bourgeois regimes, and he contrasts these with the bonapartist regime. Under the 'bourgeois king' and under the parliamentary republic, the bureaucracy was merely an instrument of the ruling class; but under cunning Louis Bonaparte the bureaucracy became a power in its own right. In a sense, says Marx, Bonaparte's regime and even the State became independent of civil society. 'Only under the second Bonaparte does the State seem to have made itself completely independent.' Was it completely independent of the bourgeoisie? Or was it only relatively independent?

'Just as the Bourbons were the dynasty of big landed property and just as the Orleans were the dynasty of money, so the Bonapartes are the dynasty of the peasants.' That sentence in part seven contains Marx's class analysis of 19th century French government. In the sentence we can substitute for 'dynasty' the word 'regime' to read: 'Just as the Bourbons were the regime of big landed property and just as the Orleans were the regime of money, so the Bonapartes are the regime of the peasants.' It is clear that a bonapartist regime is not a bourgeois one. The State dependent on a bourgeois fraction under the Orleanist monarchy and dependent on the bourgeoisie under the parliamentary republic was a state of the capitalist class, but the State under Louis Bonaparte was not bourgeois. Under Bonaparte the state apparatus was no longer a mere instrument of the economically ruling class.

We see that for Marx the class nature of a state is a function of two historical variables: the ruling class and the governing group. We now introduce distinctions he makes in part seven of *The Eighteenth Brumaire* and in part one of *The Civil War in France*. The 'state power' is the modern 'executive power'. The 'state power' serves two social groups — the ruling class and the governing bureaucracy. The ruling class holds sway in the economy; the governing bureaucracy commands the 'state apparatus' of ministries, departments, bureaus, armies, police, judges, courts.

The 'state power' also differs from the 'state edifice'. What is this edifice? Here Marx takes for granted the general meaning of the state as a 'political edifice', an organization embracing a territory and a people. But this 'political superstructure' has more than a geographical and ethnic basis: 'the superstructure's' class nature grows out of a mode of production embedded in the economic foundation and also reflects the state power and its apparatus.

The political, legal, and juridical organization of civil society is the State, but this 'superstructure' can sway in crosswinds blowing from both the ruling class and the 'state power'. When that class and this power are antagonistic forces, the result is what Marx and Engels call a state of exception. Such a state is not the state of the economically ruling class.

A state of exception is typical of transitional periods in which one social formation replaces another. From the history of revolutions in the 18th and 19th centuries Marx concluded that political and social transformations seldom if ever happen simultaneously. In periods of transition political formations do not exhibit the same class features as the economic foundations on which they rest. Only a static view of history is compatible with the vulgar Marxist notion that the political superstructure agrees in every instance with the economic structure. For Marx, the political and economic formations coincide under conditions that are stable rather than transitional. Only then is the state in bourgeois society a bourgeois state.

If a bonapartist regime goes with a state of exception — and Marx claims it does — then the corresponding state is not the normal state of bourgeois society. But only the normal state in such a society is bourgeois. Therefore, the exceptional state is not bourgeois.

In *The Housing Question* Engels describes the conditions of a bourgeois state. In his preface to the second edition and in the beginning of part one he explains the German housing shortage by the social effects of capitalism. In 1872 the German economy showed threads of petty commodity production running through a semi-feudal sector and a capitalist sector. In this patchwork the capitalist colour stood out brightly, says Engels, but was the German State bourgeois?

In section two of part two Engels describes the German State as 'the organized collective power of the possessing classes . . . against the exploited classes.' This suggests that it is not the state of a single class and that it acts neither for a single class nor for the whole society. The German State in 1872 was not an established class state but a malleable transitional one. The young and timid German bourgeoisie 'has not won either direct political domination as in France or indirect domination as in England.' Engels claims that in Germany there was an equilibrium between the landed aristocracy and the bourgeoisie – the condition for the absolute monarchy. And, alongside that condition, he also finds the condition for modern bonapartism, an equilibrium between the bourgeoisie and the proletariat. So 'the transition from the absolute monarchy to the bonapartist monarchy is in full swing.' These 'contradictory social conditions' place the governmental authority in the hands of a special caste of army officers and state officials. Is the result a bourgeois political formation? No, the process has thrown up a contradictory state. Engels' admission that 'the Prussian State is falling more and more into the hands of the bourgeoisie' shows that for him the state is not a state merely of the capitalists but rather a transitional one.

We can make a historical generalization: in established political formations the class that rules also governs, but in transitional political formations the political superstructure and economic infrastructure are out of joint.

Engels returns to this thesis in the concluding part of *The Origin of the Family*. The state 'is as a rule the state of the most powerful, economically dominant class which, through the medium of the state, becomes also the politically dominant class.' Political power becomes for this class a means of hardening its economic power by 'holding down and exploiting the oppressed class'. A 'state of slave owners' fits the slave mode of production; the landowners' 'feudal state' matches the feudal mode; and the bourgeois state suits the capitalist mode. But beyond these normal states Engels recognizes that there are so-called states of exception 'in which the warring classes balance each other so nearly that the state power, as ostensible mediator, acquires for the moment a certain degree of independence of both.' What Engels describes as a transitional state has been swallowed up by the New Left stereotype of a 'capitalist state'. Nicos Poulantzas' concept of a 'capitalist state' is a bag into which Marxists cram the liberal state, the interventionist state, the bonapartist state, the military state, and the fascist state. The state of exception has become the rule.

For Engels, both absolute monarchy and modern bonapartism are states of exception. A state with a bonapartist regime is not a bourgeois state because the bourgeoisie do not control the state power. As under Louis Bonaparte, the bourgeoisie may be the economically dominant class but it is not even indirectly the governing class. In states of exception, according to Engels, the state is relatively independent of the economically ruling class. Why? Because that class, barred from the castle where the political decisions are made, can only lay down the law in the economic field.

The Mexican left has only a superficial understanding of the Marxist distinction between normal states and states of exception. For all the left parties, the sufficient condition of a bourgeois state is a capitalist class having its own way in the economy. But for Marx and Engels this is not enough: in a bourgeois state some fraction of the capitalist class must have a hand on the reins of political power. Even though it may not occupy the throne, it must have a hold on the ruler. At least indirect political power for some sector or fraction of the bourgeoisie is a necessary condition for the capitalist state. The Mexican left has oversimplified the Marxist concept of the state by interpreting it as a mere appendage of a massive economic structure.

Sketches of a Mexican Bonapartist Regime

Other elements of the left have grasped that the Mexican political regime is not bourgeois and decided that it is bonapartist. Where did they go wrong? They either misread the Marxist meaning of bonapartism or wrongly applied this concept to the Mexican political situation. Their wrong application arose from missing the shift in the direction of history since World War II.

For centuries bureaucratic regimes had never reached more than relative independence from the economically dominant class; that is what Marx and Engels understood by a bonapartist regime. Then in the 1930s came the establishment of the first socialist society in the Soviet Union. After the war the socialist economy in the Soviet Union and Eastern Europe revealed the bureaucracy as its chief beneficiary: the bureaucrats reaped higher salaries and more privileges than any other social group. The outcome appeared as a bureaucratic mode of production; the bureaucracy came out of the closet as a new ruling class.

Even under capitalism the correlation of social forces has changed in favour of the bureaucratic elite: the corporate, political, military, educational, and labour managers are gathering ever more power into their hands. Between the managerial elite and the capitalist owners a new equilibrium has emerged — the basic condition of the new bureaucratism. And so the bureaucracy is no longer merely a bonapartist arbiter of the interests of the social classes; it is a major social force concerned with forging and expanding its own economic power. In the historical long run its revolutionary elements tend to replace the bourgeoisie at the head of the economy. That is how the PRI's left wing and some party ideologists understand the Mexican political system. They are right: the Mexican government is a post-bonapartist regime.

Equipped with these conceptual tools, we turn to the confused arguments of the Mexican left; many of these arguments assume that the state is bourgeois while guided by a bureaucratic political regime. Such arguments misunderstand this regime as bonapartist. But at least they are on the right track, and our tool box contains what we need for repairs.

Not all of these views have a Mexican origin. Their forerunner is Trotsky's analysis of the Cardenist regime in the collection of his essays *For the Socialist United States of Latin America*. On the question of Latin American bonapartism, Trotsky's influence prevails and turns up in the most unexpected quarters. We find traces of it in the work by an unorthodox Soviet writer with a following on the Mexican left, and in the views of a maverick Trotskyist with a following of his own. We find it in the documents authorized by the Trotskyist party in Mexico, and also in the official publications of the Socialist Workers' Party, a political current hostile to Trotsky and Trotskyism.

In 1920 Alvaro Obregón, the general with 20-20 vision, aimed a military rebellion at President Carranza. He did not miss and soon occupied the presidential chair. The interpretations of the Mexican State mentioned above all trace the origins of its bonapartism to Obregón's armed uprising but disagree about the outcome of the movement he founded. One view holds that the bonapartist regime gave way to a bourgeois government during World War II. Another view maintains that World War II marked a downturn for the bureaucratic regime: it slowly declined until it degenerated into a bourgeois regime in the early 1970s. A third view sees Mexican bonapartism flickering to this day, weakened but alive.

The classic statement of the first thesis is Anatoli Shulgovski's *México en la encrucijada de su historia*. In 1968 the Communist Party translated and published this work; it has sold through four printings. Its premises are the CP's original evaluation of the post-revolutionary regime as bonapartist. The party later decided that in the post-revolutionary state a bourgeois regime had been present from the beginning, but Shulgovski rejects this revision. The crusty Soviet scholar still argues that the bonapartist regime lasted for more than two decades until it gave way to a bourgeois regime during World War II.

The second thesis, that the bonapartist regime did not collapse until the early 1970s, comes from Octavio Rodríguez Araujo in *La reforma política y los partidos políticos en México*. This bearded revolutionary, whose students achieved his reinstatement after he was deprived of his teaching post, bases himself on Trotsky's discussion of bonapartism and the Mexican Revolution. Our political scientist argues that during the administration of President Luis Echeverría from 1970 to 1976 the 50-year-old bonapartist regime finally sickened under growing economic pressure from the business community. A bourgeois political offensive gave the bonapartist regime the death blow. Since 1940 the powers of the bonapartist bureaucracy were slowly fading, and the political crisis of 1968 so weakened the bonapartist regime that it succumbed to a bourgeois regime shortly after. Rodríguez Araujo still expounds these views in the National Autonomous University, where classrooms bear such names as 'Ho Chi Minh' and 'Che Guevara'.

The third thesis about Mexican bonapartism is shared by two left parties: the Revolutionary Workers' Party affiliated to that Fourth International run by the Unified Secretariat, and the Socialist Workers' Party with ties to the left wing of the PRI. These parties snarl at each other's strategies and squabble over the 'correct' understanding of the fundamental social antagonism in Mexico. But concerning the existence of the bonapartist regime and the reasons for its continuing erosion, the two find themselves in agreement. Although the Socialist Workers' Party stops short of labelling this regime as 'bonapartist', its portrait of the PRI government bears a close likeness to that of the Revolutionary Workers' Party.

All three theses distinguish between the class nature of the Mexican State and the corresponding political regime. That is their merit. Now we critically examine each.

The Regime of the Revolutionary Generals

In his work Shulgovski recalls in section two of chapter one that in the 1920s 'both the Mexican Communist Party and the Communist International claimed that the regime of revolutionary *caudillos* [government by the generals of the Revolution] was petty bourgeois and that the petty bourgeoisie — as a special social force playing a big role in Mexico's unusual conditions — had consolidated itself in power.' According to *El Machete*, the Communist Party's official organ in those years, the combined urban and rural petty bourgeoisie had picked up the sceptre of political power. Why was the intermediate petty bourgeoisie able to snap up the political sceptre from the whirlpool of the Revolution and wield it for a generation? Because neither the scrawny working class nor the tiny capitalist class was strong enough.

The resulting regime of revolutionary *caudillos*, as *El Machete* describes it, also acted as a kind of 'shock absorber in the collisions between the reactionary and the revolutionary forces.' And so the Communist Party singled out two features of the early post-revolutionary regime: its petty-bourgeois origin and its bonapartist character.

Shulgovski questions the petty bourgeois origin of the men in power but likes the party's description of the government as bonapartist. He concludes that the regime of revolutionary *caudillos* lasted from Obregón's 1920 military rebellion until ex-President Calles institutionalized the Mexican Revolution in 1929. Calles replaced the rule of the generals with that of the new Revolutionary National Party — today's PRI. During the 1920s the wrestling classes were evenly matched, and 'what stood out were the bonapartist methods of rule and the *caudillos*' clever use of the contradictions between the classes.'

Shulgovski goes on to say that the new regime initiated by Obregón was only able to hang onto power because mass support propped it up. That support came from the peasants. In this respect also the regime of the revolutionary *caudillos* looked like the bonapartist regime of Marx's The *Eighteenth Brumaire*.

But there are different types of bonapartist regime. Shulgovski cites Gramsci in distinguishing three kinds of bonapartism as 'Caesarism': besides a progressive and reactionary bonapartism there is an intermediate bonapartism with a transitional character. Through these conceptual lenses Shulgovski studies *El Machete's* picture of the post-revolutionary regime and discovers that the bonapartism of the 1920s was of the intermediate type.

In the pages that follow, Shulgovski implies that the bonapartist regime came to an end with the creation of the official party: the party's bureaucratic methods were supposed to replace the personal rule of generals tossed up by the Revolution. But in the final section of the last chapter we read: 'At the beginning of the 1930s so-called revolutionary *caudillismo*, the specific Mexican variant of bonapartism, was reborn with the domination of the bureaucratic-bourgeois elite of enriched generals of the Revolution, high government functionaries, and politicians-turned-businessmen.' In the years from 1931 to 1934 this new governing group called itself the 'revolutionary family'. The family tried to shift from the framework of alliances that had supported the presidencies of Obregón and Calles to a new set of connections. From an alliance with the labour unions the government turned a smiling face toward entrepreneurs and bankers chattering about 'free enterprise'. The revived bonapartist regime chose the capitalist road of development and urged an end to communal villages in the countryside. This road promised personal gain to the members of the revolutionary *camarilla* who hoped to become capitalists. The chameleon of Mexican bonapartism had changed from a confusing intermediate colour to reactionary black. So the bonapartist regime, says Shulgovski, did not finish up in 1929 but revived in a 'reactionary' form until the *maximato* ended in 1934.

It was replaced, he says, by a 'progressive' regime based on a new set of alliances with the popular classes. In 1935 the chameleon turned pink! Instead of the *maximato's* policy of a settled equilibrium among the main classes, Lázaro Cárdenas worked for a dynamic equilibrium. His philosophy recognized the class struggle. Shulgovski notes in the final section that Cárdenas beefed up the state economic sector to reinforce the progressive direction of his regime. The economic development of Mexico swung in a non-capitalist direction: 'To some extent we may say that the state sector helped to fortify anti-capitalist tendencies in the ranks of the Mexican proletariat.' Although Shulgovski stops short of dubbing the Cárdenas regime 'progressive bonapartism', his description of it coincides with what he understands by this term. So by implication the bonapartist regime did not end in 1934 but in 1940. At the beginning of the 1940s, according to Shulgovksi's analysis, the correlation of social forces shifted in favour of capitalism. Just as the *maximato's* switch to a reactionary bonapartism created a wave of labour and peasant insurgency, so the progressive policies of Cárdenas called forth a reaction from business groups and big landowners. Cárdenas led the nation through land reform. Then, as peasants with new lands calmed down and workers with wage hikes relaxed, the propertied classes mounted an offensive. So after 1940 President Camacho embraced the moneyed groups that wanted to industrialize Mexico with capitalist methods.

Shulgovski winds up his evaluation of the period from 1920 to 1940 with a word from Gramsci: 'In deeds Napoleon I represented the triumph of organic bourgeois forces over the petty bourgeois jacobins, and all political movements of a similar kind have led to the same result.' Shulgovski finds a similar process taking place in Mexico during the 1940s.

The Cardenist regime struggled in vain to rise above the organic and objective forces pushing Mexico into the orbit of world capitalism. The earlier bonapartist regime of 1920 to 1928 took an intermediate position, then between 1931 and 1934 a reactionary turn, and finally from 1935 to 1940 a progressive direction – but it could not win! The rule of the political-military bureaucracy finally succumbed to that of a bourgeois regime.

While the bonapartist bureaucracy sat in the driver's seat, the exploiting classes rode further back, fighting one another to get a hand on the wheel. The unstable Mexican political system careered forward. But after the semi-feudal landowners were forced out the back of the bus, the entrepreneurial class took the driver by the throat and pointed toward the system of private enterprise. Mexico passed this crossroads of its history during World War II, and the new ruling class of industrial leaders and financiers drove steadily into the future.

To explain the collapse of the bonapartist regime, Shulgovski produces a whole basket of reasons. The country began to modernize, and the private economic sector grew faster than the public sector. The government's policy of nationalizations provoked black looks and wagging fingers from the U.S. State Department. The party of the revolution divided, and a powerful current in it favoured getting along with the United States. Workers and peasants languished in government-controlled unions and leagues. The French Popular Front crumbled; the Spanish Republic bled to death. Triumphant fascism in Italy, Germany, Austria, Czechoslovakia, Greece, Portugal, and Spain encouraged a wave of reaction throughout the western hemisphere. All this put Mexico's progressive forces on the defensive. These events were blows to the political bureaucracy already reeling under pressure from Mexican and international capital.

Mexicans, however, still debate whether these blows hammered the bonapartist regime into a bourgeois shape.

Bonapartism with a Civilian Face

Against Shulgovski's thesis that the bonapartist regime ended about 1940 stand the arguments of Octavio Rodríguez Araujo. He spells out the Trotskyist usage of 'bonapartism' for Mexico's unusual conditions. 'Bonapartism' describes and explains 'the peculiar traits of the Mexican government after the 1910 Revolution, until it lost them through the process linking the national bourgeoisie to the internationalization of capital.' Octavio Rodríguez then lists the bonapartist features in the Mexican government down to 1970. How, for him, does a bonapartist regime emerge?

It emerges through a revolutionary upsurge of a proletariat that neither understands its interests nor has the strength to reshape society. The divided business class sweats in fear over the crisis undermining its mastery of the economy. Both these conditions allow the political-military bureaucracy to re-organize class alliances to maintain social peace. This relative autonomy of the state apparatus converts it into an arbiter of the class struggle. The bureaucratic referee has a double aim: to strip the moneyed interests of political power and to quiet the labouring class. In this situation the bankers and entrepreneurs surrender to a strong executive; the bonapartist ruler towers above the classes. Next, the gradual internationalization of capital brings about a qualitative change in the bonapartist political current: the balance between classes plus the bureaucracy's relative autonomy take on a post-bonapartist form. This form comes to look less and less like a bonapartist regime, for the government must give in to international lending agencies, transnational corporations, and their local stand-ins. The regime finally reveals its new bourgeois nature.

Our Trotskyist academic relies heavily on an unpublished M.A. thesis written by Carlos Sevilla at the University of Essex in 1975, *Bonapartism in Mexico: its Emergence and Consolidation*. Octavio Rodríguez claims that from 1920 to 1940 the Mexican government's bonapartist centre established different relations with society. First relation: the government's political lordship over the business community and its commanding role in the economy let it act in its own interest against the cries of bankers and merchants. Second relation: the government's alliance with workers, peasants, and petty bureaucrats put pesos in their pockets but locked them into corporative unions with state arbiters refereeing the class struggle. Third relation: the government's role as a go-between in spats between Mexican interests and foreign monopolies enabled it to dispute how much North Americans would take advantage of Mexico's economic dependency. In all these relations, our author adds, the main props of the bureaucratic regime were the peasant mass and organized labour — as under Louis Bonaparte!

What happened after the Cardenist period? Rodríguez Araujo thinks that since 1940 the bonapartist regime has undergone two big changes.

The first happened under President Avila Camacho: the bonapartist regime's power to negotiate with U.S. imperialism weakened. At the same time the regime turned from the little people of Mexico toward local business groups. 'It was during this government that . . . the bonapartist character of the Mexican State began to decline.' Rodriguez argues that the decline resulted from this fact: the flabby bureaucracy sat complacently by while the bourgeois dwarf grew up to flex powerful muscles. The lagging bureaucratic performance turned into a sideshow as the capitalist giant widened its ring in the circus of the economy.

By 1946 the bonapartist regime's actions clashed with the populist ideology inherited from Cárdenas' regime.

> From then onward the bonapartist bureaucracy's main support was not one class but its ability to negotiate among bourgeois factions and between these factions and the labour bureaucracy; the bonapartist formation rested on its position of equilibrium among the bourgeois

factions and the labour bureaucrats and no longer on its apparent
neutrality toward bourgeoisie and proletariat.

From 1946 to 1970, Rodríguez argues, the relative autonomy of the
bonapartist bureaucracy began to disappear. It was overshadowed by the
growing power of the bourgeoisie — the qualitative change in the bonapartist
regime beginning with President Alemán in 1946. This change was more than
an 'erosion' of the bureaucracy's independence. For under Cárdenas the
bureaucracy sitting on a peasant nag had been able to juggle the interests of
capital and labour with precision; but now bourgeois interests had grown so
weighty that, to keep from over-balancing, the bureaucracy threw aside the
proletariat.

The second big change happened under President Echeverría. Mexico's
most talkative president repainted the bureaucracy's bonapartist facade, but
the 1968 political crisis had hopelessly cracked it. So 'the political bureaucracy's only means of keeping its relative autonomy under the present conditions of world capitalism was to push aside its bonapartist facade and to
build a new one. This fronting is not finished but so far looks like a social
democratic regime of a new type.'

Rodríguez Araujo finds many of the old features in this new facade; he
describes the new regime as 'bonapartist without bonapartism'. In other
words, it is bonapartist in ideology but bourgeois in reality. 'The governing
bureaucracy's political hegemony over the bourgeoisie, which marks off bonapartism, no longer exists. Today the state directly represents the interests of
the bourgeoisie as in other capitalist countries.' And this means that the
political bureaucracy is no longer sole master in the National Palace: the real
political lords gather at business lunches on the Paseo de la Reforma, decide
national questions in corporate executive suites, and forge the big policies at
the Entrepreneurial Co-ordinating Council.

All of the above arguments limp through Rodríguez's pages, suffering from
the same theoretical weakness: in his list of the ingredients of bonapartism he
does not distinguish the role of the working class from that of the peasantry.
He says that against the pressures exerted by workers and peasants the bonapartist regime balances the pressure of native and foreign capitalists. He continually emphasizes the bureaucracy's role as mediator between these two
sets of forces. What this analysis therefore misses is the role of the small-
holding peasants. According to Marx, the peasantry is a class intermediate
between the proletariat and the bourgeoisie: the peasants serve as a third
force propping up the intermediary role of the bonapartist bureaucracy. This
third force is the mass basis for the bonapartist Third Position.

In *The Eighteenth Brumaire* Marx compares the thousands of French
villages to potatoes, a shapeless mass of units in a sack. Mexico's sack of
90,000 villages is shaped by government-controlled peasant leagues created
during Cárdenas' land reform. During the Revolution the sack of potatoes hit
Mexico on the head, and to this day it remains the largest single class in the

country. Failure to understand the peasantry is the recurring note in
Rodríguez's theoretical fugue on the political data of the 1970s. Our Trotskyist slips into the old error of his mentor, who was criticized by Stalin for
'underestimation of the peasantry'. Later we shall see that the Revolutionary
Workers' Party too makes the error of cramming workers and peasants into
the single classification of the 'popular classes', though in other ways the
party saves itself.

In the final section of his *Eighteenth Brumaire* Marx finds in bonapartism
five 'napoleonic ideas'. The first is reverence for small-holding property, no
matter how inefficient. The second is strong government that destroys any
institutional links between the masses and the state power. The third is an
enormous bureaucracy that upholds the regime for bread-and-butter reasons.
The fourth is the clergy as an ideological prop of the government. The fifth
is the army as society's tower of strength. For Marx all these napoleonic ideas
'are ideas of the undeveloped small holding in the freshness of its youth.'
They make up the peasantry's political ideology. But the peasantry is a transitional class doomed to extinction, so that with 'the progressive undermining of small-holding property, the state structure built upon it collapses.'

After 1920 Mexico's bonapartist regime appealed to the peasants as its
principal mass support, and its post-bonapartist successor carries on this
tradition in weakened form. In 1972 the Mexican sociologist Arturo Warman
published a book whose title spoke volumes: *The Peasants: Favourite Sons of
the Regime*. The peasants are the third force in Mexican society; they uphold
the ideology of a strong centralized state independent of the bourgeois class.
They really matter to the governing bureaucracy: now and then it distributes
land to offset the tendency toward their proletarianization. Land reform has
several political aims, and one is to limit the growth of agrarian capitalism.
The regime's peasant base must not disappear.

In this context we can understand the Mexican sociological debate between
the 'depeasantists' and the 'peasantists'. The depeasantists claim that the
peasants are turning into a class of wage labourers, but the peasantists say
that on balance the *campesinos* are not disappearing. The depeasantists see
that the bureaucratic regime promotes capitalist development replacing small
peasants with an agricultural proletariat. But the peasantists point out that
through land distribution the bureaucratic regime continually recreates the
peasantry. A bureaucratic regime, whether bonapartist or post-bonapartist,
pursues contradictory aims. In Mexico the post-bonapartist regime's economic
policy contradicts its political need for a peasant base.

Marxist theoreticians sometimes miss the importance of Mexico's largest
social group because it is an invisible class. You can drive across Coahuila,
watching the sierra pass like mountains on the moon, and never see the
million peasants in its vast ranges.

Does Bonapartism Still Survive in Mexico?
We turn to the third thesis about the Mexican state, the view held by the

Revolutionary Workers' Party and the Socialist Workers' Party. They say that after the 1968 political crisis the bonapartist regime remained in place. It is not a bourgeois regime. Why do these parties still believe in the relative auto-nomy of the PRI government?

The Revolutionary Workers' Party analyses the Mexican political system in its 1977 pamphlet *Qué es el PRT?* The document says that the workers and peasants who destroyed the 'bourgeois state' between 1910 and 1917 lacked a party acting for them at the national level. The bourgeoisie lost the govern-ment and met defeat on the field of battle. The petty-bourgeois and military commanders reconstructed the capitalist order; they became mediators in the struggle between the capitalists and the popular classes. The result was a government that kept its bonapartist head above water even after 1940, when its 'elements became increasingly bourgeoisified'.

The 1968 political crisis seemed to submerge the bonapartist regime for a moment, and the political and economic crisis of 1976 threatened it again. The party document claims that the regime's performance as umpire in the class struggle is less and less convincing, for economic dependence and foreign loans force it to favour international and local capital. Between 1970 and 1976 Echeverría tried to clean up the umpire's fair-play image, and López Portillo is in a better position to polish it, but 'the strengthening of the big bourgeoisie and the penetration of imperialism on the one hand, combined with the proletarianization of intermediate strata on the other, have whittled away bonapartism's room for manoeuvre.'

Bonapartist methods are breaking down, the document goes on, and will yield fewer results under López Portillo, since calming the workers by appeals to their prejudices no longer works. The decay of bonapartism since 1968 confronts the business class with an unpleasant fact: 'the only real historical alternative is a military dictatorship'. For the business people have no experience in governing, and the soil for bourgeois democracy is lacking. The generals wait for their cue to enter history.

For the Revolutionary Workers' Party, López Portillo's reform of the electoral process has not really changed the political system. His majesty the President still holds the sceptre of political power and bullies the Congress and the people. Under pressure his bonapartist regime has granted opposition parties the right to run campaigns, but these reforms are only partly 'demo-cratic'. So the regime weakly hangs onto power — for how long?

We have already said that the Socialist Workers' Party agrees with most of the Trotskyist view of the state outlined above. In the report of the 12th Plenum of the Socialist Workers' Party's Central Committee in September 1980 we find the key to the ongoing Mexican political crisis: 'the irreversible march of the general process of polarization into two great camps'. According to this party's analysis, at any moment 'a dangerous and decisive confron-tation may occur that could take by surprise the political leadership of the national and popular forces, and hand it the dilemma of fighting or surren-dering.' What are the two great camps? On one side, the big bourgeoisie and imperialism; on the other, the bulk of the Mexican people.

The party report maintains that since 1968 three processes have charged the Mexican political scene with tension. The fundamental antagonism 'nation-imperialism' has become a ticking bomb; the forces of private enterprise have launched a political offensive; and the working class has begun to build organizations outside the government network — unions with socialist leaders.

Growing economic dependency on foreign capital has put the nation on the defensive. The bourgeoisie's hatred of the left has filtered into the police, and the big money supports paramilitary bands that terrorize the workers. To these bad omens, says the party, we must add the counter-balancing fact that, in the struggle against imperialism, the Latin American Revolution is developing new strength. All these elements add up to a political equation for the Mexican future: the contending forces are preparing for a major confrontation.

The country is moving towards a showdown. The PRI government still controls the halls of political power, but *la grande bourgeoisie* throws a shadow over the National Palace, while behind rears the colossus of foreign capital. How long can the government stand up to business interests? 'The direction of the country by the national revolutionary sector is faced at each step with serious difficulties imposed on it by the big bourgeoisie, imperialism, and its own class limitations. These difficulties increase the chances that the governing group will defend its position by softening its policies.' There are only two ways out of the crisis: either a revolutionary government made up of the Mexican left and the PRI's 'national revolutionary sector' or a military regime that tortures and terrorizes the people.

What does this mean? The bureaucratic regime has small chance of muddling through, for its decomposition continues. The national revolutionary sector of the PRI government still stands at the helm, but the oligarchical sector has come from poop to midship and is moving toward the wheel. 'So the best and most advanced plans of the government are caught up in the web of interests woven by the big bourgeoisie in the state apparatus.'

To sum up: this third thesis has an advantage over the others we have examined in that it describes the PRI government as bureaucratic rather than bourgeois. But is the regime really about to collapse? Does it have only a transitional, bonapartist character?

The Fundamental Antagonism Is Not the Decisive One

In dependent countries the concept of the bourgeoisie embraces both its native and foreign sectors. The hostility between bourgeoisie and proletariat is the fundamental antagonism in capitalist societies — that is the ABC of Marxism. All the interpretations we have discussed assume that this is the fundamental antagonism in Mexico.

The interpretations suppose that this fundamental antagonism is the historically decisive one. By decisive we mean that the antagonism contains the germs of a new society, in this case a social order run by the labouring classes. But the history of 20th century revolutions shows that proletarian uprisings generate new labour bureaucracies and wind up losing power to them. That is the way the *Weltgeist* played its hand in Russia during the revolution of 1917 and through the decade of the 1920s; the socialist revolutions in other countries have followed suit. Have the revolutions of the 20th-Century raised up Marx's class of wage-labourers as the principal beneficiaries? No, the political and labour bureaucrats controlling the workers have reaped the harvest of higher salaries and class privileges. In this perspective the decisive antagonism is not Marx's fundamental one.

The distinction between the fundamental antagonism and the decisive antagonism in a social formation is not new — it runs through the Marxist classics. In his 1895 Introduction to Marx's *Class Struggles in France* Engels assumes that in the history of Western civilization the fundamental antagonism of ancient society was that between master and slave and the fundamental antagonism of feudal society that between landlord and serf. Yet he argues that the historically decisive confrontations were not between exploiters and exploited. The fights that decided the outcome of the historical transitions were between old and new classes of exploiters. 'All revolutions up to the present day have resulted in the displacement of one definite class rule by another, but all ruling classes up to now have been only small minorities in relation to the ruled mass of the people.' These revolutions helped replace one ruling minority by another. The new minority class then refashioned the state and the economy to suit its interests: 'Even when the majority took part, it did so, whether it knew it or not, only in the service of a minority.'

Engels adds that these features of past revolutions also appeared during the struggles of the proletariat for its emancipation. In 1848, for example, 'there were but a very few people who had any idea at all of the direction in which this emancipation was to be looked for.' To these enlightened few belonged Marx who by 1850 believed that the bourgeois republic in France had polarized society between the ruling bourgeoisie and the classes grouped around the proletariat. Engels recalls Marx predicting that 'during and after the common victory not those other classes but the proletariat grown wise by experience had to become *the decisive factor*.' Looking back with the hindsight of 1895 Engels says flatly: 'History proved us wrong.'

At the end of the 19th century Engels understood that history had not turned out as Marx expected, but he died believing that the 20th century would see the dictatorship of the proletariat. Just as Engels admitted that history proved Marx wrong about the revolution of the 19th century, so we can see that it has proved Engels wrong about the 20th.

Has capitalist society issued in majority revolutions? The new society emerging from the womb of capitalism is called real socialism; it is not the socialism foreseen by Marx and Engels as 'the lower stage of communism'. It has nothing to do with communism, but in the words of the late leader of the German Democratic Republic, makes up an 'independent social formation between capitalism and the anticipated classless society.' That was the judgment of Walter Ulbricht in an article on 'La etapa avanzada del socialismo' published in volume three of *Historia y Sociedad* in Mexico City in 1968.

We can put all this into a theoretical formula: in the historical process the fundamental antagonism between exploiters and exploited is the motor force; but the derived antagonism between rival exploiters is the guiding force. Minority revolution is still the rule.

The Contradictory State: Two Types of Bureaucratic Equilibrium

What is the exceptional state? We have seen that for Marx and Engels a balance between the classes struggling for power allows a special 'caste' to rule independently of society, a stratum made up of army officers and state officials. Between two classes in equilibrium stands the bonapartist caste with sudden power.

Centuries ago the bureaucracy was not a class. To see that, we can glance at its social composition and its members' income. In the absolute monarchies of the 17th and 18th centuries the top layers of the governing group came from the lower and middle aristocracy living off both the king's pay and ground rent. And as late as Louis Bonaparte this 'caste' embraced declassed *lumpen* elements – swindlers and adventurers – social failures who got even by looting the state. They also failed to make up a modern bureaucracy, a social group defined by its ownership of organizational expertise – a fourth factor of production. Marx's three great classes of landowners, capitalists, and wage labourers had their hands on the classical factors of production – land, instruments, and labour. The 20th century class of bureaucrats owns a fourth factor variously called science, education, organization, and expertise.

In Marx's day the governing bureaucracy of exceptional states was still a caste, but in our time the correlation of social forces has changed. In our century the professional bureaucracy has become a new class with its own interests. It owns the fourth factor of production. This factor is knowledge, personified by the political bureaucrats we have been considering and also by technocrats directing the production of surplus value. This knowledge is science in the form of 'expertise', the basis of developed forms of organization that Marx called 'co-operation'. In its elementary forms it appears as the 'work of supervision' and the 'labour of superintendence' directing the 'productive force of social labour' or 'the social productive force of labour', as you can read in the chapter on co-operation in volume one of *Capital*. But it is not labour in the sense of the classical factor of production. Nor is it, as one school of economists thinks, a form of 'human capital'.

In Third World countries now under bureaucratic regimes, the typical equilibrium among classes is not between capital and labour. It is an equilibrium between capital and 'expertise'. The capitalists preside over the economy, while the bureaucrats wield the state power – that is what marks off today's states of exception or 'contradictory states'. Under these conditions the state power is no longer arbiter in the class struggle: bonapartist regimes have given way to post-bonapartist governments. In these post-bonapartist governments the state power is not a referee: it is one of the interested parties. Today in Mexico the fundamental antagonism is *between* economic power and political power, between the bourgeois commanding the economy and the bureaucrats directing the government.

The transformation of bonapartist regimes into post-bonapartist ones has strengthened the bureaucracy, but the relative autonomy of the state power is less than ever, because the bourgeoisie has also gained in strength. It has toughened into a Hercules threatening to bend society to its will. The hardening of bureaucratic power is matched by the bourgeoisie's iron sway in production and distribution. The economic power of capital surpasses the political power of the state.

This shift in the correlation of social forces throws light on the erosion of state power. In a bonapartist regime the bureaucracy totters weakly but the capitalist class is offset by a militant proletariat. In a post-bonapartist regime the bureaucracy fortifies its class power, but the spread of capitalist production raises up the entrepreneurial class as a virtual giant. The bonapartist regime has dug a trap for itself by promoting capitalist growth.

In describing Louis Bonaparte's regime, this point is made by Marx. In part three of his *Civil War in France* he recalls the services rendered to the French bourgeoisie by 20 years of bonapartist rule: 'Under its sway bourgeois society, freed from political cares, reached a development not expected even by itself. Industry and commerce grew to colossal dimensions; financial swindling celebrated cosmopolitan orgies . . . . The state power, apparently soaring high above society, was at the same time the greatest scandal of that society and the hotbed of all its corruptions.' This reads like a description of both the Mexican 'economic miracle' of the 1950s and the widespread corruption within the 'Robberlutionary Party'. The bureaucrats used the governmental power to line their pockets.

In France this process led to the restoration of a bourgeois parliament. From 1851 to 1871 the bourgeoisie lost its political footing — temporarily! In 1871 it was not the Paris Commune of the proletariat but the ruthless Adolphe Thiers' bourgeois forces that carried the day. The bourgeois republic triumphed.

For a generation Louis Bonaparte balanced the proletariat against the bourgeoisie, but in spite of himself he nurtured conditions for the financial and industrial interests to regain command. The Mexican left sees an analogy between this process and the political journey of the PRI government. The left mistakenly sees the Mexican economic elite making short work of the bureaucracy.

Under Louis Bonaparte modern industry expanded to strengthen the capitalist sector and to undermine the peasant economy. The peasantry degenerated into a class of paupers; the military slid from the political heights into defeat by Prussia. In 1870 the bonapartist regime fell apart. From 1851 to 1870 the growth of private enterprise, the modernization of the economy, the defeat of the military — all this spurred the men of money to bear away the political prize. The business class got rid of the state of exception by reuniting the purse and the sceptre.

In world history this was the fate of all bureaucratic regimes until the Russian Revolution opened a new prospect for the political bureaucracy. In the Soviet experiment the bureaucracy stepped beyond capitalism to develop a bureaucratic mode of production. But the success of its new model only became clear to the world after World War II. In the post-war period bureaucratic regimes began to show non-bonapartist traits.

Shulgovski correctly sees a bonapartist regime in Mexico from 1920 to 1940; the Revolutionary Workers' Party and the Socialist Workers' Party correctly argue that a bourgeois regime has yet to replace it. But the thorny question is whether the post-Cardenist regimes continued to be bonapartist.

Unlike the pretorian regimes of Obregón, Calles, and Cárdenas, the post-1940 governments were civilian. After President Avila Camacho, the sway of the armed forces — what Marx called the 'culmination' of the napoleonic ideas — disappeared from the political system. Camacho abolished the military sector of the ruling party and built up the 'popular sector' to such an extent that it became as big as the labour and the peasant sectors. Beginning with Miguel Alemán, every president has come from this popular sector led by professional bureaucrats in government. Civilians have replaced the military in the president's office, and a new professional bureaucracy has replaced the self-made generals thrown up by the Revolution.

Between 1920 and 1940 Mexican society looked like Germany after the Franco-Prussian War. We have already mentioned Engels' description of the Prussian State and the rest of Germany. In his *Housing Question* he found 'alongside of the basic condition of the old absolute monarchy — an equilibrium between the landed aristocracy and the bourgeoisie — the basic condition of modern bonapartism, an equilibrium between the bourgeoisie and the proletariat.' In Mexico between the two world wars the revolutionary generals tried to offset the economic power of the semi-feudal *hacendados* by modernization and industrialization, and they beefed up the trade unions in order to keep the bourgeoisie from mounting the political throne.

After 1940 the government's mass base in the peasantry remained intact, for the slowed-down land reform did not stop altogether. But the landowners had fallen on evil days while the business community prospered. What was the outcome? The business class eclipsed both the old landowners and the emerging proletariat, so that the bureaucratic David now faces a bourgeois Goliath. In such a situation there can be no bonapartist regime.

From a Bonapartist to a Post-bonapartist Ideology

We turn to the changes in Mexican government policy with the re-organization of the official party. Alemán scrapped Cárdenas' Party of the Mexican Revolution for the re-organized Institutional Revolutionary Party. The PRI government was more than a change of facade; it was something new in Mexican political life. The equilibrium between the landowners, bourgeoisie, and proletariat was gone, and the government could no longer keep its relative independence by playing off one class against another. So a new strategy arose:

the party strengthened its 'popular sector' while encouraging capitalist growth. This bureaucratic sector was supposed to offset the growing business power.

The radical Cardenist ideology never got beyond the strategy of a 'mixed economy' and a middle road between capitalism and communism. Was this 'Mexican road to socialism' designed to replace the private sector by the public one? No, it aimed to combine the benefits of both.

The Mexican 'solution' to the conflict between individualism and collectivism shows in the *ejido* village, the basis of the co-operative sector. The Mexican village owned the land communally but assigned each peasant family a plot for its use. 'Mexican socialism' would never be more than a travesty of the new economic order in the Soviet Union and Eastern Europe. Its non-capitalist road did not aim to wipe out the social effects of the parallel capitalist road; the non-capitalist path did not aim to eliminate capitalism but to countervail it.

This bonapartist ideology was the state party's philosophy under Cárdenas. Octavio Rodríguez Araujo writes in his chapter on the PRI: 'bonapartism was an integral part of the Declaration of Principles and Programme of [Cárdenas'] Party of the Mexican Revolution.' This basic document of Cárdenist ideology recognizes that the class struggle pulsates in the capitalist mode of production. It stresses the workers' right to organizations acting for them in the contest over the surplus product and in the struggle to influence the State. It accepts the principle of a workers' democracy and a socialist regime within the Mexican constitutional system.

During the period from 1940 to 1970, the inner circles of the PRI replaced this bonapartist ideology with a new ideology. The party's 1946 principles and programme continued to recognize a class struggle and to support 'proletarian liberation', but these references disappeared in the document adopted by the party's National Assembly in 1950. In their place came softened words about 'social and economic inequalities under the capitalist system' and the 'unjust existence of classes in conditions of manifest inferiority'.

What classes are these? The working class and the peasantry, of course, but significantly the document added a third class led by the party's bureaucratic sector. The document no longer spoke of proletarian liberation; instead it proclaimed the party's promise to 'provide improved facilities for the groups belonging to the popular sector.' Although the document admitted that the state should intervene in economic matters to protect national interests, this must not interfere with the 'development of private initiative within the framework of law and public morality.'

The concept of a 'mixed economy' has also undergone revision. As Miguel de la Madrid Hurtado noted in a speech to economists in Mexico City on 27 March 1969, a mixed economy means equilibrium between the public and private sectors — nothing more. 'One hears of capitalist systems or market economies and of socialist systems or centrally planned economies. In between these two extremes we have the mixed economies that have tended to prevail . . . . These have in common only the combined elements of the two typical systems mentioned.' But in Cardenist ideology there was a co-operative sector, and this third sector goes unmentioned, as if it no longer figured in the government's plans for the future. So the big stand-off is between the private sector and the state power.

President Cárdenas' vision of the future turned on a fundamental social antagonism, the struggle between capitalists and workers. The old struggle has given way to a new one between capitalists and bureaucrats.

The Post-bonapartist Regime

This shift in the ideology of the official party mirrors a change in the correlation of social forces. From 1940 to 1970 growing bureaucratic muscles tightened into an iron grip on the State, but the native and foreign sectors of private enterprise became ever more powerful and threatened to pry it loose. Then in 1971 President Echeverría tried to reverse the direction followed during the three decades of so-called 'counter-revolution'. He preached against private enterprise, and it in turn began to thrash about in the economy. President López Portillo tried a new tack by allowing Marxist parties to organize and campaign for office. In the 1982 presidential elections the PRI government recovered its leadership of 71% of those who voted. Beyond these elections the political reform has a deeper purpose, says Pablo González Casanova in *El Estado y los partidos políticos en México*, for the opening to the left aimed to recover the government's negotiating power with native and foreign business. Can the government bring bourgeois private enterprise, both native and foreign, under control?

In this struggle the government has been losing ground, as shown by three considerations. First, during Echeverría's final years the bourgeoisie rebelled against the ideology of the Mexican Revolution and pumped through the society a contrary ideology praising free enterprise. Second, the polarization between business and government led in 1975 to the formation of a potential counter-government of the bourgeoisie – the Entrepreneurial Co-ordinating Council. And third, dependence on foreign technology escalated while the public foreign debt skyrocketed. López Portillo carried through a modest political reform; but on the ideological front, the political front, and the economic front the bourgeoisie came out ahead.

In the early 1970s Echeverría made two big efforts to recover the revolutionary legitimacy of the PRI government. He strengthened the public sector relative to the private, and in foreign policy he abandoned bilateral agreements with the United States in order to join the non-aligned nations and to support Third World revolutions. But what his regime gained by these strategies was undercut by losses in other areas.

Echeverría's strengthening of the public sector brought on the first ideological showdown since World War II between government and business. For decades the business community was loyal to the PRI, and its ideology of free enterprise only circulated in filtered form through the publications of the official party. Then in 1973 business forces broke this allegiance by flooding radio, television, movies, and magazines with propaganda about private property, the acquisitive virtues, the joys of consumerism, corruption in government, and public sector inefficiency. The powers of business financed whispering campaigns of rumour, fear, and jokes discrediting the official party. There sounded a concert of false rumours about lack of food and gasoline, attacks on school textbooks as soft on communism, and prophecies of government confiscations. For the first time the ideology of big business split from the legacy of the Mexican Revolution as interpreted by the PRI.

Carlos Monsivais' essay on 'The Ideological Offensive of the Right' sums up the government's reverses on the ideological front. The private sector has forced the following concessions: control of education outside the public schools; the final say in matters of social morality and the rights of women; the freedom to criticize all government decisions; and the right to spread demands for privatization of state enterprises.

The Mexican left also profits from this new right to publish ideas freely, but it has little money, and its newspapers' circulation is small. The bourgeois control of radio, television, movies, magazines, and newspapers is an advantage in the struggle to shape public opinion.

Echeverría's reforms also provoked a counter-attack by the forces of capital on the political front. For the first time since World War II business-people began laying plans for a government of their own. From these plans emerged the Entrepreneurial Co-ordinating Council designed to become Marx's 'executive committee for managing the common affairs of the entire bourgeois class'.

The private sector wants to take over the State. The most aggressive elements of monopoly and finance capital are ready to call on the 'party of the military' for an attack on the government palace. These elements conspire to seize power and to set up a 'national security state' modelled on Argentina's terror system and Chile's military repression. For that to happen the government must enter another big political crisis.

The government is on the defensive; it is moving to re-establish its popular alliances. In the work of González Casanova, already cited, we read that the government's 'effort sparked the [July 1978] reunion of the Congress of Work and a new social democratic programme aimed to prevent monopolistic groups from seizing control of the state'.

In foreign policy the government made its most spectacular advances: it squeezed out of its old 'special relation' to the United States. But its policy of non-alignment, its friendship with Cuba, its new attitude toward the Soviet Union, its cultural and diplomatic ties with the socialist bloc, did not widen its room for manoeuvre against Washington and the transnationals. It aided the Chilean left before and after Pinochet's 1973 coup, but this move did not buttress the State against pressure from the bourgeoisie. In an essay on 'State and Society' by Carlos Pereyra comes the summing up: 'everything gained by these measures was cancelled by the economic debacle at the close of Echeverría's administration, which led the government to kowtow to the recommendations of the International Monetary Fund.'

This economic debacle was the outcome of setbacks on the economic front. The government tried to curb the voracity of the transnationals and the ambitions of native capital, but the new laws were so cautious that they carried less clout than similar measures used by the Brazilian military. The government tried to bring off a tax reform but ran into unbreakable resistance. It tried to end the anonymous ownership of corporate stock – in vain! Investment in the public sector topped that in the private at a terrible price: the public foreign debt soared; money poured from the presses; inflation went through the roof – in 1976 the peso was devalued by half. The inflation-devaluation process concentrated income in fewer hands and slashed real wages.

During Echeverría's term the public debt exploded from four billion to twenty billion dollars, giving the international financial consortiums a vice-like hold on Mexico. The nation did not learn to make machines and technology but imported more than ever before. Mexico's dependence on foreign capital accelerated.

During López Portillo's reign the government failed to recapture the initiative. It caved in to the IMF, made concessions to the business class, and darted about looking for an exit from the crisis. It took up a strategy of better relations with big money and the foreign corporations – at a price. The price was a low-wage policy, loss of buying power, and more unemployment. The rich got richer and the poor got poorer, another setback for the government's policy of alliance with the popular classes. As Pereyra says about this turn to the right: 'The limiting of wage increases in the face of inflation and the reduction of public spending for social services aimed at a recovery in the rate of profit undercut by economic slump – but the cost was more deterioration in the miserable living conditions of the working class.'

He thinks the balance is clear. 'The government lost the ideological battle and could not carry through many of the proposed reforms . . . because the correlation of social forces and the hegemony of the capitalist sector allowed few concessions that marshal popular support.' So the 'revolutionary popular alliance' talked up by the political bureaucracy remained an idea on paper. Echeverría's political offensive began in 1970, but the government looked weaker by 1976. López Portillo also ran into trouble. He launched a political reform but suffered frightening economic setbacks. In February 1982 Mexico's high export prices and overvalued peso brought another devaluation. By 1982 the foreign debt was over 60 billion dollars. It was as if every Mexican owed over a thousand dollars to foreign creditors, more than many peasants make in a year. In August the peso was devalued again. To pay the interest on this fantastic debt with a devalued currency, the government had to hand half the federal budget to overseas creditors. In 1983 Mexico expects 14 billion dollars in oil revenues but will have to pay 14 billion in interest on the debt. The outgoing president has bowed to the IMF in exchange for a fast

4 billion, and the Fund is requiring that the government slash its deficit by half in 1983. Such a cutback in federal spending could mean a couple of million extra unemployed by the end of that year.

The PRI claims that the government directs the economy. It lies, for the bureaucracy can barely handle the bourgeois giant, getting stronger every decade. The native factory owners cut back on production, lay off workers, and smuggle money abroad. The economy's dependence on foreign investors, foreign bankers, foreign technology, and foreign trade has tied the government's hands. Is the bourgeoisie preparing its bid for political as well as economic power?

The economic imperialist penetration of Mexico grew by leaps and bounds after Miguel Alemán took office in 1946, and Echeverría was powerless to curb it. From 1970 to 1982 Mexican business made bigger profits, while the government failed to curb transnationals controlling 60% of consumer goods production. More toilet paper and kleenex were produced than newsprint and books, yet 70% of the Mexican people never feel these tissues. And they don't need them; they need schools, food, and jobs. But the IMF directors enjoying the good life in Washington are more interested in the mysteries of monetarism than the misery of the masses, and the Fund's dictates are as decisive in managing Mexico's economy as the decisions of its government.

Mexico has fallen into the trap that holds most Third World countries. States like Mexico on the periphery of world capitalism cannot survive without insertion into the world market, and this means bowing to the metropolitan centres making the big decisions. For the State to be powerful enough to stand up to foreign business, it must build an alliance with the popular classes against economic imperialism. But how far can the State go toward this alliance? The Mexican State is not master in its own economic house. As a Mexican economist explained to us: 'Our productive system is not sufficiently integrated to sustain the material life of the underlying population.' In other words, as long as Mexico is tied to world capitalism it cannot shake off dependent weakness and meet its people's needs. Caught in this trap, the government cannot mobilize the masses for the anti-imperialist struggle.

In *Bürgerliche Herrschaft in der Dritten Welt* Tilman Evers considers the underdeveloped country with an overdeveloped State. This typical Third World country is in a predicament. Its State is strong facing the native proletariat and even the local bourgeoisie, insofar as the bourgeois are 'unassociated' with the transnationals. But its State is weak before the 'associated' bourgeoisie and imperialism. The peripheral State's weak economic structure and its powerful superstructure are at odds. In section two of chapter four Evers explains why: 'the economic and political processes do not take place within the same social entity.' Evers means that the economy is controlled by a foreign bourgeoisie acting through its local associates, while the political decisions are made at home. Since the national economic space is not the basis of the State, its political superstructure must also answer to outside pressure. Evers concludes that few Third World countries can escape the determining influence of imperialism.

Since the operational bases of the peripheral State lie beyond its political control, 'the states of the capitalist periphery have no society that is strictly their own.' As satellites of the central economies, all peripheral States are weak; they are strong only within their national space. But within that space there is little economic basis for their power. So the peripheral State is undermined on two fronts: 'from outside we cannot speak of effective political control because of doubts about the state's *sovereignty*; from inside the political control is effective but there are doubts about its *nationality*.'

In section four of the same chapter Evers claims, perhaps mistakenly, that for States on the capitalist periphery the Third Position can never win hands down. 'All known examples, such as the "justicialism" of Perón and the Nasokom of Sukharno, fell under the first big industrialization push aimed at import substitution of articles for mass consumption.' Industrialization in peripheral States requires big injections of foreign capital and an investment climate with low wages. In Mexico import substitution began with Alemán. Under his influence revolutionary nationalism gave way to the ideology of industrialization at any cost. Echeverría again talked up revolutionary nationalism, he shouted everything that Fidel had said against the transnational corporations but with a difference: Castro expropriated them and Echeverría could not. Did the Mexican President's tirade change the nation's dependence?

Evers also shows how a State dragging the chain of a foreign bourgeoisie makes it heavier by asking for loans and aid from the overlord. To push the country down the capitalist road, to maintain the conditions for capitalist production, and to keep up the state apparatus, big financial transfusions are needed. A poor and backward country fails to generate this money from its own tax base: the powerful rich refuse to pay and the poor cannot. So the government seeks help abroad. The result? The government falls into an abyss of debt, prints paper money, and regularly devalues the currency. The peripheral State must also finance the army, police, education, and propaganda. This means more trips to the implacable IMF and the banks following its lead.

Third World States cannot survive in the world capitalist economy without caving in to outside pressures. As these States slide downhill they pick up momentum toward the bottom, begging loans to pay the interest on astronomical debts. Ninety-six Third World countries making up two-thirds of the world's population owe 12 international financial consortiums half a trillion dollars. Of the 96 countries, Mexico has the second largest debt. Here we have the explanation for the erosion of bureaucratic political power in Mexico City.

The giant south of the Rio Grande hangs onto its Third Position – by its teeth! It is still a big exception to the rule that bureaucratic elites in bonapartist and post-bonapartist States must finally turn into a state bourgeoisie. The explanation lies in the mass basis of the official party and its fusion with the state apparatus. For half a century the bourgeoisie has tried to crack this nut without success.

The official party still commands the loyalty of the Mexican masses; its electoral performance is even better than that of most of the parties in Eastern Europe. Since 1929 its candidates have won almost all elections at local and national levels. In the race for president and in the election for state governors and senators, this party has never officially lost a single seat. Up to the 1979 federal elections the bourgeois National Action Party, the only opposition that really mattered, had won only 129 congressional seats — the official party had won 2,327. In 40 years National Action picked up 40 townships while the government's party rolled in 27,000. Only one other 20th century party can equal that record — the Communist Party of the Soviet Union.

The re-organizations of Mexico's official party have been like those of its Soviet counterpart. In the Soviet Union the Politbureau replaced the Central Committee as the party's supreme organ, in turn replaced by the rule of the General Secretary. In Mexico the 1937-39 statutory reforms initiated the same process. The re-organized party's semi-corporatist structure unintentionally bound worker and peasant leaders to the official party in a way that ended dissidence. Internal party life slowly withered, and the National Assembly used rubber stamps. The supreme party organ was the National Council, but the Executive Council usurped its powers, only to slide under the thumb of *el presidente.*

For most Mexicans, support for the president means support for the country; and the population is patriotic. So the official party's president can easily stay in the saddle through several more political crises.

In 1920 Obregón's military takeover suspended a bonapartist regime over the classes squabbling for power. After 1940 it became a post-bonapartist regime that was not bourgeois but bureaucratic. This post-bonapartist regime sharpened the contradictory nature of the Mexican State by setting up its political power at one pole and encouraging economic power at the opposite pole. The differential between these poles discharges showers of sparks over Mexico. The polarization strengthened the bureaucratic class in its dealings with workers and peasants but weakened it in the face of the business community. The peasants are no longer the major social basis of the post-bonapartist regime, for the reinforced 'popular sector' of petty bureaucrats is becoming just as important.

To understand their importance you need to know that Mexico's work force numbers only 20,000,000 and that unofficial estimates claim that 40% of these are underemployed or unemployed. Millions of the employed are petty bureaucrats. On 24 July 1982 the Mexico City daily *Unomásuno* ran an article on the petty bureaucracy as 'One of the Most Important Elements in the Country'. The article explained that there are 1,800,000 petty bureaucrats in the civil service; another 1,200,000 in the state enterprises; another 1,000,000 working in education; and 100,000 more in the state medical system. Many of these petty bureaucrats are organized in the powerful unions of the 'popular sector'. The 600,000 teachers in the National Education Workers' Union, for example, make up the largest labour union in Latin America. These petty bureaucrats may now be more important than the peasants as a prop of the big bureaucrats running the State.

The capitalists continue to mismanage the economy so badly that the bureaucrats are forced to move against them. On 1 September 1982 a presidential decree electrified the nation:

> For reasons of public utility the installations, buildings, equipment, safes, vaults, branches, offices, property values, investments, and stocks or shares held in other enterprises, of the Institutions of Public Credit that provide banking service are expropriated in favour of the nation.

With one stroke the bureaucracy wiped out much of the bourgeoisie's financial fraction.

That was on a Saturday. By Monday the remaining industrial and commercial fractions were fighting back: the Entrepreneurial Co-ordinating Council demanded a national plebiscite on the question of bank nationalization, and the National Chamber of Commerce announced a protest strike for the end of the week. At once the government rallied hundreds of thousands for demonstrations in favour of the nationalization. During the rest of the week statements of support poured into the National Palace from countless labour unions and popular organizations around the country.

Business interests were enraged, for the dry language of the presidential decree turned dramatic with these words: 'stocks or shares held in other enterprises . . . are expropriated.' The nationalized banks held huge amounts of stock in 1,000 enterprises, including the 500 largest corporations in the nation.

During the spring and summer the government had been facing massive flights of capital, so it now decided to placate big business. On 4 September the young director of the new nationalized bank announced that it would sell off the stocks held in other enterprises. A roar of protest rose from the Mexican left, including minority groups inside the official party, but the business world called off its threatened strike.

At time of writing, the new president is taking office, and the stocks have not been sold; the left is mobilizing to keep them for the public power. But the government will sell off some in order to calm the captains of industry and bring back flight capital: Mexico is facing its worst economic crisis in a hundred years.

The nation's famous Revolution is in trouble; it stumbles from crisis to crisis. As it reaches the end of the century it will face another crossroads in its history. Who will win? Will the big bourgeoisie take over the State? Or will the big bureaucrats take over the economy?

The Revolution is still unfinished. We look to the Mexican left to shape the outcome.

Bibliography

Part I: The Mexican Revolution and Its Outcome

A. History: Mexico 1910-1976

Aguilar, Alonso, *Capitalismo y revolución en México*, Mexico D.F.: Ed. Nuestro Tiempo, 1977.

Aguilar, Alonso *et al*, 'Problemas del capitalismo mexicano', *Estrategia* (Nov. - Dec. 1976).

Aguilar, Alonso and Carrión, Jorge, *La Burguesía, la oligarquía y el Estado*, Mexico D.F.: Ed Nuestro Tiempo, 1972.

Aguilar Mora, Manuel and Hernández, Ricardo, *El PCM en la encrucijada*, Mexico D.F.: Folletos Bandera Socialista, 1977.

Alonso, Antonio, *El movimiento ferrocarrilero en México 1958-1959*, Mexico D.F.: Ed. Era, 1972.

Alperovich, M.S. and Rudenko, B.T., *La Revolución Mexicana de 1910-1917 y la política de los Estados Unidos*, Mexico D.F.: Ed. Cultura Popular, 1960.

Anguiano, Arturo, *El Estado y la política obrera del cardenismo*, Mexico D.F.: Ed. Era, 1975.

Araiza, Luis, *Historia del movimiento obrero mexicano*, (2nd. edn.), Mexico D.F.: Ed. Casa del Obrero Mundial, 1975.

Argüello, Gilberto, *En torno al poder y a la ideología dominantes en Mexico*, Puebla: Universidad Autónoma de Puebla, 1976.

Basurto, Jorge, *El proletariado industrial en México (1850-1930)*, Mexico D. F.: Universidad Nacional Autónoma de México, 1975.

Beals, Carleton, *Porfirio Díaz*, Philadelphia: J.B. Lippincot, 1932.

Boils, Guillermo, *Los militares y la política en México*, Mexico D.F.: Ed. El Caballito, 1975.

Brandenburg, Frank, *The Making of Modern Mexico*, Englewood Cliffs: Prentice Hall, 1964.

Castillo, Heberto, *Cárdenas el hombre*, Mexico D.F.: Ed. Hombre Nuevo, 1973.

Castillo Heberto, *Libertad bajo protesta*, Mexico D.F.: Federación Editorial Mexicana, 1973.

Castillo, Heberto and Paoli Bolio, Francisco, *Por qué un nuevo partido?*, Mexico D.F.: Ed. Posadas, 1975.

Cecaña, José Luis, *El capital monopolista y la economía de México*, Mexico D.F.: Ed. Cuadernos Americanos, 1963.

Chapoy Bonifaz, Alma, *Empresas multinacionales*, Mexico D.F.: Ed. El Caballito, 1975.

Clark, Marjorie, *Organized Labor in Mexico*, Chapel Hill: University of North Carolina Press, 1934.

Cline, Howard F., *Mexico: Revolution to Evolution: 1940-1960*, London: Oxford University Press, 1962.

Cockcroft, James; Frank, Andre Gunder; Johnson, Dale, *Dependence and Underdevelopment*, Garden City: Doubleday Anchor, 1972.

Cockcroft, James, *Intellectual Precursors of the Mexican Revolution 1910-1913*, Austin: University of Texas Press, 1968; Mexico D.F.: Ed. Siglo XXI, 1971.

Cockcroft, James, 'Mexico' in *Latin America: the Struggle with Dependency and Beyond*, Chilcote, Ronald and Edelstein, Joel (eds.), Cambridge: Shenkman, 1974.

Córdova, Arnaldo, *La formación del poder político en México*, Mexico D.F.: Ed. Era, 1972.

Córdova, Arnaldo, *La ideología de la revolución mexicana*, Mexico D.F.: Ed. Era, 1973.

Córdova, Arnaldo, *La política de masas del cardenismo*. Mexico D.F.: Ed. Era, 1974.

Cosio Villegas, Daniel, *El sistema politico mexicano*, Mexico D.F.: Ed. Joaquin Mortiz, 1972.

Cosío Villegas, Daniel (comp.), *Historia moderna de México*, 8 vols., Mexico D.F.: Ed. Hermes, 1948-1965.

Cumberland, Charles C., *Madero y la Revolución Mexicana*, Mexico D.F.: Ed. Siglo XXI, 1977.

Davila, Gerardo and Tirado, Manlio (eds.), *Como México no hay dos: porfirismo, revolución, neoporfirismo*, Mexico D.F.: Ed. Nuestro Tiempo, 1971.

Declaración de Guadalajara de los electricistas democráticos al pueblo de México, Guadalajara (5 April 1975).

Fehrenbach, T., *Fire and Blood: a History of Mexico*, New York: Macmillan, 1973.

Frank, Andre Gunder, *Capitalism and Underdevelopment in Latin America*, New York: Monthly Review Press, 1969.

Frank, Andre Gunder, *Latin America: Underdevelopment or Revolution*, New York: Monthly Review Press, 1969.

Frank, Andre Gunder; Puiggrós, Rodolfo; Laclau, Ernesto, *America Latina: feudalismo o capitalismo?*, Bogotá: Ed. La Oveja Negra, n.d.

Fuentes Díaz, Vicente, *Los partidos políticos en México*, (2nd. edn. 2 vols.), Mexico D.F.: Ed. Altiplano, 1969.

Furtak, Robert, *Revolutionspartei und politische Stabilität in Mexico*, Hamburg: Übersee-Verlag, 1969.

Garciá Cantú, Gastón, *Politíca Mexicana*, Mexico D.F.: Universidad Nacional Autónoma de México, 1974.

Gilly, Adolfo, *La revolución interrumpida*, Mexico D.F.: Ed. El Caballito, 1971.

Gómez A., Pablo, *Democracia y crísis política en México*, Mexico D.F.: Ed. Cultura Popular, 1976.

González Casanova, Pablo, *La democracia en México*, Mexico D.F.: Ed. Era, 1964.

Hansen, Roger, *The Politics of Mexican Development*, Baltimore: Johns Hopkins, 1970.

227

Harrer, Hans-Jürgen, *Die Revolution in Mexico*, Köln, Pahl-Rugenstein, 1973.

Horn, Hans-Rudolf, *Mexico: Revolution und Verfassung*, Hamburg: Übersee Verlag, 1969.

Huacuja R., Mario and Woldenberg, José, *Estado y lucha política en el México actual*, Mexico D.F.: Ed. El Caballito, 1976.

Huizer, Gerrit, 'Peasant Organization in Agrarian Reform in Mexico' in *Masses in Latin America*, Irving Horowitz (ed.), New York: Oxford University Press, 1970.

Huntington, Samuel P., *Political Order in Changing Societies*, New Haven: Yale University Press, 1968.

Ianni, Octavio, *La formación del Estado populista en América Latina*, Mexico D.F.: Ed. Era, 1975.

Jaramillo, Rubén, *Autobiografía*, Mexico D.F.: Ed. Nuestro Tiempo, 1967.

Johnson, Kenneth F., *Mexican Democracy: a Critical View*, Boston: Allyn and Bacon, 1971.

Von Krockow, Christian Graf, *Mexico*, Munich: R. Piper, 1974.

Lasswell, Harold, *Politics: Who Gets What, When, How*, New York: McGraw-Hill, 1936.

Lavrov, N.M., *La Revolución Mexicana*, Mexico D.F.: Ed. Cultura Popular, 1975.

Leal, Juan Felipe, *La burguesía y el Estado mexicano*, Mexico D.F.: Ed. El Caballito, 1972.

Leal, Juan Felipe, *México: Estado, burocracia y sindicatos*, Mexico D.F.: Ed. El Caballito, 1976.

Lerner de Sheinbaum, Bertha and Ralsky de Cimet, Susan, *El poder de los presidentes: alcances y perspectivas (1910-1973)*, Mexico D.F.: Instituto Mexicano de Estudios Politicos, 1976.

Lieuwen, Edwin, *Arms and Politics in Latin America*, New York: Praeger, 1960.

Lieuwen, Edwin, *Mexican Militarism: the Political Rise and Fall of the Revolutionary Army 1910-1940*, Albuquerque: University of New Mexico Press, 1969.

López Cámara, Francisco, *El desafío de la clase media*, Mexico D.F.: Joaquín Mortiz, 1971.

López Gallo, Manuel, *Economía y política en la historia de México*, Mexico D.F.: Ed. El Caballito, 1965.

López Gallo, Manuel, *La violencia en la historia de Mexico*, Mexico D.F.: Ed. El Caballito, 1976.

López, Jaime, *10 Años de Guerrillas en México 1964-1974*, Mexico D.F.: Ed. Posada, 1974.

Martínez Verdugo, Arnoldo, *Partido Comunista Mexicano: trayectoria y perspectivas*, Mexico D.F.: Ed. Cultura Popular, 1977.

Medin, Tsvi, *Ideología y praxis política de Lázaro Cárdenas*, Mexico D.F.: Siglo XXI, 1972.

Meister, Albert, *El sistema mexicano*, Mexico D.F.: Ed. Extemporáneos, 1971.

México: 50 años de revolución, Mexico D.F.: Fondo de Cultura Económica, 1963.

Meyer, Jean, *La Cristiada: la guerra de los cristeros*, Mexico D.F.: Siglo XXI, 1973.

Michels, Robert, *Political Parties*, New York: Free Press, 1962.

Millon, Robert Paul, *Mexican Marxist: Vicente Lombardo Toledano*, Chapel Hill: University of North Carolina Press, 1966.

Millon, Robert Paul, *Zapata: the Ideology of a Peasant Revolutionary*, New York: International, 1969.

Mills, C. Wright, *The Power Elite*, New York: Oxford University Press, 1957.

Moore, Jr., Barrington, *Social Origins of Dictatorship and Democracy*, Boston: Beacon, 1966.

Mora, Juan Miguel de, *Las guerrillas en México y Jenaro Vázquez Rojas*, Mexico D.F.: Ed. Latino Americana, 1972.

Moreno Sánchez, Manuel, *Crisis política de México*, Mexico D.F.: Ed. Extemporáneos, 1970.

Mosca, Gaetano, *The Ruling Class*, New York: McGraw-Hill, 1939.

Movimiento de Liberacion Nacional, *Programa y llamamiento*, Mexico D.F.: 1958.

Nearing, Scott & Freeman, Joseph, *Dollar Diplomacy*, New York: Monthly Review Press, 1966.

'Notas para el estudio de la coyuntura mexicana', *Punto Crítico* nos. 19, 22, (Aug. and Nov. 1973).

Ortiz Mendoza, Franciso, *et al.*, 'Partido Popular Socialista: esbozo histórico', *Los partidos políticos de México*, Mexico D.F.: Fondo de Cultura Económica, 1975.

Padgett, Leon Vincent, *The Mexican Political System*, Boston: Houghton Mifflin, 1966.

Parkes, Henry Bamford, *A History of Mexico*, Boston: Houghton Mifflin, 1960.

Partido Comunista Mexicano, *El Partido Comunista frente a la crísis actual: informe del Comité Central sobre el primer punto del orden del día XVIII Congreso Nacional*, Mexico D.F.: 23 May 1977.

Partido Comunista Mexicano, *Programa*, Mexico D.F.: Ed. Cultura Popular, n.d.

Partido Comunista Mexicano, 'Resolución política del XVI Congreso Nacional', *Los partidos políticos de Mexico*, Mexico D.F.: Fondo de Cultura Económica, 1975.

Partido Comunista Mexicano, 'Resolución política del Sexto Pleno del Comité Central', *Los partidos políticos de Mexico*, Mexico D.F.: Fondo de Cultura Económica, 1975.

Partido Mexicano de los Trabajadores, *Declaración de Principios, Programa, Estatutos*, Mexico D.F.: n.d.

Partido Popular Socialista, 'Declaración de principios', *Los partidos políticos de México*, Mexico D'F.: Fondo de Cultura Económica, 1975.

Partido Popular Socialista, 'Puntos esenciales de táctica y estrategia', *Los partidos políticos de Mexico*, Mexico D.F.: Fondo de Cultura Economica, 1975.

Partido Socialista de los Trabajadores, *Nueve Documentos: Cuarto Conferencia Nacional de Organización*, Mexico D.F. 26-27 March 1977.

Partido Socialista de los Trabajadores, 'Resolución del VII Pleno del Comité Central sobre la situación actual del país', *El Insurgente Socialista* (Oct. 1976).

Partido Socialista Revolucionario, *Estatutos, Programa de Lucha, Programa Socialista* . . . ., Mexico D.F.: Ed. Partido Socialista Revolucionario, 1977.

Paz, Octavio, *El laberinto de la soledad*, Mexico D.F.: Fondo de Cultura Económica, 1959.

Quirk Robert, *The Mexican Revolution: 1914-1915*, New York: Citadel, 1963.

Reed John, *Insurgent Mexico*, New York: International Publishers, 1969.

Reyes Esparza, Ramiro, 'La burguesía y el Estado', *La burguesía mexicana*, Mexico D.F.: Ed. Nuestro Tiempo, 1973.

Saldivar, Américo, *Alianzas de clase y política del Estado mexicano (1970-1976)*, Puebla: Universidad Autónoma de Puebla, 1977.

Scott, Robert E., *Mexican Government in Transition*, Urbana: University of Illinois Press, 1959.

Shulgovski, Anatoli, *México en la encrucijada de su historia*, Mexico D.F.: Fondo de Cultura Popular, 1968.

Silva Herzog, Jesús, *El agrarismo mexicano y la reforma agraria*, Mexico D.F.: Fondo de Cultura Económica, 1959.

Simpson, L.B., *Many Mexicos*, Berkeley: University of California Press, 1962.

Sindicato de Trabajadores Electricistas de la República Mexicana, *Insurgencia obrera y nacionalismo revolucionario*, Mexico D.F.: Editorial El Caballito, 1973.

Stavenhagen, Rodolfo, *Sociología y subdesarrollo*, Mexico D.F.: Ed. Nuestro Tiempo, 1972.

Tannenbaum, Frank, *Mexico: the Struggle for Peace and Bread*, New York: Knopf, 1951.

Tannenbaum, Frank, *Peace by Revolution*, New York: Columbia University Press, 1963.

Turner, John Kenneth, *Barbarous Mexico*, Austin: University of Texas Press, 1969.

Unuzueta, Gerarado, *Comunista y sindicatos*, Mexico D.F.: Ed. Cultura Popular, 1977.

Wolf, Eric, *Peasant Wars of the Twentieth Century*, New York: Harper and Row, 1969.

Womack, John, *Zapata and the Mexican Revolution*, New York: Knopf, 1969.

Zevada, Ricardo, *Calles el presidente*, Mexico D.F.: Ed. Nuestro Tiempo, 1971.

B. Theory: The Bureaucratic Class

Alasco, Johannes, *Intellectual Capitalism*, New York: World University Press, 1950.

Aron, Raymond, et al., *World Technology and Human Destiny*, Ann Arbor: University of Michigan, 1963.

Bakunin, Michael, 'Statism and Anarchy' in *Bakunin on Anarchy*, (ed. and trans. by Sam Dolgoff), New York: Knopf, 1972.

Bakunin, Michael, 'The International and Karl Marx' in *Bakunin on Anarchy*, (ed. and trans. by Sam Dolgoff), New York: Knopf, 1972.

Bazelon, David, *Power in America: The Politics of the New Class*, New York: New American Library, 1967.

Bazelon, David, *The Paper Economy*, New York: Vintage, 1963.

Bendix, Reinhard, *Work and Authority in Industry*, New York: Harper and

Row, 1963.

Berle, Adolf, *Power Without Property*, New York: Harcourt, Brace & World, 1959.

Berle, Adolf, *The 20th Century Capitalist Revolution*, New York: Harcourt, Brace, 1954.

Berle, Adolf, and Means, Gardiner C., *The Modern Corporation and Private Property*, New York: Macmillan, 1933.

Bottomore, T.B., *Elites and Society*, New York: Basic Books, 1964.

Burnham, James, *The Machiavellians*, New York: John Day, 1943

Burnham, James, *The Managerial Revolution*, New York: John Day, 1941.

Djilas, Milovan, *The New Class*, New York: Praeger, 1958.

Draper, Hal, *Karl Marx's Theory of Revolution, State and Bureaucracy*, 2 vols, New York: Monthly Review, 1977.

Engels, Frederick, *'Marx and the Neue Rheinische Zeitung (1848-49)'* in *Marx-Engels Selected Works*, vol. II, Moscow: Foreign Languages Publishing House, 1962.

Engels, Frederick, 'On Authority' in *Marx-Engels Selected Works*, vol. I, Moscow: Foreign Languages Publishing House, 1962.

Engels, Frederick, 'Socialism: Utopian and Scientific' in *Marx-Engels Selected Works*, vol. II, Moscow: Foreign Languages Publishing House, 1962.

Engels, Frederick, 'The Origin of the Family, Private Property and the State' in *Marx–Engels Selected Works*, vol. II, Moscow: Foreign Languages Publishing House, 1962.

Galbraith, John K., *The New Industrial State*, Boston: Houghton Mifflin, 1967.

Gould, Jay, *The Technical Elite*, New York: Augustus M. Kelley, 1966.

Hacker, Andrew (ed.), *The Corporation Take-Over*, Garden City: Doubleday, 1965.

Hegedus, Andras, *Socialism and Bureaucracy*, New York: St. Martin's Press, 1976.

Hodges, Donald C., 'Class, Stratum and Intelligentsia', *Science & Society*, vol. XXIII, no. 1, (Winter 1963).

Hodges, Donald C., 'Classical Economics and Marx's Theory of Social Class', *Indian Journal of Social Research*, vol. II, no. 2, (July 1961).

Hodges, Donald C., 'Elements of a Theory of Salary' *All Indian Congress Economic Review* , (March 1963).

Hodges, Donald C., 'La controverse sur la reduction du travail', *Economie et Politique*, no. 78, (Jan. 1961).

Hodges, Donald C., 'New Working Class Theories', *Radical America*, vol. V, no. 1, (Jan.-Feb. 1971).

Hodges, Donald C., 'The Human Costs of Industry', *Indian Sociological Bulletin*, vol. III, no. 2, (May 1966).

Hodges, Donald C., 'The "Intermediate Classes" in Marxian Theory', *Social Research*, vol. 28, no. 1, (April 1961).

Hodges, Donald C., 'The Relevance of *Capital* to Studies of Bureaucracy', *Telos*, no. 6, (Fall 1970).

Lenin, V.I., 'The State and Revolution' in *Selected Works*, vol. II, New York: International Publishers, 1967.

Machajski, Waclaw, 'On the Expropriation of the Capitalists' in *The Making of Society*, (ed. by V.F. Calverton), New York: Random House, 1937.

Mallet, Serge, *La nouvelle classe ouvrière*, Paris: Ed. du Seuil, 1963.

Marshall, Alfred, *Principles of Economics*, (8th edn.), London: Macmillan, 1927.

Marx, Karl, *A Contribution to the Critique of Political Economy*, (trans. by N.I. Stone), Chicago: Charles Kerr, 1904.

Marx, Karl, *Capital*, (ed. by Frederick Engels), 3 vols., Moscow: Foreign Languages Publishing House, 1961-1962.

Marx, Karl, 'The Eighteenth Brumaire of Louis Bonaparte' in *Karl Marx: Selected Works*, vol. II, New York; International Publishers, n.d.

Marx, Karl, *Theories of Surplus Value*, (ed. by S. Ryazanskaya), 3 vols., Moscow: Progress Publishers, 1968-1971.

Marx, Karl and Frederick Engels, 'Germany: Revolution and Counter-Revolution' in *Karl Marx: Selected Works*, vol. II, New York: International Publishers n.d.

Marx, Karl and Frederick Engels, 'Manifesto of the Communist Party' in *Marx-Engels Selected Works*, vol. 1, Moscow: Foreign Languages Publishing House, 1962.

Paillet, Marc, *Marx contre Marx: La société technobureaucratique*, Paris: Denoël, 1971.

Rizzi, Bruno, *Il Collettivismo Burocratico*, Imola: Ed. Galeati, 1967.

Rubin, I.I., *Essays on Marx's Theory of Value*, (trans. by Miloš Samardžya and Fredy Perlman), Detroit: Black and Red, 1972.

Schumpeter, Joseph, *Capitalism, Socialism, and Democracy*, (3rd. edn.), New York: Harper, 1947.

Shachtman, Max, *The Struggle for the New Course*, New York: New International, 1943.

Trotsky, Leon, 'The USSR in War', *In Defense of Marxism*, New York: Pioneer, n.d.

Veblen, Thorstein, *The Engineers and the Price System*, New York: Viking, 1921.

Whyte, William H., *The Organization Man*, Garden City: Doubleday, 1956.

Part II: The Continental Scope of the Revolution

Abdel-Malek, Anouar, *Esercito e società in Egitto 1952-1967*, (trans. by Goffredo Fofi), Turin: Guilio Einaudi, 1967.

Aguirre Gamio, Hernando, *El Proceso Peruano*, Mexico D.F.: Ed. El Caballito, 1974.

Alcázar, José Luis and José Baldivia, *Bolivia: otra lección para América*, Mexico D.F.: Ed. Era, 1973.

Alexander, Robert (ed. and trans.), *APRISMO: The Ideas and Doctrines of Victor Raúl Haya de la Torre*, Kent State University, 1973.

Alexander, Robert, *The Bolivian National Revolution*, Rutgers State University, 1958.

Alonso, José, 'El Peronismo en la Línea del Socialismo Nacional Cristiano, *Comunidad Nacional*, Buenos Aires (Jan.-Feb. 1967).

Alvarez Puga, Eduardo, *Historia de la falange*, Barcelona: DOPESA, 1969.

Argentina in the Hour of the Furnaces, Berkeley: NACLA, 1975.

Bambirra, Vania, ed., *Diez años de insurrección en américa latina*, 2 vols.,

Santiago de Chile: Ed. Prensa Latinoamericana, 1971.

Bambirra, Vania, *La Revolución Cubana: Una Reinterpretación*, Mexico D.F.: Ed. Nuestro Tiempo, 1974.

Bedregal, Guillermo, *Los militares en bolivia*, Mexico D.F.: Ed. Extemporáneos, 1974.

Blair, Thomas L., *The Land to Those Who Work It: Algeria, Experiment in Workers' Management*, Garden City: Doubleday, 1970.

Bodenheimer, Susanne, 'The Bankruptcy of the Social Democratic Movement in Latin America', *New Politics*, New York (Winter 1969).

Bosch, Juan,*El Próximo Paso: Dictadura con Respaldo Popular*, Santo Domingo: Arte y Cine, 1970.

Bourricaud, Francois *et al.*, *La oligarquía en al Perú*, (2nd ed.), Mexico D.F.: Ed. Diógenes, 1970.

Burke, Melvin and James M. Malloy, 'Del populismo nacional al corporativismo nacional: el caso de Bolivia, 1952-70', *Aportes*, Paris (Oct. 1972).

Cantón, Dario, *La política de los militares argentinos: 1900-1971*, Buenos Aires: Ed. Siglo XXI, 1971.

Cardoso, Fernando Henrique and Enzo Faletto, *Dependencia y desarrollo en América Latina*, (2nd edn.), Mexico D.F.: Ed. Siglo XXI, 1971.

Castro, Fidel, *La Revolución Cubana 1953-1962*, (ed. Adolfo Sánchez Rebolledo), Mexico D.F.: Ed. Era, 1972.

Ciria, Alberto, *Perón y el justicialismo*, Buenos Aires: Ed. Siglo XXI, 1971.

Clegg, Ian, *Workers' Self-Management in Algeria*, New York: Monthly Review Press, 1971.

Crozier, Brian, *Franco: A Biographical History*, London: Eyre & Spottswoode, 1967.

Ealy, Lawrence O., *Yanqui Politics and the Isthmus*, Pennsylvania State University, 1971.

Fayt, Carlos (ed.), *La Naturaleza del Peronismo*, Buenos Aires: Ed. Viracoche, 1967.

Franco, Juan Pablo, 'Notas para una historia del peronismo', *Envido* Buenos Aires (April 1971).

Frías, Ismael, *La revolución peruana y la via socialista*, Lima: Ed. Horizonte, 1970.

Frias, Ismael, *Nacionalismo y Autogestión*, Lima: Ed. Inkarri, 1971.

Frondizi, Silvio, *La Revolución Cubana: Su Significación Histórica*, (3rd. edn.), Montevideo: Ed. Ciencias Políticas, 1961.

Garcia, Antonio, *Reforma Agraria y Economía Empresarial en América Latina*, Santiago de Chile: Ed. Universitaria, 1967.

Germani, Gino, Torcuato S. di Tella and Octavio Ianni, *Populismo y contradicciones de classe en Latinoamérica*, Mexico D.F.: Ed. Era, 1973.

Gott, Richard, *Guerrilla Movements in Latin America*, London: Thomas Nelson, 1970.

Gregor, James A., *The Ideology of Fascism*, New York: Free Press, 1969.

Guillén, Abraham, *Democracia Directa: Autogestión y Socialismo*, Montevideo: Ed. Aconcagua, 1970.

Guillén, Abraham, *Socialismo de Autogestión: De la Utopía a la Realidad*, Montevideo: Ed. Aconcagua, 1972.

Gutiérrez, Carlos María, *The Dominican Republic: Rebellion and Repression*, (trans. Richard E. Edwards), New York: Monthly Review Press, 1972.

Haya de la Torre, Victor Raúl, *El Antimperialismo y el Apra*, Santiago de Chile: Ed. Ercilla, 1936.

Haya de la Torre, Victor Raúl, *Treinta Años de Aprismo*, Mexico D.F.: Fondo de Cultura Económica, 1956.

Hernández Urbina, Alfredo, *Nueva política nacional*, Trujillo: Ed. Raiz, 1962.

Hodges, Donald C., *Argentina 1943-1976: The National Revolution and Resistance*, Albuquerque: University of New Mexico Press, 1976.

Hodges, Donald C., *The Latin American Revolution: From Apro-Marxism to Guevarism*, New York: William Morrow, 1974.

Hodges, Donald C., *The Legacy of Che Guevara*, London: Thames and Hudson, 1977.

Hussein, Mahmoud, *La lutte de classes en égypte*, Paris: Maspero, 1971.

Jaguaribe, Hélio, 'Political Strategies of National Development in Brazil', *Latin American Radicalism*, (ed. Irving Louis Horowitz *et al.*), New York: Vintage, 1969.

James, Daniel, *Red Design for the Americas: Guatemalan Prelude*, New York: John Day, 1954.

Jauretche, Arturo, *FORJA y la Década Infame*, Buenos Aires: Ed. Coyoacán, 1962.

Jonas, Susanne and Tobis, David (eds.), *Guatemala*, Berkeley: NACLA, 1974.

Kaplan, Marcos, *Formación del Estado Nacional en América Latina*, Santiago de Chile: Ed. Universitaria, 1969.

Karol, K.S., *Guerrillas in Power: The Course of the Cuban Revolution*, New York: Hill and Wang, 1970.

Kohl, James and John Litt, ed., *Urban Guerrilla Warfare in Latin America*, U.S.A.: M.I.T. Press, 1974.

Ledesma Ramos, Ramiro, *Fascismo en Espana? Discurso a las juventudes de España*, Barcelona: Ed. Ariel, 1968.

Losana Aldana, Ramón, *Dialectica del Subdesarrollo*, (2nd edn.), Mexico D.F.: Ed. Grijalbo, 1969.

Losana Aldano, Ramón, *Venezuela: Latifundio y Subdesarrollo*, Universidad Central de Venezuela, 1969.

Malloy, James M., *Bolivia: The Uncompleted Revolution*, University of Pittsburgh Press, 1970.

Malloy, James M., 'Populismo militar en el Peru y Bolivia: Antecedentes y posibilidades futuras', *Estudios Andinos*, La Paz (Sept. 1972).

'Manifesto de Grupo "Octubre", *Izquierda Nacional,* Buenos Aires (May 1971).

Melville, Thomas and Marjorie, *Guatemala – Another Vietnam?*, Harmonsworth: Penguin, 1971.

Mercado, Roger, *Vida, Traición y Muerte del Movimiento Aprista*, Lima: Ed. Fondo de Cultura Popular, 1970.

Moreira, Neiva, *El Nasserismo y la Revolución del Tercer Mundo*, (with an appendix by Vivian Trías), 'Nasser: Marxismo y Caudillismo', Montevideo: Ed. Banda Oriental, 1970.

Murmis, Miguel and Juan Carlos Portantiero, *Estudio sobre los orígenes del peronismo*, (3rd edn.), Buenos Aires: Ed. Siglo XXI, 1974.

Owen, Frank, *Peron: His Rise and Fall*, London: Cresset Press, 1957.

Paris, Robert, *Les origines du fascisme*, Paris: Flammarion, 1968.

Payne, Stanley G., *Falange: A History of Spanish Fascism*, Stanford

University Press, 1961.

Peñaloza, Juan Ramón, *Trotsky ante la revolución nacional latinoamericana*, Buenos Aires: Ed. Indoamerica, 1953.

Perón, Juan D., *Latinoamérica: ahora o nunca*, Montevideo: Ed. Diálogo, 1967.

Primo de Rivera, José Antonio, *Revolución Nacional*, (ed. Agustin del Rio Cisneros), Madrid: Ed. Prensa del Movimiento, 1949.

Pumaruna-Letts, Ricardo, *Pérou: révolution socialiste ou caricature de révolution?*, (trans. Jaques-Francois Bonaldi), Paris: Maspero, 1971.

Quartim, João, *Dictatorship and Armed Struggle in Brazil*, (trans. David Fernbach), London: Monthly Review Press, 1971.

Quijano, Aníbal, *Nationalism and Capitalism in Peru: A Study in Neoimperialism*, (trans. Helen R. Lane), New York: Monthly Review Press, 1971.

Ramos, Jorge Abelardo, *América Latina: Un País*, Beunos Aires: Ed. Octubre, 1949.

Ramos, Jorge Abelardo, *Historia de la Nación Latinoamericana*, Buenos Aires: Ed. A. Pena Lillo, 1968.

Sagastume, Jorge, 'Nasserismo y Peronismo', *Fichas de Investigacion Económica y Social*, Buenos Aires (April-May 1966).

Sagastume, Jorge, 'Nasserismo y Socialismo', *Fichas de Investigación Económica y Social*, Buenos Aires (April-May 1966).

Santillana, Pablo, *Chile: Análisis de un año de gobierno militar*, Buenos Aires: Ed. Prensa Latinoamericana, 1974.

Santos, Theotonio dos, *Socialismo o fascismo: dilema latinoamericano*, Santiago de Chile: Ed. Prensa Latinoamericana, 1969.

Shieh, Milton J.T., *The Kuomintang: Selected Historical Documents, 1894-1969*, St. John's University Press, 1970.

Sigmund, Paul E. (ed.), *Models of Political Change in Latin America*, New York: Praeger, 1970.

Sigmund, Paul E. (ed.), *The Ideologies of the Developing Nations*, (2nd rev. edn.), New York: Praeger, 1972.

Souza, Ruben Dario, 'New Trends in Panama', *New Times*, Moscow, (30 September 1970).

Souza, Rubén Dario, 'Panama: New Developments', *World Marxist Review*, Prague (Feb. 1971).

Spilimbergo, Jorge E., *El Socialismo en la Argentina: Del Socialismo Cipayo a la Izquierda Nacional*, Buenos Aires: Ed. Mar Dulce, 1969.

Suárez, Andrés, *Cuba: Castroism and Communism 1959-1966*, M.I.T. Press, 1967.

Torres-Rivas, Edelberto, *Procesos y estructuras de una sociedad dependiente (Centroamérica)*, Santiago de Chile: Ed. Prensa Latinoamericana, 1969.

Trotsky, Leon, *Por Los Estados Unidos Socialistas de America Latina*, Buenos Aires: Ed. Coyoacán, 1961.

Velasco Alvarado, Juan, *La Voz de la Revolución 1968-70*, Lima: Ed. Peisa, 1970.

Villanueva, Victor, *Neuva Mentalidad Militar en el Peru?*, Lima: Ed. Juan Mejía Baca, 1969.

Waiss, Oscar, *Nacionalismo y Socialismo en América Latina*, Buenos Aires: Ed. Iguazú, 1961.

Zavaleta Mercado, René, *El poder dual en américa latina*, Mexico D.F.: Ed. Siglo XXI, 1974.

Part III: The Mexican Revolutionary Process

Aguilar Mora, Manuel, *El bonapartismo mexicano*, 2 vols., Mexico D.F.: Juan Pablos, 1982.

Aguilar Mora, 'Estado y revolución en el proceso mexicano', *Interpretaciones de la revolución mexicana*, Mexico D.F.: Nueva Imágen, 1980.

Aguilar Mora, *La crisis de la izquierda en México*, Mexico D.F.: Juan Pablos, 1978.

Alperovich, M.S. *et al.*, *La revolución mexicana: Cuatro estudios soviéticos*, Mexico D.F.: Cultura Popular, 1975.

Alperovich, M.S. and B.T. Rudenko, *La revolución mexicana de 1910-1917 y la política de los Estados Unidos*, (trans. M. Garza *et al.*), Mexico D.F.: Cultura Popular, 1960.

Barkin, David, 'Mexico's Albatross: The U.S. Economy', *Latin American Perspectives*, vol. 2, no. 2, (Summer 1975).

Barkin, David and Gustavo Esteva, 'Social Conflict and Inflation in Mexico', *Latin American Perspectives*, vol. 9, no. 2, (Winter 1982).

Bartra, Roger, *Estructura agraria y clases sociales en México*, Mexico D.F.: Era, 1974.

Bartra, Roger, 'Peasants and Political Power in Mexico: A Theoretical Model', *Latin American Perspectives*, vol. 2, no. 2, (Summer 1975).

Basáñez, Miguel, *La lucha por la hegemonía en México*, Mexico D.F.: Siglo XXI, 1981.

Campa, Valentín, *Mi testimonio: Memorias de un comunista mexicano*, Mexico D.F.: Cultura Popular, 1978.

Carmona Amorós, Salvador, *La economía mexicana y el nacionalismo revolucionario*, Mexico D.F: El Caballito, 1974.

Castaños, Alfonso, *Tiene el socialismo su prehistoria? Acerca de la naturaleza social de los países llamados socialistas*, Barcelona: Blume, 1977.

Castoriadis, Cornelius, *La société bureaucratique: Les rapports de production en Russie*, Paris: Union Générale d'Editions, 1973.

Cordera, Rolando and Carlos Tello, *La disputa por la nación*, Mexico D.F.: Siglo XXI, 1981.

Cosío Villegas, Daniel, *El sistema político mexicano*, (13th ed.), Mexico D.F.: Joaquín Mortiz, 1981.

Cosío Villegas, Daniel, *La sucesión presidencial*, (2nd ed.), Mexico D.F.: Joaquín Mortiz, 1975.

Echeverría Alvarez, Luis, 'La autodeterminación popular', *Ha muerto la revolución mexicana?*, (ed. by Stanley Ross), Mexico D.F.: Premia, 1978.

Echeverría Alvarez, Luis, 'Nuestra Revolución no ha terminado', *Ha muerto la revolución mexicana?*, (ed. by Stanley Ross), Mexico D.F.: Premia, 1978.

Evers, Tilman, *El Estado en la periferia capitalista*, (authorized Spanish translation, 2nd ed.), Mexico D.F.: Siglo XXI, 1981.

Galván, Rafael, 'Sobre la unidad de la izquierda', *Solidaridad*, no. 11, (September 1981), (originally published in the April 1977 issue).

Gandy, Ross, *Introducción a la sociología histórica marxista*, (2nd ed.), Mexico D.F.: Era, 1982.

Gandy, Ross, *Marx's Theory of History*, Austin: University of Texas Press, 1979.

García Cantú, Gaston, *Política mexicana*, Mexico D.F.: UNAM, 1974.

Garrido, Luis Javier, *El Partido de la Revolución Institucionalizada: La formación del nuevo estado (1928-1945)*, Mexico D.F.: Siglo XXI, 1982.

Gilly, Adolfo, *La revolución interrumpida*, (4th ed.), Mexico D.F.: El Caballito, 1974.

Glucksman, André, *Hacia la subversión del trabajo intelectual*, (trans. Oscar Barahona), Mexico D.F.: Era, 1976.

González Casanova, Pablo, *El Estado y los partidos políticos en México*, (2nd ed.), Mexico D.F.: Era, 1982.

González Casanova, Pablo and Enrique Florescano (ed), *México, hoy*, (5th ed.), Mexico D.F.: Siglo XXI, 1981.

Hamilton, Nora, 'Mexico: The Limits of State Autonomy', *Latin American Perspectives*, vol. 2, no. 2, (Summer 1975).

Harris, Richard L. and David Barkin, 'The Political Economy of Mexico in the Eighties', *Latin American Perspectives*, vol. 9, no. 1, (Winter 1982).

Hodges, Donald C., *Marxismo y revolución en el siglo veinte*, Mexico D.F.: El Caballito, 1978.

Hodges, Donald C., *The Bureaucratization of Socialism*, Amherst: University of Massachusetts Press, 1981.

Huacuja, Mario and José Woldenberg, *Estado y lucha política en el México actual*, Mexico D.F.: El Caballito, 1976.

Instituto de Capacitación Política, *Historia documental de la Confederacion de Trabajadores de México*, vol. 1 (1936-37), Mexico D.F.: PRI, 1981.

Instituto de Capacitación Política, *Historia documental del Partido de la Revolución*, vol. 1, PNR (1929-32), Mexico D.F.: PRI, 1981.

Instituto de Investigaciones Sociales de la Universidad Nacional Autónoma de México (ed.), *El peril de México en 1980*, (7th ed.), 3 vols; Mexico D.F.: Siglo XXI, 1980.

Interpretaciones de la revolucion mexicana, (5th ed.), Mexico D.F.: Nueva Imágen, 1981.

Labastido Martín del Campo, Julio, 'Los grupos dominantes frente a las alternativas de cambio', *El perfil de México en 1980*, vol. 3, Mexico D.F.: Siglo XXI, 1980.

Leal, Juan Felipe, *México: Estado, burocracia y sindicatos*, Mexico D.F.: El Caballito, 1976.

Lombardo Toledano, Vicente, 'El drama de México', *En torno al problema agrario*, Mexico D.F.: Partido Popular Socialista, 1974.

Lombardo Toledano, Vicente, 'Una democracia del pueblo', *Ha muerto la revolución mexicana?*, (ed. by Stanley Ross), Mexico D.F.: Premia, 1978.

Loyola Díaz, Rafael, *La crisis Obregón-Calles y el Estado mexicano*, Mexico D.F.: Siglo XXI, 1980.

Madrid Hurtado, Miguel de la, *Estudios de derecho constitucional*, Mexico D.F.: Porrua, 1980.

Martínez Verdugo, Arnoldo, *Partido Comunista Mexicano, Trayectoria y Perspectivas*, Mexico D.F.: Cultura Popular, 1971.

Marx, Karl and Frederick Engels, *Selected Works*, 2 vols., Moscow: Foreign Languages Publishing House, 1962.

Menocal, Nina, *México visión de los ochenta*, Mexico D.F.: Diana, 1981.

México 1982: Anuario económico, Mexico D.F.: Somas, 1982.

Monsivais, Carlos, 'La ofensiva ideológica de la derecha', *México, hoy*, (ed. by

237

P. González Casanova and E. Florescano), Mexico D.F.: Siglo XXI, 1981.

Moreno, Daniel, *Los partidos políticos del México contemporáneo (1916-1979)*, (7th ed.), Mexico D.F.: Costa-Amic, 1979.

Murillo Soberanis, and Manlio Fabio, *La reforma política mexicana y el sistema pluripartidista*, Mexico D.F.: Diana, 1979.

Narvaez, Ruben, *La sucesión presidencial: Teoría y práctica del tapadismo*, Mexico D.F.: Instituto Mexicano de Sociología Política, 1981.

Navarrete, Ifigenia M. de, 'La distribución del ingreso en México: tendencias y perspectivas', *El perfil de México en 1980*, Mexico D.F.: Siglo XXI, 1980.

Paré, Luisa, *El problema agrícola en México: Campesinos sin tierra o proletarios agrícolas?* (4th ed.), Mexico D.F.: Siglo XXI, 1981.

Partido Socialista de los Trabajadores, *Documentos Básicos*, Mexico D.F.: Ediciones del Comite Central, 1981.

Partido Socialista de los Trabajadores, *Instructivo para la preparación del II Consejo Nacional de Dirigentes*, (September 1977).

Partido Socialista de los Trabajadores, 'Plan Global de Consolidación y Desarrollo' (Proyecto), Mimeographed report to the 12th plenum of the Central Committee, Jalapa, Veracruz, 1980.

Peña, Rodolfo F., (ed.), *Insurgencia obrera y nacionalismo revolucionario*, Mexico D.F.: El Caballito, 1973.

Peña, Sergio de la, *La formación del capitalismo en México*, (8th ed.), Mexico D.F.: Siglo XXI, 1981.

Pereyra, Carlos, 'Estado y Sociedad', *México, hoy*, (ed. P. González Casanova and E. Florescano), Mexico D.F.: Siglo XXI, 1981.

'Polémica Política', *La República*, (December 1981).

Poulantzas, Nicos, 'The Problem of the Capitalist State', *New Left Review*, no. 58 (November-December 1969).

Qué es el PRT?, (2nd ed.), Mexico D.F.: Folletos Bandera Socialista, no. 9, (1979).

Quintanilla Obregón, Lourdes, *Lombardismo y sindicatos en América Latina*, Mexico D.F.: Fontamara, 1982.

Rodríguez Araujo, Octavio, *La reforma política y los partidos políticos en México*, (5th ed.), Mexico D.F.: Siglo XXI, 1982.

Ross, Stanley R. (ed.), *Ha muerto la revolución mexicana?* (trans. Hector David Torres), (2nd ed.), Mexico D.F.: Premia, 1978.

Sahagun Orozco, Antonio, 'La revolución mexicana, una revolución social', *La República*, (August-September 1981).

Saldívar, Américo, *Ideología y política del estado mexicano*, Mexico D.F.: Siglo XXI, 1980.

Semo, Enrique, 'Acerca del ciclo de las revoluciones burguesas en México', *Socialismo*, no. 3, (July-September 1975).

Semo, Enrique, 'Reflexiones sobre la revolución mexicana', *Interpretaciones de la revolución mexicana*, Mexico D.F.: Nueva Imágen, 1981.

Sevilla, Carlos, *Bonapartism in Mexico, its Emergence and Consolidation*, Unpublished M.A. thesis at the University of Essex, 1975.

Shulgovski, Anatoli, *México en la encrucijada de su historia*, (trans. by Armando Martínez Verdugo), Mexico D.F.: Cultura Popular, 1977.

Smith, Peter H., *Labyrinths of Power: Political Recruitment in Twentieth Century Mexico*, Princeton: Princeton University Press, 1979.

Trotsky, León, *Por los Estados Unidos de América Latina*, (ed. Dionisio Villar), Buenos Aires: Coyoacán, 1961.

Ulbricht, Walter, '*El Capital* y la etapa avanzada del socialismo', *Historia y Sociedad*, vol. 3, no. 11, (1968).

Villa A., Manuel, 'Las bases del estado mexicano y su problemática actual', *El perfil de México en 1980*, vol. 3, Mexico D.F.: Siglo XXI, 1980.

Voslensky, Michael, *La Nomenklatura: Los privilegiados en la U.R.S.S.*, (2nd ed.), Barcelona: Argos-Vergara, 1981.

Warman, Arturo, *Los campesinos, hijos predilectos del régimen*, Mexico D.F.: Nuestro Tiempo, 1972.

Zermeño, Sergio, *México: Una democracia utópica*, Mexico D.F.: Siglo XXI, 1978.

Glossary of Spanish Words

agraristas: These were the teachers, intellectuals, labour agitators, and revolutionaries who went about the countryside in the 1920s and 1930s explaining to the peasants the land reform promised in the Constitution, and who organized them to demand its implementation. Best translated as 'agrarians'.

cacique: In Mexico *caciques* are what North Americans call 'political bosses'. They have unofficial power in politics, and in Mexico are the real rulers of a locality or even a region.

centavo: A small copper Mexican coin, equal to a United States penny in 1900.

científico: Literally 'scientist', the nickname for anyone among the hundred rich advisors around the Mexican dictator, Porfirio Díaz, from 1890 to 1910. Of foreign descent, they preached the 'scientific' development of Mexico by foreign capital; they got rich through corruption, land speculation, and concessions for foreigners. A 'comprador bourgeoisie'.

ejido: In pre-Columbian Mexico, the village owned the land and assigned each peasant a plot, but he could neither rent it out nor sell it. Such a village is called an *ejido* in Mexico. The tradition of communal landholding was revived during the Mexican Revolution and lingers on to this day.

gringo: The Mexican nickname for North Americans. Sometimes used in an opprobrious manner.

gusto: Pleasure.

hacendado: Owner of a hacienda.

hacienda: A large landed estate in the country. The 'big house' was surrounded by a wall for defence, with fields outside.

mañana: Tomorrow.

manta: Course white cloth used by Mexican peasants to make simple clothes.

Mayas: Descendants of the ancient Mayas. The second largest linguistic group among Mexico's surviving Indians.

mestizo: A person of mixed Indian and Spanish descent. Today most Mexicans belong to this 'new race'.

240

Nahuatl:	The most widely spoken of the Indian languages surviving in today's Mexico, the langauge of the Aztecs.
partria chica:	The 'little nation'. This is a term used for any strongly defined region in Mexico where common traditions unite the people against outsiders.
peón:	In Mexico before the land reform of the 1930s, a peon was a person being forced to work off a debt. It has become a general term for a member of the labouring class in the countryside.
peonage:	The system of holding debtors in servitude to labour for their creditors.
porfiriato:	The period of the dictatorship of Porfirio Díaz (1884-1911).
porfirista:	A follower of the dictator Porfirio Díaz (1884-1911).
pronuncia-miento:	A political manifesto issued by a movement carrying out an armed attack on the state.
pulque:	Wine made from a native Mexican plant.
rancheros:	Small farmers. Sometimes used opprobriously for uncultured rural people in Mexico.
rurales:	The state mounted police, feared by everyone in Díaz's Mexico. There were perhaps 10,000 of them.
sierra:	Mountains. Great chains of mountains run up and down Mexico.
tienda de raya:	On every hacienda there was a store that doled out food and cloth to the peons. The *hacendado* owned the store and marked in the debt book what every peon owed him. The debt was passed down from father to son. North Americans call such a place 'the company store'.
Tierra y Libertad:	'Land and Freedom.' The war cry of the Zapatista revolution in Southern Mexico (1911-1919).
tumulto:	For centuries in colonial Mexico there were sudden uprisings of the people in the cities, always snuffed out. The word means literally 'tumult', but was used for these revolts.
Villista:	A follower of Franciso (Pancho) Villa in the northern revolution in Mexico.
Yaquis:	The Yaquis were an Indian tribe in Mexico's northwest, a proud barbarian peasant people that resisted the Spanish for ce▓▓uries. They were enslaved during the Díaz dictatorship. ▓▓iven from their lands, they were shipped to Yucatan and sold for forty dollars a head.
Zapatista:	A follower of Emiliano Zapata in the agrarian revolution in Southern Mexico.

Political Glossary

Action Group: A secret bureaucratic camarilla inside the CROM working with the Mexican government in the 1920s.

AFL (American Federation of Labor): The big labour central of craft unions in the United States during the 1920s.

Agrarian Party: *See* National Agrarian Party.

APRA (American Popular Revolutionary Alliance): Founded in Mexico in 1924, this international organization aimed to spread principles of the Mexican Revolution throughout the Continent. From its national sections emerged the populist parties which collectively are also known as the APRA.

Aprismo: The politics and strategy of the APRA.

Aprista: Adhering to *Aprismo*.

Caribbean Legion: A group of international *Aprista* revolutionaries founded in 1947 to struggle against dictatorships in the Caribbean.

CGT (General Confederation of Workers): Anarchist labour central rival to the Mexican government-controlled CROM in the 1920s.

CNC (National Peasant Confederation): Founded in 1938, this federation of peasant leagues is the largest in Mexico and is government controlled. It is the core of the peasant sector of the ruling party.

CNOP (National Confederation of Popular Organizations): This is what the Mexicans call the 'popular sector' of the ruling party. It includes the FSTSE, professional associations, women's leagues, youth groups, an organization of small businessmen, and an organization of small independent peasants who are not in *ejidos*.

COB (Bolivian Labour Central): A Marxist labour central dominated by Juan Lechín's tin miners, active in the Bolivian Revolution (1952-64) and under General Juan Torres' socialist army revolution (1970-71).

CONCAMIN (The National Confederation of Industrial Chambers): Mexican law requires all businessmen in industry to belong to an organization representing their interests. This is the chief one.

CONCANACO (The National Confederation of Chambers of Commerce): Mexican law requires all busineness men in commerce to belong to an organization representing their interests. This is it.

Corporatist: Characteristic of a corporate state, in which political and economic power is vested in organizations or corporations representing basic interest groups.

Cristeros: The religious guerrillas who fought the Mexican government from 1926 to 1929 and again from 1935 to 1938. The name comes from their war cry, '*Cristo Rey!*' or 'Christ is king!'.

CROM (Regional Confederation of Mexican Labour): The big Mexican labour central of the 1920s; it only survived its collapse in 1929 as a shadow of its former self.

CTM (Confederation of Mexican Workers): Founded in 1936, this labour central is the largest in Mexico to this day and is government-controlled. It is the core of the labour sector of the ruling party.

Cuban People's Party (PPC): An APRA-type party of importance because Fidel Castro's July 26 Movement was a left-wing split off.

Democratic Action (AD): Revolutionary *Aprista* party founded in Venezuela in 1940 by Rómulo Betancourt, an ex-communist. After taking power in 1958, the party swung rightward.

División del Norte: In 1913 and 1914 the most powerful fighting force in Mexico, the army of Francisco (Pancho) Villa. Formed by Villa in Chihuahua in 1913, it was defeated and dispersed by Obregón in 1915.

FSTSE (Federation of Unions of Workers at the Service of the State): Founded in 1938, this federation of unions is one of the most powerful in Mexico and is government controlled. The FSTSE is the core of the CNOP, which corresponds to what Mexicans call the 'popular sector' of the ruling party. The FSTSE includes the civil service unions, the teacher unions, the health worker unions, and many others.

House of the World's Worker: In the first phase of the Revolution under Madero, this anarchist labour central was founded and grew strong in Mexico City. Huerta drove it underground in 1913. In 1915 it supported Obregón, but Carranza suppressed it in 1916. For North Americans, it is the Mexican equivalent of the Industrial Workers of the World.

Labour Party: *See* Mexican Labour Party.

Labour Party in Argentina (Partido Laborista): This party was formed to help elect Perón president in 1946 and was then replaced by the Peronist Party in 1947.

Mexican Labour Party (PLM): Founded in 1919 by Luis Morones on the model of the British Labour Party. It was a nationwide organization in the 1920s.

MNR (Revolutionary Nationalist Movement): The popular *Aprista* party that led the Bolivian Revolution (1952-64).

Montoneros: Clandestine guerrilla movement of left-wing Peronism. During the 1970s it enjoyed broad support among the Argentine people. Its ideology is a mixture of Peronism and Marxism.

National Agrarian Party (PNA): Founded by Antonio Díaz Soto y Gama, this *Zapatista* peasant party advocated land reform in Mexico during the 1920s.

National Peasant League: Founded in 1926 by peasant leagues from 16 states, this radical organization dominated much of the Mexican countryside until 1930.

OAS (The Organization of American States): Through this organization the nations of the Western hemisphere are supposed to work for mutual co-operation and international alliance. The OAS is dominated by the United States.

Oligarchy: In Latin America the term 'oligarchy' refers to the traditional landed aristocracy that has dominated the Continent for centuries.

PAN (National Action Party): Founded in 1939, this party is to the right of the ruling party in Mexico. It stands for more private enterprise and a conciliatory attitude toward the Catholic Church.

PCM (Mexican Communist Party): Founded in 1919, this party is today the strongest party to the left of the ruling party, PRI. Other Marxist-Leninist parties tend to follow its lead. The PCM is especially strong among students, teachers and intellectuals.

Plan de San Luis Potosí: In this programme published from Texas in October 1911, Francisco Madero promised land reform and democracy and called for a general insurrection in Mexico on November 20.

PMT (Mexican Workers Party): Founded in the early 1970s. This party of young people has in fact a Marxist-Leninist ideology, but refuses to mention in its programme a revolutionary transition to socialism. The party prefers a populist style and programme.

PNR (Revolutionary National Party): Founded by ex-President Calles in 1929, this was the first form of the ruling party in Mexico. It later gave way to the PRM, and finally to the PRI that rules Mexico today.

Populist: From the Latin word *populus* or people. A populist appeals to all the little people against the big money — landlords, bankers, monopolies, bishops, and foreigners. Populist politics differ from classist politics by appealing to more than one class. There is petty-bourgeois populism, military populism, and socialist populism. Mao, Ho, Fidel and most successful Marxists have practiced socialist populism.

PPS (Socialist Popular Party): Grew out of a left-wing Marxist split from the Mexican PRI in the 1940s. It was originally called the Popular Party. PPS is the name of the party since 1960. For 20 years it was the main opposition to the left of the PRI. Today the main opposition is the PCM.

PRD (Dominican Revolutionary Party): Apra-type party important in the Dominican Revolution of the early 1960s, which was ended by the intervention of United States marines (1965).

PRI (Institutional Revolutionary Party): Founded by President Alemán in the late 1940s, this is a reorganised form of the ruling party. PRI is the party that rules Mexico today.

PRM (Party of the Mexican Revolution): In 1938 President Cárdenas reorganized the ruling party, at that time called PNR, to make it a workers' party and gave it this new name. The ruling party was reorganized again, along more conservative lines, into the PRI under President Alemán.

PST (Socialist Workers Party): Established in 1975, this is a social democratic Mexican party with a Marxist ideology.

Radical Party (Radical Civic Union): Founded in Argentina in 1891. Centre party. Important throughout the 20th century in Argentine politics. .

Red Battalions: In February 1915 Obregón organized 10,000 workers in Mexico City into six Red Battalions. Then he marched the industrial workers off to fight the agrarian radicals under Villa. As president, Carranza dissolved the Red Battalions (1916).

Red Shirts: In the state of Tabasco, the atheistic revolutionary governor, Garrido Canábal, organized bands of youth modeled on Mussolini's black shirts. In the 1930s they terrorized the Church and held anti-clerical marches. Garrido named his son Lenin.

Revolutionary Anti-clerical League of Mexico: Founded in 1931, many state governors were members. Unleashed a persecution of the Church across Mexico.

Ruling party: The ruling party was founded in 1929 by ex-President Calles to bring together in one organization the various elements that the Mexican Revolution had thrown into power. In 1929 it was called the PNR; in 1938 Cárdenas reorganized it into the PRM; and in 1947 Alemán again re-organized it into the PRI.

White Guards: The landowners in Mexico kept armed retainers called white guards to terrorize agrarians and kill peasants who demanded that the land reform be carried out.

Index